The Struggle with Leviathan
Social Responses to the Omnipotence of the State, 1815-1965

For Hilde, Inge and Ellen

The Struggle
with Leviathan

EMIEL LAMBERTS

◆

Social Responses
to the Omnipotence of
the State, 1815-1965

LEUVEN UNIVERSITY PRESS

Original title: *Het gevecht met Leviathan. Een verhaal over de politieke ordening in Europa, 1815-1965*
Authorized translation from the Dutch language edition published by Uitgeverij Bert Bakker
© 2011 Dutch language edition by E. Lamberts
© 2016 English language edition by E. Lamberts and Leuven University Press/Presses universitaires de Louvain/Universitaire Pers Leuven, Minderbroedersstraat 4, B-3000 Leuven (Belgium)

ISBN 978 94 6270 070 3
D/2016/1869/23
NUR: 695

CONTENTS

PROLOGUE

Any hope of subduing [the Leviathan] is false;
the mere sight of it is overpowering.
No one is fierce enough to rouse it.
(Book of Job, *41: 9-10*)

Nothing on earth is its equal -
a creature without fear.
It looks down on all that are haughty;
it is king over all that are proud.
(Book of Job, *41:33-34*)[1]

In 1651 the English philosopher Thomas Hobbes (1588-1679) published his *Leviathan*, a pioneering work in the unfolding of modern political philosophy.[2] The treatise defended the omnipotence of the State in society. The symbol of that omnipotence was Leviathan, the awe-inspiring sea monster from the *Book of Job*. Deeply affected by the chaos and anarchy that had ravaged British society during a prolonged civil war, Hobbes argued that the State should have absolute power and that the authority of the sovereign had to extend across all domains, including the religious. The prince not only wielded the highest political authority, he also determined what was good and what evil. Hobbes's thinking was innovative in that he did not trace the absolute

---

[1] Translation E.H. Palmer, et al., eds., *The Holy Bible.*
[2] Hoffman and Graham, eds., *Introduction to Political Theory*, 170.

authority of the sovereign back to a form of divine right, but to a social contract between individual citizens, who – to escape anarchy – were prepared to submit completely to the authority of the State, in exchange for protection, security and peace. In this way Hobbes provided the principle of state sovereignty with a powerful, future-oriented foundation.[3]

John Locke (1632-1704) 'liberalized' that social contract theory. He stressed that by entering into a social pact, citizens did not transfer all their rights to the State. Government had to respect their lives and property and could not impede their self-development. Locke thus put limits on state sovereignty. He was the first thinker to emphasize strongly the protection of individual rights, and can therefore be considered as the founder of liberalism, the first modern political movement in the western world.[4] His ideas were taken up and promoted by French thinkers such as Montesquieu (1689-1755) and Rousseau (1712-1778), an important development given the dominance of French culture in Europe at the time.

The most important liberal revolutions took place in France also. They led to experiments with new forms of government and encouraged the implementation of liberal ideas.[5] Above all the great revolution of 1789, which put an end to the class-based society of the *ancien régime*, gave a universal dimension to the call for 'liberty, equality and fraternity'. Following the small gains of the July Revolution of 1830, the February Revolution of 1848 finally led to a tidal wave that engulfed almost the entire European continent. The triumph of liberalism seemed assured.

Liberalism voiced the political aspirations of the emerging middle class, who opposed the established power of the absolute monarchs and traditional elites, especially the nobility and the upper clergy. It assigned a central place in the social structure to the strong, entrepreneurial individual who had to be freed from all religious, political and social constraints and be given ample opportunities to develop. Liberalism proposed a political system in which the State gave individual citizens significant space and guaranteed their inalienable rights, including civil liberties, centering on the right to freedom of opinion, as well as political liberties such as the right to vote and to petition. Political freedoms stemmed from the notion of the sovereignty of the people, which found expression in a representative, parliamentary regime. The fundamental freedoms and rights of citizens could be further protected by a separation between the executive, the legislature and the judiciary, which should prevent the exercise of arbitrary authority.

[3]   Sorrell, *Cambridge Companion to Thomas Hobbes*; Martinich, *Hobbes. A Biography*; Newey, *Hobbes and Leviathan*.
[4]   Ruggiero, *The History of European Liberalism*; Rawls, *Political Liberalism*.
[5]   Godechot, *Les révolutions (1770-1799)*; Bergeron, Furet and Koselleck, *Das Zeitalter der europaischen Revolution, 1789-1848*.

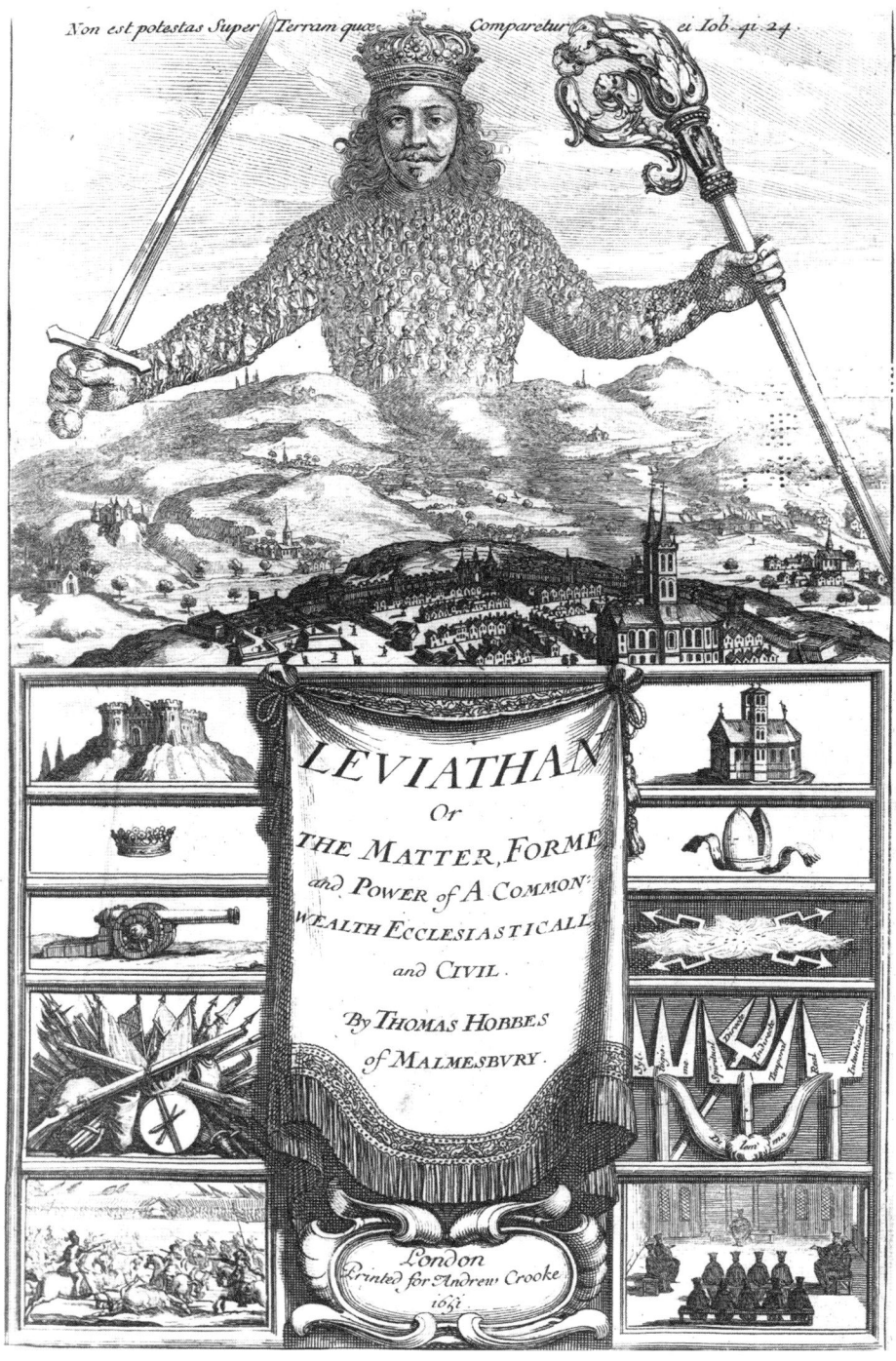

Abraham Bosse, Title page of Leviathan by Thomas Hobbes, 1651.

Liberals also attached great importance to economic freedom. They advocated a free market economy and international free trade. In a sense, they were the advocates of modern capitalism, which in the course of the 19th century became the dominant economic system. They were internationalists on the economic front, but politically they presented themselves mostly as nationalists. They became increasingly associated with national movements, which in their own way gave expression to the idea of the sovereignty of the people and were gradually becoming a political force. Nationalism would threaten the survival of multinational states while facilitating the formation of new nation states.

In the first half of the 19th century, the established powers were able to contain the pressure of liberalism and nationalism relatively well, but the wave of revolutions in 1848 opened the floodgates.[6] The prolonged and acute economic crisis, which had plunged large groups of the population into deep distress during the previous years, created an explosive situation that erupted in liberal and national frustrations. Revolutions broke out in almost all countries on the European continent. The revolutionaries forced through liberal constitutional reforms and attempted to establish new national states in Germany, Italy, Hungary and elsewhere. However, the chaos that they caused in much of Europe provoked an immediate conservative backlash.

That conservative turnaround was largely induced by the great workers' revolt that broke out in Paris in June 1848, in the wake of the February Revolution. The new republican government brutally suppressed the uprising, and inflicted a massacre that received enormous attention both in France and abroad. For the first time the ruling classes became cognizant of the 'Red Menace', the threat of revolutionary socialism. An unrelenting civil war raging for a week in the most important European capital called up the spectre of barbarian hordes threatening modern civilization. It triggered an anti-revolutionary reflex among large sections of the population. Many of those who had previously sympathized with reformist ideas and movements came to see revolutionary socialism as the logical outgrowth of liberalism and joined forces with the conservatives.

By late 1848 most reigning monarchs had already succeeded in restoring their power and rolling back many of the reforms that had been introduced. In the 1850s, authoritarian regimes would once again dominate the European continent. This was even the case in France, where the Second Republic gave way to the Second Empire under Napoleon III. Nor were any changes made to the borders; for the moment, the national movements had not succeeded in disrupting the existing international order.

Had the revolutions of 1848 then been in vain? They seemed so at first glance, but in fact they ushered in a new era. They were of great symbolic

---

[6]   Wilson, ed., *1848. The Year of Revolutions.*

value for the liberal and national movements that, following a brief backlash, again advanced relentlessly in the 1860s. During this period, a strong industrial and commercial expansion under the banner of capitalism considerably strengthened the economic power and political influence of the bourgeoisie. In the future, even conservative regimes would have to take this wealthy class into account and more or less liberalize political structures. In the same decade, national issues would come to dominate international politics.

Forced increasingly on the defensive, conservative groups strenuously resisted liberalism. They dismissed abstract liberal theories that traced the origin of the State to a supposed social contract between individual citizens. Rather, they argued, authority structures had developed organically throughout history. Social relations and political institutions that had evolved over time had to be given an appropriate place in the structure of the State, in accordance with the traditions and needs of each country. Conservatives therefore advocated a strong monarchy based on historical legitimacy, but they could not prevent the liberal, parliamentary state gradually becoming the model for political order in most European countries.[7]

However, the battle with liberalism was not completely lost, and opposition to the statism of the liberals indeed paid off. Liberal theorists endorsed the doctrine of sovereignty that had been evolving since the sixteenth century. They regarded the State as a non-voluntary organization, a timeless sovereign power, to which everyone owed obedience. The State was the only source of law and legislation whose power should, in principle, extend to all areas of social life. However, its power was limited by the guaranteed legal status of individual citizens and thus its impact on society was somewhat restricted. The rights and freedoms of citizens were expressly protected by a separation of powers, as advocated by Montesquieu, and/or by popular sovereignty, a notion espoused especially by Rousseau. He argued that there was no objection to state power being concentrated and centralized, on condition that it remained in the hands of the people and expressed the *volonté générale*. This argument would exert a great influence in liberal circles. It tied in with older bureaucratic and centralist traditions that sought to strengthen state power. However, it threatened the rights of minorities and undeniably increased the impact of the State on the lives of individual citizens, who were insufficiently equipped to resist a strong and dominant state authority. Montesquieu had already warned in this regard: 'One should not confuse the power of the people with the freedom of the people.' Nevertheless, this is what happened. From the second half of the nineteenth century, the centralized nation state would be the most common expression of a liberal statism, which was largely in-

---

[7] Harbour, *The Foundation of Conservative Thought*; Honderich, *Conservatism*; Weiss, *Conservatism in Europe*.

spired by Rousseau. The 'liberal' pursuit of restricting the power of the State thus had clear limits.

Conservatives explicitly opposed these views. Unlike the liberals, they felt that society was based not so much on individuals as on natural, pre-political groupings, such as family bonds, local communities, social class, professional organizations and church communities, which were historically and ontologically prior to the State and could claim a wide degree of autonomy. The State was indisputably the highest authority in the political sphere, but it had to take account of the social fabric, which protected citizens and helped guarantee their rights and freedoms that were too easily threatened by an omnipotent State. Many conservatives therefore wanted to erect a social buffer against the power of the State and found a powerful ally in the Catholic Church, which underwent a revival during the nineteenth century and vigorously defended both its autonomy and social influence. Conservative and ecclesiastical circles developed a 'social strategy' to curb the power of the State. In the long term they would succeed in this by joining with anti-liberal popular movements and taking advantage of social developments in European society in the last decades of the nineteenth century. In the end, after the Second World War, both the social and liberal strategies used to subdue the Leviathan would give shape to the current European sociopolitical model, which is characterized by an interplay between a well-organized civil society and a liberal democratic state structure.

The themes outlined so far form the core of this study, which in essence investigates the roots and specific character of the political order in Europe. It pays particular attention to the formation of the modern State, the implementation of its tasks and its social impact.

This rather complex subject is made accessible for a wider audience by offering a narrative about people, which is based on documentation from some thirty private archives in eight European countries. Prominent Austrian and German statesmen like Metternich, Bismarck and Adenauer are introduced, as are popes such as Pius IX and Leo XIII, prelates like Gaspar Mermillod and Wladimir Czacki, salon figures such as the Russian princess, Ekaterina Bagration and the Polish diva, Maria Kalergis, Catholic aristocrats like Anton Pergen and Scipione Salviati, businessmen such as the Dutch banker, Willem Cramer and the Belgian cotton industrialist, Joseph de Hemptinne, political agitators like Paul de Bréda, social reformers like Aloys von Liechtenstein, Karl von Vogelsang, René de La Tour du Pin and Albert de Mun. The story, however, centres mainly on the biography of the Austrian diplomat Gustav von Blome (1829-1906), a North German aristocrat from Holstein, natural grandson and protégé of the Austrian Chancellor Metternich and a declared opponent of Bismarck. In the background and out of the limelight, he played an important role on the European stage, in the political and religious as well as in the social spheres. He proved to be a transitional figure between aristocratic conservatism and sociopolitical Catholicism, which would evolve into the Christian Democracy of today. His biography sheds light on interesting political, religious and social developments that would have consequences well into the twentieth century

Biographical, social and political data are equally interwoven in this book. This is a difficult balancing act, but it has the advantage of giving the story both the character of a human document as well as of a broadly sketched historical fresco.

THE SHADOW OF METTERNICH

O n Thursday, 12 August 1852, Countess Kazakov, one of the many Russian aristocrats then staying in Paris, hosted a soirée in her residence in the Faubourg Saint-Honoré, which was attended mostly by foreign guests. As a rule, few fashionable activities were organized during the summer months in the French capital. In fact, from June onwards, the stars of the beau monde stayed on their provincial estates or in the many spas at home and abroad.[1] During that period the salons and soirées were mainly frequented by members of the foreign 'colonies'. A very noticeable group was that of the Russian aristocrats who – with the permission of Tsar Nicholas I – stayed in the City of Light. Countess Kazakov, a relative of the wealthy Demidov family, was one of those who had come to Paris in search of diversion.[2]

Among the Countess's guests was Gustav von Blome, a descendant of an old aristocratic family from the Duchy of Holstein in northern Germany. The 23-year-old nobleman had completed his law studies at the University of Berlin a year before and was preparing for a career in the Austrian diplomatic service by intensively studying French, the cultural and diplomatic language of the time. While in Paris he enjoyed the hospitality of his grandmother, the Russian princess, Ekaterina Bagration, who played an active role in society life. He had just passed the diplomatic service examination in Vienna with fly-

---

1   Martin-Fugier, *La vie élégante*, 107-109 and 115-120.
2   Blome to Pons, 9 Nov. 1854, LASH, 125.15, 613. The extensive correspondence between Blome and Pons is kept in the Landesarchiv of Schleswig-Holstein [LASH], Section 126.15, nrs. 613 (1852-1853), 614 (1854-April 1855), 615 (April 1855-Dec. 1858) and 616 (1859-1867). The repository will not be again noted in future references.

ing colours, and while awaiting his naturalization as an Austrian citizen had returned to Paris to say goodbye to his friends there.

That evening there was plenty of partying and dancing at the home of Countess Kazakov. The young Blome, described as 'witty and elegant, with a handsome appearance and a spontaneous and joyful character' did not go unnoticed. At one point he was introduced by the hostess to Count Louis de Pons, a 78-year-old French nobleman, who frequented the salons of the Russian aristocrats. The two men struck up a conversation and there was an immediate spark between them. Pons found Blome to be extremely charming in every way.[3] For his part the young man was fascinated by the amiable and refined French aristocrat and at the end of the evening escorted him to his home on the Faubourg Saint-Honoré. Pons later recalled: 'I was irresistibly attracted to you as we walked arm-in-arm down the street.'[4] This encounter was the beginning of a unique relationship that would last for more than fourteen years with hardly any loss of intensity. We know about this friendship because it led to an extensive correspondence – which has been preserved – that gives a fascinating picture of the two protagonists and their environment. The relationship between these intriguing personalities is of interest for our story because they belonged to two different cultural worlds, the German and French, whose interaction would determine the future of continental Europe. Moreover, their common history spans more than a century, allowing their comings and goings to be used to recount a *histoire de longue durée*.

Blome and Pons met one another at a pivotal moment, when post-Napoleonic Europe, which had taken shape during the Congress of Vienna in 1815, was on the point of collapse. In France, Louis-Napoleon Bonaparte, a nephew of the former French emperor, had seized power in a coup on 2 December 1851. By early summer 1852 he was preparing to proclaim the Second Empire, which was to be ratified by a plebiscite in November. The revival of Bonapartism resulted in a disruption of the established international order. Although the regime of the new Emperor Napoleon III had a clear authoritarian slant and rejected parliamentarianism, it still gave an impetus to liberal ideas such as popular sovereignty and nationalism. The conservative forces in Europe, which had just recovered from the wave of revolutions of 1848, felt uneasy about this development.

---

3   Pons to Blome, 31 March 1853: 'A pretty boy, with a gay and open face, full of spirit and elegance'; 27 Dec. 1853: 'charming enough to eat!'
4   Pons to Blome, 15 Aug. 1853.

'A special friendship'

Pons and Blome repeatedly sought out each other's company in the days follow-ing their first meeting, with the French count especially taking the initiative. On 15 September 1852, as Blome was about to leave Paris to begin his diplomatic career at the Vienna chancellery, Pons wrote: 'Only a regular correspondence will make your absence bearable.' In January 1853 Blome would leave for St. Petersburg as a diplomatic attaché and from that moment on their only contact was through their lively correspondence. In his numerous letters Pons openly and repeatedly declared his feelings of love for the young German nobleman:

> I want to be able to love you without limit. From the first glance, you have charmed and attracted me. You have a handsome appearance, which has never harmed anyone. In addition, your appearance, atti-tude and behaviour are graced with a great distinction, with that aris-tocratic cachet, that *parfum de vieille race* that I encounter so seldom these days.[5]

> Only one thing I ask of you, but I ask it with insistence: love me, be-cause that gives meaning to my life. You give lustre to my existence.[6]

The spirit of Romanticism certainly contributed to de Pons' high-flown expres-sion of his feelings, but it was clearly a homophile relationship, albeit platon-ic.[7] This can be gleaned from a number of statements and biographical details to be found in the correspondence. 'I cannot possibly entrust to you the secret of a woman's love, because I have never had it.'[8] Pons was married and had a son from that marriage, but he readily admitted that he had never been in love in his life, either because of innate inclinations or because he had never met a woman who could awaken those feelings in him.[9] Moreover, he seemed to have a weakness for other young men too, such as the young Russian prince, Alexis Galitzin, who competed with Blome for Pons' affection. However, the French count found Galitzin to be too immature and superficial.[10] In 1859, Prince Alexis married Princess Souvorov, but the marriage foundered because of his homosexuality. At the end of his life, in 1861, Pons would develop a re-lationship with yet another young man, Maxime Lefèvre-Deumier, the son of a famous sculptor, whom he adopted and made his heir.

5   Pons to Blome, 10 Nov. 1852; 10 Dec. 52: 'My glory lies in loving you with a passionate ten-derness.'
6   Pons to Blome, 26 Dec. 1852.
7   Pons would explicitly confirm this in 1861: 'For you all my love ... it is pure spiritualism.' (Pons to Blome, 21 Jan. 1861).
8   Pons to Blome, 5 Oct. 1853.
9   Pons to Blome, 7 Sept. 1854.
10 Pons to Blome, 13 March 1854.

Pons' homosexual predisposition was probably the main reason for his almost passionate love for Gustav von Blome, but he was also certainly attracted by his intellectual depth. On the other hand, one might wonder what led the young German aristocrat to respond to Pons' affection since in his later life he showed no interest in male love. The main explanation seems to be that Blome at that stage of his life had a great need for an affective bond, a father figure in whom he could confide his innermost feelings and thoughts. He had never known his mother, who had died a few days after his birth, and he had a strained relationship with his father, their characters and political choices differing like night and day. Pons was for him a sounding board as well as a role model, 'the perfect exemplar of the French chivalry of old'.[11] On the other hand, Blome kept more of a distance than did his older friend. He wrote to his grandmother, Princess Bagration: 'Pons is a fine and honourable man, with whom I get along exceptionally well. He has retained the freshness of spirit and the memory of a young man. His vivid imagination, however, plays tricks on him sometimes. So he has endowed me – I'm not sure why – with merits and qualities I do not possess.'[12] Shortly after their meeting, he wrote to Pons himself: 'The word friendship best expresses the feelings that you have aroused in me.' However, his feelings intensified in train of the busy correspondence they exchanged during their prolonged separation.[13] 'I love you as fiercely and passionately as my northern nature allows me.'[14] 'You have taught me to fuse admiration and affection into one feeling that has no name, but that I can describe as ardent, an adjective that, without you, I could hardly connect with the word love.'[15] In April 1853 Blome described their relationship thus: 'We cannot call our relationship mere friendship. It is something that cannot be named in French and that we have ourselves created. You have enriched my heart with a new feeling, which I had no inkling of before I knew you.'[16] 'Never in my life have I so idolized and cherished a living being. You are for me the ideal of *un homme de coeur et d' esprit*.'[17] His affection for Pons was not affected by his many amorous adventures: 'My love for you is of a very different kind than those little everyday passions.'[18]

11   Blome to Pons, 3 Sept. 1864.

12   Blome to Princess Bagration, 13 April 1853, LASH, 126.15, 617.

13   Blome to Pons, 25 July 1854: 'Do you know that this sweet intimacy between us, the source of my dearest pleasures, in fact grew by correspondence only?'

14   Blome to Pons, 14 Dec. 1852.

15   Blome to Pons, 26 Dec. 1852.

16   Blome to Pons, 1 April 1853.

17   Blome to Pons, 1 April 1853; 22 June 1853: 'I adore you, I worship you, I cherish you as much as it has been given to me to love, to worship, and to adore.'

18   Blome to Pons, 7 Sept. 1853; 3 Jan. 1854: 'How can you seriously ask me if I love you more than my mistresses? ... You have taken hold of my heart, how I do not know, and you occupy it so completely that you could not even leave it anymore, if you so desired.'

Both Pons and Blome felt their relationship was special. Blome declared: 'It is unique in the annals of human emotions ... At least, I have never heard talk of the like.'[19] Pons for his part wrote: 'I am more convinced than ever that our soul relationship knows no equivalent anywhere under the sun. The word "friendship" is not enough here. My relationship with you constitutes my whole life. You have become its soul.'[20]

From late 1855 to early 1858 Blome was attached to the Austrian embassy in Paris and began meeting his older friend regularly again. However, because of his busy schedule, the contacts were very fleeting, leading him at times to sigh: 'I think back with nostalgia to the time when I used to receive your graceful and charming letters regularly and I myself had more of a chance to tell you how much importance I attached to your affection.'[21] That affection persisted, even after Blome's marriage to Séphine Buol-Schauenstein. At the end of 1860 Pons described his feeling as a 'fatherly, filial, brotherly love'.[22] In November 1863 he stated: 'In the letters that I wrote to you in Russia, I used the word "love" so as to capture again the feeling you evoked in me and I will never withdraw that. The word "friendship" has become so commonplace and is so misused that it puts me off. In the absence of words that can properly express my emotional state, I have to use the most vigorous form.'[23] For his part Blome declared:

> My feelings for you have not changed, but they are no longer adorned with the youthful ornaments that could enchant you eight years ago. I grow older, and though my heart does not change, its language is more cautious. If the tender formulas of youthful friendship are more charming, then the affection of a grown man can be deemed more mature and more sustainable. It grows in value because it lies dormant in the heart for so many years and relies on a more considered judgement. A friendship of ten years cannot be eradicated, it has the strength of a fixed beacon.[24]

Because they attached so much importance to their mutual friendship, by mid-1854 Blome and Pons were already making plans to ensure their correspondence would be preserved in the same repository.[25] In April 1862 Blome confirmed that agreement: their mutual correspondence had to be a perma-

---

19   Blome to Pons, 25 July 1854; 7 April 1855: 'Our relations are so extraordinary, they will never be affected by the ordinary vicissitudes of human life.'
20   Pons to Blome, 14 Dec. 1854.
21   Blome to Pons, Jan. 1857 and 16 Dec. 1858.
22   Pons to Blome, 21 Dec. 1860.
23   Pons to Blome, 8 Nov. 1863.
24   Blome to Pons, 8 Nov. 1863.
25   Pons to Blome, 5 July 1854; Blome to Pons, 25 July 1854.

nent reminder of their unwavering friendship.[26] Following the death of Louis
de Pons, on 29 January 1867, his heirs in fact returned Blome's letters. Together
with those of Pons, they were neatly bound in three volumes and so have remained carefully stored to the present day. They are being used for the first
time in this study.

This correspondence is invaluable for reconstructing the world of Pons
and Blome. Their active lives were played out in the first and second half of
the nineteenth century respectively, and although they belonged to different
cultural spheres, they had similar aspirations. Both were confronted with a
process of modernization that threatened the old structures and values with
which they identified. Their correspondence is especially important for a better understanding of the personality of Gustav von Blome, who is the central
character in this story. He acknowledged this himself:

> It is to you [Pons] that I once entrusted all my worries and all my ex-
> pectations. You are the depository of all my youthful aspirations. The
> memories of my youth cannot ever be separated from your image. You
> occupy a central place in the most important period of my life, when my
> moral and intellectual development was proceeding ... .[27]

'The perfect exemplar of French chivalry'

The depository of Blome's youthful aspirations, Antoine-Louis de Pons
d'Annonville (1774-1867), was descended from an ancient aristocratic family
from the Champagne region.[28] His father, Pierre de Pons (1723-1805), had a
military career and at the end of the *ancien régime* was entrusted as Major-
General with the supreme command of the royal army in Alsace. Louis, his
only son, was also destined for the army. He received a very fashionable education in Strasbourg, in an international environment and a Franco-German
cultural sphere.[29] However, his future prospects were thoroughly disrupted by
the French Revolution, which in 1789 put an end to the absolute monarchy
and the privileges of the nobility and clergy. The radical reforms in politics
and religion led to the massive emigration of royalist aristocrats, the upper
clergy and dignitaries. The emigrés raised an army that, with the aid of Prussia and Austria, attempted to crush the revolution in France. At the request of
his father, Louis de Pons joined the emigré army in Koblenz, which together
with a Prussian force invaded France in August 1792, but a month later was

26   Blome to Pons, 5 April 1862.
27   Blome to Pons, 27 July 1861.
28   Pons' biography has been completely reconstructed on the basis of his correspondence
     with Blome (LASH, 126.15, Nrs. 613-616).
29   Pons to Blome, 10 Sept. 1864.

forced to retreat. The Bourbon Monarchy was subsequently replaced by a re-public, which increasingly came under the influence of radical elements. After the humiliating defeat of the emigré army, Louis de Pons continued to fight against the republic, as a cavalryman in a hussar regiment in the service of Austria. In the spring of 1796 he was taken prisoner, but he managed to escape and would later clandestinely return to his homeland, where in the meantime Robespierre's reign of terror had come to an end.

On 30 March 1797 Louis de Pons was married off by his family to a distant cousin on his mother's side, Marie-Jeanne-Antoinette de Girod de Monrond (1778-1859). He had never met his bride before, 'but she was beautiful and charming, from head to toe'.[30] The young couple settled in Avallon in Burgun-dy where they led a secluded life. A year later, their son Gaspard (1798-1861) was born, but Pons' wife was sickly and did not want a second child under any circumstances. Apparently, she was also frigid[31] and so Pons sought love else-where, mainly from the '*jolies grisettes*'.[32] He also compensated for the lack of affection by befriending younger men. All this did not prevent him from hav-ing great respect for his wife.[33]

In 1804 the family moved to Paris. In the meantime, Napoleon Bonaparte had come to power. He had averted the threat from foreign powers and consol-idated the major achievements of the revolution. He established a strong per-sonal rule and transformed the republic into an empire. As emperor he would wage an expansionist policy of conquest, but on the domestic front there was more stability and conditions became less critical for the former émigrés. Pons was more easily able to live a quiet life with his family in the capital, where he kept away from politics.[34] During the summer months he usually resided in Anjou with aristocratic friends who had suffered little during the revolution and continued with their merry lives, while Europe was being transformed by the successive Napoleonic wars into an immense battlefield.[35]

The fall of Napoleon and the restoration of the Bourbon monarchy were of course welcomed with great joy by Louis de Pons. At the end of 1814 he became an adjutant of field marshal Charles de Viomesnil (1734-1827), an old family friend who was appointed governor of Brittany. Shortly after he was promoted to lieutenant colonel, but in 1827, aged 53, he would end his mili-tary career. Meanwhile, his son Gaspard followed in his footsteps, becoming a captain of the royal guard in 1822 at the age of 24. He developed into a Roman-tic poet of some merit and was a friend of Alfred de Vigny and Victor Hugo. However, he led a dissolute life and had to contend with health problems that

30   Pons to Blome, 8 June 1854.
31   Pons to Blome, 25 Feb. 1855: 'very undemonstrative and one could not be less affectionate'.
32   Pons to Blome, 12 Oct. 1853.
33   Pons to Blome, 8 June 1854: 'She is a very distinguished women, with a superior mind.'
34   Pons to Blome, 20 Nov. 1858 and 28 Jan. 1866.
35   Pons to Blome, 28 Jan. 1866.

compelled him to resign from the army. Following his resignation he lived in seclusion in his parents' house.[36] He continued to concentrate on literary criticism and at the end of his life published his three-volume *Adieux poétiques*.

Given the above account it would appear that Louis de Pons was a typical 'noble of the sword' whose life was turned upside down by the revolution, but who got the opportunity during the Restoration to resume his former aristocratic life. He was only indirectly involved in politics and was certainly not among the hardliners whose reactionary attitude signed the death warrant of the Bourbon monarchy and provoked the July Revolution in Paris in 1830. Under the Citizen King, Louis-Philippe of Orleans, France now got a parliamentary regime that relied mainly on the support of the wealthy merchant class. Pons knew the new king personally, but nevertheless supported the so-called legitimists, who continued to defend the rights of the House of Bourbon. Like most of them, he would from now on remain entirely aloof from political life, while participating all the more actively in Parisian society life.

In the meantime his financial situation had become rosier, thanks to his wife inheriting a considerable fortune, which enabled him to lead a fashionable life. The venues of choice for the *beau monde* were the salons, of which there were many, each with a different character – artistic or political – and with an aristocratic or bourgeois audience. In all these salons the hostess played the main role. On appointed days, once or twice a week, close friends were received in the early afternoon and in the late evening the door was opened to a wider public. Conversation took precedence over entertainment. Nobody talked about hunting or horse races here, unlike in London; a familiar adage was: 'Paris is a paradise for women, a purgatory for men and a hell for horses.'[37] The salons were primarily located in the Faubourg Saint-Honoré, on the right bank of the Seine, and in the Faubourg Saint-Germain, on the left. The left quarter dominated during the Restoration, but under Louis-Philippe the balance shifted to the Faubourg Saint-Honoré, where alongside French aristocrats, foreign immigrants and diplomats held sway.[38] The salons in this neighbourhood had a pronounced cosmopolitan character. According to a contemporary observer, Paris was pre-eminently a city of foreigners where the native Parisian was the odd man out.[39] While the British set the agenda during the Restoration period, Russian aristocrats dominated the stage subsequently. They had a reputation for spending money freely, and for paying their bills, which apparently could not be said of other people. What was remarkable was that Paris, the capital of a country that had already become quite middle-class, continued to be an important venue for the feudal aristocracy of Europe.

36 Pons to Blome, 24 Nov. 1854 and 28 April 1861.
37 Mansel, *Paris, capitale de l'Europe*, 164.
38 Louis Lurine, *Les rues de Paris ancien et moderne*, vol. I, Paris, 1844, 343.
39 Mansel, *Paris*, 165.

Louis de Pons mainly frequented the salons in the Faubourg Saint-Honoré, the neighbourhood where he lived. Because of his thorough knowledge of German, he moved easily in a cosmopolitan environment, and his circle of acquaintances included a remarkable number of Russian aristocrats. He was an even-tempered man with pleasant manners, careful to avoid any provocation and able to express himself gracefully.[40] All these qualities made him, in Blome's eyes, a typical representative of the historic French aristocracy.

Despite being a legitimist, for a long time, Pons did not harbour any hostility towards the parliamentary regime but the way it functioned under Louis-Philippe – favouring a small coterie – increasingly aroused his abhorrence. The February Revolution of 1848 and the proclamation of the Second Republic led subsequently to a chaotic situation, which brought him to welcome Louis-Napoleon's coup and then the proclamation of the Second Empire.[41] 'In terms of education, instinct and sentiment I am a legitimist, but at present I am a *napoléoniste de circonstance.*'[42] Unlike his attitude to Napoleon I, he had a sincere admiration for Napoleon III, who, in his view, had brought an unprecedented stability to the country.[43] Henceforth he would regard the legitimists and their monarchical rivals, the liberal Orleanists, as troublemakers who pursued only party interests and were not able to provide strong leadership to the French nation. The concept of 'legitimacy' held little value for him.

In old age, and certainly during the last years of his life, Louis de Pons seemed to have a very pragmatic view of mankind and the world. In any case, he had always been more of a political realist than a doctrinaire extremist. Moreover, after the great revolution of 1789, he had lived through so many regimes and had seen French society alter so radically that he took a relativist approach to everything. 'I do not believe any more in what should be, but only in what to me seems likely and feasible.'[44] 'I prefer to follow my experience rather than my book knowledge. I know people and the world from the inside out. I do not have any presuppositions any more. I am nostalgic for the past, but do not exaggerate its merits.'[45] This attitude contrasted sharply with that of his young friend Blome, who would become a man of principle above all else, both in politics and religion. Pons had gradually become a spectator of the stirring events of the time. Blome by contrast, would struggle all his life to preserve the values and insights he had inherited, and to promote them in

40   Pons to Blome, 8 Nov. 1863: 'Nature has endowed me with a reasonably light-hearted character, over which sorrow has taken little hold'; Blome to Pons, 22 Sept. 1860: 'Whatever opinions you have, you always express them with a grace of spirit and a superiority of language that indicate a soul of the greatest serenity'; Pons to Blome, 14 Dec. 1854: 'I distrust myself, and fearing above all to offend anyone, I remain reserved.'
41   Pons to Blome, 10 Dec. 1852.
42   Pons to Blome, 9 April 1853.
43   Pons to Blome, 17 Aug. 1862 and 11 Nov. 1864.
44   Pons to Blome, 6 March 1853.
45   Pons to Blome, 10 Sept. 1864.

society. In Louis de Pons he found not so much a brother-in-arms, as an aristocratic soulmate, who throughout his diplomatic career acted as a sounding board for his feelings, ideas and aspirations.

The feudal lords of Salzau

Gustav von Blome was a representative of the North German feudal nobility which had hardly been affected by the revolutionary developments in western Europe. His family came from the Duchy of Braunschweig-Lüneburg and had gradually acquired extensive possessions in the Duchy of Holstein.[46] That duchy, along with Schleswig, was united in a personal union with the Kingdom of Denmark, and during the Napoleonic era it remained almost completely outside the French sphere of influence, unlike most of the other German principalities.

In 1759 Wulf von Blome (1728-1784) acquired Salzau, an estate of about 4,000 hectares near the Selenter See. It included four villages and about 600 serfs. A *fideicommissum* (a legal procedure for holding an inheritance in trust for a third party) was imposed on the domain to ensure the property would remain within the family for succeeding generations. Under Friedrich von Blome (1769-1818) the serfs became free tenants, although they continued to be burdened with onerous duties.

Several members of the Blome family held public offices in the service of the Danish royal family. Friedrich became royal chamberlain in 1812. His younger brother Otto, a general in the cavalry, was Danish envoy in St. Petersburg almost continuously from 1804 to 1841 and became close friends with Karl Robert von Nesselrode, who for decades was foreign minister in the Tsarist empire.

Friedrich's oldest son, also called Otto von Blome (1795-1884), was Gustav's father. He too chose a diplomatic career, first in the service of the Prince of Hanover and later of the Danish king. From 1822 he was delegation secretary to his uncle in St. Petersburg. In 1824 he ended his diplomatic career and devoted himself mostly to managing his estates, which he significantly extended over the coming decades.[47]

His family life was less successful. In 1822 he married Princess Sayn-Wittgenstein-Hohenstein, who came from a Rhineland family. They had two sons who died almost immediately. His wife did not seem to be able to settle in the

---

46 Hintze, *Geschichte des uradeligen Geschlechtes … Blome*; Klinger, *Salzau*.
47 In the 1850s, he also acquired, besides estates in the vicinity of his castle in Salzau, the Hagymadfalvà domain in Hungary, in the vicinity of Grofswardein (Oradea). The estate was located in a fertile agricultural area and comprised five villages, with a total of about 3,000 inhabitants (Blome to Pons, 26 May 1858).

Salzau. *Painting, c. 1850.*
[*O. Hintze,* Geschichte des uradeligen Geschlechtes der Herren und Grafen Blome, *Hamburg, 1929*]

North and their marital difficulties led to a divorce in 1826. Otto then embarked on extensive travels in Italy and France. In Paris he met the young Princess Clémentine Bagration, whom he married on 12 July 1828, a marriage that will be discussed in detail later. This new marriage, following the divorce from his first wife, was possible because Otto belonged to the Lutheran Church. From this second marriage Gustav von Blome was born on 18 May 1829. His mother died eight days after his birth. Otto von Blome then married a third wife, Juliana Friederike Sophie, Countess of Platen zu Hallermund (1811-1879), a relative on his mother's side.

In 1848 Otto encountered serious difficulties when the German residents of the duchies of Schleswig-Holstein objected to closer ties with Denmark and – under the influence of the German national movement – asked to be integrated in the German Confederation. The insurgent volunteer corps was supported by Prussian troops and for two years succeeded in heading off the Danish army and its allies. As a Danish count, Otto von Blome remained loyal to his lawful sovereign, with the result that his position in the region became untenable.[48] He left his estate for an extended period and stayed successively in Hamburg, Berlin, London and Copenhagen, while continuing to work for the cause of the Danish king. He was able to return to Salzau only after a number of years and would no longer be involved in politics. He extended his possessions even further and carried out some striking architectural projects. When his castle went up in flames in 1881, he embarked on the construction

48   Blome to Pons, 13 Feb. 1855.

of an imposing residence, which with its ninety rooms would be the largest of its kind in Schleswig-Holstein.[49] Not only was he interested in architecture, he was also musically gifted and had a number of praiseworthy compositions to his name.

Otto was above all a man of the world. He travelled regularly throughout Europe, visited the salons in the most important cities and participated in society life well into old age.[50] He had a reputation for being entertaining and witty, though he was not always very tactful.[51] He also lacked depth, and so, for example, was not taken very seriously by a prominent figure like Metternich, who nevertheless – as will be seen later – had reason enough to be favourably disposed towards him. However, Metternich believed he was untrustworthy and could not be relied on.[52] Gustav, who would take a completely different course, was also very critical of his father, whom he half-jokingly, half seriously, sometimes called 'the tyrant of Salzau'.[53] Otto was the last 'feudal' lord of Salzau. On taking over the family estate in 1884, his son Gustav would turn out to be an efficient manager, but was at the same time sensitive to social issues, and was held up by the local supervisory bodies as an example to other landowners in the region.[54]

The apprentice statesman

As already mentioned, Gustav was born on 18 May 1829 in Hanover. His parents had planned to have the delivery in Paris, but the doctors had advised against such a long journey and so it took place in Hanover. During the birth, medical instruments were used that caused heavy bleeding and eventually blood poisoning. The young mother, Marie-Clémentine died about a week later, on 26 May 1829. Gustav thus never knew his mother, but she would be sublimated in his thoughts all his life. It was partly her memory that drew him to Paris, the city where she had grown up and where he repeatedly visited his grandmother, Princess Bagration, whom he called *maman* in his letters. It was

49 It now functions as the *Landeskulturzentrum* and, among other things, has become home to a famous music festival and an orchestral music academy.
50 Blome to Pons, 18 Aug. 1858; Pons to Blome, 23 Aug. 1858, 29 Nov. 1862 and 6 May 1866.
51 Pons to Blome, 22 April 1853.
52 Metternich to Buol-Schauenstein, 13 Sept. 1852; Burckhardt, *Briefe*: 'You probably know Count Blome personally and so you have noticed that he is not lacking in intelligence, but that he is a dreamer and – although he is conservatively minded – he is not somebody on whom one can rely.'
53 Blome to Pons, 27 Dec. 1860.
54 Biczo, 'Graf Gustav von Blome', 75-79.

also one of the reasons for his later conversion to Catholicism. He never developed a strong bond with his stepmother, Juliana von Platen.[55]

According to his own testimony, the young Gustav knew what his future path would be from a very young age.[56] He came from a family of diplomats and was always listening to talk about politics. As a child he knew the names of all the political leaders in Europe. 'I fervently hoped that at some point I would exercise political power and would shine because of great political achievements and not because of military glory.' Initially he was educated privately and later attended the gymnasium in the Hanseatic city of Lübeck. At fifteen, he was enrolled in the Ritter Academy in Lüneburg, in the Kingdom of Hanover. Three years later he left for the University of Heidelberg in order to study law, the appropriate preparation for a diplomatic career. He participated full-heartedly in student life, and for years afterwards his excessive drinking bouts would cause recurring stomach problems.[57] Yet he was also very eager to learn: 'I devoured newspapers and periodicals. Liberalism, both political and religious, was fashionable in student circles. I read the great German philosophers and confessed to that vague theism which skepticism falls back on.'[58]

In Heidelberg Gustav was also influenced by German nationalist ideas. When, as noted above, the German residents in the duchies of Schleswig and Holstein rebelled against the Danish authorities in 1848, he interrupted his studies and joined the freedom fighters. He became second lieutenant in a regiment of dragoons. A short time later he was assigned as aide-de-camp to the Prussia's General Eduard von Bonin, who commanded an army of 12,000 men that, together with local forces, drove back the Danish army.[59] International pressure led to a temporary truce, but in the spring of 1849 hostilities resumed. The insurgents achieved new victories, yet still failed to reach their goal. Prussia succumbed to pressure from Great Britain and Russia and in 1850 abandoned the duchies to their fate. Schleswig and Holstein remained affiliated in a personal union with the Danish monarchy.

55   Blome to Pons, 15 Oct. 1854: 'a good and excellent creature, with a truly exemplary character that largely makes up for the empty spaces that nature has left in her mind'; Id. to id., 2 Dec. 1854: 'I consider my correspondence with my mother to be more a duty than a pleasure'; Pons to Blome, 4 Dec. 1854: 'Your stepmother's nature seems to be a little like that of a wailing dove, fearful, gentle and timid.'

56   This section is mainly based on the first volume of the diplomatic memoirs of Gustav von Blome, *Souvenirs de ma carrière politique* (237 p.) which are kept in the family's archives on the Salzau demesne (Gut Salzau, I). Further references to this document will be made under the heading *Souvenirs*, without any mention of the depository.

57   Blome to Pons, 8 May 1853; Pons to Blome, 14 May 1853: 'Count de Blome [Otto] has told me that at Heidelberg you cruelly damaged your stomach with an immoderate misuse of beer'; Blome to Pons, 28 May 1853: 'My father did not deceive you in revealing my Heidelberg follies to you.'

58   *Récit de ma conversion au catholicisme*, Gut Salzau, IX, 5.

59   Opitz, *Schleswig-Holstein*, 190-195.

Gustav von Blome. Engraving, 1849.
[*O. Hintze*, Geschichte des uradeligen Geschlechtes der Herren und Grafen Blome, *Hamburg, 1929*]

In this conflict Gustav and his father, Otto, held diametrically opposite views. Otto felt bound by his oath of loyalty to the Danish king while Gustav opted for the German national cause. The events in this revolutionary time led to discord between father and son, who were probably already estranged by the father's many absences and the lack of a real mother figure in the son's life. It would take years before their relationship again became more cordial.[60]

In 1850, Gustav left the Prussian army, and continued his law studies at the University of Berlin. His war experiences had influenced him deeply: his responsibilities as an officer and his being confronted with massacres had matured him.[61] At Berlin University, a reactionary atmosphere prevailed following the revolutionary upheaval of the previous years. Blome took a number of courses, including that of Friedrich Julius Stahl, 'who praised everything that was corporatist, historical and customary in contrast to the homogenizing and modernizing activities of state bureaucrats'.[62] He also regularly read the *Kreuzzeitung*, the newspaper of the Prussian ultra-conservatives, and so, 'little by little, I became what is called *a conservative, a reactionary*'.[63]

So, during his Berlin student days, Blome came under the influence of Prussian ultra-conservatives who emphasized order and authority, legitimacy, tradition and social cohesion.[64] Most of them turned against the modernizing State, which – in keeping with royal absolutism – wanted to treat all subjects in the same way, sidelined old private and corporative intermediate organizations and aimed at centralizing and bureaucratizing everything. The modern State persistently strove to expand its territory and its powers. The conservatives, on the other hand – in line with tradition – wanted to maintain corporative, class-based, regional communities and institutions that would impose limits on state power. In that respect their ideas showed some affinity with those of Montesquieu. They were also opponents of the national movements then emerging, which threatened the historical states and monarchies. Opposed to revolutionary nationalism, which they called an artificial invention by bourgeois intellectuals, they advocated regionalism and federalism, and even a European-wide legal order. Blome would defend such ideas his whole life.

The Prussian ultra-conservatives also accorded an important role to religion in society, but Gustav showed little interest in this, at least for the time being, his thinking being dominated by politics. He had previously been re-

---

60 Blome to Pons, 13 Feb. 1855: 'You are right not to talk politics with my father; he starts from preconceived ideas that have their source in the troubles of 1848 from which he suffered a lot'; Blome to Pons, 24 Feb. 1855 and 6 Nov. 1866: 'In this, as in so many other things, I differ from my progenitor both in taste and opinion.'
61 *Récit de ma conversion*, Gut Salzau, IX, 5.
62 Blackbourn, *The Long Nineteenth Century*, 105.
63 *Récit de ma conversion*, Gut Salzau, IX, 5.
64 Nipperdey, *Deutsche Geschichte (1800-1866)*, 313-319.

ceptive to liberal constitutional ideas, but now he evolved in a totally opposite direction: 'From now on I saw the need for a strong authority in society.' In his early youth he had already developed 'a cult of logic' and was inclined to draw the ultimate conclusions from the premises he postulated, a habit that would persist throughout his life. He no longer saw any middle ground between revolution on the one hand and order and stability on the other.

The evolution that Gustav von Blome went through was not exceptional. As already mentioned in the prologue, after the 1848 revolutions many sympathizers of the liberal cause throughout Europe moved in a conservative direction, as will be discussed later. Gustav's turnaround meant he was again taking up his family's political orientation: both his grandfather Friedrich and his grand-uncle Otto had been prominent anti-revolutionaries.

This conservative conviction greatly influenced Gustav's choice of which country to serve as a diplomat.[65] At that time, diplomacy still had a strong international character and the recruitment of diplomats was not determined exclusively by national considerations. Denmark was an obvious choice given the family tradition, but ever since the Napoleonic era the country had lost a great deal of influence and was reduced to a third-rate power. Moreover, Gustav's involvement in the revolution in Holstein had cut off that avenue. Prussia was a possibility, but not an attractive one: 'Prussia was a country of soldiers and peasants, and attracted me the least.' Princess Bagration, his Russian-born grandmother, tested the waters in St. Petersburg but Chancellor Nesselrode evinced little interest. Gustav's father did not enjoy much favour at the court of the Tsar. Nesselrode let on that Gustav was not familiar enough with the customs and traditions of the country and, in addition, could not speak the language sufficiently.

Meanwhile, the aspiring diplomat himself had already made a different choice. Austria, which then included Hungary and various Slavic and Italian territories, had in 1848-1849 gone through a major crisis, resulting in the fall and the brief banishment of Chancellor Metternich. Afterwards, Prince Felix Schwarzenberg succeeded in restoring order and providing stability to the multinational empire. Gustav opted to enter the service of the Habsburgs, the descendants of the former German emperors. In June 1851, he travelled with his father to Vienna and made a first attempt to be admitted to the Austrian diplomatic service. Schwarzenberg, however, announced that he no longer wanted to take on foreigners in the diplomatic corps. This time Gustav was not deterred; he immediately renounced his Holstein citizenship and decided to apply for Austrian nationality. As this procedure would take a full year, he resolved to go to his grandmother in Paris in order to work on his French and Italian language skills and prepare for the diplomatic service examination. However, his first application for naturalization was rejected by the Vienna

City Council. Meanwhile, Schwarzenberg had died and was succeeded as foreign minister by Karl-Ferdinand Buol-Schauenstein, who would be easier to influence through Princess Bagration.[66] What was also important this time was that Gustav was recommended by Metternich, who had returned to Vienna shortly before and was again exerting great influence behind the scenes. Gustav was given permission to take the examination with the promise that naturalization would automatically follow. This is what, in fact, transpired. He passed with flying colours and was admitted to the diplomatic service by a decree of 4 August 1852.[67] On October 30th the *Statthalterei* of Lower Austria awarded him Austrian nationality, and on November 8th he was appointed as an attaché, after which he began his internship at the state chancellery.[68]

Gustav had succeeded in his aim, not through the intervention of his father – to the contrary – but through the support of Princess Bagration and ex-chancellor Metternich. He could indeed rejoice in 'the firm support of the house of Metternich, where I was treated with particular amiability and courtesy'. Two years earlier in Brussels, he had been introduced for the first time to the former Austrian chancellor, but that brief encounter could not account for the goodwill shown towards him. Metternich's support had deeper reasons, about which Gustav was completely unaware, at least insofar as can be determined.

The naked angel

It was Blome's maternal grandmother, Ekaterina Pavlovna Skavronskaya (1783-1857), Princess Bagration, who above all gave a decisive turn to his diplomatic career. She was a prominent figure in European society life and had an eventful life.[69] She was related on her father's side to the Russian Empress Catherine I, and on her mother's side she was a cousin of Grigory Potemkin, the lover and adviser of Catherine II. At a young age she became lady-in-waiting to Empress Maria Fyodorovna, the wife of Paul I. In 1800 she was

---

66 Blome to Princess Bagration, May 1852, LASH, 126.15, 617. Karl-Ferdinand von Buol-Schauenstein (1797-1865) was minister for foreign affairs from April 1852 to May 1859. Roy Austensen characterized him thus: 'Buol was the quintessential diplomat: correct, methodical, punctual, and a master of the practice and protocol of diplomacy' ('Count Buol and the Metternich Tradition'), in: *Austrian History Yearbook* 9-10 (1973-1974), 173-193.

67 At the end of 1853, Emperor Francis Joseph I himself congratulated him on his examination (*Souvenirs*, vol. I, 10).

68 In a letter of 6 November 1852 Buol-Schauenstein had warmly recommended him to the Emperor (Biczo, *Graf Gustav von Blome*, 74).

69 On Ekaterina Skavronskaya, Princess Bagration, see: Corti, *Metternich*; Weissensteiner, *Liebe*; Bertier de Sauvigny, *Metternich*; Seward, *Metternich*; De Sédouy, *Congrès de Vienne*; de Villepin, *Le soleil noir*; Zamoyski, *Rites of Peace*. See also the historical novel by Hershan, *The Naked Angel*.

obliged to marry Major-General Pyotr Bagration (1765-1812), who came from a princely Georgian family and was at that time making a meteoric advance in the Russian army. He was a true fighting general, recklessly brave, a man with a volcanic temper and a warm heart who was idolized by his officers and men. He fell out of favour with the Tsar and joined a circle of conspirators who assassinated him in March 1801. In the meantime, Bagration had sent his young wife to safety in Dresden, the capital of the principality of Saxony. This baroque city, known as the Florence of Germany, had after the French Revolution become a privileged sanctuary for the gallant Polish and French aristocracy and the scene of a busy salon life. Ekaterina Skavronskaya, a ravishing beauty, quickly became a figure of note in that milieu. She would never return to Russia where her husband, under the new Tsar Alexander I, had a brilliant military career and would distinguish himself in the successive wars against Napoleon.

In Dresden, in late 1801, Ekaterina Skavronskaya came to know the new Austrian ambassador, Klemens von Metternich. An intelligent, ambitious, charming and elegant man, he was at that point just beginning his diplomatic career.[70] A liaison with many highs and lows ensued between them, but they became very close once again when Metternich became head of the Austrian diplomatic service in mid-1809. Meanwhile, Skavronskaya had settled in Vienna, apparently on the orders of Tsar Alexander I, who wished to put this distant relative and shrewd *salonnière* onto the diplomatic chessboard, as was commonly done in those days. The results were unexpected. On 29 September 1810 Skavronskaya gave birth in Vienna to a daughter whose name was entered the following day in the baptismal register of the Schottenkirche as Maria Clementina Defohse. The mother's name was not disclosed, but the following was recorded: 'The child's mother had already disappeared at the time of baptism and could no longer be contacted. Neither the midwife nor the godmother know exactly who the mother is. Therefore, no further information can be given about her.'[71] The child was initially entrusted to a milliner in Baden near Vienna, but she later resided regularly with Princess Bagration, who treated her like a daughter. It was known within a small circle that Clémentine – the choice of name was not accidental – was Metternich's daughter. His wife, Eleonore, soon became aware of the illegitimate child, but did not make an issue of the situation.

General Bagration himself probably never knew about his wife's pregnancy and the birth of Clémentine. In this period, Napoleon was preoccupied with preparations for his major campaign against Russia, in which Bagration

70 De Sédouy, *Congrès de Vienne*, 30: 'Thin, pale and delicate face, illuminated by deep blue eyes and framed by thinning blond hair. He is a handsome, distinguished man, who appeals to women and knows how to charm his interlocutors.'

71 Wulf, 'Salzau-Paris-Salzau', 75.

Princess Ekaterina Bagration. Aquarelle, J.-B. Isabey, 1812.
[*Paris, Musée du Louvre © RMN; Michèle Bellot*]

as commander of the Second Russian Army would play an important role. He was fatally wounded at the Battle of Borodino, near Moscow, on 7 September 1812 and died shortly afterwards, thereby acquiring the status of a hero in Russian history. On his death Skavronskaya regained her full freedom, while her daughter was able to drop her anonymity and be legitimised as Princess Bagration, as will be later discussed.

The relationship between Metternich and Skavronskaya lasted until the beginning of 1813. It also proved to be of political importance as it was used by the Tsar to inflame Metternich's anti-French sentiments, at a time when Austria was forced to form an alliance with Napoleon. At the same time the liaison provided Metternich with much useful information, thanks to Skavronskaya's extensive circle of Russian acquaintances. After the debacle of Napoleon's campaign against Russia, he cautiously steered Austrian foreign policy in a different direction and tried to forge an alliance with Russia and Prussia. Together with these countries and Great Britain, he formed a coalition that would eventually overthrow Napoleon. In this context, the Russian connections were of great importance. Love and politics appeared to go hand in hand here.

From 1813 on, Princess Bagration had to contend with a formidable rival, Duchess Wilhelmine von Sagan, for whom Metternich conceived a great passion. Both irresistible temptresses played prominent parts in the Congress of Vienna (October 1814 - March 1815), which brought together a large number of princes and diplomats to draw up a new European order after the Napoleonic wars.[72] The outside world was struck above all by the frivolous nature of this congress, with its seemingly endless festivities, balls and soirées. Very quickly the well-known remark of Prince De Ligne did the rounds: '*Le congrès ne marche pas, il danse.*' The rulers and aristocrats present shook off the nightmare of the devastating wars and returned to their frivolous lifestyle. The salons – the setting for politicizing, intrigue, coquetry and flirtation – played an important role during the conference. The most frequented salons were those of Bagration and Sagan, who – not coincidentally – had set up their residences in two different wings around the courtyard of the luxurious Palm Palace in the Schenkengasse. Both ladies vied with each other for the favour of the principal players of the Congress, and did so, it must be said, with resounding success.

Bagration was a striking beauty with golden hair and a white, translucent complexion. She usually wore very low-cut clothes that earned her the epithet of 'the naked angel'.[73] Count de la Garde Chambonas thought she combined oriental sensuality with Andalusian grace.[74] But Bagration had more to

72 Zamoysky, *Rites of Peace*, 238-259.
73 Weissensteiner, *Liebe*, 147; Desmond, *Metternich*, 49.
74 De Sédouy, *Congrès de Vienne*, 179-180.

offer than just her physical charms; she was extremely intelligent, with keen political insight, and above all had the ear of the Tsar. Furthermore, she also granted her favours to his brother, Grand Duke Constantine, as well as to several other princes. She finally entered into a more permanent (in her case a relative term) relationship with Crown Prince Wilhelm of Württemberg, who later, on his marriage to Grand Duchess Ekaterina Pavlona, would become the father of the future Queen Sophie of the Netherlands.

Ekaterina Skavronskaya was a wealthy lady, but her lifestyle during the congress was so flamboyant that it almost ruined her and she even had to ask her cook for credit. Weighed down by astronomical debts, she was placed under house arrest in June 1815 by the Viennese city magistrate. However, she managed to escape from the city and fled to the Allied headquarters, hoping that her aristocratic friends would throw her a lifeline. Apparently, she succeeded, and in all likelihood it was Alexander I who helped her out of the emergency.

At the request of the tsar she later settled in Paris, where she continued her salon activities and as a Russian agent relayed information about the ins and outs of politics under the Bourbon monarchy. Her financial situation noticeably improved: from 1825 on she rented a large residence in classical style in the Rue du Faubourg Saint-Honoré, next to the British Embassy, and bought it in 1830 for a significant sum.[75] Her salon was attended by prominent politicians and artists, including Honoré de Balzac. She continued to have a keen interest in current affairs and from the vantage point of the ambassador's box regularly attended the debates in the chamber.[76] At the time, Parisians called her 'the white cat'.

Once settled in Paris, Ekaterina Skavronskaya brought her daughter Clémentine to live with her and introduced her as Princess Bagration. The girl received a French and Catholic upbringing. In March 1825, during a stay in Paris on diplomatic business, Metternich visited Skavronskaya and appeared to be delighted about his natural daughter. A year later he began to correspond with her, and in a letter dated 6 November 1826 he formally acknowledged that he was her father. The prospect of marriage was looming and so it was important that her aristocratic background be legitimized.[77] Metternich worked on this behind the scenes. First, and without much ado, he set about changing the register of births in Vienna, but soon found this to be impossible. Princess Bagration had to make a formal notary declaration that Clémentine was her child and heir; at the same time she had to request that the name Bagration be entered in the register of births. This was done but it was not enough. In fact,

75   Jacques Hillairet, *Dictionnaire historique des rues de Paris*, Paris, 1964, vol. I, 505.
76   Mansel, *Paris*, 125; Martin-Fugier, *La vie élégante*, 217.
77   Metternich to Dorothea Lieven: 'The little one has good marriage prospects. My conscience obliges me to apply myself to this.' Cited by Wulf, *Salzau-Paris-Salzau*, 80. This account of the circumstances of the marriage is primarily based on Wulf's article.

the mother's name had not even been entered in the register and so could not be changed. The case was then temporarily shelved. However, by 1828 time was beginning to run out as Clémentine turned 18 that year and several suitors had already made overtures. Another strategy was adopted, apparently on the legal advice of the Austrian embassy in Paris. Articles 70 and 71 of the French Civil Code stated that if a birth certificate could not be presented at a marriage, a notary's deed had to be drawn up, stating where and when the birth had taken place and why a birth certificate was not available. This statement had to be signed by seven witnesses. On 10 June 1828 Princess Bagration appeared before magistrate François Pinard of the first arrondissement in Paris, and declared that her daughter Clémentine needed a birth certificate for a planned marriage. She added that the girl was the daughter of Prince Bagration, whom she had known for two months at the end of 1809, but the birth had not been entered in the register of the Russian embassy in Vienna because at the time the impending war had forced all Russian officials to leave Vienna. A proper registration was not possible later either. Skavronskaya requested that Clémentine be legally declared Princess Bagration. The witnesses were a French doctor, as well as six members of the Austrian embassy, including the ambassador in person. Clearly under orders from Metternich, they lent weight to this false declaration. Thus, Clémentine Defohse was legally declared to be Princess Bagration. All the preconditions were now met for an aristocratic marriage that would be socially acceptable.

The most successful suitor to make an appearance was Otto von Blome. After his divorce he had gone travelling throughout Europe, and from February to June 1827 he stayed in Paris for the first time. When he returned in 1828, he met Clémentine Bagration, who had made her debut. It was a *coup de foudre*. Both were deeply in love and wanted to hurry up their wedding plans, much to Skavronskaya's dismay. Otto's energetic performance, which was seen as 'inappropriate and not in conformity with his position', created a stir in the salon world. Clémentine also violated the norms of decency and, according to the rules of her social milieu, behaved with too little restraint. Skavronskaya eventually had to give in, and in June 1828 the engagement was announced; Blome was then 32 and Clémentine almost 18. On 2 July 1828 all those concerned appeared before the Paris notary Jonquoy to conclude the marriage contract, which provided for a separation of property. Clémentine received a dowry of 800,000 francs (currently equivalent to approximately 3.36 million euro), which would be paid in installments over the succeeding years. The management of the capital was entrusted to the future groom. The contract was signed by numerous witnesses: the ambassadors of Austria, Russia and Denmark, as well as some French aristocrats. On 3 July 1828 the civil marriage was concluded under French law, and shortly afterwards church weddings in both the Catholic and Lutheran rites took place.

There is little doubt that Skavronskaya and probably Metternich also would have wanted their daughter to marry someone from a higher aristocratic rank, but Clémentine could not resist the charms of Otto von Blome. It was clearly a love marriage. For Blome himself the social status of his young wife was all that he could desire. He had been informed of her legitimization, and from that protocol he could assume that Bagration was the father. Whether his wife ever told him the truth is not known. It remains an open question also whether their son Gustav, who was born a year later, ever knew about his true origins; at least there is not a single trace of this in the records that he left.

Following Clémentine's death on 26 May 1829, eight days after the birth of her son, relations between Otto von Blome and Skavronskaya were severed. Moreover, the latter also refused to pay out the rest of the dowry. However, since the marriage contract stipulated that any descendants would receive a share, Otto von Blome lodged several lawsuits against Skavronskaya, first in Paris and later in Russia, to require her to pay the trust funds to Gustav. The case dragged on for many years and was settled only in March 1846. Skavronskaya made a once-off payment of 157,000 silver rubles to Otto von Blome, who invested the capital in his domain and paid Gustav, once he reached his majority, an annual rate of three percent.[78] Relations with Skavronskaya were thus 'normalized'. This arrangement offered Gustav two advantages: he was less financially dependent on his father, and he had enough resources at his disposal to enable him choose a diplomatic career.

With her daughter Clementine married, Ekaterina Bagration herself still was in search of suitors. On 11 January 1830 at the age of 47 she married John Hobert Caradoc, sixteen years her junior, and a military attaché in the British embassy, which was housed next to her residence. He was a real dandy, nicknamed 'beau Caradoc', and was known for his amorous adventures.[79] Apparently, his marriage to Bagration brought him much financial gain.[80] In 1839 he succeeded his father as Lord Howden and carried out various diplomatic assignments in Brazil, Spain and elsewhere. He returned to Paris only sporadically, but despite this (or perhaps because of it) the marriage lasted.[81]

During the July Monarchy – and especially from the 1840s onwards – Bagration's star began to wane in the Parisian sky. She had sided with the

---

78   Wulf, 'Vormundschaftliche Rechnungsablage', Dec. 2006, 26-29.
79   *Oxford Dictionary of National Biography*, vol. X (2004), 9; William Thackeray, 5 March 1850, *A Collection of Unpublished Letters of Thackeray (1847-1855)*, New York, 1888: 'I travelled to Paris with a character for a book, Lord Howden, the ex-beau Caradoc, a man for whom more women have gone distracted than you have any idea of. So delightful a middle-aged dandy! Well, he will make a page in some book some day.'
80   Pons to Blome, 8 June 1853.
81   Pons to Blome, 3 July 1855: 'The princess is in possession of the Lord, her husband, and she acts as triumphantly about that as if he were new fruit for her'; Blome to Pons, 7 July 1855: 'She always flaunts her conjugal bliss, it rejuvenates her, and she even goes so far as to affect a great physical weariness when Milord leaves her house.'

new regime, but her salon was steeped in an overly nostalgic atmosphere and became less attractive than that of other Russian aristocrats such as Anne Sophie Swetchine and Princess Dorothea Lieven.[82] In her old age, Bagration was not particularly well preserved. According to malicious contemporaries, she looked rather like a parched and fleshless mummy, with a yellowed skin. Yet, she still wore revealing clothes and could not stop flirting and warbling like a sick hummingbird.[83] On 16 September 1852 the Austrian ambassador to Paris, Joseph Alexander von Hübner, noted in his diary:

> Just today I met Princess Bagration, who played an important role in the elegant European salon world at the beginning of this century. As soon as one crosses the threshold of the magnificent residence she occupies in the Faubourg Saint-Honoré, one finds oneself in the *Empire* of Napoleon I. A tall porter stamps his halberd on the floor, whereupon some servants, powdered and with swords on their hips rush to guide the guest into an empire salon. This is closed off with heavy yellow silk curtains that barely let the daylight in. In this salon can be found, stretched out on a low sofa and wrapped in a light gauze veil, the last survivor of the goddesses who shone at the congresses of Vienna, Aachen and Verona. But is this still a living creature? Not a drop of blood is to be detected in the dull, sallow skin of the thin face. The lustreless eyes seem lost in vagueness, but a sweet smile bids you welcome. And what exquisite manners! She is typical of the peripatetic high-society Russian ladies of yesteryear. Her epigones cannot be compared with her. And yet, the visitor is overcome with just one desire: to escape as soon as possible. One has to be oneself a mummy to be able to survive in this tropical atmosphere with its excess of perfume.[84]

Bagration and Metternich still met sporadically, including in July 1846 in the spa town of Karlsbad.[85] In May 1849 she visited the former chancellor in Richmond in England, where he was staying in exile. His granddaughter Pauline later recalled: 'It was touching to see how my grandfather, who had managed to keep a dignified and aristocratic bearing, escorted this shriveled mummy arm-in-arm to the table.'[86] People were then quite compassionate about the aged Skavronskaya, who held tenaciously to her lost youth and her past glory. But, the world in which she had glittered was gone forever. Metternich's glo-

---

82   Photiadès, 'Maria Kalergis-Moukhanow', 128-130: 'To Sophie Swetchine, this pious woman who thought she was a mystic, Lieven willingly left the kingdom of the heart; to Catherine Bagration, this odalisque of Muhammad's paradise, the realm of the senses; for herself she reserved the realm of the mind.'

83   Photiadès, 'Maria Kalergis-Moukhanow', 127.

84   Hübner, *Neun Jahre*, 75-76.

85   Sauvigny, *Metternich*, 494.

86   Seward, *Metternich*, 314; Hayman, *Pauline de Metternich*, 20.

ry days were over also, although his political legacy would remain for a long time and would continue to inspire others, including his grandson, Gustav von Blome, for whom he was a shining example.

The coachman of Europe

Klemens von Metternich (1773-1859) was a statesman of exceptional stature.[87] It is said that he dominated continental European politics in the first half of the nineteenth century, as Bismarck would in the second half. Both were conservative politicians, but they held very different views on the motives and goals of international politics. Metternich merits comprehensive treatment here, while Bismarck will be extensively discussed in the next chapter.

Metternich was a typical representative of the enlightened, elegant aristocracy, whose world had been shaken up by the French Revolution. He came from an old Rhenish family but entered the service of the Habsburg dynasty, just like his father, who for a time was a minister in the Austrian Netherlands. Influenced by the German Enlightenment and familiar with the work of philosophers like Kant, he had very broad interests, not only in politics but also in the exact and biomedical sciences. The extent to which he shared the frivolous life of his class has already been sufficiently highlighted.

The initial phase of his diplomatic career was completely overshadowed by the Napoleonic wars. Bonaparte's international policy was motivated by a desire for expansion, which brought him into conflict not only with the continental powers but even more with Great Britain. At the end of 1804, he fully revealed his imperial ambitions by proclaiming a French empire. His victory at Austerlitz (1805) led to the creation of vassal states in German territory. This resulted in a dangerous tension between France and Germany that would burden European politics for a century and a half. Napoleon reduced Prussia (1806) and proud Austria (1809) to second-class powers. He tried to strangle Britain economically by imposing a trade blockade, which required getting control of the sea lanes and coastal areas in Europe, leading to a further expansion of the French empire.

Napoleon reached the height of his power with the Treaty of Tilsit (7 July 1807), sometimes called a '*Yalta avant la lettre*'. The Russian tsar, the most powerful monarch of his time, recognized Napoleon's title of emperor and his

---

87 The following works on Metternich have been consulted: *Mémoires du Prince de Metternich*, vol. III, 225-234; Srbik, *Metternich*; Bertier de Sauvigny, *Metternich*; Berglar, *Metternich*; Kraus, *Politisches Gleichgewicht*; Sked, *Metternich and Austria*; Kissinger, *A World Restored*; De Sédouy, *Congrès de Vienne*; Zamoyski, *Rites of Peace*; Derré, *Metternich et Lamennais*; Siemann, *Metternich*; Migliorini, *Metternich*; Kronenbitter, 'Friedrich von Gentz und Metternich', 71-87; Rumpler, *Eine Chance*, 105-260; Bled, *Les fondements du conservatisme autrichien*, 51-61.

recent conquests. Both sovereigns divided Europe into two spheres of influence and promised each other assistance in supporting their claims. However, this settlement did not last long because the relationship between both countries was more competitive than cooperative. Finally in 1812, so as to put an end once and for all to Russia's ability to threaten France, Napoleon launched his fatal expedition against the Tsarist empire, which would turn into a major debacle for him.

As a young diplomat in the Austrian service Metternich followed these developments from the sidelines initially, but in October 1809 he was appointed minister of foreign affairs by Emperor Francis I. At that point, the country was at an absolute low point, following its humiliating defeat in the War of the Fifth Coalition, and was completely at the mercy of Napoleon. Metternich succeeded in arranging a marriage between Bonaparte and the Emperor's daughter, Marie-Louise, and thus Austria managed to retain a certain autonomy. It was not reduced to a vassal state but was given the status of a fully-fledged ally of France, and as such its army took part in the Russian campaign, under Austrian command.

Following the disastrous outcome of that campaign the Russian army launched a counteroffensive and Prussia allied itself very quickly with the new coalition against Napoleon. Metternich presented himself as an independent mediator, but when Napoleon's unwillingness to make concessions became obvious, he steered Austria into the allied camp. The Battle of Leipzig (16-18 October 1813) sealed the fate of the French emperor. Virtually all the German states now joined the coalition and the French lost their hegemony over Germany. The allied troops marched into France and in early April 1814 Napoleon renounced the throne, which came back into the hands of the Bourbons.

At the peace conference in Vienna (October 1814-June 1815), the victorious powers deliberated on a new order for post-Napoleonic Europe. The expansionist policies of the French emperor had completely overturned centuries-old political boundaries and structures. Moreover, they had created a European area for which broad solutions now needed to be worked out. A simple return to the *ancien régime* was neither possible nor desirable.

The Congress of Vienna redressed in a pragmatic way the disrupted balance between the five great powers, which included the defeated France. It put a brake on the hegemonic ambitions of France and Russia by strengthening Prussia and especially Austria, which became the leading powers within a newly established Confederation, a conglomerate of 39 German states intended to bring stability to central Europe. Prussia strengthened its position with the appropriation of Rhineland-Westphalia, although for the time being it would remain inferior to Austria within the German Confederation. In fact, Austria, a multinational state which for centuries had also included Hungary, the Czech Republic and Slovakia, was the leading power in German territory.

Klemens Wenzel Lothar von Metternich. Gouache, J. Einsle, 1815.
[*Private collection*]

As a result, the Austrian emperor exercised more authority over Germany than had been the case since the Peace of Westphalia (1648). Moreover, Austria regained its influence over Lombardy and also annexed Venice, thereby replacing France as the dominant power on the Italian peninsula. In proportion to its economic and military significance, Austria had become overextended, and was dependent on the support of Britain and/or Russia for its survival as a major player. Nevertheless, in the short term, the final balance was particularly positive for the Habsburgs, especially in view of their desperate situation a few years before.

Of even greater importance was that the Congress of Vienna brought about a system of collective security that would protect Europe for decades from new, devastating wars. In the previous twenty years many millions of soldiers and civilians had been killed in successive wars. Government leaders wanted to prevent a repetition of such horrors. They wanted not just to create a new balance of power, but also bring about a comprehensive and lasting peace, a higher good that would supersede the interests of individual states.

This goal was especially important for Metternich, who profoundly abhorred war and chaos. He was deeply influenced by Kant who, following Erasmus, had pleaded for a federation of states, governed by laws and treaties.[88] He strove for a balance of power in Europe that could be reached if rulers were willing to limit the autonomy of their own states and support a general system that accepted the principle of collective security. To this end, the states had to be integrated into an alliance that would replace war and violence with a widely accepted legal system aimed at resolving conflicts by diplomatic consultation. Policy had to be dictated by the directives of cosmopolitan reason and not by reasons of state or national interests. International treaties had to be supported by a canon of shared values, including respect for the rights of all states – even the smaller ones – and by scrupulous fidelity to promises and agreements. All in all, this was a very legalistic approach to international law: though based on ethical principles, it put protection of the law at its centre. In the opinion of Henry Kissinger, who later as US secretary of state would be inspired by Metternich, a shared sense of justice in his system lessened the desire to use violence, and the pursuit of a balance of power diminished the chances of doing so.

These ideas were fully approved by Tsar Alexander I and the British foreign secretary, Castlereagh, who along with Metternich were the leading figures at the Congress of Vienna. So, the Concert of Europe was created, which aimed at creating a political balance with a view to maintaining peace. The five Great Powers had regular discussions about contested issues in European politics and so began conference diplomacy. They avoided internal conflicts as much as possible and settled smaller outbreaks in remote areas by mutual agreement. The rule was that any territorial change had to be approved by all the great powers. As guardians of one another's security and as the watchmen of European peace, they claimed special rights for themselves and so in fact restricted the sovereignty of smaller countries.[89]

Immediately after the Congress of Vienna, the other great powers were above all concerned with keeping turbulent France, which had difficulty with the peace agreement, under control. As long as Metternich could count on Britain, he continued to play a leading role in European politics, earning him the nickname of 'the coachman of Europe'.[90] In the 1830s, England, then un-

88   Sofka, *Metternich's Theory of European Order*, 115-150.
89   Bridge and Bullen, *The Great Powers*; Schroeder, *The Transformation of European Politics*; Scott, *The Birth of the Great Power System*.
90   This characterization was made by the Russian tsar, Nicholas I. See Weissensteiner, *Liebe*, 164.

der liberal governments, was more attentive to the aspirations of the liberal and national movements and sought rapprochement with Orleanist France. Conservative Austria was henceforth increasingly isolated. Its position weakened also in Germany and Italy, its two natural spheres of influence, and Metternich's star began to wane.

The European Concert was increasingly perceived as an alliance of conservative sovereigns who did not seek peace so much as the suppression of national and freedom-loving governments. The Concert seemed above all to be conceived to preserve the status quo. It was very sympathetic towards the dynastic rights of sovereigns and the balance between the great powers, but it paid little heed to public opinion and political trends in the different countries. Metternich saw the emerging national movements, which were usually supported by the liberal bourgeoisie, as a threat to the European Concert. In the areas under Austrian domination, thus including Germany and Italy, he was a resolute opponent of political nationalism. He became the black sheep of the liberal nationalists who were to determine the future, and this would for a long time determine the perception of his person and his policies.

Metternich was particularly opposed to nationalism because it threatened the balance of power and peace in Europe. He also saw it – quite rightly – as a danger to the continued existence of the multinational Habsburg Empire, which in turn was an important guarantee for the balance of power in Europe.[91] The dynastic bond was the main factor of cohesion in Austria. The emperor had a special relationship with the German-speaking part of the population, but he could not afford to identify completely with just one of the nations in his realm. In Metternich's view, political nationalism was an insidious poison for Austria, although there was room for a form of cultural nationalism, provided it did not undermine loyalty to the multinational state.

Even less did the chancellor see any benefits in a liberalization of the political system, since this, in his view, would turn society over to irrational forces and possibly lead to chaos. He also rejected liberalism because, with its universal principles and formulas, it ignored the uniqueness of each country and its people. State institutions had to be adapted to the historical and economic conditions of a country and its people. In multinational states like Austria only a strong, historically legitimate monarchy could embody and guarantee the unity of the empire.

Metternich definitely favoured a powerful monarchy, but he nevertheless opposed the bureaucratic and centralist absolutism that had taken shape in Austria in the second half of the eighteenth century under Maria Theresa and especially Joseph II. In 1817 he proposed important reforms for reorganizing domestic governance. He pleaded for a federalization of the imperial state and the restoration of the traditional political entities. He seemed to be a supporter

91 Schroeder, 'Die Habsburger Monarchie und das europäische System', 178-182.

of a moderate form of historical federalism. His motto was '*Einheit in der Viel-heit*' (Unity in Diversity).[92] He also favoured reviving old consultative bodies, such as the diets, on both regional and central levels, thereby allowing for cultural nationalism and decentralized legislation.[93] However, Emperor Francis I and the leading aristocracy in Vienna opposed these proposals and opted to continue a policy of bureaucratic centralization. After that, Metternich would be less involved in domestic politics.

Furthermore, he opposed Josephinism, the ecclesiastical policy that subjected the Catholic Church to strong government control. He was willing to grant greater freedom to the Church, which had experienced a revival under the influence of Romanticism. His attitude toward religion in general and the Catholic Church in particular was otherwise dictated primarily by political considerations. The churches legitimized authority and subjected the acquisition and use of power to moral standards. The Catholic Church, which was on a collision course with revolutionary principles, was also a sympathetic partner in the defense of conservative interests. Churches could be an important stabilizing force and could be called into service in maintaining the moral and political order. In 1816 Metternich suggested that a concordat be concluded with the Holy See and some Josephinist measures against the Church be reversed, arguing that it could be given greater freedom, without it acquiring a position of priority or political influence. He was opposed to every form of political Catholicism or the reintroduction of a Christian social order, such as was advocated by Romantic conservatives and later also by his grandson Blome.[94] Ultimately, nothing came of his limited reform proposals. Francis I did not wish to give up any rights to Rome and his administration clung tenaciously to Josephinism.[95]

In Vienna Metternich would become the main victim of the wave of revolutions that engulfed Europe in 1848. He exercised little influence on domestic policy, but more than anyone he had become the symbol of a reactionary regime that opposed the liberal and national aspirations of different peoples in the Habsburg Empire. Moreover, political life in the preceding decade had been marked by a certain stasis, and a deep economic crisis contributed to the general discontent. In the wake of the February revolution in France, riots erupted in Vienna on March 13th when the government rejected petitions for liberal reforms. That same day Metternich felt obliged to resign. He managed to escape the anger of the public just in time and fled to England, where he found refuge in Richmond upon Thames. Later he would stay for two years in Brussels, under the aegis of the Belgian king, Leopold I of Saxe-Coburg.

92 On Metternich's proposals for reform, see Radvany, *Metternich's Projects for Reform in Austria*, 31-53, Sked, *Metternich and Austria*, 120-145.
93 Srbik, *Metternich*, 371-375.
94 Bled, *Les fondements*, 26-30; Wandruzska, 'Österreichs politische Struktur', 35-70.
95 Bertier de Sauvigny, *Metternich*, 285.

Meanwhile, the revolution was suppressed in the Habsburg Empire. The feeble-minded Emperor Ferdinand I (1835-1848) was forced to resign and was succeeded by his young nephew Francis Joseph I.[96] Under the strong leadership of Prince Felix von Schwarzenberg, the rebel movements in the empire were suppressed. This was achieved rather easily in Bohemia, but in Northern Italy the result was outright war with Piedmont-Sardinia. The Austrian troops, under Radetzky's command, finally succeeded in restoring order. In Hungary, the Viennese government had to enlist the help of the Russian army in May 1849, making Austria more indebted than ever to the Tsarist empire in its foreign policy.

On the domestic front, attempts were made to establish a liberal constitutional regime. Schwarzenberg himself favoured introducing ministerial responsibility, with a mostly representative function for the emperor. However, on 31 December 1851 Francis Joseph I issued the *Silvesterpatent* establishing a centralized dynastic regime. It was the beginning of a neo-absolutist policy based on an alliance between the traditional elites and the upper middle class, who had been shaken by the revolutionary agitation of nationalists and socialists. Neo-absolutism launched a process of modernization that would lead to greater prosperity, but did not grant the people the possibility of political participation. Meanwhile Metternich had already returned to Vienna, where at the end of September 1851 he was given a triumphant welcome. In the following years he continued to exercise a considerable influence on foreign policy from his palace on the Rennweg. His return was symbolic of the apparent success of the counter-revolution, not only in Austria but across Europe. The wave of revolutions, which had engulfed most continental European countries, seemed to have been suppressed and many reformers, such as the upcoming diplomat Gustav von Blome, had joined the conservatives. Still, the cards had been reshuffled, and Metternich's Europe definitely belonged to the past.

The last notes of the Concert

On 8 November 1852 Blome joined the state chancellery in Vienna, with the rank of attaché, and was introduced to the administrative aspects of diplomatic work. His northern German background did not in any way hinder his smooth integration into the team.[97] Later he would describe the few months he spent at the chancellery as being the happiest of his life. Everything was going his way: 'I was following my calling, I belonged to a great nation, I was an Austrian diplomat, albeit at the lowest rank, but what did that matter?'

96   Höbelt, *Franz Joseph I*, 1-13.
97   *Souvenirs*, vol. I, 10.

In that period Gustav was completely at home in the Metternich household.[98] He became good friends with Richard, a son from Metternich's second marriage and his oldest male heir. The two were exactly the same age and started their diplomatic careers almost at the same time, although of course as the legitimate son, Richard had an advantage over the natural grandson. He immediately started as attaché at the Austrian embassy in Paris, where in a very short time he would become first secretary. He did not have to waste his time on editing and sending dispatches.

That was to be Blome's fate. In early January 1853 he was sent as attaché to St. Petersburg, a posting that was not a bad beginning.[99] The diplomatic representation at the court of Tsar Nicholas I was of great importance because Austria's survival as a great power from now on would depend especially on Russian protection. Blome liked this first appointment for other reasons also: he had a fondness for Russia and had many acquaintances and relationships in St. Petersburg, through his grand-uncle Otto, who had been Danish ambassador for almost forty years and through his grandmother, Princess Bagration.

At that time Count Alexander Mensdorff-Pouilly, a nephew of the Belgian king Leopold I and cousin of the British Prince-Consort, Albert of Saxe-Coburg, was the Austrian special envoy to the Russian court. This three-star general would later, at a crucial moment, become foreign affairs minister and would then once again cross paths with Blome. Staffing at the Austrian delegation was very limited and was rarely at full strength, making the stay in St. Petersburg a hard school for Gustav, one of just 'drudgery, drudgery'. However, this did not stop him from pursuing additional studies, especially in philosophy and political economy, ploughing through the archives of the delegation and taking part in society life. We are well informed about his activities, insights and feelings thanks to his regular correspondence with Louis de Pons; basically, they wrote to each other every week. As might be expected, the French count particularly was very punctual. Blome's letters contain much information about the inhospitable and unhealthy climate in the Russian capital, the hard times of a junior diplomat and his social network. He complained persistently about the amount of work he had to do and his poor health, but even so he participated actively in social life and was a welcome guest in the leading salons.[100] He spent many evenings with Count Nesselrode, the Russian foreign minister, who had been a good friend of his grand-uncle Otto and who apparently appreciated him.[101] Apart from that, Blome had still other reasons to

98 *Souvenirs*, vol. I, 11-12: 'Prince Metternich with his integrity and his high conservative principles became my ideal of a statesman.'
99 Blome to Pons, end of Dec. 1852.
100 Pons to Blome, 27 Dec. 1853.
101 Pons to Blome, 28 Aug. 1854: '[Nesselrode] thinks highly of you and is happy, he says, to talk with you'; *Souvenirs*, vol. I, 20: 'Count Nesselrode has always shown great kindness to me personally.'

spend time with Nesselrode, as will be seen later.[102] In the course of 1854 political tensions meant that western diplomats were no longer welcome in the city's salons, a fate that soon befell the Austrians also.[103] Foreign diplomats as a result increasingly sought out each other's company.

During his two-year stay in St. Petersburg, Blome lost his love for Russia for various reasons, a topic that will be further discussed later. His 'exile on the banks of the Neva' ended in April 1855, when he requested and was granted extended leave for health reasons. His activities during that leave give a good picture of the lifestyle of younger aristocratic diplomats in those days. He travelled to Vienna and Paris, and finally via Prague to the Bohemian spa town of Franzensbad, where he stayed on doctor's orders for the whole month of June. It was his first lengthy exposure to one of the typical spas where the European aristocracy and the *beau monde* went in search of health and social intercourse. Of the Bohemian spas, Franzensbad was less well-known than Karlsbad, and Blome did not particularly enjoy his stay there. 'People spend the whole, livelong day there drinking water, walking and chewing hay.' In one of his letters he described the daily schedule at the spa in a very amusing way:

> Franzensbad is a stultifying place. You get up at 6 o'clock in the morning and begin with a walk. You walk around like one possessed in order to digest the water you pour into yourself every quarter of an hour. Around 9 o'clock comes breakfast, that is a cup of coffee with a piece of unbuttered bread. Afterwards, *une occupation légère*, like reading a novel or a book of poetry. You begin to yawn from the first page and by the fourth you have sunk into a deep sleep. However, it is forbidden to nap in the daytime! So, you throw the book away and throw yourself at the piano to play some Strauss waltzes, much to the despair of those sitting around who find themselves in a hall where three or four instruments are played by amateurs without any talent. To bring some more variety into your leisure activities, you smoke a cigar on the balcony, at least when it's not too windy. You amuse yourself observing the passers-by, who of course are hardly ever there, for the simple reason that your fellow water-drinkers have been condemned to the same regime as yourself. In the absence of walkers you stare at the swallows, you count the leaves on the trees, you study the signs on the houses across the street for the hundredth time, and suffer in your turn through the shrill sounds of the neighbouring pianos. This *far niente* lasts until 13.30 in the afternoon. Then it's time to dine, that is if a meal of soup with croutons or oats, a paltry piece of meat, badly cooked vegetables and a glass of pump water can be called dinner. But come, it does not matter, it's a welcome change. Afterwards you make your way to the

102 Blome to Pons, 12 Jan. and 21 Feb. 1854.
103 Ibid.

reading room to learn from the *L'Indépendance belge* that 'there is no interesting political news to report today'. Then, having filled up the time in one way or another until six o'clock, the evening walk is next on the programme. You drag yourself to a neglected park where an orchestra performs Strauss arias and dances either well or badly, but mostly badly. You walk around the trees, you make more or less large circles around the orchestra, you sit down to draw figures in the sand with your walking stick; occasionally you pull out your pocket watch and when the little hand finally reaches the figure VII, you quickly eat a fruit puree, after which you go walking again until eight o'clock. Then you rush inside so as not expose yourself to the evening breeze. Now you may go to bed, alone, all alone. This is the moment when a good Christian reviews in his mind the thoughts and events of the past day. Elsewhere, one regrets one's sins, but here you sigh as you realize that you haven't done anything, neither anything good nor anything bad. That's worse than a sin, it is *nothing*, the sad result of a vegetable life. And the doctors here dare to say that this heals the body, when in fact it kills the spirit. Come! I cannot go along with such a regime ... I have replaced the *occupations légères* that my doctor recommends with a pastime that suits my intellectual needs. Instead of banal novels and sentimental poems, I am re-reading Bastiat, my favourite writer on political economy, and I am thoroughly enjoying a new book by Ravignan about the Jesuit order. Furthermore, I am adapting a few notes that I took in Russia. So, I divide my day between useful work and the prescribed walks. When Cicero withdrew to the countryside to seek some distraction from the affairs of state, he wrote philosophical tracts. That at least was intelligent. Our modern doctors are deluded idiots in talking about *une occupation légère*.[104]

In July he visited his family in Salzau where the idyllic country life greatly charmed him, but he acknowledged, 'I think I would be very unhappy if I had to spend the rest of my life here (...) My need to move in a higher and wider sphere is too strong to be satisfied with the role of a country squire.'[105] Afterwards, he travelled with a mistress via Paris to the French seaside town of Boulogne, which at that time was also very popular among American tourists.

In August, he returned to Vienna, where, on the orders of his minister, he spent several months becoming more familiar with Austrian customs and traditions. There he frequented the 'Casa Metternich', visited the fashionable circles[106] and spent a lot of time in the offices of the chancellery.[107] Normally

104 Blome to Pons, 6 June 1855.
105 Blome to Pons, 7 July 1855. Twenty years later, in a fit of discouragement, he would express an opposite view. See *infra*, 255.
106 Blome to Pons, 30 Oct. 1855.
107 *Souvenirs*, vol. 1, 20-21: 'I retained a tender attachment to the cradle of my career. I felt comfortable with the department and all its staff.'

he should have then been assigned to the embassy in London, but totally un-expectedly – and to his great joy – in mid-November he was appointed first secretary of the embassy in Paris, his preferred city for personal, family and professional reasons. He succeeded Richard Metternich, who shortly after-wards became envoy in Dresden, the capital of the Kingdom of Saxony, where his father had begun his career.

The head of the Austrian embassy in Paris was Alexander Hübner, again an illegitimate son of Metternich.[108] He was a demanding employer and delib-erately made things difficult for his new secretary.[109] Blome became convinced that his superior had an aversion to him, but 'the opposite was true; he had discerned a lot of talent in me and decided to train me'. Hübner realized that Blome was very interested in socioeconomic issues, which he himself knew al-most nothing about, and got him to draft regular reports on the topic. He also preferred to entrust the coverage of the debates in the Legislative Assembly to him.

In March 1856, shortly after Blome's arrival, the delegation played an important supporting role for Austrian diplomacy at the International Peace Conference in Paris, which put an end to the Crimean War. For Blome this was an important experience because it was the first time that he became involved in international diplomacy so closely and at such a high level. In St. Peters-burg he had already become familiar with the issue from a bilateral perspec-tive, but now he was engaged in negotiations on an international level.

The Crimean War was provoked by Russia's attempts to take advantage of the weakness of the Ottoman Empire in order to expand its influence in the Balkans and the Middle East.[110] In July 1853 Russian troops occupied the Danubian principalities of Wallachia and Moldavia which were under Turkish control. This advance alarmed Great Britain as it threatened its commercial in-terests in the Mediterranean. The French Emperor Napoleon III now saw a per-fect opportunity to put himself forward as the defender of international law, break out of the isolation of his own country and undermine the treaty system of 1815. Turkey received the support of the western powers and declared war on Russia. It conceded severe losses, but in March 1854 received military assis-tance from Britain and France who sent an expeditionary force to the Crimea, where a long siege was fought for Sebastopol.

 This conflict put Austria in an embarrassing position. Since the crushing of the Hungarian uprising in 1849, the government owed a moral debt to Rus-sia. Moreover, Francis Joseph I and his entourage harboured a great admira-tion for Tsar Nicholas I. On the other hand, Vienna wanted to ensure freedom of navigation in the Danube estuary and opposed the expansion of the Tsarist

---

108 Engel-Janosi, *Der Freiherr von Hübner, 1811-1892.*
109 *Souvenirs*, vol. I, 21-25.
110 Bridge and Bullen, *The Great Powers*, 114-125; Yon, *Le Second Empire*, 81-84; Höbelt, *Franz Joseph I*, 28-30.

empire in the Balkans. Besides, the foreign policy of the Danube monarchy had for decades been designed to protect the Ottoman Empire with a view to maintaining the balance of power in Europe. What is more, Russia's aggression against that empire had violated the existing treaties and had broken the bond of solidarity between the conservative great powers. Austria therefore distanced itself from Russia and adopted a neutral stance. In fact, it leaned increasingly toward the western powers, while Prussia took up a much more accommodating position towards the Tsarist empire. Austrian troop movements forced the Russians to reduce their military deployment in the Crimea, and contributed to their eventual defeat. In September 1855 Sebastopol fell, following an exhausting and deadly siege. Austria then sent an ultimatum to Russia, whereupon the new Tsar Alexander II acceded to peace negotiations. The Congress of Paris at the end of March 1856 led to a settlement that included the neutrality of the Black Sea and guaranteed freedom of navigation on the Danube. Russia was also obliged to cede some territory and relinquished its claim to protect Christians in the Ottoman Empire.

The Russians were deeply humiliated by this peace, and found it particularly difficult to accept the fact that their military fleet would no longer have access to the Black Sea. Their foreign policy would henceforth be directed towards erasing this humiliation. Under Nicholas I the Tsarist empire had been the great protector of the status quo in Europe, but after 1856 upholding international order was no longer a priority for Russian diplomacy. From then on it would focus primarily on revising the treaty of 1856, and on protecting Russian interests in the Balkans and the area around the Black Sea. The relationship with Austria was poisoned forever and from now on the Danube monarchy would be abandoned to its fate by the Tsarist empire.

Although not a single shot was fired elsewhere in Europe during the Crimean War, this conflict can still be called one of the major European wars of the nineteenth century. The rupture in the alliance between the conservative eastern powers put an end to the Concert of Europe. Their understanding had held France in check for decades and had reinforced the Vienna settlement of 1815. Russia now distanced itself from the central European powers, thereby losing its leading position vis-à-vis Austria and Prussia. Furthermore, the cooperation between Russia and Great Britain came to an end, with the result that Britain largely lost its influence on continental politics. France in particular would benefit from this and would in the years to come play a dominant role in European politics. Napoleon III had succeeded in turning the structure of the treaty of 1815 upside down. The European Concert then ended in cacophony. Maintaining peace in Europe was no longer a priority now that it was obvious that a war involving several powers could still be curbed and localized. War could therefore once again be employed as a political tool to bring about territorial changes, with the right of nations to self-determination providing the catalyst.[111]

Both in St. Petersburg and in Paris, Blome defended the line followed by the Austrian chancellery in the diplomatic notes that he had to draw up about the Crimean War, but in fact he was very critical of the policy being pursued. In his view, the Danube monarchy should have spoken out more clearly against the policies of Nicholas I from the outset:

> Notwithstanding the services that Tsar Nicholas had provided us in 1849, our vital interests in the east did not warrant our supporting him. Moreover, he had broken the alliance between the three conservative powers and had offered Napoleon III the chance to put himself forward as the defender of the existing treaties. In short, neither our interests in the east, nor the just cause of the Turks permitted us to encourage Tsar Nicholas in the slightest way.

If Austria had immediately spoken out more openly against the policies of the Tsar, he probably would not have gone as far as he did. In particular, Francis Joseph I and the army leadership had initially been too lenient towards Russia. When Austria later lent its moral support to the western powers, without openly breaking its ties with the Tsarist empire, it found itself in an embarrassing position and upset both camps.[112] After the conflict had become more sharply defined, Blome clearly opted for the side of the western allies. He revealed this in private conversations and in a tract that he drew up after his stay in Russia and distributed on a limited scale.[113] As a result, he became *persona non grata* in Russia's political and diplomatic circles and pressure was put on his numerous Russian relations.

In his political memoirs, Blome would later write: 'Russia's conservative principles no longer evoked in me the admiration that I had for them during my student days in Berlin.' His position was primarily determined by the lack of respect shown for existing treaties and for legitimacy. 'I believe so strongly in the legally upheld principles that determine developments in this world that I refuse to believe that an undertaking using inadmissible means can be brought to a successful conclusion, however cleverly it is presented and justified.'[114] Only the law and legitimacy gave value and durability to power, and offered security in a world threatened by revolution and disorder. It was a view shared by a large majority of the German aristocracy at that time.[115]

---

111 Ameil, Nathan and Soutou, eds., *Le congrès de Paris (1856)*.
112 *Souvenirs*, vol. I, 20.
113 *Histoire contemporaine*, Gut Salzau, X., Memorandum on Russia's domestic and foreign policies (1852-1854).
114 Blome to Pons, 22 April 1853.
115 Pons to Blome, 8 June 1853: 'Count Platen assured me that in Germany the whole equestrian order was thinking in the same way.'

While Blome was becoming closely involved in European politics, he was at the same time going through a turbulent period in his private life. The year 1857 especially was very difficult for him. He received a lot of support from Louis de Pons as well as from a new colleague at the Austrian embassy in Paris, Count Friedrich Revertera, with whom he had forged a lasting friendship. In late February 1858, he would leave the French capital in a state of disarray to seek a way out of his troubles in Vienna.

The white fairy

At this time the young diplomat experienced a significant change in his emotional life, which had an impact on the formation of his character. In his youth he had adopted the lifestyle of many of his peers and departed little from the earlier behaviour of Princess Bagration and Metternich. Blome was an attractive, elegant young man and, according to Pons, who was certainly biased, 'charmant à croquer'.[116] Flirting with young women came easily to him; in these matters, according to his father, he did not have 'a quiet bone in his body'.[117] In his correspondence with Pons, Gustav spoke openly of his many love affairs, but always stressed that they did not stand in the way of his deep affection for Pons:[118]

> Does a man love his mistresses? One's feelings for them are fleeting, but my love for you is thoughtful, meaningful and steadfast. I only have to look at you to understand why I love you, while if I see my mistress of today coming along, I say to myself, 'is it even conceivable that I love this woman', and if I meet my mistress of yesterday, I ask, 'how is it possible that I was ever smitten by that creature?'[119]

He frequently made derogatory comments about women and in that respect was typical of his milieu. He thought of women as being poorly educated and they never inspired in him the kind of deep feelings he had for Pons.

> Desires, yes! But actually I have little respect for them. A conversation between men attracts me much more than the chatter of women. I do

116 Pons to Blome, 4 Dec. 1854.
117 Pons to Blome, 18 Jan. 1854.
118 Blome to Pons, 7 Sept.1853: 'You have got hold of my heart, I do not know how, and you occupy it so completely that you could not even get out, if you so desired. Now I occasionally rent a lodging there on the fifth floor to the wives of my friends. It's very simple... Besides, the lease is just for a term, more or less fixed. Tenants follow one another quickly enough.'
119 Blome to Pons, 3 Jan. 1854.

not find in them either logic or development or lofty sentiments ... I can pour out my heart to a man, never to a woman.[120]

According to Pons, his beloved Gustav could rightfully sing the famous song, '*J'ai des amourettes, mais n'ai pas d'amour*' ('I have dalliances, but I do not have love').[121] Otherwise, where true love was concerned, Blome behaved in a very class-conscious way: 'I am too aristocratic not to know that one cannot love somebody from a lower class.'[122] Yet on occasions, and at great length, he would sing the praises of a mistress, like the woman whom he described as 'English in her complexion, Polish in her grace, French in her esprit, German in her warmth and Spanish in her sensuality'.[123] During his stay in St. Petersburg and during the holiday period that followed, his liaisons were many and various, with only his unstable health inciting some moderation. However, these amourettes came to an end during his time in Paris when he encountered true love.

Since the summer of 1853 Blome had come to highly esteem Maria Kalergis, seven years his senior, whom he met regularly in St. Petersburg in the salon of her uncle, Count Nesselrode, the Russian foreign affairs minister.[124] She was a gifted pianist and one of the most admired divas in European society. Blome was fascinated by this talented woman and soon cherished a deep admiration and affection for her.[125]

In the autumn, Kalergis left on one of her many trips to the western capitals, but on her return in January 1854 Blome became truly lovestruck. 'She is the least feminine woman alive. She is endowed with a superior mind, which nature in principle reserves only for our gender. She compels admiration and her attraction even for the most recalcitrant is irresistible, because she does not have the typical female weaknesses, yet retains the charming sophistication that delights us in women.'[126] A cry of alarm soon followed: 'I begin to fear that I'm in love for the first time in my life.'[127] Blome became obsessed by Kalergis, who 'is a man in her thinking and judgement and a woman in her

120 Blome to Pons, 26 Sept. 1853.
121 Pons to Blome, 19 Feb. 1855.
122 Blome to Pons, 19 Oct. 1852.
123 Blome to Pons, 2 Dec. 1854.
124 On Kalergis, see: Photiadès, 'Marie Kalergis-Moukhanow'; La Mara [Ida Maria Lipsius], *Marie von Mouchanoff-Kalergis*; Szenic, *Maria Kalergi*.
125 Blome to Pons, 7 July 1853.
126 Blome to Pons, 12 Jan. 1854.
127 Blome to Pons, 21 Feb. 1854: 'It could be love, do you understand? That would be terrible. A whole future of suffering and nameless emotions!'

grace and fine sensitivity'.[128] She brought out the best in him. In the meantime, Pons had obtained more information about her in the Parisian salons and could confirm that she was an exceptionally talented woman, and was beyond reproach.[129]

Because of the great influence Kalergis would exert on Blome, it is worth examining her personality more fully. Countess Maria Nesselrode (1822-1874) was of German-Polish descent. Because her parents' marriage had broken up, she was raised in the family of her uncle, Chancellor Nesselrode. At sixteen she was married off to the wealthy Jan Kalergis, who came from an Italian-Greek background, but within a very short time, the marriage, which had produced a daughter – Marie – ended. An amicable, though not a legal, separation followed. For a while Maria continued to live in St. Petersburg where she had a spacious residence. Then the plutocrat Anatoly Demidov (1812-1870) courted her, but plans for a wedding stumbled on considerable opposition from his mother and eventually came to nothing. In the meantime, Maria Kalergis evolved into a talented pianist.

From 1842 on, Maria began to travel and quickly developed a great liking for a nomadic life. In 1844 she went on a long trip through Italy, where she met the Polish sculptor and poet Cyprian Norwid (1821-1883), the most intellectual writer among the Polish emigrés. He fell hopelessly in love with her, but it was an unrequited love. The following year Kalergis settled in Paris, which became her base for regular trips to Warsaw, St. Petersburg and the spa town of Baden-Baden. On her travels she met many famous contemporaries and became a well-known society figure. She was able to use her strengths – her beauty and charm, her piano playing, her artistic and political baggage – to great effect in the highest circles.

Her salon in the Rue d'Anjou in Paris was frequented mainly by writers, painters and musicians. Franz Liszt, with whom she had already become close friends in 1843, introduced her to Frederic Chopin. She became one of his favourite pupils.[130] Music went on to occupy an increasingly prominent place in her life, through her association with Chopin, Liszt, Rossini and Hans von Bülow. Chopin in turn brought her in contact with the painter Eugène Delacroix who spent a lot of time in her company. Famous writers were also fascinated

---

128 Blome to Pons, 6 March 1854: 'I live in her and for her. My day is divided into two parts, the hours before and the hours after I have seen her. It is a kind of unparalleled idolatry ... The influence that this woman exercises over me is entirely exemplary. She lifts me up morally, she definitely makes me a better person, she arouses in me feelings and tastes of such a higher order so that I feel closer to heaven since I have known her.'

129 Pons to Blome, 20 March 1854: 'Beauty, mind, talents, superior in everything, seductive, irresistibly attractive ... One would think her to be without reproach. Very cold by temperament, very much mistress of herself. A very devout Catholic, with a burning zeal and limitless kindness, this star cannot but light up those who come near her.'

130 On the relationship between Chopin and Kalergis, see: Rambeau, *Chopin*, 856-858.

Maria Kalergis. Engraving from an aquarelle by M. Delessert, c. 1850.
[*Private collection*]

by her, such as Alfred de Musset, who courted her, and Théophile Gautier who in 1848 dedicated a poem to her, *Symphonie en blanc majeur*. Heinrich Heine, whom she met later, stated 'this is not a woman but a monument, a cathedral of the God of Love'. He too dedicated an ode of praise to her, *L'Eléphant blanc* (1851). The adjective *blanc* in both poems refers to the beautiful creamy white tint of her skin, which was the reason for her appellation as the 'white fairy'. Poets and novelists further praised the Venetian golden sheen of her blond hair, the violet blue of her eyes and her tall, regal stature.

Kalergis clearly had much success in artistic circles, but in Paris she was still primarily known as the niece of Chancellor Nesselrode. She herself did not wish to play any political role, but she was well informed about European politics and her salon therefore attracted many diplomats and politicians. In the late summer of 1848, General Louis-Eugène Cavaignac was one of her most faithful visitors. After the army, under his command, had put down the workers' uprising in Paris in June, he became head of the executive branch, with almost dictatorial powers. He fell headlong in love with Kalergis and asked her to marry him, but his mother proved more powerful than the dictator and put a stop to this plan, to Kalergis' great disappointment. It was the second time that a potential mother-in-law had sabotaged her chances of remarrying.

The influence of the salons waned under the Empire. Moreover, the Crimean War forced many Russian *salonnières* to leave Paris. During her sporadic visits back to the city, Kalergis scaled back her social activities. She was also spending more time during this period in Warsaw and St. Petersburg, where Blome met her. His passion for her became a true obsession. He was, as already noted, particularly fascinated by her 'masculine' qualities: 'It is clear that nature made a mistake when it brought forth this miracle.'[131] His work as a diplomat began to suffer from this hopeless love, but he awoke from his dream world on learning that Emperor Francis Joseph I had made very laudatory remarks about him and had great expectations of him. To Pons' satisfaction, Gustav distanced himself from Kalergis at the end of April 1854, in order to once more devote himself fully to his duties as a diplomat. Nonetheless, love kept gnawing away at him.

When Kalergis returned to Paris a few months later, Gustav called in Pons as a *postillon d' amour*.[132] Pons performed this task very quickly and seemed very impressed: 'I think she is not a man-woman, but a woman with a sparkling spirit, a lot of grace, a sound judgement, a charmingly natural manner and simplicity. In Parisian society today there is not one lady who can be compared with her.' He also had an encouraging message for Blome: 'She loves you very much, she says, like a dedicated sister. She greatly appreciates your feel-

---

131 Blome to Pons, 19 April and 8 Sept. 1854. He characterized her as 'French in her way of thinking, German in her seriousness and Polish in her enthusiasms'.
132 Blome to Pons, 12 Aug. 1854.

ings, your excellent and loyal character, your many outstanding qualities.'[133] Some time later, he wrote: 'The more I meet her, the more I approve your taste, judgement and discernment.'[134] But a short time later came less favourable reports: 'I find her to be rather cool and aloof, very sensitive to expressions of approval, no matter from whom.'[135] And, 'I get the impression that she is strongly attracted to celebrities.'[136] Blome's interest in her appeared to diminish and he asked Pons to drop the matter and make no further contacts: 'Let the river flow to the sea and the top of the fir tree grow towards the azure sky. Time will tell.'[137] Gustav looked for compensation in a few new amourettes.

Still, the fires continued to smoulder and when Blome was assigned to Paris in late 1855, he resumed close contact with Kalergis. The diva began frequenting the salon of Princess Bagration, even though she disliked both the hostess, whom she described as a nemesis, as well as the brooding atmosphere in the house.[138] For a year she and Blome were very intimate with each other,[139] although there was certainly no talk of a sexual relationship. Marriage was apparently considered for a time,[140] but in the spring of 1857 thunder clouds appeared on the horizon and the relationship came increasingly under pressure.[141] We can only guess at the exact reasons for this. A sharp conflict between Gustav and his father, with a possible threat of disinheritance, may have played a role – a topic that will be discussed later. However, the most likely cause was a clash of personalities. Pons' final judgement on Kalergis was that 'she is a coquettish but unfeeling woman, who is also arrogant and vain'.[142] In addition, behind a surface equanimity she was rather gloomy, whereas Blome himself was at that time restlessly seeking a balance in his own life. Opposite likes also stood in the way of a lasting relationship. Blome increasingly took less and less pleasure in the society life in which as a diplomat he had to par-

133 Pons to Blome, 28 Aug. 1854.

134 Pons to Blome, 13 Oct. 1854.

135 Pons to Blome, 7 Sept. 1854.

136 Pons to Blome 13 Oct. and 7 Nov. 1854.

137 Blome to Pons, 2 Dec. 1854.

138 Photiadès, *Maria Kalergis-Moukhanow*, 127.

139 Pons to Blome, end of Jan. 1856: 'You have spoken to me about someone who loved you and who sacrificed her former way of life just to please you...' In May Kalergis organized a dinner to celebrate Blome's birthday (Pons to Blome, 16 May 1856). When Kalergis fell seriously ill in February 1857, Blome was beside himself (Blome to Pons, 18 Feb. 1857).

140 The fact that she was still formally married to Jan Kalergis was not an obstacle for her. Maria Kalergis had already considered divorcing her husband so as to be able to marry again eventually.

141 Blome to Pons, 4 April 1857: 'My heart is still in the poor state that you used to know.' That year Kalergis didn't do anything to celebrate Blome's birthday. 'She does not spoil me and I only receive these delicate attentions from you' (Blome to Pons, 18 May 1857). 'She likes only what is unexpected and out of the ordinary' (Blome to Pons, Sept. 1857).

142 Pons to Blome, 5 Nov. 1857.

ticipate.[143] For a *salonnière* such as Kalergis that would have been problematic. Furthermore, his political views differed from hers considerably.[144]

Apparently the liaison ended tempestuously. Pons was delighted with the break and Otto Blome shared that feeling.[145] They would reconcile only five years later when they met by chance in the spa town of Karlsbad.[146] Thereafter their paths no longer crossed, although Blome would still have sporadic contact with her daughter Marie, who in the same year 1857 married the Austrian diplomat, Franz Coudenhove.[147]

Following the marriage of her daughter, Maria Kalergis once again began to travel more. Her base was now mainly Baden-Baden, the most fashionable health resort in Europe, where she had close ties with various European monarchs.[148] Music, which she called the poetry of her existence, continued to dominate her life. She used to say, proudly, 'when I sit at the piano, kings fall silent'. Unfortunately, however, her mental and physical health began to suffer. After the death of her husband in 1863, she opted for more security in her life and married the eleven-years younger Sergei Muchanov, a Russian official who later would become director of Warsaw's theatres and imperial palaces. From 1868 on she resided permanently in this city where she would play an important cultural role. After her untimely death in May 1874, Liszt – one of her favourite composers – composed his 'First Elegy for Cello and Piano' in her memory.[149]

It is remarkable that Blome managed to attract the attention of this widely celebrated diva and develop a strong emotional bond with her, which almost led to marriage. This was not something one would expect given his closed nature.[150] Pons affirmed this: 'You are far more predisposed to be loved than

143 Blome to Pons, 30 Oct. 1855 and 16 Feb. 1859.

144 Kalergis was more liberally and constitutionally minded (Photiadès, *Maria Kalergis-Moukhanow*, 182), whereas Blome was a fervent opponent of constitutionalism.

145 Pons was glad 'to know that Renaud has removed the ties that bound him to the enchantress' (Pons to Blome, 7 Dec. 1857).

146 Blome to Pons, 10 June 1862: 'I met a wealth of acquaintances and who was there in the front row? Madame Kalergis! I had not seen her for five years. Our meeting was not without emotion. For my part, at least, I have no difficulty in admitting that she is still able to exert a great influence on me.' Kalergis also reports on this in a letter dated 10 June to her daughter Marie: 'Blome came to my house last night – we are reconciled; he seemed easier and calmer than before' (La Mara, *Marie von Mouchanoff-Kalergis*,106).

147 He had contacts, for instance, with the Coudenhove-Kalergis family in Ischl in May 1863 and in Rome during Vatican I. Maria Coudenhove-Kalergis would become the grandmother of Richard Coudenhove-Kalergis, the founder of the pan-European movement during the interwar period.

148 See the correspondence with her daughter, Marie, published by La Mara.

149 'Elegy for Cello, Piano, Harp and Harmonium' (17 June 1874, Weimar). Kalergis also had close relations with Richard Wagner, who dedicated his opera *Tristan und Isolde* to her.

150 Blome to Pons, 29 Nov. 1852: 'I am not very expansive by nature'; Blome to Pons, 28 Dec. 1858: 'I am extremely stiff ... so I have always been.'

to love. You will never be a Werther, because as a German you are cold and distant, but not dreamy.'[151] Moreover, as already noted, Blome and Kalergis differed from one another in a variety of ways, yet there were enough similarities between them to account for their mutual attraction. Blome clearly had musical talent: his singing was praised[152] and he was a proficient pianist.[153] His elegance, his intellectual depth and his social background probably also played in his favour. Like Kalergis, he was a cosmopolitan who felt equally at home in the Latin and Slavic worlds as in the Germanic. For his part, he was probably attracted by the versatility of Kalergis, who was both an artist and a society figure, as well as a sophisticated observer of European politics.

This relationship, despite ending so heatedly, had a lasting impact on Blome. In the first place it changed his condescending opinions about women. Moreover, his relationship with Kalergis, which he valued highly, put an end to his amorous adventures. His association with the 'white fairy' had a lifelong effect in another respect: the diva, who as the daughter of a Polish mother was a fervent Catholic, played a role in his conversion from Lutheranism to Catholicism, which would be of exceptional significance for the rest of his life.

The long path to Rome

During his stay in Paris Blome joined the Catholic Church, a well thought-out move that came after much deliberation. There is little reference to it in the correspondence with Pons, because the old French aristocrat was a conventional Catholic who did not trouble himself with religious matters. He called himself religious but was guided primarily by humanistic considerations.[154] Our main information about Blome's evolution on the religious front and specifically about his transition to Catholicism comes mostly from what he himself wrote later in life.[155] Admittedly, this information should be considered critically, but it still paints an interesting picture of his religious odyssey.

Like the vast majority of the North German aristocracy, the Blome family belonged to the Lutheran Church. Princess Bagration was Russian Orthodox, but had her daughter Clementine raised as a Catholic in Vienna and Paris. Incidentally, religion did not matter much in those circles. 'The atmosphere that surrounded me was anything but religious.' The young Gustav did attend the usual religion classes, but they failed to excite him: 'I was not a disbeliever,

---

151 Pons to Blome, 21 Oct. 1855; Id. to id., 7 Sept. 1854: 'Platen is always telling me that you push reserve to its utmost limits, that you are never unbuttoned. This is a virtue in diplomacy, but it is not one for intimate company.'
152 Pons to Blome, 27 Dec. 1853 and 17 June 1855.
153 Pergen to Cramer, 13 Nov. 1872, NKDC, *Cramer*, 434, 12 C.
154 Pons to Blome, 4 April 1860; 17 Sept. 1860.
155 *Récit de ma conversion au catholicisme*, Gut Salzau, IX, 5.

but the supernatural was of absolutely no interest to me.' During his secondary school studies in Lübeck, his religious indifference was both deliberate and systematic. While at the lycée in Lüneburg, encouraged by an older fellow student, he began to read the German philosophers Kant, Fichte, Schelling and Hegel. 'At home I had been indifferent, in Lübeck a mocker, and in Lüneburg I became a *raisonneur.*' Later, at the University of Heidelberg, he delved further into German philosophy and fell under the influence of a vague theism.

His participation in the first Schleswig-Holstein War of 1848-1849 led him to make a volte-face. Not that he became a devout Christian immediately, and he scandalized even his fellow officers with his anti-religious statements. However, the confrontation with massacres during the war engendered a greater seriousness in him and he began to search for direction in his life. At the University of Berlin, he encountered an environment that was reacting against the political as well as the anti-religious ideas of the democrats. He was surrounded by students who did not question the fundamental truths of Christianity, although this did not mean that they were deeply religious. Gradually he began to believe in a 'creative and rewarding God', but he still had no idea what the word 'cult' meant.

In 1851 he came across the book *Von Babylon nach Jerusalem*, in which Ida Hahn-Hahn, a distant relative, described her conversion to Catholicism.[156] It was a revelation for him. 'For the first time I realized that outside the Lutheran orthodoxy, which interested me so little, there was also another form of Christianity, which was anything but outdated and seemed to exercise a great attraction to questing spirits.' He had just begun to study Luther's writings and felt that their consequences led directly to modern philosophers like Kant and Hegel. Moreover, he thought Protestantism was deficient in logic, a major defect in his eyes. Conservative considerations also led him to have little sympathy for Luther's rebellious stance with its unmistakable political implications. It is striking that he approached the question of religion from a predominantly political perspective: in his opinion, Protestantism could hardly contribute to political order and stability and he became convinced of 'the inadequacy of Protestantism and its affinity with revolution'. 'I abhorred liberalism. The so-called Reformation already contained a hefty dose of it. I had contempt for the constitutional regime and in a number of countries I discovered a striking analogy with the Lutheran church organization. I had a great longing for authority, but found that the so-called reformers had undermined its foundation.' He saw the Reformation as having had a disastrous in-

---

156 In the German-speaking world, Countess Ida Hahn-Hahn (1805-1880) was one of the most widely read women authors. She wrote many edifying novels and travel books, especially about the Arab world.

fluence on the political and social organization of Europe.[157] He respected the Catholic Church, which he valued as 'a centuries-old institution with a strong hierarchy', a beacon in a world adrift. The Church of Rome did not withdraw from public life, but instead exercised a conservative influence on society and was a guarantor for the maintenance of order and stability. One cannot stress enough the fact that Blome's growing interest in the Catholic Church was primarily inspired by political motives. He was, in fact, now 'a statesman in the making', with an overriding interest in political and social issues.

The change in his religious position did not mean that he immediately took steps to become a Catholic. During his first long sojourn in Paris, he didn't make the slightest effort to familiarize himself with the Catholic faith, he never entered a church, and never talked about religion. However, he did feel some sympathy for the religion to which his mother had belonged.[158]

Once he entered the Austrian diplomatic service, he found himself in a more Catholic atmosphere than he ever had been before. He was obliged to delve into Church-State relations and political relations with the Holy See, and thus became acquainted with Austrian Catholic traditions. During his stay in St. Petersburg, he resolved to get to know the Russian Orthodox Church better. Almost by chance he met Andrei Muraviev[159] who was an intermediary between the Eastern patriarchs and the Metropolitan of Moscow and was very involved in theological questions. He explained the tenets of his church to Blome, but always in a polemical tone against Rome. Challenged by this, Blome felt compelled to defend the Catholic Church, but first he had to deepen his knowledge of Catholicism. Muraviev, 'the only person in the world who has ever taken the trouble to convert me to his religion', did not realize that he was pushing Blome, whom Catholics had never bothered with thus far, into the arms of Rome. The young diplomat left St. Petersburg as a committed Catholic, convinced that the truth was indivisible and that it was to be found in the Catholic Church. Conversion to the Orthodox Church did not hold any attraction for him given its subordination to state authority and its weakness as an independent player in society.

For now religion remained largely a theoretical exercise for Blome. 'My reason asked for it, but my will was not yet prepared to submit, my mindset was still worldly.' For the moment he did not have the courage to break with his libertine lifestyle. However, he continued with his religious reading and,

---

157 He also came under the influence of a book by Auguste Nicolas, entitled *Du protestantisme et de ses rapports avec le socialisme* (1852).

158 *Récit de ma conversion*, Gut Salzau, IX, 5: 'Her image remained always with me in the town and in the house where she had lived.'

159 Andrei Muraviev († 1874) was deputy procurator of the Holy Synod and had a reputation of being very anti-Catholic. His staunch anti-Catholicism also incited Prince Ivan Gagarin to convert to the Church of Rome. See C. Evtuhov and S. Kotkin, eds., *The cultural gradient: the transmission of ideas in Europe, 1789-1914*, Lanham, 2003, 45 and 53.

not surprisingly, had a special preference for ultramontane, anti-liberal writers. For example, he came to admire greatly the work of the French journalist and polemicist Louis Veuillot, 'who chases down today's enemy to his last stronghold, instead of limiting himself to the defense, as overly cautious lawyers do'. Later he would establish a close relationship with Veuillot.[160]

On his appointment as secretary of the embassy in Paris, Blome began preparations for his conversion. However, he had to immerse himself in diplomatic files and was so busy that he was continually postponing his religious plans. 'After my work at the embassy I visited the salons, all the salons, of all kinds.' After a few weeks he took Maria Kalergis into his confidence and asked her to put him in touch with the famous Jesuit, Gustave-Xavier de Ravignan.[161] Blome had already read some of his work and was very impressed. He had never before been in contact with Jesuits, but had read many of the pamphlets directed against them. Curiously enough, these had aroused his sympathy for the Jesuits because 'it is not the worst fruits that the wasps gnaw'. It should be noted that, unlike most of his fellow Jesuits, Ravignan belonged to the liberal Catholic wing, indicating that at this time Blome did not attach much importance to the growing dissension in the Catholic camp.

Kalergis introduced Blome to Ravignan, who found the young diplomat sufficiently interesting to instruct him himself. Two to four times a week he received him in his austere, small cell. There were few gaps in Blome's knowledge of doctrine, but he knew almost nothing about liturgy and related matters. He had never attended a Catholic Mass and was unfamiliar with Catholic devotional practices. Ravignan realized that he had to form the heart rather than the reason of this convert. In March 1856, he decided that the time was ripe for reception into the Catholic Church, but Blome drew back because he had not had a chance to warn his father. So he decided to become a Catholic secretly and delay announcing his conversion. His reception into the Church took place on Tuesday, 18 March 1856, in a small chapel in the Rue des Sèvres. Besides Ravignan, the only other person present was Maria Kalergis. A few months later he was confirmed by Monsignor De la Bouillerie, bishop of Carcassonne, also in the presence of an intimate circle of people.

Blome's conversion was certainly not an isolated case in the German world, as we shall see later. Thanks to the influence of Romanticism, many

---

160 See Chapter III.
161 After a brilliant career as a lawyer, Xavier de Ravignan (1795-1858) entered the Jesuits and became a famous preacher. Along with Lacordaire, Montalembert and Dupanloup, he devoted himself to the defence of ecclesiastical liberties and freedom of education. Kalergis, a fervent Catholic, was in touch with Ravignan from whom she got much support. 'He taught her patience and resignation. He gave her advice that enabled her endure her solitude. Ravignan used to say: "Loneliness is the homeland of the strong."' (Photiadès, *Maria Kalergis*, 416).

prominent figures became Catholic during this time. Some harboured a deep admiration for the Christian Middle Ages, others were attracted by the rich liturgy and devotional practices of the Catholic Church, and others again by its communal character that distinguished it from the more individualistic Protestantism. Sociopolitical factors, however, carried the most weight for Blome, in particular the Church's anti-revolutionary posture and its support of the established order.[162]

For the moment only Kalergis and a friendly colleague at the Austrian embassy knew about Blome's conversion. Then Gustav cautiously informed his father, who reacted very negatively to the news. Although Otto von Blome had hardly any interest in religious matters, he strongly objected to the conversion of his only son, who once again had wandered off the beaten track, and even threatened to disinherit him. In that period also the split with Maria Kalergis occurred, but whether there was a connection between the two events is not clear. Ravignan was a great support for Gustav in those difficult days, dissuading him from wild plans to renounce his inheritance and to join the Jesuits.[163] Gustav found himself in what seemed like a hopeless situation. He asked permission of his ambassador to return to Vienna, where he wanted to apply for a paid position in the state chancellery. Until now, as was customary for young diplomats, he had not received any remuneration; diplomats at a higher grade did get an allowance, but were obliged to draw on their own funds in order to keep up to the standards expected of them. If Gustav were to be disinherited, he would no longer have any prospects for a successful diplomatic career and would be better off immediately taking on a more modest administrative function, for which he would be well paid.

In February 1858, shortly before Blome's departure, Ravignan fell seriously ill and his condition deteriorated to the extent that all visits were forbidden. However, because Gustav had built up such a close relationship with him in the preceding months, he was allowed to go to Ravignan's death bed to make his farewell. This moving event was described a few years later in a biography of Ravignan by the Jesuit priest Armand de Ponlevoy. Blome himself gives some additional information about this episode, but there is a trace of hagiography about his narrative: 'I was allowed to receive his last blessing and – with firm conviction – he predicted rehabilitation with my family, a successful career and an imminent, unexpected marriage.' Ravignan advised the

162 Blome to Revertera, 6 Feb. 1859, HAH, IV, 56, 32: 'If the Church cannot provide for a regeneration of society, then the last days of humanity are at hand'; 20 Sept. 1860, ibid.: 'God will punish humanity because Europe without the Church will descend into barbarism once again.'

163 *Récit de ma conversion*, Gut Salzau, IX, 5: 'He [Ravignan] replied that one did not become a priest in order to prove anything to the world, nor because one lacked resources to embrace or continue a fashionable career; [he said] that I absolutely did not have a vocation for the priesthood.'

young diplomat to marry one of Buol-Schauenstein's daughters, about whom he had heard many good reports. He died four days after Blome had left.[164] In later life Blome would continue to venerate him as a saint.[165]

On his return to Vienna, Blome threw himself into the social circuit in order to forget his troubles. The 'Casa Metternich' once more offered a safe harbour.[166] There he came into contact, almost by chance, with Séphine Buol-Schauenstein, whom Ravignan had pointed out to him.[167] They immediately hit it off, and by the end of March Blome was already asking the minister of foreign affairs for permission to court his eldest daughter, with a view to marriage, provided, in his words, that 'my father will provide me with the necessary financial resources for now and later'. Buol agreed and then Blome travelled to Salzau with a heavy heart.[168] On April 10th, he was picked up in Kiel by his father. 'The salutations were very cool, but when I brought him up to date on my marriage prospects, the ice was broken and he made a complete turnaround.' The prospect of his son entering a prestigious aristocratic Austrian family through the proposed marriage explained Otto Blome's change of heart; at least, he no longer threatened to disinherit his son. The religious issue would be avoided for months in the conversations between the two.[169]

On 1 September 1858 Gustav Blome married Séphine Buol-Schauenstein, whom he described as 'blonde, beautiful, touchingly sincere, kind, gentle and very pious'. Her piety was important and the religious factor was of major importance in this marriage, which Ravignan to some extent had arranged. Although the social status and wealth of the future bride were also important factors, it was still a marriage of love.[170] Much later Blome would testify about his wife: 'Since our marriage, she has fully measured up to the ideal of a Christian wife: a model of piety, gentleness and self-sacrifice as a woman, mother

164 The Austrian ambassador Hübner reported the following in his diary (Hübner, *Neuf ans*, vol. II, 117): '26 Feb. 1858. The death of Father Ravignan, which took place yesterday, is a huge loss for the Jesuits of France ... He was a holy man, who had a talent for words'; Blome to Pons, 10 March 1858: 'It is for me a very painful loss and although I might have been prepared for it for a long time, I could not hold back my tears when I read the fatal news in the papers.'

165 Blome to Pons, 17 July 1859: 'A grace from on high radiated from Father de Ravignan's face and it was his understanding of divine things that gave him this marvellous wisdom in worldly matters.' In 1862 Blome would name his son Xavier after him.

166 Blome to Pons, 10 March 1858.

167 *Récit de ma conversion*, Gut Salzau, IX, 5: '... almost without any initiative on my part, but under the auspices of my holy Father de Ravignan, from whom I seemed to receive useful assistance throughout the whole course of the events that preceded my engagement'.

168 Blome to Pons, 3 April 1858.

169 Blome to Pons, 26 May 1858; Pons to Blome, 5 June 1858.

170 Blome to Pons, 5 Sept. 1858: 'I love my wife as I have never loved before, or believed could love'; 26 March 1860: 'No doubt, I shall appear ridiculous to many people in admitting that I am becoming more in love with my wife every day, and yet nothing is more true.'

and partner.'[171] At the end of September, the young couple was triumphantly welcomed in Salzau, where they spent a few weeks of their honeymoon.[172] Only in late December 1858 would Blome resume work.

Before his marriage, there was some talk of a return to the embassy in Paris, but because it was not the practice in the Austrian diplomatic service for married diplomats of lower rank to be given a foreign posting, Blome was assigned to an important political function in the state chancellery. Among his new colleagues were several other converts, with whom he quickly got along very well.[173] The least Catholic and least steadfast in his principles, according to him, was his father-in-law, Buol-Schauenstein.

Still it was with Buol that the Blome couple travelled to Rome at the end of 1859 to spend the winter there and above all to meet with Pope Pius IX. It was an eventful trip, which Gustav reported on extensively to Pons. Obviously he was thrilled with Rome: *la maîtresse de l'Univers, la cité reine* ('the mistress of the universe, the queen of cities').[174] He was mostly interested in the ancient and artistic Rome, but he also occasionally frequented the salons and was impressed by the grandeur and luxury of the Roman aristocracy.[175] Still, it was mainly the private audience with the Pope that most impressed the convert. Like so many others who met Pius IX for the first time, he was struck by 'the immense goodness in the eyes of the Holy Father', although he added, interestingly, 'I do not know why, but I would have liked to see more firmness there.'[176] That feeling would be confirmed in his later, frequent contacts with this Pope, for whom he would nevertheless continue to have great admiration. Meanwhile, a long, arduous road had been traversed and the Rome of the popes would be a guiding light for Blome for the rest of his life.

At the age of thirty Blome's life had taken a definite turn. His previous relationship with Maria Kalergis and his marriage to Séphine Buol-Schauenstein put an end to his frivolous youth. This development ran parallel with his conversion and was also affected by it. His search for unshakeable principles that could provide an anchor in a world adrift had led him to the Catholic Church, which he saw as called to play an active role in social and political life. He would follow the guidelines of the Church in his public and private life with the zeal of a convert and an iron will. Indeed, the era of aristocratic libertin-

---

171 *Récit de ma conversion*, Gut Salzau, IX, 5.

172 Blome to Pons, 7 Oct. 1858.

173 Blome was deputy to Baron Otto Meysenbug who, like Ludwig von Biegeleben and Marx von Gagern, was a convert. 'On religious matters, we were in perfect agreement' (*Souvenirs*, vol. I, 83).

174 Blome to Pons, 20 Jan. 1860.

175 Blome to Pons, 14 Feb. 1860: 'The finest residences in Paris, London, Vienna and St. Petersburg still appear shabby alongside the Corsini, Borghese, Doria, etc. palaces. These truly are the dwellings of grand nobles and as for the diamonds of the Roman princesses, those of my grandmother have to humbly give way, and that is saying a lot.'

176 Blome to Pons, 20 Jan. 1860.

ism, exemplified by Princess Bagration and the young Metternich, was almost over. Across Europe, the aristocracy adopted a more bourgeois, puritanical value system, while at the same time the majority supported the Christian churches in the expectation that they would bolster the established order.[177] Blome's evolution fitted within that framework. At the end of the 1850s it became necessary to bring together all the conservative forces as liberal and national movements had begun a new offensive. The Italian war of 1859 gave the signal for this.

The resurgence of Italy

This war, preceding Blome's trip to Rome, sounded the death knell for the Metternich system, which had already been eroded by the Crimean War, and at the same time dealt a severe blow to Austria's status as a great power. Blome was at this time employed at the state chancellery, in the department that oversaw relations with embassies in western and southern Europe and where he became familiar with European politics. Views diverged somewhat within that department. Some dreamed of restoring the Holy Roman Empire under the Austrian emperor, while others favoured a 'Catholic' Franco-Austrian alliance. Blome himself had a preference for the traditional Austrian policy of balance. Neither the German Confederation nor Napoleonic France aroused much confidence in him.[178]

He used his time at the state chancellery to study the important political correspondence of the previous decades, especially Metternich's diplomatic missives, yet 'what especially interested me and taught me a lot more, were my almost daily conversations with the old prince in person'. Immediately after his return from Paris in 1858, his contacts with the 'Casa Metternich' on the Rennweg became more frequent.[179] His conversion to Catholicism and his marriage to Séphine Buol were viewed very positively in the circles of the former chancellor. In his new official capacity Blome acted from now on as an intermediary between the state chancellery and Metternich. Buol-Schauenstein was still providing the former chancellor with the most important diplomatic documents and – so as to avoid a daily correspondence – he used his son inlaw as a go-between. Not infrequently, the young diplomat lingered for hours in the office of the elderly prince, who would then discuss in detail his views

177 Lieven, *The Aristocracy in Europe*, 134-161.
178 *Souvenirs*, vol. I, 78-83.
179 Blome to Pons, 26 Feb., 10 March and 28 Dec. 1858, 16 Feb.1859; Metternich to Buol-Schauenstein, 21 June 1858: 'Your future son-in-law is a young man endowed with the happiest of qualities' (Cited Burckhardt, *Briefe des Staatskanzlers Fürsten Metternich-Winneburg*, 206).

The Italian Principalities, 1848-1859.

on the issues at hand. Those discussions aroused Blome's admiration even more – if that was possible – for Metternich's versatility, intellectual qualities and great gifts of character, which rendered him the model of the ideal statesman.[180]

In the last months of his life, in the period leading up to the Italian war, the aged Metternich was deeply involved in political negotiations at the highest level. On 12 May 1859 the Emperor dismissed Buol-Schauenstein as foreign minister and, at Metternich's suggestion, appointed as his successor Bernhard von Rechberg, at the time Austrian envoy to the German Confederation.[181] In the days following, Metternich recommended Blome to the new minister as 'a young official in whom he could place all his trust and who would be able to give him all the information he would need at the beginning of his term in office'. Rechberg followed Metternich's counsel, and on taking office immediately appointed Blome as his *chef de cabinet*, a position that had not existed previously in the state chancellery. The young diplomat was, of course, delighted with this new assignment: 'I now had the opportunity to spend more time than ever with Metternich, since Count Rechberg continued to seek his advice on all important issues.'[182] But that would not last for long more, as the former chancellor's health declined at the end of May and he died on 11 June 1859.[183] For Blome it was a great personal loss.[184] He had felt at home in the 'Casa Metternich' and lost in the great statesman his main political mentor.[185]

Meanwhile, Austria had landed in a major crisis. The advance of the national movements put the multinational state under a lot of pressure, both internally and externally. The Hungarians, Czechs and Poles were almost continuously causing unrest within the state: they opposed German dominance in the central government and demanded greater autonomy. From the outside, Austria's dominance was especially threatened by Italian and German nationalism. It was the Italian issue that would come to the forefront in European politics in the late 1850s, mainly due to Napoleon III and Camillo Cavour.[186]

---

180 *Souvenirs*, vol. I, 84-85.
181 Johann-Bernhard von Rechberg (1806-1899) was foreign minister from May 1859 to October 1864. See: Engel-Janosi, *Graf Rechberg*; Srbik, *Metternich*, vol. II, 512-514.
182 *Souvenirs*, vol. I, 149.
183 *Souvenirs*, vol. I, 148-149.
184 Blome to Pons, 17 July 1859, LASH, 126.15, 616: 'For me, in particular, it was a terrible blow. I saw the prince almost daily, he lavished me with kindness and I revered him as the most perfect being I had ever met after my saintly Father de Ravignan ... He was wisdom incarnate.'
185 *Souvenirs*, vol. II, 244: 'I still [1875] passionately love Austria, the traditional Austria, the Austria of Prince Metternich, the Catholic and conservative Austria of my dreams!' See also Blome's articles on Metternich in *Das Vaterland*, 3 and 17 July 1883.
186 Bridge and Bullen, *The Great Powers*, 126-145; Rumpler, *Eine Chance*, 369-373; Hearder, *Italy in the Age of the Risorgimento*; Riall, *The Italian Risorgimento*; Davis, *Italy in the Nineteenth Century*; Montanelli, *L'Italia del Risorgimento*, Milan, 2004.

The Italian peninsula was divided up into a large number of small and medium-sized principalities and since the sixteenth century had been the object of a power struggle between France, Spain and Austria. Napoleon I was finally able to bring the entire region under his control by annexing the northern territories and setting up vassal states. He set in motion a process of economic and political modernization, but that soon backfired on him. The spread of liberal and national ideas inspired a movement that aimed at a *Risorgimento*, a resurgence of the Italian people. This movement wanted to bring about both a sociocultural revival as well as a political unification of the peninsula. It had a romantic and revolutionary impact and for a while had great success in intellectual and bourgeois circles. However, it still carried little political weight and could not prevent Austria replacing France as the dominant power in Italy after the Congress of Vienna. The Habsburgs now exercised direct authority over Lombardy-Venetia and, through dynastic family ties, they also controlled the principalities of Tuscany, Modena and Parma. Moreover, the Papal States, the secular property of the papacy in central Italy, and the southern Kingdom of Naples-Sicily, which was governed by a subsidiary branch of the Bourbons, were in fact dependent on Austrian support. In order to be free of Austrian domination, the Italian patriots could only pin their hopes on the northwestern Kingdom of Piedmont-Sardinia, which had remained outside the Austrian sphere of influence.

During the period of the Restoration, rebellions repeatedly broke out in various Italian principalities, but were suppressed, mostly with foreign aid. The formula *Italia farà da sé* ('Italy will take care of itself') proved ineffective. Against the background of the revolutions of 1848, riots erupted from Sicily to Piedmont, which were directed against Austria or the local rulers, but dynastic disunity and political-ideological disputes prevented a concerted action. Piedmont-Sardinia was the region that was most engaged in the struggle against Austria, but on two occasions its army suffered a crushing defeat by the troops of Field Marshal Radetzky. Thus in the summer of 1849 the revolutionary phase of the *Risorgimento* came to an end. In almost all the Italian principalities the political reforms that had been introduced were scaled down or simply withdrawn.

After 1849, only the Kingdom of Piedmont-Sardinia retained its liberal constitution and an elected parliament. For this reason it would become even more the preferred refuge of Italian patriots. Camillo Cavour, who in 1852 became leader of the government in Turin, managed to convince the moderate national-liberals that Italy could be most easily unified from above by extending the power of the Kingdom of Piedmont-Sardinia, possibly with foreign aid. He tried to put the Italian question on the diplomatic chessboard for the first time by entering the Crimean War, but had little success. In 1856 there were no indications that Italian unity would be a reality within the next five years. The opponents of Austrian rule were much too weak: they were divided between federalists and unitarians, monarchists and republicans and moreover did not yet have much support among the population at large.

Napoleon III would lend a helping hand as he was sympathetic to the Italian cause. Moreover, he wanted to use the country to further undermine the state system of 1815 and to restore French hegemony over the Italian peninsula, thereby also reinforcing the position of his country in the Mediterranean area. In July 1858, at Plombières, he signed a secret treaty with Cavour, which planned the first war of aggression in Europe since Napoleon I, this time against Austria. The agreement included the following provisions: France would annex Savoy and Nice; Sardinia would acquire Lombardy, Venice, the duchies of Parma and Modena and the northern part of Romagna; in central Italy a new state would be formed around Tuscany, under French protection; the Papal States and Naples-Sicily would remain; the four listed Italian states would together form a confederation, chaired by the pope. With this last provision, Napoleon III wanted to satisfy French Catholics. He was firmly counting on his ability to exert sufficient influence on the central and southern Italian territories and thus replace Austria as the hegemonic power in Italy.

The French emperor insisted on one important condition for his participation in a possible war: Austria would have to be identified as the aggressor. In the following months, the government in Vienna was confronted with a relentless flow of military provocations from the Italian side and finally succumbed. Francis Joseph I behaved like an officer whose honour had been violated and fell into the trap, something Metternich had expressly warned about. On April 23rd, the Emperor sent an ultimatum to Piedmont-Sardinia, demanding an end to the provocations. When this ultimatum was rejected, he himself declared war on April 29th. Then, as stipulated in the agreement, France entered the conflict on Piedmont-Sardinia's side.

The Danube monarchy was extraordinarily ill-prepared for this confrontation. The Crimean War had taken a heavy toll on the empire's finances and its credit rating weakened. The army's arsenal left much to be desired. In addition, the Hungarian and Polish units proved unreliable and the command was substandard. Austria could not count on the help of allies either. It belonged to the German Confederation, which however under Prussian pressure remained neutral in the conflict because Austria itself had joined in the hostilities. Furthermore, the German states were reluctant to defend Austrian possessions outside the German area. Russia, which the Viennese government had repudiated during the Crimean War, also remained aloof. Austria's political, diplomatic and military system then failed completely.[187] Vienna had pinned all its hopes on a recovery of the mechanism of the European Concert, but was abandoned to its fate by the other great powers. Although Francis

187 Rumpler, *Eine Chance*, 369-370; Brose, *German History*, 277-278.

Joseph himself was in large part responsible for this debacle, he made his foreign minister Buol-Schauenstein the scapegoat and dismissed him summarily. As already mentioned, Bernhard von Rechberg was charged at that moment of highest need with the impossible task of searching for a way out of the diplomatic tangle. He undertook a final but futile attempt to persuade neutral Britain to take a more lenient approach to Austria.[188]

Meanwhile, the military operations in Lombardy did not proceed as hoped. The army was hampered by floods in the Po Valley and by an incompetent command. In late May Francis Joseph I decided to travel to northern Italy himself and join his troops. On June 4th, his army suffered a narrow defeat by the French in a fiercely fought battle at Magenta. Many Italian districts and towns then turned against the Austrian rulers and joined the cause of Italian unity. The Austrian army retreated eastwards, under the personal command of the Emperor. On June 24 the Austrian and Franco-Sardinian troops clashed at Solferino, the bloodiest encounter since the Battle of Leipzig in 1813. The Austrian army was turned back with heavy losses, but the toll of human lives was particularly high in the other camp also.

All the while, central Italy was in turmoil. The Habsburg rulers were driven from Tuscany and Modena, the Bourbons from Parma, and the papal administration in Romagna was under threat. Cavour incited the Hungarians to revolt. A general revolutionary war threatened and that spectre spurred the protagonists in the conflict to come to a quick agreement. Bypassing Cavour, Napoleon III directly contacted Francis Joseph I. He rightly feared a German attack from the Rhineland under Prussian leadership, if the war with Austria were to continue: anti-French sentiment in the southern German principalities could easily lead to such an outbreak. Moreover, Napoleon III wanted to prevent Piedmont-Sardinia from becoming too strong and the continued existence of the Papal States from being threatened, something that French Catholics especially feared.[189] On the Austrian side the military situation was not hopeless, but a financial collapse loomed. Francis Joseph I also had to worry about possible revolts in some territories of his empire, especially in Hungary and Polish Galicia. Moreover, Prussia took advantage of the situation to reinforce its own position within the German Confederation, which a continuation of the war would further reinforce.[190] Apparently, Vienna could no longer secure its influence in Germany and Italy simultaneously, and Francis Joseph I finally chose for the German rather than the Italian option.[191]

---

188 On the orders of his minister, Blome drew up the memorandum that was to serve as a guide for Prince Paul Esterhazy, the Austrian ambassador in London. He evaluated the operation thus: 'In relying on England, Count Rechberg made a mistake in the date, by a quarter of a century at least.' (*Souvenirs*, vol. I, 154).
189 Milza, *Napoléon III*, 350-358; Yon, *Le Second Empire*, 84-86.
190 Nipperdey, *Deutsche Geschichte, 1866-1918*, dl. I, 692-695.
191 Rumpler, *Eine Chance*, 371.

The ball was now in the diplomats' court. Rechberg was twice summoned to the imperial headquarters in Verona, and on the second occasion he was accompanied by his *chef de cabinet*.[192] Blome was appointed 'diplomatic secretary' to the Austrian delegation that worked out the terms of a truce with the French on July 8th in Villafranca. He drew up a report of the discussions, as well as the draft agreement, which was later refined in a personal correspondence between the two emperors. Napoleon III and Francis Joseph I finally met one another on July 11th at Villafranca to seal the agreement, which was confirmed by the Treaty of Zurich (10 November 1859). Its main provisions included the following: Austria would cede Lombardy to Piedmont-Sardinia; the Habsburg rulers of Tuscany and Modena would be restored to power; the Austrian emperor as governor of Venice would become a member of an Italian confederation led by the Pope – a provision that ensured Francis Joseph could still exert some influence in Italy. The most important consequence of the agreement, however, was that with the loss of Lombardy a substantial part of the political and economic balance in the make-up of the Austrian state disappeared.[193]

Many provisions of the Villafranca and Zurich treaties would remain a dead letter, however. The signatories had not taken account of the national fervour in Italy and of the position of Britain, which wanted to prevent France from threatening its interests in the Mediterranean at all costs. Popular uprisings in Modena, Tuscany and northern Romagna led to referenda in which an overwhelming majority of the population voted to join the Kingdom of Piedmont-Sardinia. Britain's liberal government introduced a non-intervention principle to which the French had to acquiesce. Nothing came of the proposal to create an Italian Confederation under papal leadership. The principle of self-determination recalled legitimist claims and traditional power politics. At the end of 1859 there were still only three independent political entities on the Italian peninsula: the Kingdom of Sardinia, the much-reduced Papal States and the Kingdom of Naples-Sicily. Venice and its surrounding districts remained in Austrian hands.

However, the national momentum did not weaken, but rather strengthened. In early May 1860 Garibaldi with his thousand Redshirts landed in Sicily and in a few months brought about the fall of the Bourbon regime in Naples. The republican *condottiere* was given a free hand by the British, who wanted to counteract French influence in southern Italy. Cavour was not keen to annex the impoverished south, but when Garibaldi threatened to overrun the Papal States, which would inevitably lead to French intervention, the Sardinian troops marched south. While passing through the Papal States, they defeated a papal volunteer army at Castelfidardo on 18 September 1860 and overpow-

192 On this episode, see also Lamberts, 'A Peculiar Heir of Metternich', 193-220.
193 Rumpler, *Eine Chance*, 364.

ered Umbria and the Marches. They then joined up with Garibaldi's revolutionary forces in the south. This intervention prevented Naples from becoming a hotbed of political instability, which would have threatened the rest of Italy. Plebiscites endorsed the annexation of Umbria and the Marches – formerly papal territory – and of Naples-Sicily to the Kingdom of Piedmont-Sardinia. In March 1861 a newly elected parliament in Turin proclaimed the *Regno d'Italia*. Rome was to be the capital city, but the Eternal City and the surrounding Latium remained in the hands of the Pope who refused to surrender his temporal power. Thus arose the 'Roman question', which for decades would cause major tensions between the papacy and the Kingdom of Italy.

The Italian unification process was set in motion in 1859 primarily by considerations of power, but it was driven by a popular fervour that became unstoppable over time. The outcome was certainly not what Napoleon III had foreseen. The unification of Italy went much further than he desired and, thanks to Great Britain's diplomatic moves, French influence on the peninsula declined. France now had to cope on its southern border with a unified state that could easily make common cause with its enemies. Great Britain gained most from the new situation: Italy was now liberated from Austrian as well as French influence and that meant that British trade interests no longer faced any threats in the Mediterranean. Austria was totally shattered. The Italian *Risorgimento* set in motion a process of decline that in the long term would lead to the downfall of the Habsburg monarchy. In the next few years it would renew its focus on Germany and make every effort to consolidate its supremacy there in the vain hope of thereby regaining its influence over Italy, if only partially.

Blome was closely involved in the developments in Italy. The campaign of 1859 was a traumatic experience for him as it was for so many Austrian soldiers, politicians and diplomats. He was adamantly opposed to the Villafranca agreement: though he had helped to draw it up, he had done so completely against his will. After the peace talks, he returned to Vienna with Rechberg and with Richard Metternich who was also involved in the deliberations. Totally exhausted by the tropical heat in Verona and surroundings, he sighed, 'this African sun can later be invoked as an excuse for the shameful peace that we have just signed'.[194] On the way back, he also had an acute attack of dysentery. According to his own testimony, it was largely due to the good care of Richard Metternich that he reached Vienna safely, albeit physically and mentally exhausted.[195] He was then given the painful task of explaining to the Austrian embassies the motives for a peace that he himself considered to be so humiliating. He was of the opinion that Austria was on a slippery slope by giv-

---

194 Blome to Pons, 17 July1859.
195 *Souvenirs*, vol. I, 168. During this period Blome carried on an intense and friendly correspondence with Richard Metternich (NAP, Metternich, *Acta Richardiana*, No. 160).

ing into a national revolution, which Napoleon III also supported for strategic and diplomatic reasons.[196]

The first phase of the Italian unification process was a very painful experience for Blome as it heralded the decline of the great power Austria, his chosen fatherland.[197] In addition there was the threat of revolutionary nationalism, which he saw at work in Tuscany, Parma, Modena and Romagna. That threat became even more acute in the second phase of the unification process, with the actions of Garibaldi's Redshirts in southern Italy. The establishment of the Kingdom of Italy, which claimed Rome as its capital, increased the pressure on what remained of the Papal States, the Patrominium Petri. The Roman question, which challenged the temporal power of the Pope and threatened his freedom as head of the universal Church, would be the main factor in mobilizing a militant, predominantly anti-liberal Catholic movement in which a decade later Blome would be a prominent player.

However, this was not his first priority as long as he was actively involved in Austrian diplomacy. He now had to conclude with regret that the Metternich system had collapsed, as was almost symbolically illustrated by the death of the former chancellor. Nevertheless, Blome remained convinced that the treaty system of the Concert of Europe was the best guarantee for the preservation of peace and stability in Europe. He noted with dismay that international politics was increasingly being dictated by national considerations and was slowly making more use of war and violence as a political tool.[198] In line with Metternich he would stubbornly continue to oppose this. In a similar way, he went on the offensive against political liberalism, which in his eyes was a breeding ground for revolutionary nationalism.

In his concrete vision of the position of the Habsburg monarchy in Europe, Blome like Metternich believed that collaboration with Prussia in the context of the German Confederation was desirable. Together, the two German powers could form a buffer against the hegemonic ambitions of France and Russia. Blome's distrust of Russia had grown considerably during his stay in St. Petersburg and, though he had a deep sympathy for France, he was wary of the expansionist and revolutionary accents in Napoleon III's foreign policy. In his view, Austria had to do its utmost to uphold its dominance in Europe and in northern Italy, in order to safeguard the temporal power of the papacy. After 1859, this could be done only indirectly by maintaining Austrian influence in Germany. A major difficulty, however, was that this was being challenged by Prussia, which had gradually become an important economic and political power and struggled with Austria for supremacy in the German area. Prussia

---

196 *Souvenirs*, vol. I, 171-173.
197 Blome to Richard Metternich, 3 Nov. 1859, NAP, Metternich, *Acta Richardiana*, No. 160. 'The sick man at this time is not the Grand Turk, it is our Empire. Do not have any illusions about that.'
198 *Souvenirs*, vol. I, 95 and 112.

was also a conservative power, but its new chancellor Bismarck would enter into an alliance with nationalism and to some extent even with liberalism. This modernization strategy of conservatism was at odds with the Metternich model and would prove very successful in the short term. The alternative, which Blome would choose, would bear fruit only in the longer term.

BISMARCK'S MOVE

On Monday, 24 July 1865 the Prussian King Wilhelm I travelled with his entourage from Salzburg to the spa at Gastein, where he was enthusiastically welcomed by the mayor and local dignitaries.[1] It was the king's third visit to this Austrian resort, south of Lend.

The Gastein valley, surrounded on the west by the Stubnerkogel and on the east by the Graukogel, is famous for its pleasant, mild climate. The Gasteiner Ache, a wild mountain river, tumbles down the flanks of the Graukogel and at the centre of Badgastein forms a waterfall with a drop of nearly one hundred and fifty meters. The numerous hot springs in the area have been famous since the fifteenth century for their healing properties, especially for rheumatism and arthritis. By the first half of the nineteenth century Gastein had grown into a renowned spa resort, whose visitors included artists such as Franz Schubert and Johann Strauss Jr.

In 1863 the Prussian king had chosen the resort because it was difficult to reach and easy to secure. Indeed, the year before he had been attacked in his favorite spa town of Baden-Baden, and General Helmuth von Moltke had recommended Gastein as an alternative. An added benefit was that this location was only 120 kilometers away from Bad Ischl, the permanent summer residence of the Austrian emperor. This offered an opportunity for reciprocal courtesy visits and possible political contacts, an opportunity that was taken

---

1   On the spa at Gastein see: Rohrer, *Kurorte*, 17-40; Niel, *Die grossen k.u.k. Kürbaden*, 28-39.

both in 1863 and 1864 to deal with disputes that had arisen between the two great powers in connection with the German question.[2]

When in the summer of 1865 Wilhelm I and his entourage descended on Gastein for the third time, relations between Prussia and Austria were particularly tense and were even threatening to erupt in war. This time, a meeting between the two rulers was far from certain. In a final attempt to avert a rupture, Count Mensdorff, the Austrian foreign minister, proposed to his Prussian colleague, Otto von Bismarck, that he would send a confidant of the Emperor to Gastein in order to come up with a solution for the main bone of contention between the two great powers: the governance of the duchies of Schleswig-Holstein, which had been taken from Denmark in 1863.

The Austrian ambassador in Bavaria was charged with this delicate task. He arrived in Gastein on the evening of Thursday, July 27th and next morning began the difficult discussions with Bismarck. The negotiating partners met in the Hotel Straubinger, a hundred meters from the waterfall, whose drumming, monotonous noise created a threatening atmosphere.[3] Every day there were two rounds of discussions, each lasting two to three hours. The two men sat opposite each other at a large table, smoking cigars almost continuously. Most of the time Bismarck fiddled with a big Spanish knife that he used for cutting his cigars, and perhaps on this occasion for intimidating his discussion partner. Every evening there was a dinner with the king and his courtiers; after two days the ice was broken and the atmosphere thawed, although the tone remained stiff, even snappish, during the negotiations themselves. Bismarck was more forthcoming at the gambling table in the late evening hours.[4] At that time, Bad Gastein did not boast a casino, but the local physician, Ströll, was an excellent host and offered the important guests the accommodation they desired. Meanwhile, the outside world, including the entourage of the Austrian emperor, was completely unaware of what was happening at the spa, despite the fact that the German and international press was buzzing with rumours. That the Austrian envoy had not immediately returned to Vienna was considered for a while to be a good sign, but at the beginning of August diplomats and journalists got the impression that the discussions in Gastein

---

2   From 1871 to 1888 Wilhelm I, then German emperor, spent his annual holiday in Gastein. His arrival was the highlight of the season every year. His court would descend on the spa with a large number of luggage carts, as even the silver cutlery was brought from Berlin. In those years Francis Joseph I made frequent courtesy visits to the German emperor. The Kaiser Wilhelm Promenade is now one of the landmarks in Gastein.

3   Bismarck to his wife, 14 Aug. 1865: 'Bächlein, lass dein Rauschen sein [Wilhelm Müller]. Little brook, let your rushing be! That wish is appropriate for my room day and night also. You can breathe again when you reach a place where you do not hear the infernal noise of the waterfall.' (Cited in: *Otto von Bismarck. Werke in Auswahl*, ed. G.A. Rein, vol. III/1, letter 429).

4   Steinberg, *Bismarck*, 232.

Gustav von Blome. Photograph, c. 1863.
[*Vienna, Österreichische Nationalbibliothek*]

had reached a dead end. The Austrian envoy then hastily left the spa to go to Ischl, where Francis Joseph I was impatiently waiting for him. When that news was made public, the leading stock exchanges in Europe took a dive. A war between the two German powers seemed inevitable, possibly sparking ramifications elsewhere in Europe.

The Austrian envoy in question was Gustav von Blome, who had been ambassador in Munich since December 1863.[5] At the time of the negotiations in Gastein he was barely 36 years old, but despite his youth, he had already become a top diplomat and enjoyed the full confidence of the Emperor. Otto von Bismarck, his opponent, was then 50 years old and since September 1862 minister-president and foreign affairs minister of Prussia. Seen from a contemporary perspective, the young Blome was hardly a match for the experienced Bismarck, but Bismarck had not yet proved himself, and had not yet made the political choices that would lead to his future successes.

The meeting between Blome and Bismarck at Gastein is interesting for our study in several respects. Given Blome's origins and history, the encounter can to some extent be seen as a confrontation *par personne interposée* between Metternich and Bismarck, the most influential continental European politicians of the nineteenth century. The pragmatic *realpolitik* of Bismarck, whose primary aim was to expand Prussian power, would forge a link between conservatism and nationalism, consecrate the nation state and strengthen the power of the State. His counterpart had a preference for a more ethical and internationally oriented policy and for a multi-layered state and society. This seemed to be a politics of the past, contrary to the *Zeitgeist*. Nonetheless, Blome would continue to defend it stubbornly. The contrast between the two visions came fully to light in the German question, and led to a sharp confrontation between Austria and Prussia.

The struggle for Germany

Tensions between Austria and Prussia had a long history.[6] The German Confederation, which had been set up by the Congress of Vienna as a loose confederation of thirty-five principalities and four free cities, was, in fact, dominated by the multinational Habsburg Empire. The Bundestag, the only central

5　The details about the negotiations with Bismarck are derived from *Souvenirs*, vol. II, 57-69 and from Blome's memoirs, *Historique des négociations qui aboutirent à la Convention de Gastein. Ma campagne diplomatique de l'été 1865*, 83 p., LASH, Section 126.15, nr. 622.

6　Srbik, *Quellen zur deutschen Politik Österreichs, 1859-1866*, vols. I and II; Bridge and Bullen, *The Great Powers*, 146-159; Brose, *German History*, 264-285; Nipperdey, *Deutsche Geschichte (1800-1866)*, 674-714; Blackbourn, *History of Germany*, 225-258; Rumpler, *Eine Chance*, 386-402; Zöllner, *Geschichte Österreichs*, 404-411; Höbelt, *Franz Joseph I*, 31-38.

body, had its seat in Frankfurt am Main and was little more than a gathering of envoys who came together under Austrian leadership. Before 1848, the Confederation, through Metternich's influence, functioned principally as a repressive instrument against the liberal, national movements, which the Austrian chancellor saw as posing a danger to the conservative order in Central Europe. At the time German national sentiment was less vigorous than it had been during the Napoleonic era; although still popular in intellectual and bourgeois circles, the German Confederation did not evince the slightest sympathy for it. The Confederation did not in any way promote a national identity and was associated by the public with the selfish dynastic interests of the reigning German princes.

The wave of revolutions in 1848 brought the liberal, national forces to the forefront. In most German principalities liberal constitutions were drawn up that granted ample freedoms and political participation to citizens. At the same time patriotic leaders tried to bring about German unification under a liberal flag. They gave this task to a nationally elected parliament, which met in May in the Paulskirche in Frankfurt am Main to work out a constitution for a unified Germany. The crucial question was whether or not the planned German nation state should include Austria. Parliament wanted to integrate only the German part of the Danube monarchy, but this was not acceptable to the Viennese government; it therefore finally opted for the formula of a Lesser Germany, that is a German state under Prussian leadership but with close ties to Austria. After the constitution was drafted in the spring of 1849, the Prussian King Frederick William IV was elected emperor. However, he refused the crown, because he did not want 'to have to pick it up out of the gutter', or, put more elegantly, to receive it from the hands of a parliament. In the meantime, the tide had turned: the radicalization of the revolutionary movement had provoked strong repression, and the princes and their courts had gradually recovered their confidence. A conservative reaction was already evident in late 1848, which led to the withdrawal or modification of liberal constitutions and the appointment of conservative governments. The Frankfurt parliament was dispersed and the unification of Germany – under a liberal banner – had failed thoroughly. Events had shown that a large section of public opinion favoured a Lesser German state under Prussian leadership. However, most of the reigning German princes were not supportive. The medium-sized states, the *Mittelstaaten*, were apprehensive about the expansionist ambitions of militaristic Prussia and eventually accepted the restoration of the German Confederation, which was pushed through by Austria with Russian help.

Austria now regained formal leadership of the Confederation, but its relationship with Prussia would henceforth be severely strained. The rivalry between the two great powers emerged on several levels, especially with regard to economic development at a time when the economy was picking up considerably. Prussia had significant industrial assets with its Rhineland provinces. Through the *Zollverein*, a customs union under its leadership, it bound the other German states ever more closely to itself. It could also count on some goodwill from the liberally minded in the *Mittelstaaten* because it had not completely abolished the constitutional reforms of 1848. By contrast, Austria under neo-absolutist rule revealed itself once again as a conservative power. When the Danube monarchy became entangled in the web of the Crimean War and practically sided with France, people in western Germany, where a strong anti-French mood prevailed, felt that Austrian foreign policy did not serve German interests. The Crimean War thus brought the German question again to the foreground. Prussia attempted to use these developments to gain equal status within the Confederation, but ran up against Austrian unwillingness to make the slightest concession in that regard. When the Italian war prompted anti-French patriotism to flare up, German patriots looked especially to Prussia in order to achieve their objectives and not to beleaguered Austria, which was seen more as a European than a German power. In 1859 the Lesser German *Nationalverein* was founded, which strove for the unification of Germany under Prussian leadership. Three years later, a Greater German *Reformverein* was established, which wanted to maintain the existing state system under Austrian leadership. Tensions came to a climax, especially because Francis Joseph I, following his defeat in Italy, was determined to regain lost ground in the German territories.

However, before the Danube monarchy could again pursue an active foreign policy, it first had to put things right at home.[7] The defeat in the Italian war had discredited neo-absolutism and exposed the major weaknesses of the regime, in particular the financial chaos and unrest among several ethnic groups. The Imperial Council, which thus far consisted of appointed members with an advisory role, was expanded in March 1860 with representatives from different parts of the empire and was commissioned to draw up a constitution. Within the Council serious tensions emerged between the German centralists, who hitherto had set the agenda in the empire, and the federalists, who were demanding greater autonomy for the different peoples. This opposition largely paralleled the controversy between liberal-minded politicians and conservative particularists. The liberals wanted to give the intelligentsia and the merchant class an important voice in political life through a centralized parliamentary system. The conservative federalists on the other hand favoured more regional autonomy and the preservation of the traditional intermediary structures. Many of them were aristocrats and exerted great influence within those institutions and levels of government. The Emperor initially chose to take the federalist side in the conflict. On 20 October 1860 he issued the *Oktoberdiplom* by which he retained his usual prerogatives in foreign and

---

7   Rumpler, *Eine Chance*, 373-380.

military policy, awarded a mostly advisory power to the Imperial Council and expanded the powers of the provincial diets. This amounted to a significant decentralization and the recognition of the historical rights of the different sections of the empire.

Blome worked behind the scenes on this arrangement. Following the Italian war, he had been given extended leave of absence and only on 10 August 1860 had he again resumed his position as *chef de cabinet*, pending an appointment to a diplomatic posting.[8] At that time he was not particularly busy, and from the sidelines became involved in the constitutional reforms in his own country. 'I had the necessary time to participate behind the scenes in the constitutional debate. I enjoyed the confidence of some of the main protagonists and was able to follow the secret manoeuvers closely.' He was an ardent supporter and advocate of traditional liberties and of extensive decentralization. He had already noted in his diary in 1857: 'Civil liberty and decentralization: there lies the future of Europe.' In 1875 he would add: 'I recognize in that entry the core of the principles that I would honour for the rest of my life.'[9] It should be noted that he mentions only 'civil' and not 'political' freedom. In fact, he was very suspicious of the liberal strategy that aimed at linking popular sovereignty with bureaucratic centralism. By restricting the right to vote to the propertied classes, the wealthy bourgeoisie, which in fact constituted only a small minority in the empire, aimed at acquiring a predominant position in parliamentary representation; by taking over the apparatus of the centralized state, they would succeed in expanding their power over the whole empire and all sectors of society.[10]

The genesis of the *Oktoberdiplom* was fraught with difficulty, but the federalists were altogether delighted with the compromise reached. However, their euphoria was short-lived. The German centralists, who were widely supported by the Viennese merchant class, had an important weapon at their disposal: the granting of credit to the ailing state coffers, since the big financiers refused to give the necessary loans. Yet another fact led the Emperor to change direction: he had to rely on the support of the German liberal bourgeoisie in his realm in order to pursue a more active German policy. A cautious liberalization of the regime would also improve Austria's image in the German Confederation. Anton von Schmerling turned the *Oktoberdiplom* in a liberal, parliamentary and centralist direction. The *Februarpatent* (1861) put a definitive end to royal absolutism in Central Europe. The Imperial Council was transformed into a parliament with broad legislative powers and henceforth would consist of two chambers: an *Abgeordnetenhaus* (House of Depu-

8   *Souvenirs*, vol. I, 194.
9   Entry for 5 July 1857 from a lost diary of Blome's. He copied this passage into his *Souvenirs*, vol. I, 48.
10   *Souvenirs*, vol. I, 206-235; *Mémoire sur les phases administratives de l'Autriche de 1848 à 1870*, Gut Salzau, II.

ties) elected by the provincial diets and a *Herrenhaus* (House of Lords) whose members were appointed by the emperor. The members of the provincial diets would henceforth be elected on the basis of census suffrage. Ministerial responsibility was not yet introduced and the emperor's power remained dominant.[11] However, the new constitutional arrangement met with widespread resistance. The Hungarians boycotted it because of its centralized nature, and the Slavic parts of the empire also protested vociferously. A few years later, in September 1865, the Emperor would suspend the *Februarpatent* and would again seek an agreement with the provincial diets. The task of working out a balanced system of government that would do justice to all sections of the empire proved well-nigh impossible, due to the traditional predominance of the more developed and richer German territories and the particularism of the strong Hungarian minority. In general one can conclude that domestic issues and foreign policy interacted continuously, as was also the case in the German question.

Over the next few years Blome would be closely involved in settling the German question. On 7 November 1860 he was appointed special envoy and minister plenipotentiary to the Hanseatic cities of Hamburg, Lubeck and Bremen. That in itself was not an important posting but Rechberg wanted to keep him close by so as to entrust him with any special assignments that might arise. Thus ended Blome's 'lower career'. He was quite happy with the way things worked out: 'Only eight years in the lower grades! That's a brilliant promotion for someone who does not have the special privileges that come from a princely background or strong support in the Court.' He was now paid for the first time, although the amount allocated barely sufficed to maintain his stables and carriages.[12] Fortunately he had his trust money as well as a legacy from Princess Bagration, who had died in 1857. Moreover, in 1865, a small fortune would come his way through his wife, on the death of his father-in-law, Buol-Schauenstein.[13]

From his vantage point in the Hanseatic cities, Blome was asked to observe developments in northern Germany, and especially to keep an eye on Prussian machinations. He also monitored events in Schleswig-Holstein, his birthplace, where yet another confrontation between the German residents and the Danish government would finally lead to a new nationalist upsurge. In addition, he used his stay in the Protestant north to defend the interests of the local Catholics there. This was not part of his diplomatic mission, but it was consistent with his militant Catholic position, which he did not hide.[14]

Francis Joseph I wanted at all costs to consolidate the leading role of Austria in the German Confederation. He remained basically faithful to Metter-

11   Kriechbaumer and Bussjäger, eds., *Das Februarpatent 1861*.
12   *Souvenirs*, vol. I, 236.
13   *Souvenirs*, vol. II, 2.
14   *Souvenirs*, vol. II, 3-9.

nich's vision: with Prussia as the junior partner, the Danube monarchy should and could guarantee the existing order and stability in Central Europe. The problem was that Prussia was no longer satisfied with a minor role. The *Mittel-staaten* were also discontented and wanted a greater say in the leadership of the Confederation; moreover, their governments had to take account of liberal public opinion which was calling for the reform of confederal institutions in a more parliamentary direction. In October 1861 Friedrich-Ferdinand von Beust, minister-president of the Kingdom of Saxony, proposed such a reform to the *Bundestag*. Prussia responded in December of that year by again resurrecting the plans for a Lesser German union. Austria could not remain passive any longer.

In mid-December, Rechberg summoned Blome to Vienna with the utmost urgency and informed him that the Emperor wanted to entrust him with a confidential mission to the *Mittelstaaten*.[15] He had to provide assurances to the sovereigns of those states that Austria was determined at all costs not to give up its historically acquired position as the premier German power and that it would counter any attempt to establish a parliamentary German empire under Prussian leadership. He had to make clear to the *Mittelstaaten* that if they wished to maintain their independence, a weak Austria was not in their interests. He was tasked with concluding an agreement with those states declaring they would not accept any settlement that excluded Austria. For its part, the Danube monarchy vowed not to accept a reform of the Confederation that would jeopardize the independence and equality of the German sovereigns.

It was an extraordinarily delicate mission. It also involved great risks for Blome's own career because of the serious tensions in the Austrian government between Schmerling and Rechberg. He therefore insisted that the mission be explicitly formulated as having been ordered by the Emperor. His letter of introduction to the princes noted that 'he enjoyed the full confidence of the Emperor and was fully informed about the views of his government'. During the month of January Blome visited four states, starting with Bavaria, where he stayed the longest and where he encountered the most resistance. Bavaria was the most important *Mittelstaat* and, because of its geographical location was less fearful than the other principalities of the hegemonic aspirations of Prussia. It took a lot of effort to persuade the government to sign a joint protocol (22 January 1862), but Blome was successful to the extent that the Bavarian King Maximilian II himself added an article to the protocol that would later have considerable consequences. It provided that the governments of the *Mittelstaaten*, through their ambassadors, would hand over identical notes (*Identische Noten)* rejecting Prussian proposals for reform of the Confederation. The other *Mittelstaaten* endorsed the agreement reached with Bavaria

15   *Souvenirs*, vol. II, 10-23. A short time later Blome wrote a report on this mission: *Curieux épisode de ma vie (1862)*, 13 p., Gut Salzau, III.

without much trouble; feeling threatened by Prussia and pleased that Austria was finally giving a sign of life, their governments pledged their support.

On 3 February 1862 Blome returned to Vienna, the secrecy of his mission still intact. Shortly afterwards the ambassadors of the *Mittelstaaten* indeed handed over their *Identische Noten* to the Berlin government, which aroused great consternation.[16] Blome received high praise from the Emperor and Rechberg; even the liberal deputies in the Imperial Council congratulated him on the results he had achieved. At the end of December 1863, at the age of 34, he received an appropriate reward by being appointed ambassador to Munich. 'That post was very desirable for someone of my age ... Within the diplomatic corps, Munich was seen as the most important of the secondary postings.'

In those years, Austria still had a number of assets for consolidating its leading position in Germany. The *Februarpatent* had given the State a more liberal profile, which enhanced its prestige in the Confederation. Prussia on the other hand had to contend with some major domestic issues. Wilhelm I, who took over as regent in 1858, initially followed a moderate course, but on becoming king in 1861, began to defend his privileges forcefully, especially on the military level. The liberals on the other side were becoming increasingly powerful in the urban centres and had gained a majority in the *Landtag* (House of Deputies). They wanted the army – and especially the military budget – to be brought under parliamentary control. An acute constitutional crisis ensued, which would drag on for years. In desperation, in October 1862, Wilhelm I appealed to Otto von Bismarck to advance royal interests. Until this point Bismarck had mainly made a diplomatic career. He was known as a reactionary and at the same time as a ruthless power politician.[17] He also had a reputation as being a staunch opponent of Austrian hegemony over Germany; during the ten years he was Prussian envoy to the Confederation in Frankfurt, he had become convinced that over time there would be no place for Austria in Germany. His appointment did not enhance Prussia's image in the other German principalities: once again it was profiling itself as a reactionary and militaristic state.

Developments in Prussia then presented Austria with both opportunities and risks in its attempt to establish its position in the Confederation. The Viennese government worked out some proposals to modernize the functioning of the Confederation while still maintaining its confederal structure, but again and again Bismarck succeeded in torpedoing them. A final Austrian proposal was submitted to a congress of German princes in Frankfurt in mid-August 1863, which took some account of the wishes of the *Mittelstaaten* but above all secured Austrian hegemony in the Confederation. For that reason, Bismarck

---

16   *Souvenirs*, vol. II, 22: 'The *Identical Notes* led to a bomb-like explosion.'
17   Pflanze, *Bismarck and the Development of Germany*; Gall, *Bismarck, the White Revolutionary*; Feuchtwanger, *Bismarck*; Lerman, *Bismarck*; Steinberg, *Bismarck*.

opposed the proposal, arguing that given Prussia's economic power and in-creasing political weight, it could no longer be regarded as a second-class power and should be treated equally to Austria. Moreover, its hegemonic in-fluence north of the Main Line had to be recognized. Prussia absented itself from the congress of the princes, with the result that it was a complete failure. It was now crystal clear that Austria could no longer secure its position in the Confederation through diplomatic channels. Bismarck would risk everything to expand the power of Prussia and sideline Austria, and to that end made deft use of the Schleswig-Holstein controversy, which had been inflaming passions since the end of 1863.

The Schleswig-Holstein hotbed

The duchies of Schleswig and Holstein, located in the south of the Jutland peninsula, had for decades been a source of ethnic contention. Though joined in a personal union with the Danish crown, culturally and historically they belonged to the German territories.[18] This was particularly true of the more southern Holstein, which had been part of the Holy Roman Empire and as such became a member of the German Confederation in 1815. The northern duchy of Schleswig had been predominantly Danish-speaking initially, but since the fifteenth century had come increasingly under German influence. Although Schleswig was historically inseparable from Holstein, it was not a member of the German Confederation. This complex legal situation was put under strain with the emergence and growth of national movements both in Denmark and in Germany. The Danes made valiant efforts in Schleswig to counteract and even turn back the process of Germanification, but met with much resistance on the German side. Tensions in the duchy were already playing an important role in the German national movement in the 1840s. Nevertheless, it was the Danish government that went on the offensive in 1848. In the broader context of a constitutional revision, it wanted to integrate the duchies and especially Schleswig in the Danish kingdom. This led to the insurgency in which Blome participated. The rebels demanded that the duchies be more fully integrated into Germany, but with the intervention of the great powers were forced to back down. The London Protocol (8 May 1852) virtually restored the former situation: Schleswig and Holstein remained an indivisible whole connected to Denmark in a personal union and subject to the same rules of succession.

In the 1850s, the Danish government's continuation of its language policy in Schleswig aroused sustained protest on the German side. In 1863, national tensions were further exacerbated by new constitutional reforms in Denmark

18   Opitz, *Schleswig-Holstein*, 184-205; Lange, ed., *Geschichte Schleswig-Holsteins*.

The Duchies of Schleswig-Holstein, 1848-1864.

and by a disputed succession in the duchies, which resulted in an almost inextricable tangle.[19] The impetus was the promulgation of a new constitution in Denmark that was also to be applicable to Schleswig, and would amount to its full integration into Denmark. The result was an upsurge of nationalism in Germany that invoked the indivisibility of the duchies in support of its cause. German nationalists now demanded nothing less than the annexation of these territories into the German Confederation. When a dispute about the succession arose after the death of the Danish king Frederick VII at the end of 1863, the house of Augustenburg, with the support of liberal opinion in the

19   Nipperdey, *Deutsche Geschichte*, 704-714; Blackbourn, *History of Germany*, 243-248.

Mittelstaaten, claimed the succession in the duchies. A head-on collision ensued between the Danish and German national movements, but they were not the only players in the conflict. After all, the question also had a European dimension: the London Protocol of 1852 was being put at risk and the international balance of power was threatened.

The overriding question for Austria and Prussia was whether they would allow their policies to be determined primarily by public opinion, or whether they would behave like European powers. Bismarck, who had come to power in Prussia shortly before, deliberately chose the second option.[20] In his view, the London Protocol had to be respected and he had little difficulty in persuading Austria of that viewpoint. Respect for international conventions was indeed paramount for the Viennese government; moreover, for reasons of self-preservation, it had little sympathy for national movements. By adopting a legalistic standpoint Bismarck also hoped to prevent Russia and Great Britain from interfering.

Prussia and Austria asked the new Danish king, Christian IX, to repeal the provisions of the new constitution concerning the duchies and to respect the treaty provisions of 1852. This claim was rejected, and on 1 January 1864 the disputed constitution came into force. The Confederation's troops then occupied Holstein, and in Kiel Frederick von Augustenburg declared himself ruler of the two duchies. Apart from the Confederation troops, Prussian and Austrian armies also operated in Schleswig as well as in Holstein. The Danish army was no match for that superior force. In May, an armistice was signed and negotiations started in London, with the other major powers also participating. However, no immediate result was forthcoming and battle was resumed at the end of June, but after three weeks the Danish troops finally had to cease hostilities. Meanwhile, the objectives of the belligerents had shifted. A return to the pre-war situation no longer seemed possible: Austria, like Prussia, had come to the conclusion that a personal union between the duchies and the Danish crown was no longer feasible. The Treaty of Vienna (30 October 1864) forced Denmark to cede Schleswig and Holstein, along with the Duchy of Lauenburg, to Prussia and Austria. The Danish monarchy thereby lost two-fifths of its territory. From now on the future of the duchies would be a German affair, but would primarily depend on the victorious powers, Prussia and Austria, with the Confederation on the sidelines. It was a major achievement for Bismarck to have brought the duchies finally and decisively within the German sphere of influence, without Russia or Britain intervening, all of which marked a big change from 1849. The German patriots would credit the 'reactionary' Bismarck with this achievement.

The duchies were provisionally ruled jointly – as in a *condominium* – by Prussia and Austria, but it was clear that this arrangement could not last

20   Lerman, *Bismarck*, 91-113.

long. The pressing question was whether Schleswig and Holstein would in the future form a new *Mittelstaat* within the German Confederation under Augustenburg's administration, or whether they would be incorporated into neighbouring Prussia. Bismarck was not willing to tolerate having on the Prussian border a new *Mittelstaat* that would be an instrument in the hands of a German Confederation under Austrian hegemony. The duchies could form a new *Mittelstaat* only if they were willing to link their fate with that of Prussia. When Augustenburg's reluctance to accede to his demands became obvious, Bismarck resolutely opted for annexation, but had to proceed cautiously as both the *Mittelstaaten* as well as Austria wanted to prevent it.[21]

At the end of 1864 the Danube monarchy was in an absurd situation. It was politically weakened because its actions in the duchies had alienated it from its natural allies, the *Mittelstaaten*. It was linked to Prussia, yet opposed the annexation tendencies of this great power and its aspiration to gain hegemony over northern Germany. Long negotiations between Bismarck and Rechberg in Vienna's Schönbrunn Palace foundered in the summer of 1864 on Austria's resistance to accepting the dominance of Prussia north of the Main Line. The Viennese government had not yet realized that it no longer had the economic, military or diplomatic means to maintain its dominance over Germany. It even wanted to counteract the influence of the Berlin government on the remote peninsula of Jutland, Prussia's backyard, where it did not have any strategic interests to defend and which, moreover, it could only retain with difficulty. The dispute over the northern duchies became more and more a central issue in the struggle for hegemony over Germany. In those circumstances, continuing a policy of appeasement with Prussia made little sense. On 29 October 1864 Francis Joseph I dismissed Rechberg as foreign minister and replaced him with Count Alexander Mensdorff-Pouilly.[22] The latter would strive to regain lost ground in the Confederation by giving unconditional support to Augustenburg, with the aim of having Schleswig-Holstein recognized as a new *Mittelstaat*. The Vienna state chancellery therefore changed direction once again, implying that it preferred to pursue a collision course with Prussia.[23]

This decision did not have to lead immediately to war, although Bismarck increasingly began to consider the possibility. In that event, he wanted to prevent the armed conflict from acquiring an international, European dimension and Austria from finding allies. The revolution against the Tsarist regime in the Russian part of Poland in 1863 offered a good opportunity to strengthen Prussia's international position. Bismarck sided with Russia, thereby improving his relationship with that country. For his part, the French emperor, Napo-

---

21 Eyck, *Bismarck*, vol. II, 11-37; Winkler, *Der lange Weg nach Westen*, vol. I, 161-173.
22 Blome warmly welcomed the appointment of Mensdorff, having served under him in St. Petersburg (Blome to Mensdorff, 29 Oct. 1864 in: Srbik, *Quellen*, vol. IV, 354-355).
23 Elrod, 'Realpolitik or Concert Diplomacy', 84-97.

leon III sought to exploit the Polish revolution so as to bring about a revision of Europe's political map, but following the suppression of the uprising, he lost his role as arbitrator in European politics. In addition, he had his hands full at this time with military operations in Algeria and Mexico. Great Britain also faced serious problems in its empire; moreover, the Foreign Office seemed to have little confidence in Austria as a counterforce to France and Russia. According to British diplomats, only Prussia could give Germany the power necessary to resist a possible expansion of the two great powers. Prussia would have little to fear from Russia and Great Britain in the near future, while Austria could expect little of them.[24]

Even so, Bismarck did not encourage fraternal strife in Germany and still held the door open for a negotiated settlement, even though the chances of success were minimal. Disputes and frictions mounted between the two occupying forces in the duchies, aggravating irritations on both sides. In a note dated 22 February 1865 Bismarck made clear to Austria that he would renounce his plan to annex the duchies only if they were bound hand and foot to Prussia. Austria rejected the proposal as its conditions made it impossible to reconcile the status of Schleswig-Holstein with the ground rules of the Confederation, and instead supported the motion in favour of Augustenburg's succession introduced by Saxony and Bavaria on April 6th in the *Bundestag*. Thus, Prussia's plans for annexation were thwarted. The voting however revealed that all the northern German states, with the exception of Saxony, supported Prussia and that the Main Line was already a reality. Unwilling to negotiate with the Confederation, Bismarck threatened to cancel Prussia's membership. The Viennese government then decided to administer the *condominium* henceforth in such a way that the interim arrangement would be almost untenable for Prussia, thereby forcing it to come to a settlement. However, all that was achieved was that the honour of Wilhelm I was offended. A *definitivum* in accordance with Austrian wishes was seen as a humiliation by Berlin, and the *provisorium* was increasingly difficult to endure. On May 29th the possibility of war was discussed for the first time at the Prussian royal council.[25] The *Doppelherrschaft* was in danger. Both Prussia and Austria were willing to sacrifice conservative solidarity for the sake of their power ambitions.

At the same time, the Danube monarchy was again faced with an internal crisis due to ongoing unrest in Hungary. On June 26th, under pressure from the conservatives, the Emperor dismissed the Schmerling government and a month later dissolved the Imperial Council. Constitutionalism was buried, at least temporarily, and the empire had to function without a parliament in the difficult days ahead. On July 30th, the Emperor gave the green light for the formation of a conservative government, led by Richard Belcredi, with Mensdorff

---

24 Bridge and Bullen, *The Great Powers*, 150-160.
25 Eyck, *Bismarck*, 51-60.

continuing as foreign minister.[26] Bismarck welcomed the fall of Schmerling, as this damaged the liberal reputation of Austria in the *Mittelstaaten*. It also gave the impression that, given the concessions promised to the Hungarians, the Danube monarchy would shift its focus towards the East and would be less willing to resist Prussia on the German question. Bismarck tested Austria's resilience with a number of provocative notes in which he denounced Augustenburg's agitation in Holstein for which he held the Viennese government responsible. His last note sounded very warlike and contained a virtual ultimatum. It was in that context that Francis Joseph I and Mensdorff decided to make a last-ditch effort to keep the peace by sending Blome on a mission to Gastein at the end of July 1865.

The Convention of Gastein

Why was Blome charged with this extremely delicate mission? Normally Mensdorff himself would have gone to meet Bismarck, but the government crisis did not allow him to leave the capital. Inviting Bismarck to Vienna did not seem like a good idea, because he could then indirectly influence the formation of the new Austrian government. A third possibility was to entrust the mission to Ludwig Biegeleben, the specialist on German affairs at the state chancellery, but he was *persona non grata* in Berlin. In their quest for a skilled negotiator, with sufficient knowledge of the issues and the necessary political weight, whom they could trust, the Emperor and his minister finally came to Blome. He was very familiar with developments in Schleswig and Holstein as he came from that region himself. Thanks to his secret mission to the *Mittelstaaten* in January 1862 and his diplomatic posting in Bavaria, he had learned much about the pitfalls of the German question. Moreover, he enjoyed the confidence of Mensdorff with whom he had worked in St. Petersburg. The Emperor also valued him highly because of his work during the Italian campaign in 1859 and his successful mission in early 1862. Finally, the choice of Blome was apparently also influenced by the Hungarian Count Moritz Esterhazy, the éminence grise of the state chancellery and a Metternich sympathizer.[27]

Otherwise, Blome was not quite on the same wavelength as his government. In his view, Austria staked too much on its dominant role in Germany and had ventured too far in the Schleswig-Holstein question. He believed that Vienna should have defended the integrity of the Danish monarchy much more stubbornly. Contrary to his convictions of 1848, he thought that the duchies

26   Rumpler, *Eine Chance*, 380-383.
27   See the note on Moritz Esterhazy (1807-1890) in *Österreichisches Biographisches Lexikon*, vol. I, 1957, 269-270. On the role Esterhazy played in the choice of Blome as negotiator, see Eyck, *Bismarck*, 73-74.

would have been better off staying within the Danish sphere of influence. In May 1864 the Vienna government had changed its mind and had accepted the separation, making what had been a European issue an exclusively German question. In order to offer a counterweight in this new context to the expansionist wishes of Prussia, Austria could only rely on the *Mittelstaaten*, which were under pressure from national liberal opinion. Support for Augustenburg was the price that had to be paid, even though his claims lacked legitimacy and the dreaded 'democracy' loomed behind him. Blome's position was thus largely determined by ideological considerations but was also dictated by a form of *realpolitik*. When the issue was reduced to a purely German affair, Vienna had to accept that Prussia, as a North German great power, could legitimately exert influence in this neighbouring region. At the end of 1864 Blome was already in favour of ceding a large part of Schleswig to Prussia. He carried on a confidential as well as an official correspondence with Mensdorff once he entered office, in which he stated repeatedly that the Viennese government had to give priority to good relations with Prussia, and, if necessary, had to sacrifice the duchies and transfer them to Berlin. A good relationship between the two leading conservative German states was both strategically and ideologically desirable as the *Mittelstaaten* were powerless and unreliable allies.[28] Blome met with strong opposition from his good friend Biegeleben, who had been the chief architect of the Austrian change of direction,[29] and felt that annexation would only fuel the Prussian desire for expansion.[30] Blome was not convinced but declared himself ready to cooperate loyally with the policy worked out by Vienna. In all likelihood, the final choice for him as a negotiator was also motivated by the consideration that he, probably more than any other Austrian diplomat, could create the necessary goodwill to work out a last-minute compromise.

In mid-July, while on holiday with his family in Lindau near Lake Constance, Blome was summoned urgently to Vienna, where he was prepared for his mission through discussions with Rechberg and Biegeleben and through an audience with the Emperor. He had to try to discern whether Prussia was truly serious about its war plans. In order to avoid fraternal strife, he could possibly agree to a temporary settlement that would be acceptable to Prussia on condition that guarantees were obtained for a final settlement in line with

---

28 See Blome's diplomatic correspondence with the Vienna state chancellery: Srbik, *Quellen*, vols. III and IV.

29 Both had maintained good relations since 1852. Biegeleben to Blome, 26 Nov. 1864 in: Srbik, *Quellen*, vol. IV, 428-429: 'I know of no one whose opinion, even on an ancillary matter, I would so unwillingly deviate from as yours.' On the diplomatic stand of Biegeleben, see: Elrod, 'Realpolitik or Concert Diplomacy', 88-95.

30 Biegeleben to Blome, 5 March 1865 in: Srbik, *Quellen*, vol. IV, 584-585.

the Austrian position. Foreign diplomats in Vienna deemed his assignment to be 'difficult' and the chances of success as 'doubtful'.[31]

We have precise information about Blome's discussions in Gastein thanks to an unpublished account that he himself drew up a few months later. It contains many interesting details that have not been incorporated thus far in the historical literature. While a certain critical distance is necessary, the previously known details included in the account are in line with the published sources and the scholarly literature, so one may assume that the story is sufficiently reliable.[32]

Blome arrived in Gastein on Thursday, July 27th and next morning began discussions with Bismarck. The latter started with a long exposé of his complaints, the most grievous being the vote in the *Bundestag* on April 6th. In his view, Austria had then de facto abandoned the alliance with Prussia and from that day Berlin had to prepare for a rupture. Moreover, Bismarck could not accept that the liberal party, which he opposed with all his might at home, would prevail in neighbouring Holstein. Augustenburg had also challenged the two monarchs by acting as a legitimate sovereign. Finally, Austria had taken too little action against the revolutionary actions in the duchies. Wilhelm I and his army felt offended by the pretender and the constant pressure of his party, a situation that could not continue. If the Austrian government together with the Prussian king refused to suppress this disorder, then he would do it alone. This was an argument by a conservative statesman with which Blome personally could concur. Remarkably, the honour of Wilhelm I played an important role in this matter – the princes were still a significant factor in the politics of the eastern powers. Just as the wounded honour of Francis Joseph I had been a factor in the outbreak of the Italian war, so the honour of Wilhelm I repeatedly determined the orientation of Prussian politics in the German question.

Contrary to his own personal conviction, Blome had to publicly defend Augustenburg's candidacy. He laid special emphasis on the fact that it was supported by the local population, a consideration that in fact carried little weight for him personally. He accused Prussia of exaggerating the incidents of the previous months and of using them to push through an annexation, something Austria could not tolerate. Bismarck replied: we are willing to accept a final settlement that does not include annexation, if Austria drops Augustenburg and we get the reparations we are demanding. The two negotiat-

31   Bray, Bavaria's envoy in Vienna, to Pfordten, 27 July 65 in: Srbik, *Quellen*, vol. IV, 802-803.
32   Blome, *Historique des négociations qui aboutirent à la Convention de Gastein. Ma campagne diplomatique de l'été 1865*, LASH, section 126.15, nr. 622. See also *Souvenirs*, vol. II, 57-80. Published sources: Srbik, *Quellen*, 5 vols.; Bismarck, *Gedanken und Erinnerungen*, vol. II, 1-31; Vitzthum, *London, Gastein und Sadowa*, 85-95. Literature: Stadelmann, *Das Jahr 1865*; Zweybruck, ed., *Bismarck und Österreich*, 45-55; Eyck, *Bismarck*,73-90; Lerman, *Bismarck*, 91-113; Nipperdey, *Deutsche Geschichte (1800-1866)*, 768-780; Kitchen, *A History of Modern Germany*, 108-112; Rumpler, *Eine Chance*, 392-396.

ing partners then explored all the possible formulas for a final settlement, but to no avail. Above all, the options that included a role for Augustenburg were rejected: Wilhelm I was too offended by his attitude, as he made clear in a lengthy private conversation with Blome, in which he emphasized the importance to him of Prussia, the smallest of the great powers, upholding and respecting his rank. Blome was in complete agreement and succeeded in pacifying the king so that the ice was broken and a slightly friendlier climate prevailed during the talks. Wilhelm I appeared open to the argument that the two conservative great powers had every interest in working together, a view that General Edwin von Manteuffel especially voiced in his immediate circle. Although the general's reactionary position was too extreme even for Blome, he nevertheless thought of him as a suitable ally with whom some agreement was still possible.

To what extent did Bismarck allow himself to be guided by ideological considerations in his foreign policy, and how much importance did he attach to the defense of conservative values and the existing social and political order? The historical literature on this subject is extensive. Bismarck's conservative disposition cannot be doubted. Even in the 1850s he was known as a reactionary, and his aim throughout his whole life was to maintain the social and political dominance of the nobility and military monarchy. In addition, his foreign policy was primarily directed at consolidating and increasing the power of the Prussian monarchy. It was for him a matter of course that Prussia should acquire hegemony at least over northern Germany, something that Austria, which pursued a more active German policy after 1859, wanted to prevent. Ideological considerations did not prevent Bismarck from doing his utmost to realize his concrete political goals. His conservatism concerned only Prussia, whereas Metternich's was universal, intended to benefit not just one throne, but the entire legal system that had been handed down at both national and international levels. Bismarck was prepared, if necessary – should an agreement with Austria not be feasible – to collaborate with the liberal nationalists, not in establishing a liberal unitary state but in extending Prussian influence in (northern) Germany.

For the Prussian chancellor politics was primarily a matter of defending interests, not ideas. In fact, he espoused a *realpolitik* that was critical of ideals, theories, doctrines and principles. On taking office as minister-president, he had stated in parliament: 'Not by speeches and majority decisions will the great decisions of this time be taken – that was the big miscalculation of 1848 and 1849 – but by blood and iron', a statement that would subsequently take on a life of its own. Politics was concerned with states, their power and their interests. Bismarck observed all the social and political forces and checked to see how they could be used to extend Prussian power. In his view, principles

such as legitimacy and international conservative solidarity should not determine the international policies of his country.

His counterpart held a completely different view. Blome belonged to the
school of Metternich and had the same vision of international law. He strongly
believed in absolute moral principles, even in the political arena, where law,
justice and respect for international treaties should be primary. 'It is always
ideas that triumph.'[33] 'Only moral force leads to sustainable power.'[34] That
same adherence to principles was clearly evident both in his personal life and
in his political conduct. Because of the rigidity of his ideas, which were at
odds with the *zeitgeist*, he would get the reputation of being an 'interesting
eccentric'.[35] The Saxon envoy in Paris, Albin von Seebach, would even call him
'the will-o'-the-wisp of Austrian diplomacy', but he had his reasons for that as
Blome challenged the policies of the Saxony *Mittelstaat* and despised Beust,
its minister-president.[36] If the young Austrian diplomat already had a singular
reputation at that time, then it certainly was no worse than that of Bismarck,
who was seen by his colleagues in the Prussian cabinet as an arrogant, ambitious, jealous and petty man. In wider circles, the Prussian chancellor was
seen as a maverick, a solitary figure who did not hesitate to lie and never could
be trusted completely, an opportunist of the first degree. Blome formed the
same impression during his discussions: 'He is not a statesman but a reckless
gambler with a lucky hand.'[37] 'For this minister every means is acceptable if it
achieves its ends; he would, if necessary, make common cause with revolution
in order to thwart revolutionaries.'[38] He is 'an energetic, ruthless man, who
can still cause a lot of harm'.[39]

In late July Bismarck and Blome were still having exploratory talks which
the latter found particularly difficult because while he personally stressed
conservative solidarity between the great powers, in public he had to advocate the transfer of power in the duchies to Augustenburg, the candidate of
the German liberals. During the discussions Blome learned through a coded
telegram that in the previous weeks Bismarck had entered into negotiations

33 Blome to Pons, 19 Oct. 1860.
34 Blome to Pons, 12 Sept. 1860.
35 Höbelt, 'Bismarcks widerwilliger Widerpart', 175: 'an interesting but eccentric figure,
    known for his extreme formulations'.
36 Blome to Mensdorff, 29 Jan. 1865 in: Srbik, *Quellen*, vol. IV, 541-543. In this letter Blome
    calls Beust an incompetent, unreliable conspirator and a serious threat to his country. In
    a letter to Biegeleben on 1 Jan. 1865 (Srbik, *Quellen*, vol. IV, 494), Blome criticized Beust's
    liberal sympathies. On the sharp confrontation between Blome and Beust in 1867-1868, see
    infra, 120.
37 *Souvenirs*, vol. II, 67.
38 *Historique des négociations*, p. 4, LASH, abt. 126.15, nr. 622.
39 Mensdorff to Esterhazy, 20 Aug. 1865 in: Srbik, *Quellen*, vol. V/1, 18. Mensdorff agreed with
    Blome's judgement of Bismarck: 'He is not a statesman in the true sense of the word, nor a
    smart fellow, but an energetic, ruthless man, who can still cause a lot of harm.'

with the Italian government with a view to opening up a second front against Austria in the event of war. When he challenged Bismarck on this, suggesting it was very strange that he and Garibaldi were prepared to march together against Austria, Bismarck readily concurred and replied: 'You march with the German revolutionaries; why then should we not be allowed to march with the European revolutionaries?'[40]

The talks followed each other in quick succession, but no progress was made. The existing *provisorium* had become untenable, while a *definitivum* in conformity with Austrian desires did not stand a chance. For that reason Blome occasionally proposed the idea of proceeding to a definitive division of the duchies between the two great powers that could assert their right of conquest in these areas. He had already conceived this plan while preparing for the negotiations before his departure from Vienna. It went against the wishes of the *Mittelstaaten* and also violated the principle of the indivisibility of the principalities, over which war had been waged. For Blome, however, it was a matter of finding a basis for a possible understanding between the two great powers. He had little trouble with Prussia expanding its power, provided there were compensations. Austria could eventually still transfer to Augustenburg the territory that it would acquire through redistribution and thereby withdraw honourably from the hornets' nest of northern Germany. Bismarck, however, repeatedly dismissed the suggestion.

The talks dragged on. Bismarck made some concessions on some unimportant matters, but when he refused to confirm those agreements in writing, Blome decided on July 31st to suspend the negotiations and leave empty-handed for Vienna. After dinner on Sunday, he informed General Manteuffel that war was inevitable if no other way out could be found, and that he would make a farewell visit to Bismarck that very evening. As he hoped, Manteuffel discussed the burning question with the chancellor the same afternoon. On Sunday evening Blome took his leave of Bismarck, but just at the moment of departure, Bismarck held him back, saying, 'Well, let us share! Are you authorized to negotiate on this basis?' Blome replied that his plan was a personal one and had never been discussed in Vienna, but that, provided the conditions were acceptable, he would defend this solution to his government. Bismarck then asked him to postpone his departure in order to continue discussing the proposal the next day, after he had consulted with the king. The king was willing to agree with the plan, under certain conditions. The concrete terms of a possible agreement were then discussed further. Bismarck had a preference for Holstein, but Blome was able to convince him that annexing Schleswig to Prussia would offer greater military benefits and would lead to fewer problems with the German Confederation. The chancellor also claimed the smaller duchy of Lauenburg, which had also been taken from Denmark. Moreover, he

---

40 *Historique des négociations*, p. 10, LASH, section 126.15, nr. 622.

wanted to take over Kiel in Holstein as a naval base. The king, for his part, was charmed by the prospect that Prussia would acquire sovereignty over a territory where his troops had achieved military success and informed Blome that he approved further negotiations on this basis.[41] So on Tuesday, August 1st, the Austrian envoy left for Ischl to report back to the Emperor.

Francis Joseph I was sympathetic to the proposal and felt it deserved serious consideration, though he was taken aback and expressed surprise several times that Bismarck would agree to a possible division. The next day Mensdorff arrived, but he kept a low profile and suggested the matter be referred to the full Belcredi government, which had just taken office. Blome was given the opportunity to defend his proposal to the cabinet. The new ministers were pleased that there was still a chance of an agreement and, overall, were in favour of the proposal but Mensdorff remained reticent.[42] Blome urged his superior not to present the question to the department heads in the state chancellery and especially not to Biegeleben, who was the architect of the policy in favour of the Confederation and would probably go on the defensive.

The final decision was taken at a special cabinet meeting on Saturday, August 5th, which was presided over by the Emperor himself. Mensdorff especially remained doubtful and recommended breaking off negotiations, a move that in his view would not necessarily lead to warfare. However, the Emperor was of the opinion that a rupture without war would result in the worst possible outcome. Austria would have to arm itself considerably without reaping any real benefits. The minister of finance could only confirm that the state finances were in a lamentable state. On their side, the Hungarian ministers, supported by Esterhazy, declared that maintaining peace was necessary for the pending negotiations with the Hungarian politicians. Mensdorff was outvoted and Blome was commissioned to travel back to Gastein, to continue negotiations on the basis of the approved text.

According to Blome's own report, the council of ministers expressed support for a definitive redistribution of the duchies. However, contrary to what had been agreed, Mensdorff presented Biegeleben with the draft text, which had been drawn up after the meeting of the council of ministers. Beigeleben was very disappointed because his position had not been endorsed, and he therefore made a substantial change in the text, adding the word 'temporary' to the article on the distribution of the duchies. As a result, the ultimate fate of Schleswig and Holstein remained uncertain. Furthermore, the scope of the agreement had been completely changed, and so, instead of bringing about peace, it could only broker a political truce. In those circumstances the smallest pretext could be used in the future by both sides to provoke a war. The proposed amendment was apparently motivated by the desire not to completely

41 *Historique des négociations*, p. 27, LASH, section 126.15, nr. 622.
42 On Mensdorff's attitude, see: Höbelt, 'Bismarcks widerwilliger Widerpart', 167-180.

Otto von Bismarck. Engraving of the painting by A. Chappel, c. 1870.
[*E. Duyckinck,* A Portrait Gallery of Eminent Men and Women, New York, *1873*]

dissipate the credit of the Danube monarchy with the *Mittelstaaten*: the indivisibility of the duchies was not definitively abandoned and a solution according to the wishes of the majority in the Confederation still remained possible. Blome protested strenuously against the amendment and threatened to
give up his mission, but Mensdorff and even Esterhazy rallied behind the new
version. Blome reluctantly allowed himself to be persuaded and once again
presented his objections in his farewell audience with the Emperor, who in
the meantime had been briefed by Esterhazy. Francis Joseph I advised him to

propose the provisional settlement to Bismarck but not to insist on it if he had any objection.[43]

On the evening of Wednesday, August 9th, Blome arrived back in Gastein. To his great surprise, Bismarck immediately accepted the provisional distribution of the power of governance over the duchies. The eagerness with which he did so confirmed the Austrian ambassador in his belief that his government had made a fundamental error.[44] The discussions about Lauenburg and especially about the naval base in Kiel in Holstein were much more difficult. Eventually Blome succeeded in ensuring that Austria would be financially compensated for giving up its claims to Lauenburg. He was also inclined to allow the Prussian troops a comprehensive logistical infrastructure in the Kiel area, but on that point was rebuked by his government and especially by Francis Joseph I. Finally, the two parties agreed that only Prussian naval forces and not ground troops would be stationed around Kiel. This concession weighed heavily on the Prussian king, although he seemed to be pleased about the acquisition of Lauenburg.

On Sunday, August 13th the agreement was ready and on Monday afternoon it was signed by Bismarck and Blome. Meanwhile, it was agreed that the two sovereigns would meet in Salzburg on Saturday, August 19th to formally ratify the convention and to confirm their lasting friendship. Mensdorff reported to Esterhazy that the princes were delighted war had been avoided, although in his view nobody was happy about the compromise that had been reached. In particular, the senior army officers, on both the Prussian and Austrian sides, scoffed at the agreement,[45] presumably because they were being temporarily denied the pleasure of displaying their military prowess. The minister himself was convinced that a definitive solution had not been brought any closer by the new *provisorium*; in this he was correct, but it was largely his own doing. However, he expressed his satisfaction to foreign diplomats and praised Blome's negotiating skills.[46]

---

43 Afterwards, the Emperor would repeatedly declare to Blome that he preferred the first project, but had not insisted on it because he had had too much confidence in Esterhazy's judgement (*Historique des négociations*, p. 68, LASH, section 126.15, nr. 622).

44 Blome to Mensdorff, 14 Aug. 1865 in: Srbik, *Quellen*, vol. V/1, 5-12.

45 Mensdorff to Esterhazy, Salzburg 20 Aug. 1865 in: Srbik, *Quellen*, vol. V/1, 18.

46 Fugger to Ludwig II of Bavaria, 24 Aug.1865 in: Srbik, *Quellen*, vol. V/1, 26: 'Mensdorff seemed very satisfied with the outcome of the negotiations in Gastein. To one of the German delegates he expressed the opinion that its success was due completely to the adroit actions and negotiating skills of Blome, who had to endure a hard struggle in the negotiations with Bismarck. In diplomatic circles, the agreement is considered to be highly beneficial for Austria, while the local press assigns all the advantages to Prussia.' According to Blome, the state chancellery was very satisfied with the outcome. Biegeleben had received his *provisorium* and Mensdorff was glad that this turbulent period was over (*Souvenirs*, vol. II, 67-68).

In a detailed report to Mensdorff, which was also given to the Emperor, Blome noted that they had gained some time and that it was perhaps still possible to consolidate the precarious relationship with Prussia. In his view, Bismarck was prepared to cooperate with Austria in defending a common conservative policy, but nevertheless gave priority to conservative interests in his own country. If he came to see that he had to pursue the expansion of Prussian power in order to neutralize liberal opposition to his policies, he would not fail to do so. According to Blome, Austria had to support Bismarck in his conservative politics and avoid further friction with regard to the duchies. Maintaining friendly relations with Prussia was compatible with Austrian interests, and at the very least would win them time. A war could not be ruled out and had to be properly considered, but it would not erupt before spring 1866 and would require careful preparations. In the meantime, the *Mittelstaaten* could be assured that, given the preliminary nature of the solution, not a single principle had been abandoned, no rights had been violated and that the agreement concluded had kept the peace in Germany and even in Europe.

Still, the convention was very badly received in the *Middelstaaten* where people were convinced that Austria had suffered a great political and moral defeat. The Prussian propaganda machine did everything to reinforce that impression. In southern Germany it was felt that Prussia had taken a major step towards the annexation of Schleswig and probably of Holstein also. Prussia would never relinquish the advantages it had acquired. Augustenburg himself was aware that his chances of succession had markedly dwindled. The liberals especially were outraged. Nonetheless, Blome himself was not perturbed. In his view Austria should not sacrifice too much to the *Mittelstaaten*, as again and again it had been shown that they were of little use to the Danube monarchy. Moreover, if it came to resisting the expansionism of Prussia, they would ultimately side with Austria.

The agreement Blome had negotiated with Bismarck would be overwhelmingly judged by historians as a fruitless and even clumsy attempt to prevent a fraternal conflict between the two German powers. The general view is that in Gastein Bismarck had bought the time he needed to make the necessary diplomatic and military preparations for the inevitable conflict.[47] Blome's defense against this view was that while the temporary nature of the arrangement indeed caused tensions to continue smouldering, Austria also had been given a chance to better prepare for the conflagration.[48]

47 Bismarck to Goltz, 16 Aug. 1865, cited in Otto von Bismarck, *Werke in Auswahl*, ed. G.A. Rein, vol. III/1, Berlin, 1965, letter 432.

48 Blome to Revertera, 11 Dec. 1898, HAH, IV, 56, 32. In this letter Blome comments on the *Gedanken und Erinnerungen* of Bismarck. He notes with satisfaction that the former German chancellor endorses what he himself had proposed in 1865-66 but had not been able to push through, namely that in order to isolate Prussia, Austria in 1865 should have accepted the definitive and not just the administrative division of the duchies.

'The world is collapsing'

Thus, the Gastein Convention had resolved little. From now on Prussia and Austria got less in each other's way in the duchies, but no final choice was made between the formation of a new *Mittelstaat* under Augustenburg and annexation to Prussia. At the end of 1865 frictions and mutual irritation surfaced again.[49] In particular, demonstrations in Holstein in favour of Augustenburg drove the two great powers apart. Clearly, Prussia could not count on public opinion in the duchies to push through its plans for annexation; it had to hope for an agreement with Austria, but the Viennese government was anything but forthcoming since it was supported by most of the *Mittelstaaten*. Bismarck came to the conclusion that only a rupture and presumably war with Austria could offer a solution. The conflict, however, had to be given a wider dimension and be focused on the division of power between the two great powers within the Confederation. At the end of February 1866 both Vienna and Berlin started preparing for war. Prussia renewed contact with Italy, with a view to concluding an offensive alliance treaty that would force Austria into a war on two fronts, while the Danube monarchy looked for military support from the *Mittelstaaten*, especially Bavaria and Saxony.

Austria's position in Germany was fairly strong because it could count on the governments of the major *Mittelstaaten*, which feared Prussian expansionism, and because of its clear support for Augustenburg; it could even count on some sympathy from the liberals, who despised the reactionary Bismarck. However, on the European level the standing of the Danube monarchy was extremely weak, a significant factor as the German question was also a European matter in which all the major powers felt involved. Ever since the Crimean War, Austria no longer had any friends in Europe; as noted earlier, it could no longer count on Russia and Great Britain. A crucial question was what attitude Napoleon III would take. His influence on both the domestic and foreign fronts had weakened considerably, but precisely because of that he coveted diplomatic and possibly military success. He tried to play the two powers off against each other, allowing both to hope for his help in exchange for compensation. In any case, he was counting on a long war, in which he would serve as arbitrator.[50]

For the moment, the situation had not gone that far. In April 1866, in order to put his war aims on a higher alert, Bismarck seized on an initiative by the *Mittelstaaten* to discuss reforming the Confederation once again. In an attempt to win over public opinion for his own position, he proposed to allow the federal parliament be directly elected by universal male suffrage. That

49 On the run-up to the Austro-Prussian war, see: Stadelmann, *Das Jahr 1865*, 65-78; Blackbourn, *History of Germany*, 143-259; Nipperdey, *Deutsche Geschichte*, 775-781; Rumpler, *Eine Chance*, 392-396; Lerman, *Bismarck*, 105-113; Winkler, *Der lange Weg*, vol. I, 173-200.
50 Bridge and Bullen, *The Great Powers*, 150-155; Milza, *Napoléon III*, 539-543.

Austria would not agree was to be expected, but even liberal opinion in the *Mittelstaaten* dismissed the proposal as a sham. Meanwhile, enthusiasm for war grew on both sides. On April 21st Austria began to call up its reserve troops and ten days later Prussia started to mobilize its army.

As the Austrian ambassador in Munich, Blome followed these developments closely. He had to ensure that Bavaria would provide maximum support for the policies of the Viennese government and would contribute its share to the war effort. Bavaria, however, proved to be a difficult partner. It dreamed of forming a third force in Germany together with the surrounding principalities, and accordingly aimed at reforming the Confederation. When war was all but inevitable, the government in Munich tarried in mobilizing its troops and refused to place them under Austrian command. Finally, in late June Vienna concluded a military agreement with Bavaria, but Blome was not involved; he was completely opposed because such an agreement, were it successful, would tie down the Viennese government and would yield little benefit.[51]

More important was the role Blome played as Mensdorff's counsellor in the crucial months before the outbreak of the war. His position deserves analysis as he was considered to be an important expert on the German question and his advice was regularly sought by the minister. During the negotiations in Gastein, Blome had still aimed at achieving a rapport with Prussia, but now he apparently came to the conclusion that the chances of that were unlikely, at least as long as Bismarck remained in power. Still, Vienna could not set its hopes on the fall of the chancellor, as this would inevitably lead to a liberal takeover in Prussia and a unitary Lesser Germany with a parliamentary regime. No single government in the *Mittelstaaten* was strong enough to reject such a programme.[52] The choice was then either war or revolution. With Bismarck in power, war was unavoidable; should he fall, then revolution would put an end to Austrian influence in Germany. Only war would give the Danube monarchy a chance to survive as a leading power (*Präsidialmacht*) in Germany, consolidate the conservative order in Europe and preserve Rome for the Pope, something that Blome considered of great importance. All in all, he thought Bismarck was still Austria's least dangerous opponent: 'Whoever succeeds him will have all of Germany behind him, and we cannot withstand that in peacetime, nor probably even by means of war.'[53] This comment indicates that Blome's stance was strongly determined by ideological factors, but that his expectations now were different from those he had in Gastein, as he no longer believed in Bismarck's peaceful intentions.

In late April Blome spent about ten days in Vienna, and together with Biegeleben pushed for speedy action, but Austria had to be careful not to de-

---

51 See Blome's diplomatic correspondence in Srbik, *Quellen*, vol. V/1 and V/2.
52 Blome to Biegeleben, 7 April 1866 in: Srbik, *Quellen*, V/1, 438-439. See also: Elrod, 'Realpolitik or Concert Diplomacy', 94-95.
53 Blome to Biegeleben, 15 April 1866 in: Srbik, *Quellen*, vol. V/1, 494-495.

clare war itself. Mensdorff held off for the moment. 'A war at any price cannot be our policy.'[54] A major problem was that Vienna could not delay the decision too long because of the deplorable condition of the state treasury. The country could not afford an endless period of mobilization. When in early May Mensdorff asked for his advice, Blome recommended provoking Prussia by convening the diet in Holstein and proclaiming Augustenburg as sovereign. An alternative was to allow the Confederation decide the future of the duchies.[55] 'When we need a war but cannot declare it, we have to force the opponent to do it.' Clearly, at this juncture Blome was truly bellicose, believing that 'a revolution causes even more blood to flow, undermines the prosperity and, above all, the moral strength of a nation, while a war reinforces both'.[56] That war itself could provoke a revolution was, he said, a delusion.[57] This view would be gainsayed by the Paris Commune uprising of 1871 and the revolutions at the end of the First World War.

In late May the Prussian statesman Anton von Gablenz made a final attempt to save the peace by suggesting that Germany be divided into two spheres of influence, with the Main as the boundary, and that the succession in Schleswig-Holstein would go to a prince from the Prussian Hohenzollern dynasty. Bismarck wanted to give the proposal a chance, but in Vienna, the war party now finally had the wind in its sails and the lamentable condition of the state finances did not allow any further delay. There was even talk of convening a European peace conference, but that initiative was subtly torpedoed by Esterhazy. Blome also did not want to hear about it: 'War, we need war, only war.'[58]

On June 1st, the Viennese government followed Blome's suggestion and put the decision on the future of the duchies into the hands of the Confederation. It also announced that the diet of Holstein would be convened with the aim of electing Augustenburg as ruler. This unilateral measure, which contravened the *provisorium*, was quite rightly seen by Prussia as a provocation and Bismarck declared that the Convention of Gastein had been violated. On June 9th, Prussian troops entered Holstein and prevented the diet from meeting. On June 14th, a majority in the *Bundestag* decided to mobilize the confederal army against Prussia, which retaliated by declaring the Confederation to be dissolved. There was no turning back. The main *Mittelstaaten* were on the side of Austria, which a few days earlier had signed a secret treaty with France whereby Napoleon III promised to remain neutral on condition that Austria

54 Mensdorff to Esterhazy, 22 and 23 April 1866 in: Srbik, *Quellen*, vol. V/1, 529-530: 'Blome and Biegeleben are pushing for war.' See also: Elrod, 'Realpolitik or Concert Diplomacy', 94-95.
55 Blome to Mensdorff, 5 and 16 May 1866 in: Srbik, *Quellen*, vol. V/2, 596 and 684-685.
56 Blome to Mensdorff, 20 May 1866 in: Srbik, *Quellen*, vol. V/2, 723-724.
57 Blome to Mensdorff, 16 June 1866 in: Srbik, *Quellen*, vol. V/2, 896-897.
58 Blome to Mensdorff, 29 May 1866 in: Srbik, *Quellen*, vol. V/2, 802-803.

ceded Venice and its surroundings to Italy.[59] Italy had itself concluded an alliance with Prussia on April 8th and was therefore the only country that was guaranteed some spoils of war.

Most observers reckoned on a protracted war that would probably not be limited to the two great German powers.[60] The general expectation was that Austria, supported by most of the *Mittelstaaten*, would win. Even Berlin's stock exchange was confident of such a victory. Indeed, on the southern front the Austrians quickly got rid of the Italians[61] but the northern front was much more important. The Prussian army defeated the troops of Saxony, Hanover and Hessen without much trouble. After that, the main force, divided into three army corps, left for Bohemia, and not Moravia as the Austrians had expected. The Prussian army made clever use of the railway and telegraph services and advanced much more quickly than anticipated. The three army corps each followed a separate route, with the intention of coming together at the last moment to fight the main Austrian force. They were sighted on July 2nd in the area around Sadowa/Königgrätz where one of the most important battles of the nineteenth century took place, involving nearly 450,000 soldiers. Initially, the Austrian army, which had an excellent cavalry and artillery, successfully countered the assault by the Prussian troops, but when it left its defensive positions, it was attacked on the flank by a Prussian army corps that had been delayed in reaching the battlefield. In the late afternoon, the Austrians were forced to retreat.

The Battle of Königgrätz/Sadowa dealt a severe blow to the Habsburg monarchy and aroused great consternation throughout Europe. On hearing the news, the papal secretary of state Antonelli exclaimed, '*casca il mondo*' ('the world is collapsing'). Contemporaries realized immediately that this was an important turning point in European history, but still this battle did not immediately herald the end of the Austro-Prussian war. The Danube monarchy still had a large army, which withdrew in an orderly fashion in the direction of Vienna, while the southern army also marched towards the city. A cholera epidemic was raging in the ranks of the Prussian army. There was also the possibility of an intervention by Napoleon III, which the Austrian diplomatic mission did everything to promote, but to no avail. Napoleon III was totally surprised by the unexpected turn in the war; moreover, he was seriously ill and he let the opportunity pass to prevent the formation of a German empire under Prussian leadership. His decision was also influenced by his desire to remain true to the principle of nationality, which had also determined his Ital-

---

59   Blome was strongly opposed to that treaty. See *Souvenirs*, vol. II, 101.
60   On the Austro-Prussian War, see: Craig, *The Battle of Königgrätz*; Lerman, *Bismarck*, 115-123; Nipperdey, *Deutsche Geschichte*, 781-788; Rumpler, *Eine Chance*, 399-400.
61   The Italian territorial army was defeated near Custoza in the region of Verona on June 24th; the Italian fleet was defeated two weeks later near the island of Lissa in the Adriatic Sea.

ian policy. He offered to mediate in the conflict, an offer Bismarck eagerly accepted, knowing that Prussia had no interest in destroying Austria completely.

Blome was one of the many who were shocked by the defeat at Sadowa.[62] His world also collapsed: 'I was overcome with grief. I had been convinced that God would support our just cause, that Austria was called to restore the Christian order in Europe.' That prospect now went up in smoke. To his good friend Pons, he wrote: 'I am a nervous wreck, I can hardly even write letters anymore. I cannot speak about unimportant things and even less can I talk about what afflicts me. You know that nothing is closer to my heart than the cause that Austria is defending.'[63] Yet he did not lose heart. He called for 'a war to the death', saying, 'it is better to perish with weapons in hand than to retreat in a cowardly manner, after having given up one's rights'.[64] But he foresaw that the 'cowards', Mensdorff and Esterhazy, would back down. When recalled by his minister to Vienna for consultation in mid-July, Blome urged further resistance. 'But no, perseverance, that eminent virtue of our ancestors, I could not find it any longer in the Vienna of those days.'[65] The Emperor and his government decided to start negotiations with Bismarck. Mensdorff wanted Blome to be the Austrian negotiator, but he was reluctant on the grounds that he would be a useless peace negotiator, since he ardently supported the continuation of the war. The ambassador in Berlin, Count Karolyi, was then charged with the delicate task.

Meanwhile, Napoleon III and Bismarck had already worked out the broad outlines of a possible agreement: Austria would be removed from Germany; Prussia could incorporate most of the territories above the Main and would, with the remaining northern states, form a North German Confederation; the southern German principalities would remain independent.[66] These provisions were further elaborated in the preliminary Peace of Nikolsburg (26 July) and were subsequently endorsed by the Peace of Prague (23 August). Bismarck's lenient treatment of Austria is striking, and he did not demand much more than what he had previously pursued through diplomatic channels. King

---

62 *Souvenirs*, vol. II, p. 105. What was particularly painful for Blome was that his father sympathized with the Prussian cause. See Blome to Pons, 2 April 1866: 'I am warning you that Blome Senior is in the opposing camp. He supports Prussia, and wishes that Holstein would be annexed by Bismarck.' The estrangement between father and son subsequently worsened.

63 Blome to Pons, 7 July 1866.

64 Blome to Séphine Buol, 4 July 1866, cited in *Souvenirs*, vol. II, 104.

65 *Souvenirs*, vol. II, 108.

66 Prussia annexed several principalities such as Hanover and Nassau in northern Germany. Saxony and a few other smaller principalities above the Main continued to exist, but united with Prussia to form the North German Confederation. The southern German states maintained a semi-autonomous status, but they were quickly put under pressure to cooperate closely on military and economic matters with the North German Confederation. However, a South German Confederation was not formed, because its neighbouring states feared Bavaria's eventual domination.

Wilhelm I and the army staff wanted to annex several border areas of Austria and impose high war reparations on the country, but Bismarck realized that the Danube monarchy was still in a position to resist harsh peace terms. He also counted on it – 'a good chess piece on the European chessboard'[67] – as a future ally. In any case, he did not want to create a feeling of revanchism that would drive Austria into the arms of France. The Danube monarchy thus lost its influence in Germany, just as it previously had lost influence in Italy. The latter process was also completed by Vienna remaining loyal to the previous agreement with Napoleon III and – despite the victories gained against the Italians – ceding Venice and environs to Italy.

The Austro-Prussian war, which would later also be called the 'Seven Weeks' War', was without doubt the most important event of the nineteenth century in Central Europe. Austria was no longer part of the German Empire and so eight hundred years of history came to an end. The dream of the Holy Roman Empire was finally over. Moreover, the weakening and later collapse of the Danube monarchy put the balance of power and stability in Central and Eastern Europe at risk. This would have dramatic consequences in the next century for the whole of Europe: it played a role in the run-up to the First World War, the expansionist policy of the Nazi regime before and during World War II and the occupation of Eastern Europe by the Soviet Union after 1945.

Leviathan redivivus

The victory over Austria significantly increased Prussia's power. The kingdom now formed a contiguous area from East Prussia to the Rhine. It completely dominated the newly established North German Confederation, which was conceived as a union of states, an alliance of ruling sovereigns, albeit 'an alliance of the dog with the fleas'.[68] Sovereignty lay with the *Bundesrat*, an executive body composed of representatives of the governments. There was also a *Reichstag*, elected by universal male suffrage but with only limited legislative powers. As chairman of the confederation, the Prussian king was given the authority to determine foreign policy, declare war and make peace. He exercised exclusive supervision of the army, which was not subject to the control of the *Reichstag*. The prestige of the armed forces had grown tremendously thanks to the resounding victory over Austria and would continue to increase in the coming years. In the new state structure, the relationship between civil and military authority was clearly not balanced.

The success of Bismarck's foreign policy ensured that the constitutional conflict in Prussia itself, which had dragged on for years, now came to an

67   Rumpler, *Eine Chance*, 401.
68   Lerman, *Bismarck*, 130.

end.[69] Government and parliament were reconciled, forgave one another and ironed out their differences. Bismarck had succeeded in winning over a majority of the liberals to his policy which brought German unification significantly closer. The National Liberals were now ready to support the state government and the military monarchy. The victory at Sadowa laid the foundation for the formation of a German national state, but at the same time it slowed down the liberalization process in Prussia and soon after in the rest of Germany also. Only the most convinced liberals continued to believe that constitutional liberties were more important than a national unity forged by 'blood and iron'. The *Altkonservativen* or ultra-conservatives, to whom Bismarck himself had once belonged, objected for other reasons to the state of affairs. They opposed the removal of the legitimate rulers in the annexed areas, the establishment of a *Reichstag* elected by universal suffrage, and the excessive nationalism. In order to extend Prussia's power, Bismarck had turned to the people, a move that was revolutionary in itself. However, when revolution was at hand, he thought it was better to start it oneself than to undergo it, and for that reason he was sometimes called a 'white revolutionary'. Due in part to his policies, nationalism evolved from being an ideology of opposition to one of integration.

The principle of nationality now became the leading point of reference. The war with Austria had become a clash between 'the right of a nation to a national state' and 'the right of the community of states to an institutionalized consensus', which Austria had advocated for decades. The concept of the nation had prevailed and the nation state would henceforth be the principal actor in international politics. The conviction grew that the interests of the national states had primacy over international law, and that the states could now better rely for their security on their own military power than on treaty rights. That entailed huge risks for international security, as would soon become evident.[70]

The forceful expansion of Prussian power was perceived as a threat by France, which had been taken by surprise by the course of events. Napoleon III initially resigned himself to the new situation and welcomed the principle of nationality. However, the left-wing opposition, led by Adolphe Thiers, accused him of fostering, with his ill-considered foreign policy, the formation of two redoubtable neighbouring states, Italy and now the North German Confederation, with the result that France was in danger of being pushed aside altogether in European politics. French national pride was wounded and Sadowa was widely perceived as a humiliation. Napoleon III therefore went in search of compensation for the loss of face, but met with no sympathy from the other powers. Attempts at rapprochement with Austria were also unsuc-

69 Lerman, *Bismarck*, 123-127; Nipperdey, *Deutsche Geschichte*, 790-803.
70 Bridge and Bullen, *The Great Powers*, 126-128.

cessful: the Danube monarchy was licking its wounds and lying low. Eventually, the French government would be tempted to go to war against Prussia.[71]

Most historians believe that Bismarck did not want this war, at least not in the short term, but that he considered it and did little to avoid it. In any case he did not deliberately seek war in order to complete the unification of Germany, which he expected would take place gradually, for example with the renewal of the *Zollverein* in 1877. The southern states were all linked with northern Germany through military and trade agreements, but public opinion in those areas was for the time being strongly hostile to Prussia, which was associated with higher taxes, militarism and a repressive authoritarianism. That was expressed in popular circles as *Steuerzahlen, Soldatwerden, Maulhalten* ('paying taxes, enlisting, shutting up').[72] Bismarck himself had little sympathy with the southern Germans: their Catholicism, their particularistic traditions and dynastic pride could cause major problems. In any case, time would tell. An eventual war with France could accelerate the process and would create a national momentum that could change the whole equation.

And so it transpired, with France providing the catalyst.[73] A dispute about the succession to the Spanish throne was the occasion for the outbreak of hostilities. Bismarck seized the occasion to get France into trouble but it was the French who made it a matter of war. On 19 July 1870 Napoleon III declared war on Prussia. Contrary to what was generally feared, it did not become a European-wide conflict. Austria remained neutral, as did Britain, which distrusted Napoleon III because of his plans to annex strategically important Belgium. The southern German states felt more threatened by France than by Prussia; as expected, they were swept along by a national fervour and almost immediately sided with Berlin. Within a very short time, Prussia and its allies managed to concentrate a large army on the border and go on the offensive. The French army was well equipped, but its organization revealed major flaws: it was spread out and its main force was trapped in the fortress of Metz. Napoleon III put himself at the head of an auxiliary army to relieve the fortress, but on 2 September 1870, he was defeated at Sedan and surrendered with his army. This immediately led to the end of the Second Empire in France.

A provisional government declared the Third Republic and, contrary to Bismarck's hopes, decided to continue the war. The French troops were driven further into a corner. In late October the fortress of Metz surrendered and the Prussian troops then pushed on without much difficulty to Paris, which they surrounded and besieged. Meanwhile, radical Republicans had called

---

71   Milza, *Napoléon III*, 539-544 and 574-593; Yon, *Le Second Empire*, 96-101.
72   Nipperdey, *Deutsche Geschichte*, 794.
73   On the Franco-Prussian War, see: Howard, *The Franco-Prussian War*; Wetzel, *A Duel of Giants*; Rak, *Krieg, Nation und Konfession*; Lerman, *Bismarck*, 144-160; Nipperdey, *Deutsche Geschichte, 1866-1918*, vol. II, 55-84; Kitchen, *A History of Modern Germany*, 113-130; Winkler, *Der lange Weg*, vol. I, 201-212.

for a *levée en masse*, a mass mobilization. In several regions guerrilla warfare broke out and snipers were deployed against the Prussian troops. Reprisals followed, creating an extremely grim atmosphere. The long siege of Paris aroused feelings of mutual hatred. This war was different to that of 1866 which had been fought only by soldiers; now national sentiments were inflamed and the entire population felt involved in this battle of life and death. The nation state mobilized all its forces to achieve its objectives, in this case in order to defend itself against a foreign enemy.

Unlike the Prussian army command, Bismarck did not want a war of complete destruction, hoping rather for a political agreement with the interim government. It assented to a ceasefire only on 28 January 1871, when the population of Paris was almost starving and several break-out attempts had failed. Shortly afterwards, an *Assemblée nationale,* elected by universal male suffrage, met in Bordeaux and appointed Thiers as head of the executive power. On February 26th, the newly elected parliament approved demanding conditions for peace: giving up Alsace and northern Lorraine, as well as paying a huge war indemnity. This arrangement would be confirmed by the Treaty of Frankfurt on May 10th. The annexation of Alsace-Lorraine, which Bismarck demanded mainly for strategic reasons, inflicted deep wounds in France and would create a strong revanchism.

Almost immediately the peace settlement provoked a fierce reaction from the population of Paris, which had doggedly endured a months-long siege and now felt humiliated and abandoned. A confrontation ensued between the new government and the Parisian population. Other factors also played a role here. The *Assemblée,* which had been elected by universal male suffrage, consisted mostly of monarchical and conservative delegates. *La France profonde* indeed differed in many respects from republican Paris. When the new government, with the support of parliament, passed a number of anti-social and conservative measures, Parisians revolted on March 18th and installed a people's government in the capital, *le conseil général de la Commune.* The Commune uprising would later be honoured by Karl Marx as the first proletarian revolution, but it was hardly inspired by his ideas and had a strongly anarchistic bent. After peace was officially concluded with Bismarck on May 21st, Thiers launched the battle for Paris. It would last a full week and became known as *la Semaine sanglante* (the Bloody Week*):* more blood flowed than even during the repression of June 1848.[74] However, the effect was similar: all over Europe, many wealthy citizens, and not just the traditional elites, were seized by a fear of revolutionary socialism. Once again a social outburst provoked a conservative response.

74 Serman, *La Commune de Paris (1871)*; Gould, *Insurgent Identities: Class, Community and Protest in Paris from 1848 to the Commune*; Amicabile, *La Commune de Paris.*

In an analogous way, the Prussian victory also contributed to a strengthening of the Right in Europe and again enhanced the prestige of the monarchies. Even in France, where a republic was proclaimed, attempts would be undertaken for many years to restore the monarchy. Prussia had the strongest monarchy, which now acquired the imperial title. The foundation of the German empire was indeed a remarkable result of the Franco-Prussian war. The southern German states now agreed to be part of a German empire under Prussian leadership. The dream of a Lesser Germany had been realized. On 18 January 1871, just before Paris surrendered, the empire was proclaimed in the Hall of Mirrors at Versailles. It was a confederation of sovereign princes, and was given an organizational structure closely resembling that of the North German Confederation, with an authoritarian and militaristic slant, and ceding only modest concessions to liberal constitutionalism. This was not the ideal of the 1848 revolutionaries who had hoped for the formation of a national, liberal empire.[75] The new state was largely an artificial construct, created in an atmosphere of militarism and war, and was not the result of an organic or evolutionary process of unification. In that respect, it did not meet the expectations of the ultra-conservatives, to whom Bismarck had once belonged. While predominantly German, the new empire included many ethnic minorities, and would in addition be plagued by sharp social and political contradictions. It was held together by an authoritarian system of government with a militaristic slant. That was the dark side of Bismarck's impressive performance, who in five years had succeeded in bringing about a powerful German empire that in the coming decades would play a dominant role in continental European politics.

The period 1866-1871 was an important turning point in European history. In a short time the balance of power on the European continent had changed radically. The new German empire became the dominant great power, while Austria was relegated to the second division and as time went on would increasingly align itself with Berlin. Isolated for twenty years in European politics by Bismarck's skillful maneuvers, France sought compensation overseas, through an active colonial policy. The latent antagonism between France and Prussia/Germany, which went back to Napoleonic times, now turned unusually sharp and would burden European politics for many decades. From 1871, the European state system was once more defined in conservative legitimist terms, but the turbulence of the preceding decade left indelible traces. States now relied primarily on their military power and made shifting alliances according to their own national interests. The notion of a supranational interest, the pursuit of an international legal order that could guarantee a lasting peace had almost disappeared.[76]

75   Volker, *Die nervöse Grossmacht*, 29-38.
76   Bridge and Bullen, *The Great Powers*, 175-182.

Nationalism had become the dominant political force in Europe and partly thanks to Bismarck's support, it was now also taken up into conservative ideology. The nation state had become not only the cornerstone of international politics, but also the all-determining factor in domestic politics. It dominated all spheres of social life and claimed the right to deploy all citizens in furthering its goals. In times of war, it controlled even the life and death of its subjects through a process of militarization, including the introduction of personal conscription. The State was seen as both the source of law and the true conscience of the nation. Bismarck's conservatism, unlike that of his former allies, had become not only more nationalistic but also more statist with his growing appreciation for the modern state as a crucial power factor.[77] The liberals also endorsed the principle of a strong State, although they were of the opinion that, within its comprehensive scope, it had to respect the inalienable rights of individual citizens. For its part, socialism, which was then expanding rapidly, would soon abandon its predominantly apolitical, anarchistic position and come to rely on the State in order to improve the situation of the working class. The Leviathan had arisen from beneath the waves and was preparing for the starring role it would later play in the fascist and communist utopian states.

The multinational Danube monarchy was not a nation state, but increasingly it had to take account of the national movements in the historical areas of the empire.[78] A solution had to be found for the Hungarian question in particular. With the loss of its dominant position in Germany, the empire naturally turned more to the east, and now more than ever had to consider the Hungarians, who had been demanding greater autonomy for decades.

At the end of 1866, the Belcredi government was still at the helm. It was the last government to cling to the idea of a supranational state with federalist leanings. In its view it was dangerous to allow the principle of nationality to determine the institutions of the state. Its policy was designed to take account of the historical territories of the country, without damaging the unity of the state, and so while expressing understanding for the aspirations of the Slavic minorities, it did not want to give the Hungarians any preferential treatment. However, the Hungarians were putting the stability and even survival of the Danube monarchy at risk and were making far-reaching demands, to which the Emperor, out of necessity, had to accede.

Francis Joseph I turned to an outsider, Friedrich Ferdinand von Beust, former Saxon minister-president, to resolve the problem. He appointed him minister of foreign affairs on 30 October 1866 and more than two months later minister-president in place of Richard Belcredi. Beust had the support of the

---

77 Lerman, *Bismarck*, 35.
78 On the constitutional developments in the Danube monarchy, see: Rumpler, *Eine Chance*, 403-422; Zöllner, *Geschichte Österreichs*, 411-420; Höbelt, *Franz Joseph I*, 57-70.

German liberals, who occupied a dominant position in the non-Hungarian part of the empire. In his view, the government could not satisfy all the minority groups and had to rely on the strongest elements, the German and Hungarian sections of the population. He therefore agreed with the dualistic solution that the Emperor had worked out in the meantime, namely the transformation of the empire into a Dual Monarchy. In mid-February 1867, Francis Joseph I proposed a separate government for Hungary and together with the Hungarian diet proposed an *Ausgleich* (great compromise). This was accepted in December of the same year by the parliament of Cisleithania, the non-Hungarian section of the empire. The German liberals were willing to agree to this transformation of the state, provided a constitutional state would once again be established in Cisleithania.

In the Dual Monarchy, Cisleithania and Transleithania (Hungary) would henceforth enjoy broad autonomy, each with its own parliament and government. The central government would be responsible only for foreign policy and national defense. Matters of common interest would be discussed annually by 'delegations', each consisting of sixty delegates from the two parliaments. A limited joint ministerial council would be responsible only to the emperor, but would have to report annually to the delegations. In fact, it was still the emperor, especially through his foreign minister, who gave shape to the international policy of the Dual Monarchy.

The German liberals and the Hungarians were united in their rejection of a tripartite division of the empire that would include a similar solution for the Slavic peoples. In Cisleithania the Galician Poles would acquire more autonomy, but the Czechs abstained and in the 1870s would boycott even the functioning of the new institutions which then came to be completely dominated by the German liberals.

In 1867 a constitutional pact between the parliament, the government and the monarchy in Cisleithania was signed. This *Verfassungsreform* was mainly the work of an industrial-capitalist and intellectual bourgeoisie, who did not want to weaken the centrally controlled state but rather to transform it into a constitutional state, under the rule of law. The liberal bourgeoisie, together with the bureaucrats, favoured increasing state control. The *Dezemberverfassung*, which was accepted by the Imperial Council on 21 December 1867, laid down basic civil rights, expanded parliament's rights of oversight and reinforced the independence of the judiciary. The Imperial Council would, as foreseen in the *Februarpatent* of 1861, continue to be composed of two chambers: the *Abgeordnetenhaus* and the *Herrenhaus*. The members of the *Herrenhaus* had hereditary seats, or were appointed for life by the emperor. The deputies were elected through a system of corporate representation, in which the population was divided into electoral classes, with separate representation from the large estates, rural areas, cities and chambers of commerce. This electoral system mainly benefited the German urban bourgeoisie and the big landowners, because the right to vote was linked to census suffrage.

The liberals, who favoured a strong centralism, nevertheless had to accept that the *Länder* still retained substantial rights. The protection of all the vernaculars was upheld and German was not given the status of an official language in Cisleithania. Another important point was that ministers were responsible to the emperor and not to parliament. The monarch could also, in a case of emergency, govern without parliament. The *Dezemberverfassung* thus bore all the hallmarks of a compromise.

In comparison with the Third Republic in France or with the parliamentary monarchies in Great Britain and the Low Countries (Belgium and the Netherlands), the regime still had many authoritarian characteristics, as was also the case in the new German empire. Nevertheless, a number of steps towards a liberal, parliamentary regime had been taken. This corresponded to the general pattern: liberalism had made great strides throughout Europe during the economic boom of the 1860s. This development was also evident in the Danube monarchy, where a precarious balance had been found between liberal aspirations and traditional structures. A major difficulty remaining was that the Dual Monarchy had not found a satisfactory solution for the nationality problems either in Cisleithania or in Hungary, so that Francis Joseph I could say, '*In meinem Reich geht die Krise nicht unter*' ('In my realm, the crisis never ends'), an allusion to Charles V's dictum, 'In my kingdom the sun never sets.'[79]

The Catholic Church as a counterpower

In the space of two years, the Danube monarchy had fundamentally changed. Metternich's Austria was no more. The empire was no longer a prominent player in European politics and was transformed into a constitutional Dual Monarchy. This proved to be a major problem for Blome who, though not Austrian by birth, had chosen this state for ideological reasons and he resolved now to take some time off from politics. When, after the Peace of Nickolsburg, the Viennese government finally recognized the Kingdom of Italy, which had annexed large areas of the Papal States and threatened the position of the Pope in Rome, he decided to withdraw temporarily from the diplomatic service. He turned down offers to be ambassador in St. Petersburg or Berlin and asked for

79   Vocelka, 'Die Gegenkräfte des Liberalismus in der Donaumonarchie', 123.

leave for an indefinite period.[80] Over several months he travelled throughout Europe, and at the beginning of November 1866, he settled in Vienna, with the intention of leading a studious life.

Blome could now afford to live without working. As a diplomat with an inactive status he received a modest, reduced salary, but he also had much more important sources of income. In 1863 he had acquired the demesne of Montpreis in Styria (Steiermark), which included 750 acres of farmland and a forest of 1,750 hectares. That same year he also took over the management of his father's Hungarian estate. Furthermore, he came into possession of half of a sizeable inheritance from his father-in-law, who had died at the end of October 1865. He was now rightly considered a wealthy man, though his income was not comparable to that of the great Hungarian magnates or of the leading feudal families.[81] In 1867 the Blomes had four children, three of them boys, to be followed by four daughters in the coming years. Maintaining this large family, educating his sons, marrying off his daughters, together with economic hardship and an unfortunate investment policy would in time eat into the family fortune[82], but for the moment there were absolutely no reasons to worry.

Blome still corresponded regularly with his faithful friend, Louis de Pons. He seized every chance to visit him in Paris, especially on the occasion of his name day on the 15th of August.[83] He also asked him to be godfather to his second son. Their correspondence, as before, was mainly concerned with personal and family matters, and the tone was more than friendly. As might be expected, Pons in particular displayed his feelings: 'I still love you as much as in the Russian period. With my "love" (friendship is too weak a word) has come great respect for your character.'[84] After his last visit, in September 1866, Blome wrote: 'I do not know why, but I love you so much and more than ever, but I don't get to show it as much as before.'[85] The correspondence between them hardly ever included any mention of political or diplomatic issues.

Remarkably enough, religious topics did not often come up for discussion either. In that matter they clearly held different views. For Pons, reli-

---

80   *Souvenirs*, vol. II, 109. In his capacity as ambassador in Munich, Blome had by late 1865 already criticized Bavaria's recognition of Italy. See Blome to Mensdorff, 12 Nov. 1865 in: Srbik, *Quellen*, vol. V/1, 104-106; Blome to Pons, 18 Nov. 1865: 'You see that I'm writing to you still upset by Bavaria's recognition of Italy. No more principles, dignity or moral sentiment. The century has taken everything away, it piles ruins upon ruins and I look in vain for what it is rebuilding.'

81   An article in the British newspaper *The Telegraph* (Feb. 1868) estimated his annual income at 1 million francs [about 4.2 million euro], but according to Blome himself, that figure was grossly exaggerated (*Journal*, Note 12 Feb. 1868, Gut Salzau, V).

82   See *infra*, 255-257.

83   See for example: Blome to Pons, 25 Aug. and 28 Oct. 1863.

84   Pons to Blome, 17 Aug. 1862.

85   Blome to Pons, 30 Sept. 1866.

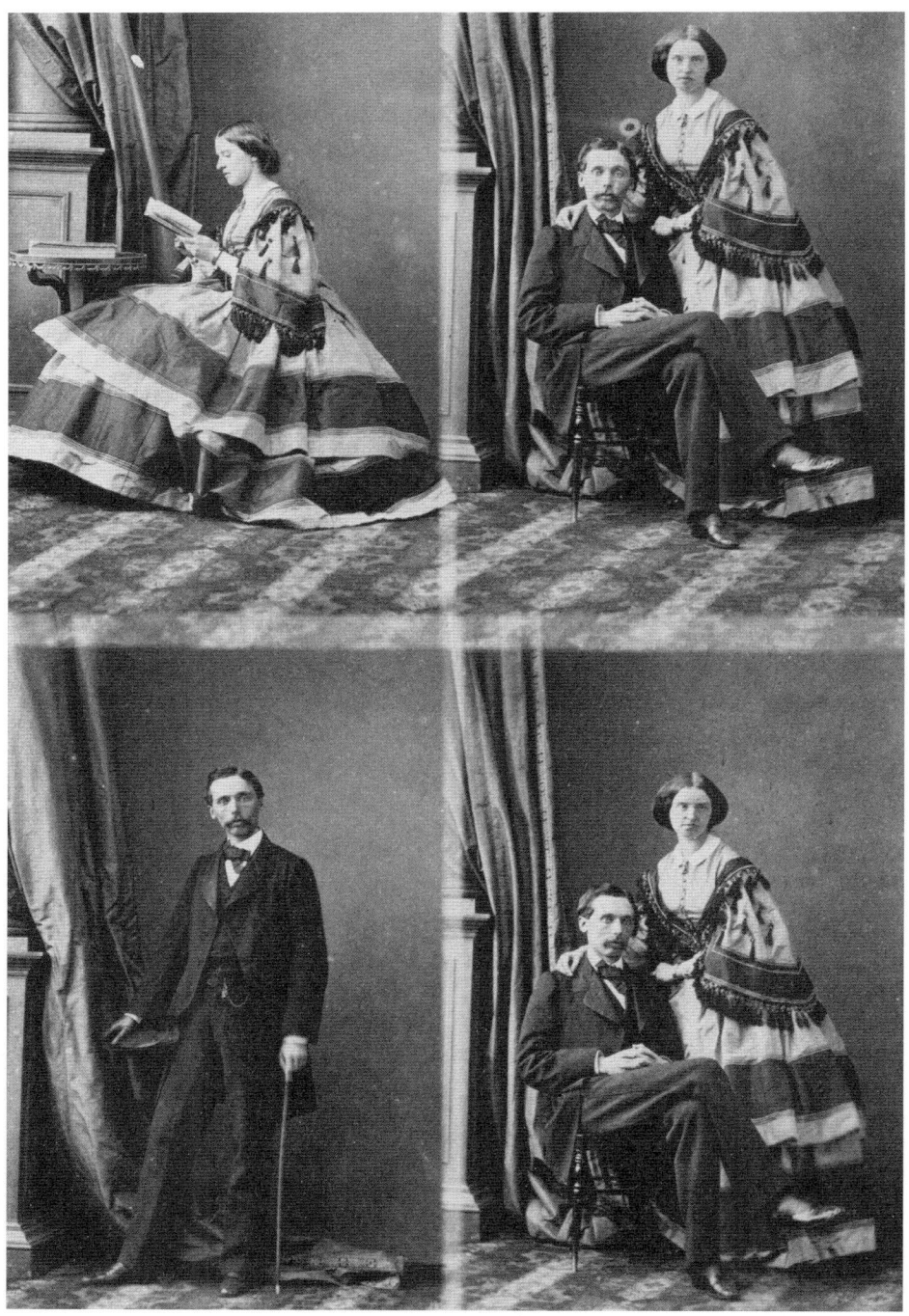

Gustav von Blome and Séphine Buol-Schauenstein. Photograph, A. Disdéri, 1858.
[*Paris, Musée d'Orsay/©RMN (Musée d'Orsay); René-Gabriel Ojéda*]

gion was not so important and, like most of his contemporaries in France, he was something of a Gallican.[86] Blome, for whom religion had become all-important, had gradually developed into an ardent ultramontane Catholic.[87] Pons repeatedly criticized this: 'You have become a Catholic and I can only applaud your religious zeal, provided it stays within limits, because even in the best of cases exaggeration is a fault.'[88] He found that Blome had become too one-dimensional: 'You push all your feelings and emotions to the limit.' Blome readily concurred: 'I cannot deny that I am often sharp in my judgement. I adhere strictly to principles and am always ready to shout "*fiat justitia et pereat mundus*".'[89] He deliberately chose to adopt an unyielding attitude: 'Even if I have to wage opposition all my life from a minority standpoint, I will not stop saying that the right path is that of the law, and especially that of the church.'[90] 'Impartiality is not possible when faced with a choice between good and evil, truth and falsity.'[91]

In the last letter that Pons wrote on 17 November 1866, he described with great lucidity the young man for whom he fourteen years before had conceived a true passion:

> I will not hide the fact that the excessive earnestness that has taken hold of you saddens me. In your youth you already had the typical characteristics of a German, but your cool and aloof manner was tempered now and then by a milder expression. At the moment – without your being aware of it – you radiate such a chilly seriousness that I am overawed by it. We understand one another very well, but differ considerably in the expression of our feelings. Has that to do with a certain exaltation of your religious convictions? You are an outspoken opponent of what is now called 'liberalism' and that makes you gloomy. As a statesman you are disappointed, as a convinced and dutiful Christian you are wounded. It makes those who love you think back with nostalgia to the time when you were less perfect in the eyes of the world.[92]

86   Pons to Blome, 19 Sept. 1854: 'It is impossible to be less of a theologian than I am. A good Roman Catholic, attached to my religion (though not observing practices as much as I should), I only want to have a simple faith. I do all I can to believe, and to this end at least I absolutely refuse all religious discussion.' Id. to id., 4 April 1860: 'Without having your fervour... I remain faithfully subject to the laws of the Church, and I carry out its commandments to the best of my abilities.'

87   See also the remark by Maria Kalergis, following her meeting with Blome in Karlsbad: 'He appeared to me to be more simple-hearted, calmer than before, yet very absolute in his ideas, a champion of the Church of a kind that the world does not often supply.' (Maria Kalergis to her daughter, 10 June 1862, cited in La Mara, *Marie von Mouchanoff-Kalergis*, 106).

88   Pons to Blome, 4 April 1860.

89   Blome to Pons, 22 Sept. 1860.

90   Blome to Pons, 5 April 1862.

91   Blome to Pons, 26 March 1860 and 26 Feb. 1862.

92   Pons to Blome, 17 Nov. 1866.

Pons died on 29 January 1867, shortly before his 93rd birthday. As agreed, his adopted son, Maxime Lefèvre-Deumier de Pons, returned Blome's letters to him, and so they were preserved for posterity, a permanent testimony to a very special friendship.

Blome's firmness of principle, which Pons thought exaggerated, made him thus decide to take a break in his diplomatic career. That decision took even more definitive form when Mensdorff was replaced as minister of foreign affairs by Beust, for whom Blome felt a profound aversion, both for political and personal reasons.[93] Beust had been one of the most active protagonists of liberal politics in the *Mittelstaaten*. His character was completely opposite to that of Blome, who called him an opportunist, a political adventurer and a corrupt man. Moreover, he saw him as a tool of the freemasons.[94] Beust, on the other hand, was apparently convinced that Blome was very influential and tried to win him over to his side. On 23 December 1866 he arranged his appointment as privy councillor, an honorary title given to state officials as a reward for exceptional services. Even more important was Blome's appointment on 1 April 1867 as a member of the *Herrenhaus*. Both honours were awarded by the emperor, but the initiative came from the ministry of foreign affairs. The news of his nomination to the *Herrenhaus* reached Blome while he was staying in Paris and came as a complete surprise: 'My appointment can only be seen as an exceptional favour, especially considering my political opinions, which I have never kept secret.'[95] Though Blome was honoured by the nomination, he was irritated by it at the same time. He was after all an opponent of the constitutional, parliamentary system, and only with difficulty could he participate in it. On his return to Vienna he went to visit Count Kuefstein, the grand marshal of the court, and explained his objections to him. The court dignitary emphatically asked him to accept the appointment, if only to avoid causing scandal – in fact, the appointment had already been made public by imperial decree. In addition, the grand marshal believed that Blome could serve the cause well by joining the side of the defenders of the law and the monarchy in the *Herrenhaus*. The appointment also did not require an oath of allegiance to the constitution that was then being readied, but merely a promise to respect

93 Diary entry for 4 Nov. 1866, cited in *Souvenirs*, vol. II, p. 110-111: 'The appointment of Beust has angered me (...) I consider this choice to be more baneful than the deplorable handover of Venice and the terrible defeat of Königgratz; I consider it to be the beginning of the end, and I am afraid that Beust might become the Necker of Austria.'

94 *Souvenirs*, vol. II, p. 112; *Journal*, note 5 Nov. 1867, Gut Salzau, V: 'I found him to be lightweight, superficial, and above all completely selfish. He never looks at you directly and he tries to hide his lack of principles under a flow of words delivered with extreme volubility.' Blome accused Beust of having been the first to introduce phenomena like corruption and bribery into the elections (*Journal*, Notes 11 and 18 Dec. 1867). According to Blome, Beust also accepted bribes from the Belgian financier Langrand-Dumonceau in exchange for financial benefits (*Journal*, Notes 13 Oct. 1868, 22 Jan. and 2 May 1870, Gut Salzau, V).

95 *Souvenirs*, vol. II, 120.

existing laws. Blome allowed himself to be persuaded, but during the usual audience with the Emperor after he took his seat, he stated unequivocally that he was actually an opponent of the parliamentary regime, felt no calling for such a career and also had no talent for it. The Emperor replied, 'just join the assembly; there you will get ample opportunity to render service to the Crown and the good cause'. Blome resolved not to interfere in constitutional issues and to engage only in religious and social matters.[96]

The *Herrenhaus* began its deliberations on 20 May 1867. Blome took part in the first sessions only, then excused himself for health reasons, and went to stay in the spa town of Karlsbad until the end of October. By that time most of the constitutional laws that would lead to the *Dezemberverfassung* had been put to a vote. Blome did not join in with any faction in the upper house as he did not come from one of the historic *Länder* and only felt called to defend his principles. He was closest to the federalists who supported wide-ranging autonomy for the *Länder*. He was indeed vehemently opposed to parliamentary and bureaucratic centralism and to an overly strong state power.[97]

From the end of 1867 a few proposals were discussed in the *Herrenhaus* that were crucial for Church-State relations.[98] Blome was fully involved in these debates and even took a leading role. For him, the religious issue had become all-defining. In a world undergoing so many shocking changes, both social and political, the universal and ancient Catholic Church was a pillar of strength, and it alone would be able to hold out in the catastrophe to come. Its monarchical form of governance gave it great inner strength. It defended universal moral values that also had to give a moral compass to social and political life. It had to be given the possibility of exercising its beneficial influence in society without constraint. It had turned against the principles of the French Revolution of 1789 and was therefore the preferred ally of everyone who strove for order and stability. In a diplomatic note in early 1865, Blome had expressed his opinion that the big battle looming was not that between Austria and Prussia, but between the supporters and opponents of papal sociopolitical teaching.[99] His views caused a stir at the time, but made very clear that for him the ideological struggle was more important than the fight in the

---

96 *Souvenirs*, vol. II, 121-126.

97 Blome's profound dislike for parliamentarianism and the principle of state omnipotence is evident in various diary entries in 1866-1867. In an entry for 20 May 1866 he called the parliamentary debates 'loquacious outpourings of revolutionaries'. See also: *Souvenirs*, vol. II, 123: 'In my opinion, the constitution was execrable, parliamentarianism a detestable system, centralization a curse. It was always my conviction that the religious and social point of view dominates all others. I wanted to devote myself exclusively to that perspective, and not initiate serious discussion on secondary issues.'

98 Vocelka, *Verfassung oder Konkordat?*

99 Blome to Biegeleben, 1 Jan. and 5 March 1865 in: Srbik, *Quellen*, vol. IV, 494 and 584-585. See Eyck's sarcastic commentary, *Bismarck*, vol. II, 74.

political arena. When it came to a conflict between principles, there was no place for an intermediate solution:

> Between the revolution and the Church there is no middle ground. Between the principles of 1789 and the principles of the Gospel, between disorder and order, lies and truth, the violation of treaties and the preservation of peace, between all this there is no middle ground. One cannot make compromises with the revolution: one is either for it or against it.[100]

With that attitude Blome threw himself into the debates about the place of the Church in the Danube monarchy. As might be expected, his participation did not go unnoticed.

In Cisleithania nearly 80 percent of the population was Catholic, and the Church was still very influential there.[101] It was closely intertwined with the apparatus of the State, although its position was a minor one. A church-friendly climate prevailed under neo-absolutist rule, and in 1855 a concordat was signed with the Holy See that was very favourable to the Church. It was given more freedom, and retained control of key sectors such as the registry of births, marriages and deaths, marriage regulations and education, sectors which in most western European countries had already been put under state supervision. The Austrian liberals opposed those regulations and in 1867 used their newly acquired dominant position to demand a lifting of the concordat. However, it was a state treaty and could not simply be unilaterally put aside.

Meanwhile, the *Dezemberverfassung* of 1867 included articles that guaranteed freedom of religion, proclaimed the exclusive and comprehensive legal sovereignty of the state and assigned the government an important role in organizing education. The liberals then rightly argued that several provisions of the concordat were contrary to the new constitution, and therefore, before negotiations with Rome got under way, they wanted to render a number of articles in the concordat inoperable. They proposed extending the competences of the civil government in the area of marriage legislation and putting education under state control. Heated discussions ensued both in the media and in parliament. The disputes took less acute form in the *Abgeordnetenhaus*, where the liberals had a large majority, but flared up in the *Herrenhaus*, which was predominantly conservative.

Shortly after his return from Karlsbad, Blome was chosen as a member of the commission dealing with the disputed bills in the *Herrenhaus*.[102] Along

---

100 Blome to Pons, 24 Aug. 1862.
101 Leisching, 'Die römisch-katholische Kirche in Cisleithanien', 34-47.
102 On Blome's participation in the debates in the *Herrenhaus*, see: *Souvenirs*, vol. II, 126-211; *Journal*, notes 1867 and 1868, Gut Salzau, V.

with Cardinal Rauscher, archbishop of Vienna, he soon became the linchpin of the minority group that strenuously resisted the proposed reforms. This group found itself facing a coalition of liberals and former Josephinists who wanted to push the Church out of the official sphere and at the same time keep it under control. The opposition managed to prevent a unilateral lifting of the concordat, but had to back down in the area of marriage and education legislation. With the support of the Emperor's entourage, they almost succeeded in delaying the 'anti-religious' laws, but nevertheless failed at the last moment. For a long time it was not certain on which side the balance would fall; this uncertainty also explains the doggedness with which the debate was conducted in the *Herrenhaus*, as well as in the press and even on the street. Blome acted more and more as a spokesperson for the minority, and therefore came in for sharp attack in the liberal press. Even the British quality newspaper *The Telegraph* devoted a critical article to him.[103] It portrayed him as a Peter the Hermit, preaching a crusade against liberalism. Incidentally, the same newspaper had words of appreciation for his 'northern thoroughness and southern vivacity', as well as for his 'aristocratic versatility': 'He can be a Frenchman with the French, an Englishman with the English, a Russian with the Russians, a German with the Germans.'[104] The debates in the *Herrenhaus* reached a climax between 19 and 21 March 1868. The tribunes were packed and stormy demonstrations were organized in front of the parliament building. The disputed bills were finally approved by a narrow majority, after which the liberals were welcomed with great acclaim and the conservatives were booed. That evening a crowd gathered in front of Blome's home, but fortunately remained calm. Thanks to the campaign launched against him, he had become 'the most hated and at the same time the most formidable leader of the Catholic party'.

Blome's speeches in the *Herrenhaus* covered many legal and technical matters, but they also expressed general views that were very typical of his outlook.[105] With regard to the concordat, he obviously called for respect for the existing treaties, which could not be unilaterally terminated by any one party. He was also of the opinion that a conflict with the Church would have disastrous consequences for the State. However, he particularly opposed State omnipotence. In his view, those who 'practised the cult of the State' believed that the State absorbed the rights of all to itself, while on the contrary it should respect everyone's rights, those of other states, individuals, families, corporations and churches. With regard to the school question, Blome pointed to the natural rights of the family in the upbringing and education of children. The

103 *Journal*, note 12 Feb. 1868, Gut Salzau, V.
104 *Souvenirs*, vol. II, 208-209.
105 'Die katholischen Stimmen des österreichischen Herrenhauses. Reden gehalten in der Ehegesetz-Debatte am 19, 20 und 21 März 1868', *Katholische Stimmen aus Österreich*, vol. III, Vienna, 1868, 30-40; 'Reden gehalten in der Schulgesetz-Debatte am 30. März 1868', ibid. 13-18.

State had to take these into account and was also obliged to respect the freedom of the Church in that domain. He pleaded above all for an area that would be free of state intrusion and filled with the traditional social entities. That the Catholic Church had an overly dominant place in society and threatened to overwhelm other denominations was, apparently, less problematic for him. In his eyes, the Church was best suited to be a counterpower to the modern State, which interfered too much in the lives of its citizens and paid too little attention to the protective social fabric that had taken shape over time.

On 25 May 1868, the Emperor signed the 'anti-Church laws' which were henceforth known as the 'May Laws'. He had serious qualms of conscience about the new legislation, but he fulfilled his constitutional role and endorsed parliament's decision. Blome thought that the Emperor had been too lenient on this crucial issue. At the time Francis Joseph I let slip the remark, 'Blome is the only one who has shown great strength of character', but he was not inclined to return the compliment.[106] He would never see the Emperor again. In previous years, he had been having more and more doubts about Francis Joseph's political decisions, but the fact that the sovereign had now finally turned in favour of the liberals and confirmed their anticlerical politics was too much for him to accept.

All in all, the May Laws were moderate and moreover would not be rigidly enforced. They introduced civil marriage, but still allowed Catholics to have only a church wedding. The laws put schools under state supervision, although religious education provided by the clergy remained mandatory. Two years later, the liberal government would unilaterally terminate the Concordat of 1855. That happened, as will be explained later, on 30 August 1870, in response to the decrees of the First Vatican Council. Some time later, in 1874, through the Emperor's agency, a law came into force that granted a privileged status to the Church and affirmed its interrelationship with the State. The Catholic Church would for decades remain a mainstay of the regime of Francis Joseph I.[107]

However, the opposition to the May Laws formed the beginning of a Catholic opposition movement that would gradually gain strength.[108] Remarkably enough, opposition to the anticlerical government policy was stronger in lay circles than among the bishops, most of whom – in the tradition of Josephinism – were still very law-abiding. Resistance to this compliant attitude grew under pressure from militant lay circles, and here international events played an important part. It was the Italian question and the threat it posed to the Papal States that led to the initial mobilization of the Catholic faithful. In February 1860, the *St. Michaelsbruderschaft* (Confraternity of St Michael) was

106 *Journal*, entry for 16 March 1868, Gut Salzau, V.
107 Pfleger, *Gab es einen Kulturkampf in Österreich?*; Höbelt, *Franz Joseph I*, 71-76.
108 Röhrig, 'Die katholische Kirche', 205-208.

founded in Vienna, dedicated to defending the temporal power of the Pope and the social influence of the Church.[109] It would later spread widely outside the capital and help foster the establishment of other militant Catholic associations. Then, in 1868, widespread opposition to the May Laws grew, which, together with the Italian question, created the impression that the Church both at home and abroad had been put on the defensive and had to be defended by the people. The mobilization of the Catholic population had great potential, and the Church could still count on broad support in the 'real country', support that could be tapped, provided modern mobilization techniques were used.

Blome was soon convinced that Catholics had to be mobilized in order to defend the freedom and influence of the Church, both internationally and domestically.[110] Such mobilization would also benefit the conservatives in Austria whose only chance of being widely accepted depended on an affiliation with the Catholic movement. Just as Bismarck had contracted an alliance with nationalism in order to achieve his conservative targets, so Blome opted for an alliance with the Church, which could no longer rely on the political elite and certainly not on the then liberal governments, but still commanded wide support among a large section of the aristocracy and the broader public. That potential had to be tapped in order to restore the conservative and Christian order. Here he was venturing further than had his great role model Metternich, who had spoken out against any form of political Catholicism.

During his stay in Vienna, Blome became actively involved in the Catholic associations that were then slowly developing. At the beginning of January 1868 he made a remarkable speech to the *Ressource*,[111] a sociocultural association for conservative Catholic notables which he himself had helped set up a few years before. Under the title *Zeitgemässe Betrachtungen* he updated an 1846 publication by the French politician, Charles de Montalembert. This was remarkable given that Montalembert, who will be extensively discussed later, was the most prominent liberal Catholic layman in continental Europe, while Blome clearly belonged to the ultramontane opposition movement. Montalembert's tract included a call to French Catholics to form their own political movement and to use all legal means within the existing parliamentary system to defend the rights and liberties of the Church. Catholics were citizens of the State and therefore had rights which they had not fully availed of yet. No government would do anything for the Church, unless it was forced to do so under pressure from Catholic opinion. Significantly, Blome omitted some passages referring to the principle of popular sovereignty and the advantages of

109 Wolny, *Chronik der Erzbruderschaft vom heiligen Erzengel Michael in Wien.*
110 Blome to Pons, 22 Sept. 1860.
111 *Zeitgemässe Betrachtungen. Vortrag, gehalten im Wiener geselligen Vereine (Ressource) von Graf Blome*, (Katholische Stimmen aus Österreich, vol. I), Vienna, 1868.

the parliamentary system, but he fully supported the call by Montalembert to combine all the Catholic forces in social and political life. 'Let us cease being only a part of history. Let us rely only on ourselves and people will then rely on us. Yes, we can do this, when we decide to do so ... ' This speech showed that Blome, as well as Montalembert, gave priority to the struggle for the freedom of the Church and felt that it should be fought with whatever political means were available.

In Vienna Blome was a board member of the *St. Michaelsbruderschaft* and dedicated himself to promoting all sorts of activities in favour of the Papacy. He also secretly lent his cooperation to the leading Catholic newspaper, the *Volksfreund*. Both before and after the debates in the *Herrenhaus*, he travelled to Rome, Paris and London, where he came into contact with leading Catholic prelates and lay people. He spent two weeks in early January 1868 in Rome, where he visited secretary of state Antonelli, among others.[112] An audience with the Pope was, of course, also on the agenda. Blome was becoming an increasingly important figure on the international Catholic scene, a role for which he was particularly well equipped, given his history and extensive knowledge of languages. Moreover, his social status opened all doors for him.

In the end he decided to leave Vienna and settle in Rome, where he wanted to put himself at the service of the papal cause. In the circumstances, a career in the diplomatic service no longer seemed possible to him, and the reasons for his resignation were still valid. He waived his retainer salary and was given the status of a minister plenipotentiary in disponibility. He would never return to diplomacy, and that was a great sacrifice for him. At the end of his political memoirs in 1875, he sighed:

> Oh, it took me a lot of effort to forego every type of political career, given that every door in that direction was wide open for me. I must say that it is a sacrifice that I still have to make time and again, a bitter sorrow that I still feel every day. But one must be prepared – if necessary – to sacrifice one's ambitions, passions, well-being, peace and even one's life for one's principles.[113]

For the moment, he also ceased to participate in parliamentary activities in the *Herrenhaus*. He no longer wanted to sit in parliament following the adoption of the anticlerical laws, but if he remained in Vienna, he could not always stay away from the *Herrenhaus* without giving an explanation that would offend the Emperor. A further stay in the capital would bring him into conflict with a principle that he wanted to respect at all costs, namely 'the principle of

112 *Journal*, entry for 20 Jan. 1868, Gut Salzau, V. He then still regarded Antonelli as 'the foremost statesman of the contemporary world'.
113 *Souvenirs*, vol. II, p. 246.

authority in society'. That is why in November 1868 he settled with his family in Rome, to await better times and 'to drink from the source of all wisdom'.[114]

Leaving Austria was difficult for him, as he wrote in 1875:

> Oh, I still love Austria very much, the traditional Austria, the Austria of Prince Metternich, the Catholic and conservative Austria of my dreams! But the new situation that had been created corresponded so little to my ideal ... and I saw so few opportunities to respond effectively to the dominant trends that it seemed to me wiser to seek shelter and solace in the common fatherland of all those who have lost theirs or have reason to be unhappy about it.

In the next few years he would play a role in the highest echelons of ecclesiastical politics and would become an important figurehead of militant ultramontanism, which was gaining ground on liberal Catholicism. This new phase in his career would provide him with the opportunity to make one last attempt to restore a Christian political order in Europe.

---

114 *Souvenirs*, vol. II, p. 245: 'I had the intention to refresh and strengthen myself at the fountain of all wisdom, while waiting for a turnaround to take place at home, and then return to my battle station in more favourable circumstances.'

THE CATHOLIC CHURCH
IN BATTLE MODE

Around noon on Thursday, 20 August 1863, one day later than scheduled, Count Charles de Montalembert arrived in the congress hall of
the minor seminary in Mechlin (Belgium), where the first international
Catholic congress was taking place.[1] As he entered, the three thousand participants, who were eagerly awaiting his arrival, stood up and chanted: 'Long live
Count de Montalembert, long live the son of the Crusaders!' This staged welcome was an allusion to a famous speech in 1844 by de Montalembert which
he had concluded by proclaiming, 'we are the sons of the Crusaders and we
will not yield to the sons of Voltaire'. In the late afternoon he delivered the first
part of his planned speech.[2]

The refectory and reading room of the boarding school, which had been
transformed into a large congress hall, were crammed full and the heat was
so unbearable that some windows were broken to let in fresh air. Under the
title *A free Church in a free State*, Montalembert made an impassioned plea for
reconciliation between the Catholic Church and democracy, and for an acceptance of modern civil and political liberties. His speech did not initially meet
with much enthusiasm, but gradually he got the crowd on his side by referring to the many benefits that modern freedoms had bestowed on the Belgian
Church. The second part of his speech would specifically deal with freedom

---

1   Lamberts, 'Catholic Congresses', 215.
2   Montalembert, *L'Eglise libre dans l'Etat libre*; Id., *Journal intime inédit*, vol. VII; Aubert, ed.,
    Correspondance entre Charles de Montalembert et Adolphe Dechamps; Id., 'L'intervention
    de Montalembert au congrès de Malines en 1863', 1950, 525-555; Latreille, ed., *Charles de
    Montalembert*; Van Isacker, *Werkelijk en wettelijk land*; Cattaneo, *Montalembert*; Dumont,
    ed., *Montalembert et ses contemporains*.

of conscience, a very delicate subject in Catholic circles. Then, because of the late hour, the topic was postponed until the following day.

Montalembert returned the same night to his hotel in Brussels where he made some modifications to his text. Following a proposal by the Belgian archbishop, Cardinal Sterckx, he introduced into his speech a clear distinction between dogmatic and civil tolerance. On the afternoon of Friday, August 21st he returned to the conference room in Mechlin, where at the time Archbishop Wiseman of England was delivering a monotonous report on the state of the Catholic Church in his country. Then Montalembert shook the audience awake with a challenging speech on freedom of conscience. The scenario of the previous day was repeated: initially the speech was greeted with 'silent attention and a striking reserve', but – as the speaker himself noted in his diary – 'the speech ended around eight o'clock to thunderous applause and an enthusiasm that moved me even more than it charmed me and made me more happy than proud'.[3] Montalembert was delighted with the broad support he received because he was aware that he had taken a big risk: 'Never was a more daring speech made by a Catholic.' Most of the Belgians in the audience were enthusiastic about his carefully constructed and virtuoso speech, but among the foreign delegations there was a lot of criticism of the scope of his statements, which roundly contradicted the discourse of the Roman curia. Montalembert knew that Rome was working on a document on freedom of conscience and his speech in Mechlin was intended as a shot across the bow. However, there was a real risk that a cannonade would follow.

When the organizers of the Mechlin Congress had asked Montalembert to speak, he had accepted the invitation, albeit after some hesitation, because it offered him the chance to break through the isolation in which he had ended up in France. In the 1840s he had acquired great fame as a champion of the Catholic cause in parliament, but during the Second Empire he had opposed the authoritarian regime of Napoleon III and was politically silenced. Within Catholic circles, he was also being increasingly attacked by the radical ultramontane movement –'that fanatical and servile school that enchains the Church everywhere to despotism' – and by its figurehead, the journalist Louis Veuillot. Government censorship deprived him of the chance to go on the defensive and defend his ideas in a public forum; for that reason he wanted to use the opportunity that was offered to him in Mechlin. There, in front of an international audience, he would be able to defend his conviction that Catholics had to accept modern society, democracy and freedom of conscience. He regarded this as his political testament and, in retrospect, he could say with satisfaction: 'Now I can pronounce my *nunc dimittis*.'

In liberal Belgium Catholics enjoyed exceptional freedom, thanks to the new state that they, together with the liberals, had created in 1830 following

3   Montalembert, *Journal intime inédit*, vol. VII, 634.

Charles de Montalembert. Oil on canvas, A. Pichon, 1879.
[*Versailles, Châteaux de Versailles et de Trianon/©RMN (Châteaux de Versailles); Gérard Blot*]

the break with the Netherlands. An almost unlimited freedom of association and assembly allowed meetings like the Mechlin congress to take place. In addition, wide educational freedom was granted, making possible the development of an extensive network of Catholic schools at all levels. A typical outcome of this educational freedom was the minor seminary at Mechlin, where numerous international and national Catholic congresses would later take place. It was a diocesan boarding school that offered a humanistic and philosophical training to future priests. The building complex consisted of a conglomeration of old patrician houses and made a great impression on Montalembert. It was in many ways a suitable stage for his ode to freedom.

The French historian Georges Weill later described Montalembert's Mechlin speech as 'the most complete and powerful expression of liberal Catholicism in that generation'.[4] Its central thesis was that Catholics had to accept liberal democracy, along with the freedoms that characterized it, if only because there was no returning to the *ancien régime*.[5] Moreover, modern liberties offered the best guarantee for the independence of the Church and that, for Montalembert, was the crux of the matter. In particular, he interpreted the formula 'a free Church in a free State', as he wrote in the published version of his speech, as 'a free Church in a free country'. The Church could and should no longer rely on special privileges. Rather, its freedom was now dependent on general freedom, which it should not fear. Every extension of political and civil liberties would enhance that freedom and any restriction would damage it. So it was in the Church's interest to endorse those freedoms, thereby helping at the same time to curb the inherent dangers of democracy, which could lead both to revolution and to despotism. Montalembert pointed explicitly to the tendency towards the centralization and concentration of power in the modern State, which had more resources than ever to establish its domination. The Church could be a buffer against this and thus serve the cause of freedom. Freedom needed religion just as religion needed freedom.

Montalembert followed the same line of argument in that section of his speech dealing with the delicate problem of freedom of conscience. He explicitly stated that he was demanding freedom of conscience primarily *against* the State, which had no jurisdiction in matters of faith and only had to guarantee freedom of worship. Freedom of conscience was the most precious of all freedoms: 'It deserves the utmost respect and demands an absolute commitment.' Though many Catholics did not agree, their Church needed this freedom to develop and thus be able to combat both despotism and demagoguery. Collusion with absolutist regimes would only compromise the Church and curtail its freedom; to expect exclusive protection from such regimes was counterproductive and, furthermore, hypocritical. Catholics could not demand freedom

4   Introduction by Le Guillou in: Montalembert, *Journal intime inédit*, vol. VII, 25.
5   Montalembert, *L'Eglise libre dans l'Etat libre.*

for themselves and deny it to others at the same time: 'Exclusive liberty is only a privilege, and freedom that is not afforded to others is tantamount to a form of betrayal.' He added: 'The *ius commune* is the only refuge for religious freedom today.' The mutual independence of Church and State was a regulative principle in modern society, and did not have to lead to an absolute separation, much less to mutual enmity.

Montalembert then was fully aware that by rejecting exclusive State protection for the Church in Catholic countries, he was going against the Church's teaching. He therefore emphasized repeatedly that he was speaking as a politician and historian and not as a theologian. As a politician, he could only conclude that liberal democracy was the future and that the freedoms it introduced had largely contributed to the revival of the Catholic Church in the most developed countries in Europe. The Church should draw the obvious conclusions from this and henceforth turn to the 'people', which for him meant the bourgeois middle class. In that way it could best secure its freedom and resist the State's omnipotence.

This, remarkably, was also the essential objective of the ultramontanes, the opponents of liberal Catholics. Both movements in fact were striving for the same goal: to strengthen the autonomy of the Church, which implied resisting State omnipotence. But they differed in their strategies, largely because of their divergent concepts of freedom: the ultramontanes clung to a privileged freedom, while the liberal Catholics resolutely accepted general freedom.

The sweet fruits of freedom

The Catholic Church's struggle for independence was part of its traditional view on society, whose starting point was the understanding that Church and State were pursuing different objectives: the Church looked after the spiritual welfare of mankind and the State took care of the material side. On matters where the two overlapped, the Church claimed precedence over the State because of its higher nature and purpose. In their specific domains both powers were autonomous, but relied on mutual support and cooperation since they operated in the same society.[6] However, the perfect balance in Church-State relations was rarely achieved. Medieval theocracy had compromised the independence of the secular authority, while the later emergence of national principalities led to the Church being subordinated to the State. The spread of Protestantism furthered this development, as the principle of *cujus regio, eius religio* led to the emergence of Anglican, Lutheran and – to a lesser extent – Calvinist state churches under the supervision of their sovereign. The Catholic Church remained largely a supranational church and defended to the utmost

6   Lecler, *L'Eglise et la souveraineté de l'Etat*.

its autonomy from the authority of the State. In the struggle against Protestantism, the Holy See was for Catholics a visible sign of the Church's unity and a touchstone of orthodoxy. Furthermore, its opposition to internal deviant movements such as Jansenism reinforced the doctrinal and disciplinary authority of Rome over the local churches. However, the opposing forces put up a strong fight. Regalism appealed to absolute State sovereignty in order to keep the Catholic Church in a subordinate role and to loosen the ties between the national churches and Rome. Thus, in France, the main Catholic country, Gallicanism left little room for the claims of the Holy See.

The French Revolution of 1789 brought great changes.[7] It quickly turned against the clergy, one of the pillars of the *ancien régime*, and broke the religious monopoly of the Catholic Church by introducing religious freedom. It also put an end to its political and economic power and with the introduction of the *constitution civile du clergé* subjected it to strict state supervision. Fierce opposition to these measures led to an escalation and even to real persecution of the Church. In these difficult times, the Holy See became a refuge for the French Church. The Concordat of 1801 between Pius VII and Napoleon laid the basis for an organizational recovery. It subjected the Church to permanent State supervision, while at the same time allowing the Holy See a greater input. Shortly afterwards Napoleonic ecclesiastical policy led to new tensions with Rome. The French emperor went so far as to incorporate the Papal States into the French empire, thereby conferring a martyr's halo on the Pope and laying the foundations for a papal veneration that would characterize ultramontanism in the coming decades. The Pope emerged stronger from the revolution, and this not only in France. A decision by the Congress of Vienna led to his resuming possession of his principality in central Italy and becoming a modest player in the European Concert. Even more important was that he had in the meantime extended his influence over the local churches, and that he had become the main defender of their autonomy from State authority, which was being increasingly asserted and was often hostile to the Church.[8]

The prestige of the papacy also grew thanks to a remarkable religious revival, which was also evident on the Protestant side.[9] The destructive effects of the French Revolution, felt all across Europe in the wake of the Napoleonic wars, widely undermined belief in the rational principles to which the revolutionaries had appealed. Trusted frameworks and structures were destroyed or had lost their significance. In these circumstances religion offered many a safe haven, and for others it gave new meaning to their sense of identity. Conservatives saw in religion a support for the social order. The influence of Romanticism, with its preference for emotion, the subconscious and magical-mythical

---

7   Plongeron, ed., *Les défis de la modernité*, 301-478.
8   Gilley and Stanley, eds., *World Christianities c. 1815-c. 1914*, 13-29.
9   Atkin and Tallett, *Priests, Prelates and People*, 110-120; McLeod, *Religion and the People*; Plongeron, ed., *Les défis de la modernité*, 627-792.

powers, also had a significant impact. Belief was regarded as an autonomous, animating force, was brought openly into the public sphere and directed towards social activism.

The revolutionary period was followed by an explosion of religious energy which, remarkably enough, was more of a grassroots development. The dismantling of the ecclesiastical structures ensured that lay people increasingly came to the fore, including quite a number of women whose opportunities for social advancement had hardly been improved by the revolution. Religious brotherhoods and devotional associations flourished. An intense popular piety was expressed in a renewed veneration of the saints, in processions and in pilgrimages.[10] Many charitable organisations and new religious congregations were founded. In addition, the secular clergy restored parochial structures. The hierarchy within the Church was strengthened: parish priests were henceforth more subject to the bishops, who in turn came under stricter oversight by the papal curia. The curia succeeded in bringing the religious revival under its control and using it for its own purposes. Still, the revival was above all an affair of the people and the initiatives and structures it inspired had a more democratic character than those of the *ancien régime*.

As a matter of course, the Catholic revival had political consequences, especially in countries where constitutional reforms had been implemented and public opinion could exert pressure on policy. This happened first in countries where Catholics were a minority and were discriminated against by a Protestant majority. The political initiatives of Catholics had an emancipatory, democratic undertone, as was the case in Great Britain where Catholics were still denied access to public office. Daniel O'Connell's mobilization of the Catholic minority resulted in the passing of the Emancipation Bill in 1829. That example inspired their co-religionists in the United Kingdom of the Netherlands where the Catholic Church felt patronized by the predominantly Protestant government of William I. His policy, inspired by the German *Staatskirchentum*, evoked a fierce response from a Church that in the previous decades had already been evincing a strong desire for independence. A decade later it was the turn of the Rhineland where Catholics were resisting the church policy of Protestant Prussia.

Catholics then wanted to withdraw from State control and demanded greater freedom for their Church. In countries where they were a minority, they could not claim an exclusive freedom and could do nothing else but appeal to the general freedoms and – if necessary – push for their extension. In this way a rapprochement with the liberals took place, which was facilitated by the fact that liberalism in many countries in that period, under the influence of Romanticism, had been stripped of its Voltairean, anticlerical tenden-

10   Heimann, 'Catholic Revivalism in Worship and Devotion', 70-83.

cies. Thus the way was paved for a liberal Catholicism that would make use of modern liberties to bring about independence for the Church.[11]

France and the Southern Netherlands (today's Belgium) played a leading role in this development. In the latter region Catholics and liberals concluded a coalition in 1827 that would become known as 'unionism'. The unionists demanded the introduction of a regime of freedom. When William I's government refused to accede to that request, a revolution broke out in Brussels in September 1830 that led to the establishment of an independent Belgian State. Within a very short time a constituent assembly produced a liberal constitution, which awarded many liberties to the Church as part of a broad general freedom. Liberals and Catholics mutually agreed to a benevolent separation between Church and State. The Church was freed from all State supervision and made immediate use of this to strengthen its structures and expand its activities in the areas of education and charitable work. For most priests and leading Catholic politicians, cooperation with the liberals was a tactic that yielded the Church many benefits, although they did not in principle advocate modern freedoms. Many among the younger clergy and the Catholic bourgeoisie, however, went a step further, and confessed their hopes for a far-reaching reconciliation between the Church and liberalism, the consequences of which they were prepared to accept. They were influenced in their opinions by the Breton priest, Félicité de Lamennais, who from 1829 had propagated a consistent liberal Catholicism.[12]

In France, Catholicism was, in the words of the Concordat of 1801, 'the religion of the majority of the population'. So it was not from a minority position that an increasing number of Catholics there demanded greater freedom for the Church. The support of the Bourbon regime was assured, but in line with Gallican tradition, the government interfered constantly in ecclesiastical affairs. The objections to this were best expressed by the talented writer Lamennais. Nobody was as anti-Gallican, ultramontane and supportive of the Pope as he was. Nobody defended the Church with such fervour or upheld its rights against the State so resolutely. Nobody emphasized its supremacy so vehemently or insisted so urgently on the all-inclusive role it should play in society. He struggled more and more against the meddlesome church policy of the Bourbons and finally came to the conclusion that the cause of the Church had to be separated from that of the monarchy. An intense need for religious freedom drove him to the people, among whom the yearning for freedom was strongest. In his view, the monarchy had sacrificed religion in favour of its own interests, but the Church's freedom would be guaranteed by the people.

11   Schmidt and Schwaiger, eds., *Kirchen und Liberalismus im 19. Jht*; Gadille, ed., *Les catholiques libéraux au 19ᵉ siècle*.

12   Haag, *Les origines du catholicisme libéral en Belgique*; Lamberts, *Kerk en liberalisme in het bisdom Gent*.

The Church therefore had to enter into an alliance with political liberalism. From 1829 on, in a number of high-profile publications, Lamennais outlined these ideas, which were partly inspired by events in the Belgian region. He surrounded himself with young people like Montalembert and proclaimed his liberal Catholic ideas in a periodical with the expressive title *L'Avenir*, which also became well-known outside France. However, he met with far more opposition than acclaim. So, as a champion of the ultramontane case, he decided to call upon the Pope and travelled with some loyal followers to Rome to plead his case there. But, the moment was ill-chosen. The new pope, Gregory XVI, only just a few months into his pontificate, was facing a liberal revolt in the Papal States and was under strong pressure from the conservative courts on whom he depended for the restoration of his temporal power. He would not consider making an accommodation with revolutionary liberalism. In his first encyclical, *Mirari vos* (15 August 1832), he spoke out bluntly against the basic liberal principles and implicitly against Lamennais' ideas. He rejected the idea that the Church needed a spiritual rebirth. If it was in a deplorable condition, then that was due not to any internal weakness but to the machinations of its enemies. In order to resist these, the core principles of traditional papal teaching had to be implemented, namely the religious monopoly of the Church in Catholic countries and an alliance between throne and altar. The Pope put greater confidence in the princes than in the people. He did not want the Church to be assigned the role of guiding mankind towards liberal and social conquests. Catholics in Belgium wondered whether *Mirari vos* in fact condemned their new, liberal constitution. However, the bishops felt that the constitution belonged to the domain of positive law and offered the Church an acceptable compromise. Belgian liberal Catholics then withdrew behind their constitution, which seemed to offer sanctuary from papal censure.

Lamennais had great difficulty in submitting unconditionally to the encyclical. Almost imperceptibly he began to distance himself from the Church, spurred also by an inner religious crisis. In the end he chose to remain loyal to his political ideas. If the Church did not want to be a guide for mankind, then mankind had to build its future on its own. God's kingdom on earth, characterized by freedom, love and justice would be brought about by the victory of the people. He outlined this eschatological expectation in *Paroles d'un croyant*, which was published in April 1834. The literary qualities of this book and its democratic tenor ensured its rapid distribution. This time Rome hit back hard and in the encyclical *Singulari Nos* of 25 June 1834 the Pope explicitly condemned the ideas of Lamennais, who shortly thereafter broke definitively with the Church and moved more towards a humanitarian socialism. His young supporters were left disheartened. Most of them, like Montalembert, would not abandon their liberal Catholic beliefs but gave them a more pragmatic orientation.[13]

In Belgium the conservatives used the papal encyclicals to repress the democratic movement among the clergy. That was also the wish of the first Belgian king, Leopold I of Saxe-Coburg, who expected the Church to support his conservative policy. With the help of the papal nuncio in Brussels and of newly appointed conservative bishops, the clergy that sympathized with the ideas of Lamennais were forced into line in a heavy-handed manner, in what was a troubled, even tragic episode in the history of the Belgian Church. The liberal Catholic, democratizing movement lost momentum and increasingly the Church began to cooperate with conservative unionist governments.[14] As a consequence, the liberal bourgeoisie got the impression that unionism was becoming a cover for the power regained by the upper clergy and the aristocracy, and they started their own political party with an anticlerical programme. The party came to power in 1847 and made every effort to restore the independence of the State authority and reduce the political influence of the Church. Thus began a clerical-liberal confrontation that would mark Belgian politics for a long time. In order to defend itself against the liberal government's policies, the Church could fall back on its free status. In general, it remained faithful to the constitutional pact signed in 1831.

The free status that the Belgian Church had acquired was an inspiring model for Catholics in other countries. The slogan '*la liberté comme en Belgique*' ('freedom as in Belgium') was regularly to be heard not only in France but also in the Rhineland. Referring to Belgian education legislation, in 1837 Montalembert launched a campaign in France against the government's monopoly of secondary education. This awakened Catholic public opinion and led to the formation of an embryonic Catholic party, which at the end of the 1840s was able to exert pressure on government policy.

The temptations of power

Liberal Catholics, who continued to put their trust in freedom, felt heartened by the election of a reformist pope in June 1846. The previous pope, Gregory XVI, an austere Camaldolese monk, had pursued a conservative policy in unison with the European Concert. In the Papal States, he had refused to allow any form of popular participation, not even the involvement of lay people in the administration. High expectations arose immediately on the election of the

---

13 Derré, *Lamennais, ses amis*; Le Guillou, *L'évolution de la pensée religieuse de F. de Lamennais*. On Lamennais' influence over Belgian Catholics, see: Jürgensen, *Lamennais und die Gestaltung des Belgischen Staates*; Simon, *Rencontres mennaisiennes en Belgique*.

14 Haag, *Les droits de la cité*; Lamberts, *Kerk en liberalisme*, 154-266.

Pius IX. Lithograph, N. Maurin, 1848.
[Leuven, KADOC]

new pope, Giovanni Maria Mastai, who took the name Pius IX.[15] At 54 years of age, he was still relatively young. An amiable man with a warm personality and great charisma, he would be the most 'priestly' pope of the century. He felt that the Church should not accommodate itself too readily to political regimes. As Archbishop of Imola, he had gained a lot of pastoral though little political experience. He sympathized vaguely with the cause of Italian unification, was inclined to implement a number of necessary reforms in the Papal States, and even wanted to move towards introducing a constitutional regime. His election was enthusiastically received all over Europe and especially in Italy. Metternich for his part was aghast: 'A liberal pope: that was the last thing we could have foreseen!'

15   Aubert, *Le Pontificat de Pie IX (1846-1878)*; Martina, *Pio IX (1846-1878)*.

In the spring of 1848, *Pio Nono* was obliged to make a difficult choice. As already mentioned, a revolt against the Austrian government had broken out in Lombardy and Piedmont-Sardinia came to the aid of the insurgents. The Pope was under great pressure to support the Italian cause and to deploy his modest military force on the side of the Sardinian army. Eventually he decided against this because he considered that as head of a universal Church preaching peace and reconciliation, he could not take part in an offensive war, especially against a Christian nation. That decision cost him all credibility with the Italian nationalists. When a revolt broke out in Rome in November 1848, he narrowly managed to flee the city and found refuge in Gaeta, under the protection of the reactionary king of Naples. A republic led by Giuseppe Mazzini was then proclaimed in Rome, but an intervention by the great powers – primarily republican France – in July 1849 put an end to this regime and made possible the Pope's return. A French expeditionary corps would continue to guarantee the protection of his temporal power.

In April 1850 Pius IX returned to Rome. He had lost his 'liberal' image and was intent on not yielding an inch to those who invoked the revolution of 1789. From now on, his bitter experiences as a secular ruler would considerably influence his political and religious views. He distanced himself more and more from liberal Catholics, but still he did not become a mere copy of Gregory XVI, as many Romans feared. His warm personality made his administration bearable, and outside of Italy his prestige remained high. The alliance with the Catholic revival north of the Alps continued.[16] Catholic opinion already acted as a shield for the papacy, as its efficacious pressure on the French republican government had proved. Pius IX continued to put his trust in the Catholic people, which in his eyes was the carrier not so much of freedom as of religion.

Otherwise, Pius IX hardly engaged in political matters. During his pontificate, the policies of the Holy See, both on the domestic and foreign levels, were determined mainly by Cardinal Giacomo Antonelli, who had come to the fore during the exile in Gaeta and became secretary of state, the highest official in the curia.[17] He was a shrewd diplomat, but he lacked vision and failed to steer developments. Antonelli's policy consisted mainly of making compromises and buying time. He was a master at resolving minor problems and at toning down the bold statements of the Pope, who paid no heed to diplomatic language. Unlike Pius IX, the secretary of state had little confidence in the mo-

---

16   Horaist, *La dévotion au Pape*; Papenheim, 'Il pontificato di Pio IX e la mobilitazione dei cattolici', 137-146.

17   Aubert, *Le Pontificat de Pie IX*, 85: 'He was one of those prelates with a thoroughly lay outlook, for whom the interests of this world are more important than those of the other, but he joined an easy manner with a sincere faith (...). All his life he remained a parvenu, greedy for money, obsessed by the Italian idea of "creating a family" (...) and actually he left a nice fortune to his natural children.' On Antonelli (1806-1876), see: Falconi, *Il Cardinale Antonell*; Coppa, *Cardinal Giacomo Antonelli*.

bilization of the Catholic people and continued to rely more on governments. It remains a remarkable fact that these two totally different personalities worked together for more than a quarter of a century, a collaboration made possible solely by a clear division of labour between them. Moreover, Antonelli was able to create a vacuum around himself, which made him indispensable.

The Pope's primary goal was to strengthen the unity and resilience of the Church and erect a dam against the laicising culture of the time. In this regard, the proclamation of the dogma of the Immaculate Conception in 1854 was particularly important. That dogma held that the Blessed Virgin Mary, unlike the rest of humanity, had been born without original sin. By emphasizing the purity of Mary, the Pope wished to remind the modern world of original sin, and the need for penance and mercy. He also wanted to fight against the contemporary belief in human perfectibility. The new dogma was explicitly directed against rationalism and also against the elimination of religion from public life. It gave a strong impetus to Marian devotion, which would be practised on a massive scale in many places of pilgrimage, Lourdes being the most prominent example.[18]

There was a connection between the reference to original sin and the issue of religious freedom. Liberal Catholics were convinced that the truth and appeal of the faith were so great that it would prevail in a climate of freedom. Their opponents, by contrast, held the view that because of original sin, human beings were inclined to evil and had to be adequately supervised and supported in order to remain on the right path. They believed that the lower classes especially would remain Christian only if error and evil were kept in check with State support. This thinking was at the core of the ideology of the ultramontanes who promoted collaboration between Church and State. They explicitly followed the anti-liberal line of Pius IX and, unlike liberal Catholics, advocated a privileged freedom for the Church.[19] Moreover, the concept of general freedom had been discredited by the political uprisings and social unrest of 1848.

Nevertheless, Catholics had taken some advantage of the wave of revolutions in 1848. In the predominantly Calvinist Netherlands, following the example of Belgium, they made an alliance with the liberals and in a sweeping reform of the constitution were given a similar free status. In Prussia also, the Catholic Church acquired greater freedom through the constitution of 1850. Consequently, in his 1852 treatise *Des intérêts catholiques au XIX siè-*

18 Fiorentino, *La questione romana*, 55-60; Id., 'Dalle Stanze del Vaticano, 285-290.
19 Liberal Catholics were also 'ultramontanes' in the original sense of the term: proponents of an independent Church under papal leadership and thus opponents of regalism/Gallicanism. On ultramontanism, see: Weiss, 'Der Ultramontanismus', 821-877; Lamberts, ed., *De kruistocht tegen het liberalisme*, 11-63; Voisine and Hamelin, ed., *Les ultramontains canadiens-français*; Fleckenstein and Schmiedl, eds., *Ultramontanismus. Tendenzen der Forschung.*

cle, Montalembert could with good reason claim that the revival of religion in the previous decades had been mainly advanced by a regime of political freedom. He would further develop this position in his speech at Mechlin in 1863. He proclaimed similar views in the periodical *Le Correspondant*, from 1855 the mouthpiece of a liberal Catholicism that still found approval among the French Catholic intellectual and upper middle class, the Orleanist aristocracy and a minority of the episcopate.[20]

The vast majority of the ecclesiastical hierarchy and faithful in France, however, supported the authoritarian regime of Napoleon III, which treated the Church with great benevolence. The main spokesman of this anti-liberal, ultramontane movement was the above-mentioned journalist Louis Veuillot, a former ally of Montalembert.[21] Like many, he had changed direction after the 1848 revolution. He transformed the newspaper *L'Univers* into a tribune for a fiery, theocratic ultramontanism, and soon gained the explicit support of Pius IX. For Veuillot, liberal Catholicism was a 'deviation of the rich' who had lost touch with the people. He was a spokesman for the lower clergy especially and soon emerged as the most influential layman in France. He wrote in the vivid language of the people, but he was also an accomplished stylist and a sharp polemicist. For him, zeal was not compatible with either caution or moderation, and to make compromises was in fact to betray one's conscience.

In the late 1850s a sharp polemic broke out between *L'Univers* and *Le Correspondant*, and thanks to the prominent position of the French Church, it resonated widely internationally. Veuillot, a born fighter, spared none of his opponents, Montalembert least of all. In 1859 he would break with Napoleon III whose Italian policy, in his view, constituted a real threat to the Papal States. The government banned the further publication of *L'Univers*, but Veuillot then wrote several tracts relentlessly attacking his liberal Catholic opponents, which were widely distributed.

This was the background to Montalembert's two speeches at the Mechlin Congress of 1863. They were intended largely as a counterattack against the '*veuillotins*', who were also on the rise in Belgium, although the climate there for the time being remained favourable to liberal Catholics. Montalembert regarded these speeches as his political testament, but they subsequently proved to be more of an elegy for the liberal Catholicism of his time.

The Brussels nuncio immediately denounced Montalembert to Rome, as did the Italian delegation at the Mechlin Congress and some French bishops. It quickly became clear that a storm was brewing and a number of religious and political personalities in Belgium came to Montalembert's defence. Initially

---

20   Cattaneo, *Montalembert*; Finley, *The Liberal Who Failed [Montalembert]*; Kenny, 'The Correspondant', 243-260.

21   On Louis Veuillot (1813-1883), see: Brown, *Louis Veuillot*; Pierrard, *Louis Veuillot*; McMillan, 'Remaking Catholic Europe', 112-122.

Secretary of State Antonelli sent a reassuring response. The Roman Jesuit journal *La Civiltà Cattolica*, a major mouthpiece of the Holy See, also responded very moderately. In its commentary on modern freedoms, it introduced a distinction between *thesis* and *hypothesis* that would afterwards become quite famous. The thesis stated that modern freedoms were to be rejected in principle, and had been repeatedly condemned by successive popes. The hypothesis was that since they were enactments defined specifically by time and context, they could be accepted and used in the service of religion. According to the periodical, Montalembert had the tendency to overly praise these freedoms, but here he had been expressing a personal opinion which he had submitted to an eventual judgement of the magisterium.[22]

In October, pressure from French ultramontane circles mounted. It soon became clear that the Pope himself was deeply concerned about Montalembert's public stand and that he was not inclined to accept the principle of religious equality in Catholic countries. He hesitated for a long time to act against Montalembert because of his great merits and service to the Church. However, when the French count was so careless as to write a letter of self-justification to Antonelli, Rome was obliged to speak out. The Holy Office was commissioned to examine the speech and it was the consultor Luigi Bilio who was assigned the case.[23] He drew his inspiration from theologians of previous centuries to affirm that tolerance could only be permitted in order to prevent evil – for example political instability – or to obtain a greater good, but this should be allowed only temporarily and to a limited extent. He rejected the argument that the Church should once and for all dispense with calling on State power to support the truth. He recommended that Montalembert be condemned indirectly in a private letter from the Pope, advice that was followed. Papal censure was for Montalembert the most painful ordeal of his life, as he revealed in his reply, but he loyally submitted to the reprimand. This was not the end of his agony however. A continuing source of worry was the Pope's suggestion that a more public statement would soon follow on the issue of modern freedoms.

The idea of taking a firm stand against the many intellectual currents that threatened the Church had been discussed for some time in curial circles. The Pope himself became increasingly convinced that there was a close link between the principles of the French Revolution of 1789 and the destruction of religious and moral values. A list of errors to be condemned was already circulating in 1860 in the highest ecclesiastical circles. In June 1862 the Pope received advice on this from more than 300 bishops, but the affair leaked out and the plan to publish such a list was temporarily shelved. The Mechlin Congress of 1863 reactivated the issue. Rome was not happy either about

---

22 *La Civiltà Cattolica*, 17 Oct. 1863.
23 Martina, *Pio IX*, dl. II, 320-325; Martina, 'La confutazione di Luigi Bilio', 55-69; Id., 'Verso il Sillabo', 137-181; Ciampani, 'Un cardinale Barnabita', 353-358.

a theology congress organized in Munich by Ignaz von Döllinger in September 1863 in which the participating German theologians demanded freedom of research in all areas in which Church dogma was not at stake. Döllinger fought for freedom *within* the Church, while Montalembert stood up for the freedom *of* the Church by appealing to modern liberties. The position of the German theologians threatened to weaken the Church on the level of doctrine, precisely at a time when it was being forced to defend itself against external attacks. For their part, modern liberties gave free rein to the opponents of the Church, which in different countries was itself the victim of regalistic government measures that weakened its structures and limited its scope for action. A particularly painful development for the Pope was that the Sardinian secularizing laws of the 1850s were introduced at that time in those areas of the Papal States which at the end of 1860 had been annexed to the Kingdom of Italy. Those laws included the confiscation of Church property, the abolition of a large number of religious orders, the government's right to censor episcopal pastoral letters and to supervise private education and theological studies. Pius IX felt that the freedoms that had benefited many local churches north of the Alps were now being used by the liberals to implement a systematic policy of secularization.

In the summer of 1864, Bilio was charged with editing a comprehensive list of errors that was then thoroughly updated by a commission of cardinals. He was also asked to draft an accompanying encyclical. On 8 December 1864, ten years after the proclamation of the dogma of the Immaculate Conception, the encyclical *Quanta Cura* was published with the *Syllabus Errorum* attached.[24] The *Syllabus*, in particular, with its list of eighty errors, caused a great sensation, if not consternation. It was the most controversial papal document of the nineteenth century, and remained so even well into the twentieth century. It did not contain any new position: the errors formulated were taken from former papal documents and speeches, thus giving a good picture of the positions taken by the Pope in the previous eighteen years. The fact that they were brought together in a catalogue had an enormous impact. Their short and concise wording, separated from the context of the original document, left little room for nuance and had a provocative effect. This is best reflected in the final proposition, which seems to capture the whole tenor of the *Syllabus*: it declares that 'the Roman Pontiff cannot reconcile himself and come to terms with progress, liberalism and modern civilization'. Thus the impression was created that the Church was firmly placing itself outside modernity. The passage in question was taken from a speech of March 1861 in which Pius IX had vehemently protested against the anticlerical measures of the new Italian

---

24   On the history and impact of the *Syllabus Errorum*, see Martina, *Pio IX*, dl. II, 287-356; Christophe and Minnerath, *Le Syllabus de Pie IX*; Martina, 'L'Eglise, la société moderne et les droits de l'homme', 595-612.

government. He declared that he could not reconcile himself with progress, liberalism and modern civilization when they ran counter to the faith and trampled on the rights of the Church. However, the general public was not interested in those nuances. Neither Bilio, nor the Pope, nor any cardinal had realized that this last proposition was dynamite and indicated that the Papacy was out of touch with the world, to say the least.

Most public attention focused on the propositions condemning liberalism. In fact many more 'errors' were linked to naturalism and rationalism, which affected belief in God. Even more propositions again defended the freedom of the Church against the State and were directed against Gallican and regalistic views. So the *Syllabus* rejected the omnipotence of the State, stressing that its authority was not unlimited, that it was subject to morality and that its duty was to pursue a just ordering of society. The State also had to respect the autonomy of the Church, since it was a perfect society and should have all the means necessary to achieve its own goals.[25] According to a German formulation, the Church was a *vorstaatliche* (or pre-state) entity and should not be subordinated to any civil authority in fulfilling its spiritual mission.[26] Several propositions in the *Syllabus* were directed against the liberal governments in Europe and South America that saw the State as the only source of law, and therefore wanted to control the Church's activities. The document also defended the temporal power of the Pope as a guarantee of his spiritual independence as leader of the world Church.

Considerable attention was paid to the issue of freedom of conscience. This was not explicitly condemned in the *Syllabus*, but it was repudiated in the encyclical *Quanta Cura*, which took over the terminology of Gregory XVI in *Mirari vos* (1832). The doctrine pointed out that the Church and political authorities could adopt a tolerant attitude towards non-Catholics, but could not give them the same rights. In countries with a Catholic tradition, the State had to give the Church a public status and provide legal protection for the moral norms taught by the Church. At that time most Protestant and Orthodox countries applied similar principles and the confessional State remained a reality, although it came under growing pressure. The papal magisterium distrusted the subjective rights of the individual which were considered to be a source of religious indifference. Only a few referred to the dignity of the human person as the foundation of a Christian justification of freedom of conscience.[27] That line of thinking would a hundred years later form the basis of *Dignitas Humanae*, the solemn declaration on religious freedom issued during the Second Vatican Council (1965).

---

25 Van Megen, *The Concept of Perfect Society*.
26 Christophe and Minnerath, *Le Syllabus*, 90-98.
27 That was the case for example with Mgr. Henri Maret, dean of the Theology Faculty at the Sorbonne, who belonged to the moderate Gallican camp.

The major problem in Church-State relations at the time was that both powers kept each other in a stranglehold. The Church, which had gained in strength with the religious revival, did everything it could to free itself from the state custody to which it had been subjected in previous centuries, but at the same time it did not want to break off links completely with the State. So it pursued a maximalist programme: it requested both freedom and protection. Conservative governments were prepared to offer it some protection, but in exchange demanded some form of state supervision. Liberally influenced governments, on the other hand, were not inclined to give the Church any form of protection but they also begrudged it complete freedom, fearing its anti-liberal approach and its counter-revolutionary potential. The liberal bourgeoisie increasingly used the State as an instrument for their own advantage, and had the uneasy feeling that the Church, which could still count on broad popular support, was an impediment to their absolute domination. They therefore wanted to continue using the power of the State against the Church. So, the Church still had the ambition of laying its hands on the State, and vice versa. This stalemate could only be broken when Church and State were prepared to let go of one another, whereby the Church would relinquish state aid and the State would recognize the Church's freedom of action. Montalembert made a case for this at the Mechlin Congress of 1863, but he was rebuked by the encyclical *Quanta Cura*. Even most liberals were unwilling at the time to support his views, views whose time would come only in the second half of the twentieth century.

For now, that point had not yet been reached. The unnuanced formulations of the *Syllabus* and especially of the last proposition caused a huge stir. In France the government forbade the bishops to distribute the Pope's texts, even though most of his statements were directed against the situation in Italy, Germany and Latin America. Only one government, that of Queen Isabella of Spain – the most maligned of governments – openly expressed its consent. Liberal Catholics were distraught. They read the papal documents as condemning every form of liberalism and offering a doctrinal justification of radical ultramontanism. A mood of triumph prevailed in the latter camp, whereas many moderate clerics and lay people were devastated.

The situation was saved by Monsignor Dupanloup, Bishop of Orléans. He added an interpretation of the *Syllabus* to a tract he had written defending the temporal power of the pope, in which he put the most contentious propositions in their documentary context and explained the nuances. With regard to modern freedoms, he went back to the distinction between thesis and hypothesis already formulated in the *Civiltà Cattolica*, which justified the practical acceptance of those freedoms. The tract was instantly a huge success: in just a few weeks, hundreds of thousands of copies were sold. More than 600 bishops from around the world expressed their agreement with the views of the Bishop of Orléans. Even the Pope, shocked by the stormy reaction to his encyclical and the *Syllabus,* was relieved and at the beginning of February 1865 sent Dupanloup a letter of approval.[28]

For liberal Catholics what could be saved had been saved, but it was clear that the ultramontanes had the upper hand. The *Syllabus* was immediately interpreted in a flexible manner, but still it gave expression to the obdurate mentality that dominated in the curia and that was fully supported by Pius IX. The Church had equipped itself for the struggle against the *Zeitgeist* and against the modern State. Some Catholics would also literally take up arms and enter the fray in support of the papacy.

The Pope's crusaders

This study has repeatedly emphasized the important role played by the *Risorgimento* and the unification of Italy in the shifts in international politics and the orientation of Church policy. The Papal States, which originally included Lazio, Umbria, the Marches, Abruzzi and Romagna, had become simply an insurmountable obstacle in completing Italian unification. Once the Kingdom of Piedmont-Sardinia took over the leadership of the *Risorgimento*, the annexation of the Papal States and especially of Rome, with its great symbolic value, seemed almost inevitable.

Pius IX, however, was not prepared to give up his temporal power for various reasons. First, the papacy had legitimate rights in that region, which his predecessors had governed almost continuously since 756. A second, much more important consideration was that the Pope's political autonomy was a guarantee for his spiritual independence. In addition, Pius IX had little faith in the Sardinian government which had carried out a marked anticlerical policy in the 1850s. A final factor was that the Papal States supplied a large part of the income necessary for the governance of the universal Church, although that argument paled in significance when the most prosperous region, the Romagna, fell to Piedmont-Sardinia in 1859. On the other hand, the exercise of secular power saddled the papacy with major problems. Modernizing and laicizing the administration proved to be a difficult task in this priestly state, which was increasingly perceived as an anachronism. Moreover, the *monsignori* responsible for the administration were too involved in worldly affairs, the most striking example being the secretary of state, Antonelli, the highest administrator after the Pope. Finally, the struggle for the survival of this State threw too dark a shadow over Church policy.

---

28 Félix-Antoine Dupanloup (1802-1878) was Bishop of Orléans from 1849. O'Connell, 'Ultramontanism and Dupanloup. The Compromise of 1865', 200-217; Martina, *Pio IX*, II, 349-356; Aubert, *Le Pontificat de Pie IX*, 254-260.

Still, Pius IX received massive support from the faithful throughout the world for the defense of his temporal power. Under his immediate predecessors, the great powers had helped maintain the Papal States, based primarily on the principle of legitimacy. Since the flight of Pius IX to Gaeta in late 1848, the role of international Catholic opinion had become more important. Catholics were mobilized in support of the ousted Pope, and in France this proved so successful that the republican government was persuaded to send an expeditionary corps to Rome to restore the Pope's authority. Austria, Bavaria and Naples also intervened, but it was the French who, pressured by Catholic opinion, now offered the most effective protection for the survival of the papacy's temporal power. Anti-liberal Catholics regarded the Pope as a victim of the revolution and defended his legitimate rights while liberal Catholics also took up his cause, convinced that his temporal power was an essential guarantee of his spiritual autonomy.[29]

With the loss of Romagna in 1859, the papal finances, already burdened by large debts, were threatened with major problems. As a result, on the initiative of the Catholic laity in North Western Europe, Peter's Pence was reintroduced. The faithful from around the world were asked to contribute financially to the maintenance of the pope's temporal power and to the financing of the universal Church. National, regional and local committees were formed in many countries for the collection of donations. Most contributions were modest and for that reason were called *das Scherflein der Armen* ('the mites of the poor') in German-speaking regions. The gifts were seen as a public act of devotion and faith and formed a solid basis for the defense of the papacy. In the 1860s they covered almost a quarter of the state budget.[30] More well-endowed donors subscribed to papal loans, which were issued regularly up until 1866. Moreover, the Pope received additional donations from national churches on the occasion of major religious celebrations and events in Rome, so that bankruptcy could be avoided.[31]

Rising expenditure on the military put further pressure on the papal budget. That the Pope could no longer count on the great powers to protect his temporal power had gradually become obvious. So, in order to ensure a minimum state of preparedness, the papal administration decided to reorganize and strengthen the military, which at that point was almost non-existent. The task was entrusted to a Belgian prelate from an upper aristocractic background, Xavier de Mérode, a brother-in-law of Montalembert.[32] Before embarking on an ecclesiastical career, as a French army officer de Mérode had

---

29 Viaene, 'Catholic Mobilisation', 135-143.
30 Donations came mainly from France (40 %), Belgium (10 %), Italy (10 %) and the Netherlands (6 %).
31 Klieber, 'Geld und Soldaten für den bedrängten "Papst-König"', 65-122; Pollard, *Money and the Rise of the Modern Papacy*, 21-45.
32 On Xavier de Mérode (1820-1887), see Martin, 'Pie IX et Mgr de Mérode', 3-27.

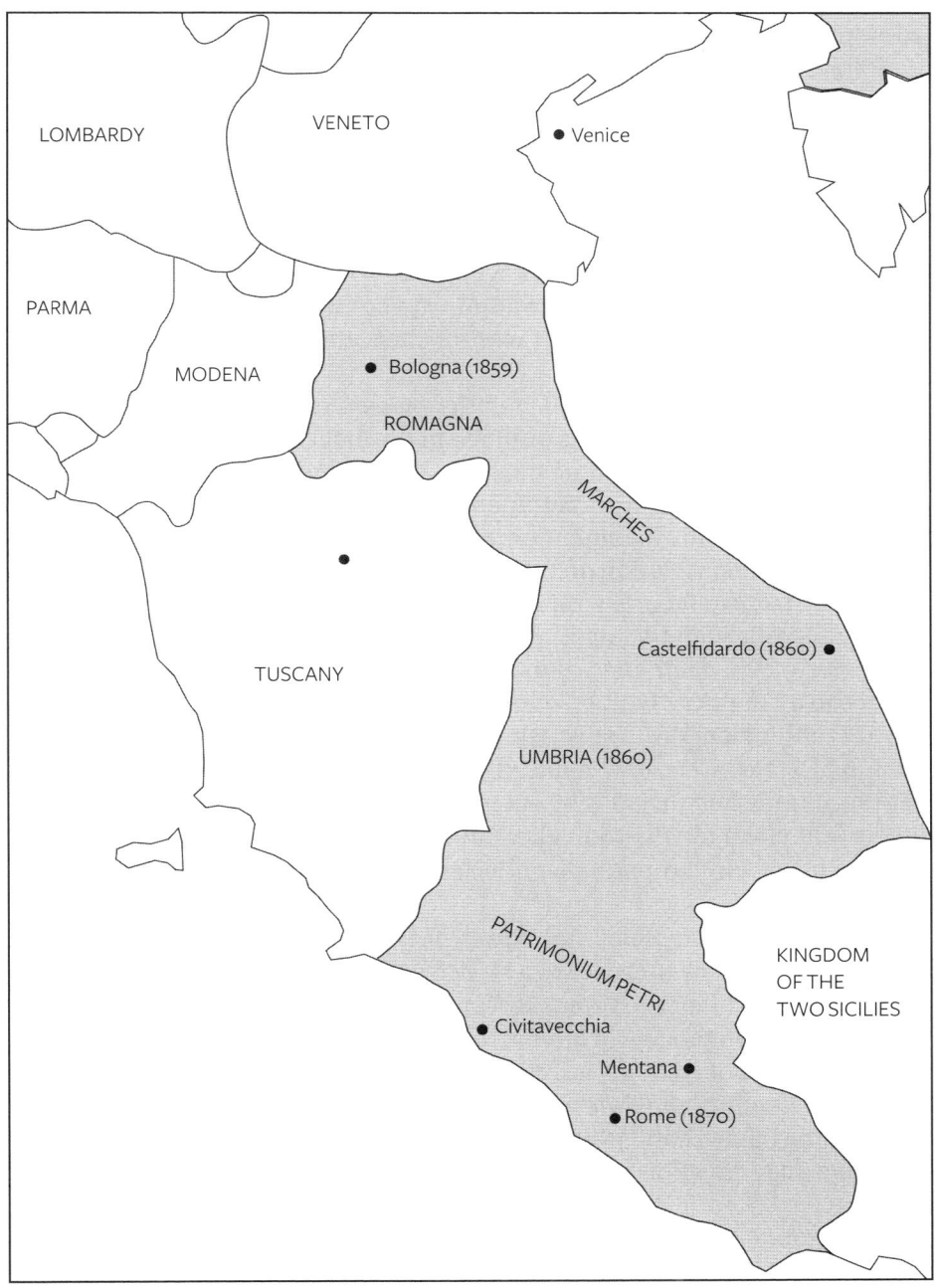

Papal States (1859-1870).

participated in several campaigns in Algeria and thus had more knowledge of military affairs than the other Roman *monsignori*. The Pope promptly appointed him minister of war. At the same time he entrusted the French general Christophe Lamoricière with the supreme command of the papal forces. Since the residents of the Papal States were not enthusiastic about the possibility of conscription, volunteers were invited to fill out the ranks.[33] A Franco-Belgian battalion, soon to be joined by Dutch volunteers, formed the kernel of the new corps. Remarkably, the Francophones in the battalion included many legitimist aristocrats whose motivation was not only religious but political: the sacred authority of the pope was for them the ultimate consecration of legitimacy.

The papal army was still only in the process of being reorganized when its mettle was put to the test. As outlined in the first chapter, Garibaldi and his Redshirts invaded the Kingdom of Naples in the spring of 1860, and pushed through in a northerly direction, upon which the Piedmontese army invaded the Papal States with the intention of cutting off the *condottiere*. The papal army opposed this violation of its territory and on 18 September 1860 engaged in battle near Castelfidardo with a force that was six times stronger. Two thirds of the Franco-Belgian battalion were killed. When a Piedmontese general saw the names of the dead and wounded, he remarked, 'this looks like a list of invitees to a Louis XIV ball'.[34] Following this defeat, the Marches and Umbria joined the Kingdom of Italy, which was officially proclaimed on March 14th. The Papal States were now reduced to Lazio, the region around Rome, and were surrounded on all sides by enemy territory. The Kingdom of Italy immediately laid claim to what remained of the papal territories and on 27 March 1861 the newly elected parliament declared that Rome, finally, was to be the capital of Italy.

From now on the temporal power of the pope came under very severe pressure and only the presence of a French expeditionary corps, funded by the papal treasury, still offered some form of protection. Napoleon III had set the Italian unification process in motion, but he could no longer afford to alienate the leading Catholic circles in France from his regime and so felt obliged to continue defending the *Patrimonium Petri*. In addition, the continuing mobilization of the Catholic people remained necessary. The papal administration intensified its efforts to collect Peter's Pence and recruit volunteers for the army.

De Mérode returned the Franco-Belgian battalion to its former numerical strength and indeed even expanded it. The volunteers were henceforth called

33 On the papal volunteer army, which has been extensively covered in the literature, see: Guenel, *La dernière guerre du pape*; Sawallich, *Die Geschichte der päpstlichen Armee*; Raggi, *La nona crociata*; Coltrinari and Trogu, 'Atanasio de Charrette' 72-92; Zaal, *De vuist van de paus*.

34 Guenel, *La dernière guerre*, 35.

'Zouaves', a reference to their new uniform, which was borrowed from that of an Algerian combat unit founded by Lamoricière. However, in the succeeding years, the Zouaves did not have much to do and essentially led a monotonous garrison life. Their military activity was limited to combatting the many bandit gangs that plagued the countryside around Rome, while the French expeditionary corps guarded the country's borders. Mgr. de Mérode failed to shape a coherent strategic plan for the army and would eventually be forced to resign by his rival, Antonelli. In fact, Rome had no ideas about a future direction for the papal army.

The September Convention of 1864, which was concluded between France and Italy, changed this. According to this agreement, the Italian government promised not to attack the *Patrimonium Petri* and to make every effort to thwart attempts in that direction by third parties – clearly Garibaldi was being referred to here. It would also take over the debts of the territories that had been taken from the Papal States. Under these conditions, France would withdraw its troops within a period of two years.[35] This Convention aroused consternation in Rome and in the Catholic world. It had been concluded without the knowledge of the Pope, who was still the main stakeholder. The dominant feeling was that Napoleon III was no longer willing to protect the temporal power of the papacy. Nobody attached any credence to the assurances of the Italian government; the expectation was that under the pretence of restoring order, it would take the first opportunity to hide once again behind the actions of revolutionary radicals like Garibaldi, and would then proceed to annexation.

The Convention ensured that the papal army was further strengthened. It was placed under the leadership of the Swiss general Hermann Kanzler and the recruitment of volunteers was accelerated. The number of Zouaves increased from 500 in 1864 to 2,500 in 1867, with the Franco-Belgian battalion still constituting the core of the force. The total papal army then included about 13,000 troops, among whom were the 1,000 soldiers of the so-called *légion d'Antibes* who were recruited in France with the consent of Napoleon III and signalled his continuing involvement in the papal cause. This unit, also known as the 'Roman legion', was fully integrated into the papal army, unlike the expeditionary force of 8,000 men that, as had been agreed with the Italian government, left Roman territory in late 1866.

Once the French troops had withdrawn, the dreaded expectations were realized. The Italian government came increasingly under pressure and had to deal with the challenge posed by anti-monarchist extremists. It tried to come to a compromise with the Pope, but he resolutely continued to refuse any discussion of his secular power. In the autumn of 1867 Garibaldi began to make a move, under the slogan '*Roma o morte*'. He called for an uprising in Rome

35 Milza, *Napoléon III*, 508.

and recruited volunteers to attack the *Patrimonium Petri*. Since the *condottiere* had public opinion behind him, the Italian government could do little and informed Napoleon III that it felt obliged to occupy the *Patrimonium Petri*. The French emperor made clear that he would intervene in that case and immediately sent a new expeditionary army to Rome. Garibaldi then tried to provoke an uprising before the French troops arrived, but he failed miserably.

On October 23rd, Garibaldi took over the command of his volunteer army, which, like the Zouaves corps, had an international composition. As in the Spanish Civil War seventy years later, two multinational armies, each with a pronounced ideological motivation, faced off against each other. Instead of marching immediately on Rome, Garibaldi decided to first take the border town of Monte Rotondo. That took more effort than expected, giving the French troops time to disembark in Civitavecchia. Rome was now out of danger, but General Kanzler wanted to use the situation to deal definitively with Garibaldi's troops. On 3 November 1867, with the backing of the French expeditionary force, he engaged them in battle near the village of Mentana, and inflicted heavy losses on them. This signalled the end of Garibaldi's revolutionary career. He would not be able to claim credit for the conquest of Rome, although he undoubtedly made a major contribution to Italian unification.

The papal army's victory in Mentana was the antipode of the defeat at Castelfidardo. This victory had proved the usefulness of the Zouave army which, with the help of the well-trained French expeditionary army, armed with the most modern rifles, had been able to combat irregulars and brigands. An attack by the Italian army was not to be expected as long as the French government continued to provide guarantees for the survival of the *Patrimonium Petri*. Provided the European political situation did not radically change, the Pope would likely be able to maintain his position for some time. That demanded considerable expenditure on military spending, which from 1867 swallowed up almost half the annual budget.

After the boost at Mentana, the papal committees in many countries stepped up their activities. The composition of the Zouaves corps became increasingly international and at the end included volunteers from twenty-five countries, with remarkably strong contingents from France, the Netherlands, Belgium, Ireland and Canada. Their weaponry was improved with war material from English and Belgian arms factories, which the national papal committees arranged to provide. They also stepped up their efforts for Peter's Pence.

Through the papal committees more and more prominent Catholic lay people descended on Rome. They built up relationships in curial circles and came into contact with each other. Most of them were convinced ultramontanes and many had legitimist sympathies. Thus a basis was created for international collaboration between prominent laymen who for various reasons associated themselves with the papal cause and wanted to devote their efforts to it.[36] One of them was Blome, who in November 1868 had settled with his family in the Palazzo Simonetti in Rome. He had already become involved in the activities of the *St. Michaelsbruderschaft*, such as recruiting Zouaves and fundraising for the Holy See. When he moved to Rome, he became an important point of contact for the leading figures in the papal committees in Austria.[37]

However, Blome became primarily involved in 'high politics'. In the spring and summer of 1869 he travelled throughout Europe and made contacts in various countries with church and political leaders.[38] In settling practical matters, such as recruiting Zouaves and fundraising, he could call on the services of Count Anton Pergen, who will play a prominent role in the later stages of this story. He was ten years younger than Blome and became virtually his *alter ego*.[39] He came from an old Lower Austrian family and had received a military training. He was a military attache in the Austrian embassy in Bavaria during the ambassadorship of Blome, whom he admired greatly and whose political and religious ideas he shared. On becoming embassy secretary in Rome in 1867, he volunteered to be the contact person for the *St. Michaelsbruderschaft*.

Because of his support for the Pope and his close relationship with Blome, Pergen ran into difficulties with Beust and in September 1868 resigned as a diplomat. That was not very difficult for him because he – like Blome – could not give his assent to the anticlerical policy of the new Austrian government. In January 1869 he went to live as a private individual in Rome, and joined Blome's entourage, acting as an intermediary between General Kanzler and the *St. Michaelsbruderschaft*. He was also involved in Blome's network and gained access to the highest ecclesiastical circles. Through his chivalrous attitude, his warm and charming personality, his commitment and dedication, he succeeded in winning over Pius IX and even Antonelli. His decision to devote the rest of his life to the papal cause was motivated primarily by religious considerations, whereas in Blome's case, political considerations were also significant, as was even more true of the legitimists who took part in the crusade against liberalism.

---

36 Viaene, 'Catholic Mobilisation', 150-156.
37 Klieber, 'Solidaraktionen österreichischer Katholiken', 653-679.
38 Information about his activities during this period comes from fragments of his *Journal*, Gut Salzau, V. Notes were kept for the period from 5 November 1867 to 25 October 1868 and from 30 October 1869 to 12 June 1870.
39 On Anton Pergen (1839-1902), see: Weinzierl-Fischer, 'Aus den Anfängen der christlichsozialen Bewegung in Österreich', 468-486; Bled, 'Les correspondants français du comte Pergen', 1-8. His extensive archive, which is preserved in the state archives in Vienna, forms an important source for this book. (HHSA, *Pergen*). Information about his stay in Rome in 1867-1870 comes primarily from his correspondence with the Austrian diplomat Palomba and with Eduard Stillfried, chairman of the *St. Michaelsbruderschaft*. Blome's diary also includes a number of details in this regard.

The legitimists in the ranks

French legitimism, the political movement that remained loyal to the Bourbon monarchy, seemed an anachronistic and, at best, a nostalgic affair in a society in the throes of industrialization and urbanization. During the Second Empire of Napoleon III the legitimists were politically marginalized in the beginning, but their following grew as the Emperor's popularity declined and as they adjusted their programme and strategy.

The legitimists supported the claims to the throne of Henri d'Artois, Count of Chambord (1820-1883) who, as Henry V, was for them the legitimate king of France. He had lived in exile since 1830 and after a while settled in Frohsdorf, in the vicinity of Vienna. There Chambord presided over a small court and kept in touch with his supporters in the French provinces. Indeed, it was not so much in Paris, but in rural areas such as Brittany, Anjou and the small towns of the Languedoc that the legitimists still had a large following, especially among the local aristocracy and the *vieille et bonne bourgeoisie*. In the first years of the reign of Louis-Philippe they still dreamed of a counter-revolution, but after 1832 they opted for constitutional opposition. They gradually strengthened their position at the local level, rejuvenated their constituency and adjusted their programme, becoming advocates of a representative, decentralized and social monarchy.[40]

Under the Second Republic the legitimists leaned towards the *parti de l'ordre*. Like Louis de Pons, many of them were subsequently happy with the authoritarian rule of Napoleon III which provided the stability they desired, and they had fewer problems with the regime than the Orleanists, who supported a liberal constitutional monarchy. Chambord, their pretender, was in favour of a strong monarchy that would not be subordinate to parliament.[41] However, he was not a supporter of royal absolutism. He developed an organic vision of society that respected both the traditional freedoms and intermediate bodies, and he favoured decentralization. His growing interest in the social question was also remarkable. He was very sensitive to the social implications of industrialization and to the increasing poverty of the working class. That reconciliation with the Orleanists was not forthcoming had to do not only with dynastic interests but also with a different vision of society: legitimism was less liberal than Orleanism, socially as well as politically.

The legitimists not only turned against the centralized State, they were also prepared to abandon the Gallican tradition and give more latitude to the Church. From about 1860 onwards, the so-called clerico-legitimists came to the fore. They were mainly middle class and joined the movement, often un-

40 de Changy, *Le mouvement légitimiste sous la Monarchie de Juillet*; Multon, 'Géographies et mémoires', 129-144.
41 Bled, *Le Lys en exil*, 205-218.

der clerical influence.[42] Indeed, it was noteworthy that Chambord himself became politically active only after the Italian war of 1859. He then urged his supporters to join the papal army. Many of them died at Castelfidardo, and that defeat intensified their dissatisfaction with the policy of Napoleon III who had abandoned the Pope at such a crucial moment. From then on they rallied unconditionally to the side of the Church and started an active campaign against the empire. In December 1866 Chambord published a manifesto in which he described the papal cause as being of vital importance for society and freedom, and he promised that the Church would enjoy wide autonomy under his administration.

The legitimists then ceased striving for the restoration of the *ancien régime*. For them, noble titles and privileges were not relevant any more; the ruling classes had to derive their moral authority from education and virtue, not from birth and wealth. A new aristocracy, with the requisite social and moral leadership qualities, had to control the anarchic passions of the masses. This came increasingly to be perceived as an urgent imperative because of the growing social unrest in the country, which indeed would soon erupt. The legitimists turned not only against egalitarianism, but also individualism. They dedicated their energies to establishing and strengthening intermediary collective structures, such as professional associations, production cooperatives and mutual aid societies. They also felt that society could not be saved without defending the social and political power of the Church. A Christian social order had to come about that would resist individualism, bridge class antagonisms and slow down social disintegration. These views would exert an undeniable influence in the long term.[43]

A very colourful figure among the clerico-legitimists was Count Paul de Bréda.[44] Initially a diplomat, he held posts in Washington DC, Darmstadt, Rio de Janeiro and Constantinople successively. This experience gave him a thorough knowledge of world politics and an extensive knowledge of languages. Around 1866 he resigned from active service because – in his own words – he encountered too much opposition due to his legitimist and ultramontane views.[45] He came from an impoverished aristocratic family and, too poor to survive without a regular income, he opted for a career in journalism in order to earn a living. He had the requisite skills – he was a good writer and was well-trained in many areas – but in fact it was an occupation beneath the level of his abilities. At that time, the social standing of journalists, with a few exceptions, was not very high. When Louis Veuillot got permission from

42 Kale, *Legitimism*, 19-44.
43 Kale, *Legitimism*, 89-110; Locke, *French Legitimists*, 140-180.
44 On Paul de Bréda (1830-1891), see: Bacht, 'Ein verschollenes Tagebuch', 397; Knoll, *Der soziale Gedanke im modernen Katholizismus*, 110-111 and 114-115. See also the analysis by Georges Goyau, *infra*, 268 n56.
45 Bréda to Cramer, 7 May and 12 June 1871, NKDC, *Cramer*, 434, 12 a, III.

the government in 1867 to restart *L'Univers*, Bréda, who had bought a modest country house in Dornbirn (Vorarlberg), offered his services as a correspondent for Germany and Austria. His contributions, which appeared under the pseudonym 'Agréval', very quickly garnered high praise from Veuillot. It was probably through his participation in *L'Univers* that Bréda first came into contact with Blome. The two former diplomats, who were almost contemporaries, with similar views and careers, immediately struck up a friendship. Although Bréda's social standing was much lower than Blome's, his intellectual prowess made up for this. Very soon Blome invited the *Dornbirnien*, as Bréda would frequently be called by his friends, to air his views in *L'Univers* and especially his criticism of the state of affairs in Austria.

Besides journalism, Bréda looked for a supplementary source of income and, at the same time, another outlet for his energy. In several instances, he acted as an agent for Chambord, thereby earning an occasional financial perk. In late 1868 he became involved in some of the pretender's business transactions. At his request, he also lent a helping hand to the Carlists who were attempting to seize power in Spain. These operations brought him into contact with the Dutch financier Jan Willem Cramer, another colourful character who will play an important role later in this story.

The history of Carlism fits perfectly with that of French legitimism because these two movements not only had a similar ideology but also strove to restore a Bourbon descendant to the Spanish and the French thrones respectively.[46] After the Napoleonic era the Spanish Bourbons were brought back to power. They managed to survive longer than their French relatives, though not because they were excellent rulers; in fact, they acted despotically, became embroiled in unsavoury financial scandals or led dissolute lives. The latter was especially true of Queen Isabella, who was a notorious nymphomaniac, but she compensated for this by displaying a deep devotion. Dissatisfaction with her policy eventually became so great that in September 1868 the army declared a *pronunciamento* and expelled her from the throne. Spain now had to look for a new king. A constitutional *Cortes*, with a progressive and liberal majority, opted for a moderate monarchy and went in search of a democratic king. According to Juan Prim, the central figure in the provisional government, this was equivalent to a 'search for an atheist in heaven'. Parliament excluded the Bourbons from the throne, thereby also cutting off the Carlist branch of the family which had already claimed the throne at gunpoint in the 1830s. The Carlists, named after the former pretender Don Carlos, were very traditionalist and 'apostolic', and even more conservative than the French legitimists.[47] Following the expulsion of Isabella, they again laid claim to the throne and

46   Dumons and Multon, ed., *"Blancs" et contre-révolutionnaires*.
47   Holt, *The Carlist Wars in Spain*, 225-245; Callahan, *Church, Politics and Society in Spain*, 196-208 and 248-278.

had an attractive candidate in the youthful Don Carlos, the grandson of the last pretender.

However, because of the power relations within the *Cortes*, constitutional opposition could offer little relief for them in the short term. In any case, following a long tradition, insurrection came to mind more readily in Spain than in other European countries. The Carlists wanted to take advantage of the power vacuum and began to prepare for a coup that would bring Carlos VII on the throne, but they first had to find the necessary financial resources. Jewish bankers, such as the Rothschilds, showed no interest and talks with British bankers, who initially seemed somewhat more obliging, failed. So, they ended up with the Belgian financier Langrand-Dumonceau, who called himself the Napoleon of the European financial system. One of his business partners, the Dutch banker Jan Willem Cramer, made a strong case that he could provide the Carlists with a loan of thirty million francs [126 million euros], with in addition a commission of five million francs [21 million euros] for himself. Cramer had been keeping up contact for a long time with Chambord, who was also entangled in Langrand-Dumonceau's web. Through the French pretender, he met Bréda whose political experience, linguistic skills and familiarity with legitimist circles led Cramer to recruit him as a fundraiser for the Carlists. Bréda was certainly not immune to the financial aspect of the agreement, although he claimed that he, like Cramer, was primarily driven by a passion for the cause of the monarchy and the Church.[48] High ideals demurely veiled greed, in one out of dire necessity, and in the other from habit.

The collaboration between Cramer and Bréda would become very intense and would prove sustainable. They soon would shift their attention to other areas. Though they came from different backgrounds, their ideas were largely similar and above all they shared certain characteristics: a vigorous dynamism, a lack of realism and a pronounced tendency to overestimate themselves. We have detailed information about their relationship because Cramer, who as a businessman had a well-equipped secretariat at his disposal, kept his documents carefully and had what for that time was an ingenious system for copying his outgoing letters.

The correspondence between Cramer and Bréda provides a good insight into the campaign for raising a loan for the Carlists, which had Chambord's moral support.[49] It exposes in an interesting way the twilight world between politics and finance. As a matter of course, the pair first went in search of funds in legitimist circles. Bréda also traveled to England, where he attempted to win over prominent churchmen, and in France, he launched a campaign in the Catholic press. He also maintained frequent contacts with Don Carlos

---

48 Bréda to Cramer, 1 April 1869, NKDC, *Cramer*, 434, 12 a, I.
49 Letters from Bréda to Cramer, in NKDC, *Cramer*, 434, 12 a, I and II; letters from Cramer to Bréda, in NKDC, *Cramer*, 14, 1.

himself who was then living in Paris, occasionally providing him with political advice. However, the fundraising met with little success. Initial encouraging responses repeatedly came to nothing, and in the end, only a sum of 200,000 francs [840,000 euros] was collected. The same amount was donated to Don Carlos by an uncle, the Duke of Modena, and the pledge of the jewelry of his wife Margarita generated another 100,000 francs [420,000 euros]. With these meagre resources, he launched the uprising, which his advisers believed could no longer be delayed. In late July 1869, together with some loyal followers, he went to Spain, there to take up the leadership of the rebel movement. In Catalonia, Navarre and the Basque country, the Carlists launched a number of uncoordinated actions, but they quickly fizzled out. At one stage Cramer was instructed to send a steam boat with weapons from Liège to the north of Spain, but presumably nothing came of this because by the beginning of September the insurgents were already drifting away. Don Carlos retreated to the Geneva region. In the succeeding years, his supporters restricted themselves to constitutional parliamentary opposition. In the summer of 1870, the succession to the Spanish throne would give rise to the Franco-Prussian War. Finally, in January 1871 the crown was offered to Amadeo, the second son of the Italian King Vittorio Emanuele II, but he quickly tired of playing the role of a constitutional monarch in turbulent Spain and two years later renounced the throne. After that, the Carlists had a real chance of seizing power.

For Cramer and his second-in-command Bréda, the Spanish campaign ended with a whimper. In September 1869 the Dutch financier closed the Paris office, which had been the centre of operations. Bréda, who had devoted himself relentlessly to the cause, was disheartened but soon recovered: 'I never lose courage for long.'[50] That trait would stand him in good stead throughout his life. Shortly after, in collaboration with Cramer, he would dedicate himself with great zeal to other big plans: the creation of an international Catholic newspaper and an international Catholic bank. Indeed, Catholic internationalism flourished remarkably during this time of increasing nationalism and it became necessary to provide it with modern means of action. The Cramer-Bréda duo could certainly not be accused of a lack of vision. The only question was whether they were the most suitable people to carry out such plans, and that was certainly an issue in the case of Cramer, given his earlier history. Nevertheless, his unbridled vigour and assertiveness would give an important boost to Catholic internationalism at a crucial moment.

---

50   Bréda to Cramer, 4 Sept. 1869, NKDC, *Cramer*, 12 a, II.

Flirting with capitalism

During this period, when industrialization was developing and the credit system was expanding, a number of people made an effort 'to Christianize capitalism', the above-mentioned Jan Willem Cramer (1817-1884) from Amsterdam being one of them.[51] He was a physician by profession, but business was in his blood. As his name indicates, he came from a *kramer* or chandler family in German Westphalia, though his father had succeeded in pulling himself up in the world and had acquired a certain prosperity. Jan Willem studied medicine, but he also had a special talent for languages.

> 'He spoke and wrote French and Dutch with equal ease and also had excellent German, Latin and Italian. In his native tongue, he was a considerable stylist who constructed smooth and graceful sentences, a born improviser and to some extent he could even be called an artist with words. He was also a captivating speaker.'[52]

He was able to realize these talents by combining his medical practice with journalism and in 1846 became the principal assistant to Judocus Smits, chief editor of the leading Catholic newspaper *De Tijd*. He worked on the paper from 5 to 8 in the morning and from 10pm until midnight; in between he visited his patients. Over a period of eleven years, he wrote more than one thousand articles, mainly on the situation of Catholics in the Netherlands. Even all that was not enough for him. Very soon he came to play a leading role in a Catholic youth committee that pushed for collaboration with the liberals, with the aim of obtaining wider freedoms for the Catholic Church through constitutional reform.[53] 'He beat the drum of liberal Catholicism with sparkling virtuosity and boisterous passion.'[54] If he had had his say, the Catholics would have gone over to the liberal side completely. Following the constitutional reform, he campaigned with his committee for the restoration of the Catholic episcopal hierarchy in the Netherlands. He also combatively crusaded for freedom of education and even went so far as to deny the State the right to be involved in education at all. His energetic efforts were not appreciated by everyone and many in his circle began to think of him as an insufferable character, who 'carried away by his own successes, presents himself as an Atlas bearing Catholicism in the Netherlands on his shoulders'. Another commentator put it thus: 'Acting the big shot, stirring up controversy, pushing himself forward:

---

51   Beekelaer, *Rond grondwetsherziening*; Peijnenburg, *Judocus Smits en zijn tijd*, 110-125; Id., *Johannes Zwijsen*, 141-146; Rogier. *Katholieke herleving*, 258-266; De Valk, 'A Struggle behind the Scenes', 387-408.
52   Rogier, *Katholieke herleving*, 259.
53   Beekelaer, *Rond grondwetsherziening*, 39-54.
54   Rogier, *Katholieke herleving*, 47.

Jan Willem Cramer. Photograph.
[Nijmegen, KDC]

such actions characterize this propagandist and agitator.'⁵⁵ Church authorities became increasingly irritated by his headstrong and ceaseless activity. In reorganizing their church province and integrating the Catholic population into the nation, they had to take serious account of the sensitivities of the Protestant majority for which the physician-journalist had little regard. Another

55   A remark by Gerard Brom, cited in Beekelaer, *Rond grondwetsherziening*, 218.

cause of unease was the way he jumped from one ideological extreme to the other during the 1850s: from ardent liberal to great admirer of Napoleon III and from liberal Catholic to rabid ultramontane. Judocus Smits had difficulty with these swings and found that Cramer 'lacks firmness in his opinions, is prone to all views and is influenced by those with whom he last spoke; he is like an organ, faithfully reproducing every note that is played'.[56] Still, Cramer's ideological development was more deeply grounded and was not that unusual, as has been demonstrated several times in this book. The revolutionary events of 1848 had led many liberals to change course, though in Cramer's case nothing happened in moderation, and his turnabout was therefore all the more pronounced. By 1857 he had created so much disarray and tensions with the bishops were so high that he withdrew from Catholic organizational life and from *De Tijd*.

Later his attention shifted to the world of finance, which was booming at the time, but he did not abandon his commitment to Catholicism. In his view, Catholics should not leave the financial sector to liberals and Jews. The latter were traditionally very active in the money market and indeed had built up a strong position in the banking world in many countries as well as in international finance. According to Cramer, Catholic banks and other financial institutions could support the Church, strengthen its organization and press and also come to the aid of the Pope, who from 1860 was experiencing growing financial difficulties in governing the Papal States and the universal Church. Thus began a new phase in Cramer's career, one with a more international orientation. This gives the story of his life, in the words of the historian L.J. Rogier, 'a sensation similar to that of a crazy car ride (...) hurtling from mountains to valleys, from dazzling successes to compromising failures, from almost fabulous wealth to the disgrace of bankruptcy'. The wealth he acquired in the mid-1860s, 'meant that anybody with a fantastic plan for large-scale and revolutionary improvements in the Church, the fatherland, or Amsterdam found in him an enthusiastic and highly eloquent driving force'.[57] Many of those plans were never implemented or fizzled out, as was the case with the Carlist loan, but those failures were obscured by some resounding successes, which – at least temporarily – yielded him great wealth. Above all, his collaboration with the Belgian financier Langrand-Dumonceau would make him a wealthy man for a decade or so.

The life of André Langrand-Dumonceau (1826-1900) was, if such is possible, even more colourful and turbulent.[58] This man, who would fit perfectly in a novel by Balzac, began his career as a street trader and served for some time in the French Foreign Legion. In 1847 he started a small agricultural insur-

---

56   Peijnenburg, *Smits*, 116.
57   Rogier, *Katholieke herleving*, 258-260.
58   Jacquemyns, *Langrand-Dumonceau*, 5 vols.

ance company, and other insurance companies soon followed in Belgium, the Netherlands and Austria, some of which still exist. He gradually built up the first pan-European insurance empire. In the early 1860s he launched major mortgage and land credit companies in Central Europe, especially in the Danube monarchy. He wanted to exploit land that lay dormant and create a class of affluent farmer-owners. Accordingly, he bought up the land of the aristocracy on a massive scale and divided it into smaller plots which he then sold on to tenants for an annual installment. He raised the capital for these large-scale operations from bonds sold by his companies on the western European capital market. His system thus consisted of transferring capital from countries where it was abundant to regions where it was scarce and expensive. It was an ingenious plan that would help to take the business of land and mortgage credit out of the hands of loan sharks, notaries and other money traders. That was the positive side of the story. The negative side was that the continuous creation of new companies eventually resulted in an opaque conglomerate of insurance, property and mortgage companies that operated on a pyramid scheme. The capital collected from the new companies was used to discharge the deficits of already existing companies, an operation that regularly reappears in the financial world. However, all this remained concealed from the public for the time being. Langrand manipulated public opinion with large-scale advertising campaigns, lured shareholders with exceptionally high dividends and shamelessly bought diplomats, politicians and civil servants. In this way he established an impressive financial empire within a very short time. His prestige soon approached that of Rothschild, Pereire, Laffitte, Oppenheim, Bischoffsheim and other big bankers. He won the trust of prominent aristocrats, kings and even emperors like Francis Joseph I and Napoleon III.

Langrand-Dumonceau deliberately carried on his capitalist activities under a Catholic and conservative banner. At the Congress of Mechlin in 1863, one of his colleagues declared from the gallery: '*il appelle les capitaux au baptême pour les christianiser*' ('he calls capital to baptism in order to Christianize it'). Langrand pretended that he wanted to build up a Catholic financial system that would counterbalance the dominance of the Jewish bankers. Land ownership, he said, was more important than movable property and had to be distributed in order to strengthen the fabric and moral values of society. These ideas struck a sensitive chord not only among the aristocracy and upper bourgeoisie, but also in Church circles. In 1864 he was entrusted with the organization of a new papal loan.[59] As an extra boost, he received a laudatory papal *breve* (brief) and afterwards, as a reward, the title of papal count. However, the new loan was not a success. The target had been 50 million francs [210 million euros], but only 20 million was pledged. Many wealthy Catholics

---

59 Pollard, *Money and the Rise of the Modern Papacy*, 35-36; Jacquemyns, *Langrand-Dumonceau*, vol. III, 501-510.

were expecting the end of the Papal States and, not interested in investing in a lost cause, they left it largely to fail. If they in fact came on board, it was more out of devotion than for profit. In smaller countries like Belgium and the Netherlands, the response could still be said to have been satisfactory, but in larger countries like France and Austria, the results were miserable. The local clergy and Catholic opinion made a clear distinction between the papal loans, which were mainly intended to pay off the debts of the Papal States, and Peter's Pence, which supported the operations of the universal Church. For them the latter initiative was much more important and they wanted to give it priority. Ultimately, the Holy See would also make that choice, thereby indicating that its future would depend primarily on broad Catholic support.[60]

If the papal loan of 1864 could be said to have been a relative success in the Netherlands, this was due largely to Jan Willem Cramer. His Catholic convictions led him to become involved in Langrand's initiatives. He succeeded in using his many contacts in Catholic circles to promote the papal loan successfully. Langrand valued his efforts and in September 1865 appointed him co-founder and director of the Dutch Society for Land Credit (*Nederlandse Maatschappij voor Grondkrediet*), a subsidiary of the General Bank for the Promotion of Agriculture and Public Works (*Algemene Bank ter bevordering van de Landbouw en de Openbare Werken*). The Dutch Society was completely subordinated to the General Bank and served its interests primarily. Its director was essentially just a straw man, and knew it, but he was royally rewarded. He was given management positions in some of Langrand's other companies and was also entrusted with the campaigns for promoting his business empire in the Netherlands. As director of the Dutch Society he designed grandiose projects, including the impoldering of the Zuiderzee and comprehensive urban development plans in Amsterdam. However, he could not even begin to carry out any of them. They would later be taken up again and implemented by other companies and local authorities.[61]

Although the papal loan of 1864 had not been a great success, Langrand-Dumonceau made every effort to take advantage of his good relations with the curia. He sought Roman support for a plan to capitalize much of the vast church properties in Austria-Hungary. In 1866-1867 the sale of the government-expropriated monastic property in the new Italian state was put on the agenda.[62] The extensive lands of the abolished monasteries, worth about two billion francs [8.4 billion euros], had to be converted into marketable securities. A third of the proceeds of this transaction would be paid to the Italian state, which was virtually bankrupt, and the remainder would benefit the Church. In addition, Langrand expected the operation to raise sixty million francs [252

---

60   Viaene, 'The Roman Question', 148-149.
61   Jacquemyns, *Langrand-Dumonceau*, vol. II, 443-450.
62   Id., vol. IV, 123-193.

million euros] for himself. But the plan never materialized. At the last moment the Holy See rejected the agreement made with the Italian state because it was incorporated in a fundamental law that was hostile to the Church. In the background were other considerations, such as a growing distrust of Langrand-Dumonceau's financial constructions and a deep-seated aversion to modern capitalism. Cramer followed the negotiations with the curia closely and was also occasionally directly involved. Eventually this Italian affair gave its *patron* nothing but trouble: instead of a profit of sixty million, Langrand posted a loss of two million francs. Moreover, his prestige was severely dented. He just changed tack then and began to focus more on public works, especially railway concessions in Austria-Hungary, where the economy had been booming for seven years.

At that precise moment, his empire began to falter. In early 1868 he was obliged to launch a call for funds with a request that the still unpaid shares be deposited into his key businesses. That led to a collapse of their stock market value. To make matters worse, his main business partner, the princely house of Tour and Taxis, decided to withdraw from his businesses. As guardian of that family's minor children Emperor Francis Joseph I was involved in this operation.[63] He put severe pressure on Langrand and in early May 1868 forced him to acquiesce in the takeover of Tour and Taxis's shares. In order to keep his head above water, the great financier was obliged to take on additional heavy loans. According to Blome, as compensation, the Austrian emperor promised Langrand that major railway concessions and other public works in the Dual Monarchy would be entrusted to his companies.[64] Chancellor Beust, in return for bribes, had already made similar commitments.[65]

In October 1868 a press campaign against Langrand got underway and in the same month a judicial investigation on charges of fraud and extortion was opened against him in Belgium. A major scandal erupted. The liberals consciously fanned the controversy, as many Catholic politicians – especially those with a liberal Catholic orientation – were extensively involved in Langrand's companies. Their liberal opponents did not let the opportunity pass to bring them down, jeering, 'Christianizing capital means putting the sign of the cross over it'. The settlement of the judicial process would take more than ten years. Langrand fled Brussels and succeeded in bringing his personal accounts and all his movable possessions to safety. He sought refuge in Paris, Rome and London successively, and finally left for the United States in 1872, where he stayed with a business partner, Henry Amy, a banker of Belgian origin. Meanwhile, the Belgian courts announced the failure of his business (1870) and sentenced him to ten years imprisonment (1872), but he remained

63   Jacquemyns, *Langrand-Dumonceau*, vol. IV, 345-365.
64   *Journal Blome*, entry for 22 Jan. 1870, Gut Salzau, V.
65   *Journal Blome*, entry for 18 Dec. 1867, Gut Salzau, V.

beyond the reach of the law and would spend the last years of his life in France and Italy.[66]

During the judicial investigation, Emperor Francis Joseph I and chancellor Beust were regularly mentioned, but they managed to keep out of the firing line. Blome devoted much attention in his diary to this financial scandal and appeared to be well-informed about the true facts. Obviously, his judgement on the corrupt practices of Beust was scathing,[67] but he also had completely lost his trust in the Emperor.[68] Further, he despised the Catholic politicians who swarmed around Langrand and who had made a commodity of religion. The story about the Christianization of capitalism disguised a boundless greed that could only wreak damage on religion.[69] Moreover, Blome increasingly opposed capitalism on principle, as will become evident in his later career. He would soon direct his opposition not only against political liberalism, but also against the liberal economic model.

For that reason, it is remarkable that at the end of 1870 he began to collaborate closely with Jan Willem Cramer. He, after all, had been one of the most loyal employees of Langrand and had been badly affected when the business empire collapsed.[70] The Commercial Court of Amsterdam had begun the liquidation of the Dutch Society for Land Credit (*Nederlandse Maatschappij voor Grondkrediet*) in March 1869, a process that would take many years, and cost Cramer most of his fortune. He was also involved in the bankruptcy settlement of some of Langrand's other companies in which he had played a minor role. For a long time he managed to keep his involvement in this unsavoury history hidden from Blome and his friends. When the story eventually broke, he masterfully played the role of the injured innocent.[71] The fact that he was never brought before the court for dishonest practices played in his favour; he only had to bear the shame of bankruptcy, which damaged him mainly in his own country, without it putting an end to his business activities.

Even when Langrand-Dumonceau's ruin had become a fact, Cramer toyed for a while with the idea of setting up an international Catholic bank

---

66 Jacquemyns, *Langrand-Dumonceau*, vol. V, 160-295.
67 *Journal Blome*, entry for 18 Dec. 1867, 13 Oct. 1868, 22 Jan. and 2 May 1870, Gut Salzau, V.
68 *Journal Blome*, entry for 28 June 1870, Gut Salzau, V: 'He does not know how to distinguish any more between an honest man and a scoundrel.'
69 *Journal Blome*, entry for 31 May 1868, Gut Salzau, V.
70 Jacquemyns, *Langrand-Dumonceau*, vol. II, 229.
71 Although Bréda was aware of what was going on, Cramer downplayed his involvement to him also. See Cramer to Bréda, 14 Feb. 1870 NKDC, *Cramer*, 24, I, 22: 'I can wash my hands of everything that goes on in Brussels.' See also: Cramer to Schérer-Boccard, 11 Dec. 1870, BCUF, *Schérer* LD, 5; Cramer to Hemptinne, 21 Nov. 1871, NKDC, *Cramer*, 24, I, 753. Contrary to his claims, in the succeeding years Cramer maintained contact with Langrand-Dumonceau and with some of his business partners, including the Belgian banker Amy in New York. See *infra*, 256-257.

in support of the Catholic press and organizations.[72] However, following the Waterloo of the Napoleon of finance, that was an unrealistic project, which even a fantasist like Cramer was forced to acknowledge. Afterwards, the spectacular stock market crash of May 1873 in Vienna would not only herald a prolonged economic downturn, but would also bring financial capitalism into discredit. Sporadic attempts were still undertaken – especially in France – to establish a Catholic financial system, but those attempts failed repeatedly.[73] They were not sufficiently supported by Catholic opinion, which moreover espoused anti-capitalist views. The flirtation with capitalism was thus of short duration and left a bitter aftertaste.

The canonization of the papacy

However, socioeconomic issues did not dominate the ecclesiastical agenda at that time. Rather, all attention was focused on the battle against philosophical and political liberalism, which was then in full swing. In order to rally the Church around the chair of Peter and to better equip it for the defence of its autonomy and social influence, Pius IX took the initiative of convening an ecumenical council that would enter history as the First Vatican Council. Specifically, the Pope wanted to gain the support of the entire episcopate for the main guidelines of *Quanta Cura* and the *Syllabus Errorum*.[74] By choosing Rome as the venue, he drew attention to the city's function as the centre of Christendom, which was a welcome bonus at a time when the last remnants of his temporal power were being threatened.

At the end of 1864 Pius IX submitted his intentions to several cardinals and bishops. Encouraged by their positive responses, he announced the final decision in June 1867, when more than 500 bishops from around the world were gathered in Rome to commemorate the martyrdom of the Apostle Peter. Preparations for the council were made by the curia, who called on Italian experts above all. The Roman authorities excluded German theologians in particular from the preparatory committees as they were considered to espouse overly progressive ideas. The Pope decided early on not to invite any Catholic heads of state, a decision that marked a significant break with the past.

Church circles harboured high though diverse expectations of the upcoming council, the first general assembly of Catholic bishops since the Council of Trent (1545-1563). The ultramontanes hoped it would ratify the views and convictions of Pius IX and further strengthen papal authority. Bishops in the Gal-

72   See *infra*, 174.
73   Jacquemyns, *Langrand-Dumonceau*, vol. IV, 337-344.
74   On Vatican I, see: Aubert, *Vatican I*; Christophe, *Le Concile Vatican I*; Hasler, *Pius IX (1846-1878)*; Schatz, *Vaticanum I, 1869-1870*; Aubert, *Le Pontificat de Pie IX*, 311-367; Martina, *Pio IX*, vol. III, 111-232.

lican tradition championed greater autonomy for the national churches and a weightier role for the episcopate. Along with liberal Catholics, they wanted the Church to adapt cautiously to modern society. Both liberal Catholics as well as ultramontanes attached great importance to the Church's independence from and supremacy over the State, while the Gallicans had more respect for the autonomy and singularity of the civil authorities, which they recognized as having certain supervisory rights over the Church.

Even before the council actually started, opinions were polarized about a possible definition of the dogma of papal infallibility. The doctrine of the infallibility of the supreme magisterium in matters of faith was broadly accepted within the Church, but the question was whether it should be solemnly promulgated as dogma at a time when rationalism and relativism dominated the intellectual climate. It went totally against the *Zeitgeist* and would further deepen the gap between the Church and modern society. In the first preparatory conciliar documents, the issue was given a somewhat peripheral role, but it was gradually forefronted by the Jesuit periodical *La Civiltà Cattolica*. In particular, an article of 6 February 1869, containing an urgent petition from French priests for the proclamation of papal infallibility, caused great consternation and triggered a fierce controversy that very quickly overshadowed all other issues. The pressing question was whether the upcoming council would come to a definition of infallibility and if so, how broadly it would be defined. The issue poisoned the pre-conciliar climate.

Proponents of infallibility hoped that an explicit proclamation of the dogma would strengthen the position of the pope and hence the unity of the Church, at a time when it was being put on the defensive by movements and governments hostile to the Church. The most radical among them wanted the declaration to have a broad application, going beyond the realm of faith and morals to include the area of social teaching. Specifically the *Syllabus Errorum* had to fall within its scope. This would allow them to deal with liberal Catholics, who could then be branded as heretics. For ultramontane bishops in German-speaking territories, the infallibility statement was also a weapon against theologians like Döllinger who defended academic freedom. On the other hand, many French and especially German bishops considered a definition to be superfluous and – even more so – inopportune. One of the most prominent figures in this group was Dupanloup, Bishop of Orléans, who had acquired great international prestige as a defender of the temporal power of the papacy. A small minority of the world episcopate even opposed the principle itself. Over time, a coalition between Gallicans and liberal Catholics emerged and appealed to the public and governments to bring the ultramontane offensive to a halt. That in turn further encouraged the doggedness with which their opponents pursued their goal, with growing support from the Pope.

The council was opened on 8 December 1869 at an impressive ceremony in St. Peter's Basilica. More than 750 council fathers were present, most from Latin Europe, which was still for the time being the centre of the Church. The bishops set up four committees to work on the conciliar texts. The proponents of the infallibility statement were very well organized and made sure their opponents hardly featured in those committees. As the debates were beginning in St. Peter's Basilica, they launched a campaign to put the theme of infallibility on the agenda. Petitions in favour got 450 signatures, while those against garnered only 136. On 1 March 1870 the council leadership finally decided to recommend to the council fathers that the issue be brought up for discussion. Meanwhile, tempers became severely heated; public opinion was mobilized, while the minority called on friendly governments to exert pressure.

Pius IX, who thus far had allowed the council a great deal of freedom, took umbrage at this development and now lent his full support to the 'infallibilists'. They went to work on ensuring the issue was given priority treatment, so as to prevent external pressure from becoming too great. Although many moderate cardinals and bishops, including council leaders, were not in favour, on April 29th, following the unanimous approval of the dogmatic constitution *Dei Filius*, the Pope announced that the debate on the infallibility question would begin immediately. From then on, the discussion focused on the scope of the dogma: to whom and to which matters did infallibility apply? A lengthy and heated debate ensued, in which the minority was able with some effort to voice its views, and cardinals such as Bilio and Guidi exerted a moderating influence. Finally, on July 18th, after many trials and tribulations, 535 council fathers approved the constitution *Pastor Aeternus*, which ratified infallibility. Many members of the minority had left Rome the previous day, a clear indication that the infallibility statement could not count on a moral consensus within the Church. The deep gulf between the council fathers could not be bridged afterwards, because the council was interrupted by the outbreak of the Franco-Prussian War. A short time later Rome was occupied by Italian troops and complete chaos ensued. Almost all the bishops would in the end endorse the infallibility statement, but in a number of countries minority groups broke away from the Church. These so-called 'Old Catholics' were often supported by their governments, as will be seen later.

The constitution *Pastor Aeternus* confirmed the primacy of the pope within the Church, but also left room for the authority of the bishops, 'who lead their flock like true shepherds'. It wanted once and for all to put an end to the possibility of appealing against the pope at a ecumenical council. It also opposed any restriction by secular governments on the exercise of papal authority. It declared the pope to be infallible in matters of faith and morals, but only when he was speaking for the whole Church; he had to make certain that pronouncements *ex cathedra* were in accordance with scripture and tradition and were broadly supported by the bishops. Such a solemn proclamation of an irrevocable doctrine would remain an extremely rare event, and indeed after 1870 happened only once again, with the proclamation of the dogma of the Assumption of Mary (1950). The proclamation of papal infallibility then had mainly a symbolic significance. It strengthened the institutional unity of the Church at a time when nationalism was exerting a centrifugal effect and the protective environment of a Christian society was disappearing. Social factors had been the primary motives for the infallibility declaration. The Church of Peter presented itself as an unshakeable pillar, a bulwark of security in a society that seemed adrift and restless. *Pastor Aeternus* emphasized the element of authority within the Church, while the constitution *Dei Filius* stressed the certainty of a transcendental – yet rationally justifiable – faith. Authority and certainty had been key terms in the conciliar debates.

Pius IX was more involved than any other in the debate on papal infallibility, which revolved around strengthening his authority over the universal Church. He had no sympathy for the rejection of infallibility itself, but understood people's doubts about the timing of its promulgation. As mentioned previously, his attitude towards the conciliar minority hardened when they sought support from liberal public opinion and from governments hostile to the Church. He repeatedly intervened afterwards to expedite the handling of the issue or to amend weak spots in the texts submitted. Nevertheless, he eventually contented himself with a definition that was much less broad than what he originally had envisioned.

During the council, the elderly Pius IX revealed all the facets of his complex personality.[75] The council fathers and observers who stayed in Rome all judged him very differently. Almost nobody was immune to his spontaneity, sweetness and cordiality. Conversely, many said that he could act very emotionally and impulsively and could be merciless with his opponents.[76] He was a very pious and deeply religious man, with a mystical disposition, but he was too easily taken in by stories of visions and prophecies. His theological knowledge was rather limited, and his political insight, as mentioned earlier, even more so.[77] During the council he increasingly treated opponents of infallibility as personal enemies, and even went so far as to call them tools of freemasonry. Doubts about his person dominated among the anti-infallibilists who accused him of an unhealthy illuminism, megalomania and despotic tendencies, while some even queried his sanity. That did not prevent his being idolized by the

---

75   See above all Hasler, *Pius IX*, 25-155.

76   Dupanloup to Leo XIII, late 1878, CARAN, AB, 19, 525: 'a hot-tempered, even aggressive character'; 'Is it certain that he has always taken the necessary precautions, counselled by Christian providence, to avoid being deceived?'

77   Xavier de Mérode: 'The Pope does not understand anything about the fundamental conditions of modern society.' (Cited in: Le Guillou, *Charles de Montalembert. Journal intime*, vol. VII, entry for 24 Sept. 1864).

Catholic masses for whom he had become a cult figure, and the aura of infallibility now bestowed on him could only confirm this trend.

The Pope was obviously admired and almost adored by the radical ultramontane bishops and laymen who remained in Rome for the duration of the council. As already noted, the papal committees had led to the formation of an international network of militant lay people, many of whom had found their way to Rome during the 1860s. The council offered them the opportunity to extend their international contacts and to reinforce their ideas. Rome was also swarming with *hommes d'oeuvres*, journalists and dignitaries who met one another along with the council fathers and the diplomats in the Roman salons. Most of the Roman aristocrats were supporters of the pope and of the infallibility declaration. Kindred spirits met each other in the palaces of the Borghese, Rospigliosi, Salviati and Odescalchi families. The salon of the devout and very wealthy Princess Sofia Odescalchi-Branicka was an especially important venue for prelates, papal diplomats and aristocrats.[78]

The most influential lay people on the 'infallibilist' side were Veuillot and Blome. Diary entries[79] that have been preserved for that period give us a good idea of the frequent contacts the latter maintained with diplomats, the Jesuit editors of *Civiltà Cattolica*, and the leading figures of the radical group within the conciliar majority: Henry Manning, Archbishop of Westminster, Ignatius von Senestrey, Bishop of Regensburg[80] and Gaspard Mermillod, Suffragan Bishop of Lausanne-Geneva. Blome got along particularly well with Mermillod, an internationally renowned preacher. Thanks to his status, the former diplomat also had easy access to Antonelli. Prelates such as Manning sent him to the secretary of state to urge him to take a more resolute stance on the infallibility question, and he had occasional audiences with the Pope himself, who apparently deeply appreciated him.

Blome closely followed developments within the council. His personal view was obvious: the council had to reinforce the authority of the Holy See and win approval for the infallibility statement.[81] Once the decision was made

78 Von Hutten-Czapski, *Sechzig Jahre Politik und Gesellschaft*, 8-15. Other prominent noble ladies, mostly of foreign origin, received sympathizers of the council's minority in their salons. The 'infallibilists' called them '*les commères de l'Eglise*' (the gossips of the Church), or, a term that was even more popular, the 'matriarchs'. That epithet, which was coined by Bréda apparently, soon made the rounds in all the European salons. See Bacht, *Ein verschollenes Tagebuch*, 391-393; Franco, *Appunti storici sopra il Concilio Vaticano*, 264-267.

79 *Journal Blome*, diary entries from 30 Oct. 1869 to 19 May 1870, Gut Salzau, V. The diary then breaks off until the beginning of September.

80 Ignatius von Senestrey, *Wie es zur Definition der päpstlichen Unfehlbarkeit kam.*

81 *Journal Blome*, entry for 23 Jan. 1870, Gut Salzau, V: 'If the Council does not restore the authority of the Holy See in its fullness, we will be weaker than before against the revolutionary deluge; but if before its prorogation, the Council were to do nothing but define infallibility, we would be strong enough from now on to inherit the legacy of liberalism that is already dead.'

to give priority to the issue of papal infallibility, he noted with dismay that it would be limited to matters of faith and morals. 'As a result, the propositions of the *Syllabus* will not be infallible and all that concerns relations between Church and State will remain vague and unclear ... That will be a victory for the *Césariens*', a reference to the supporters of State omipotence.[82] For Blome clearly the main task was to endorse the Church's independence from the State, and he regretted this would not fall under the principle of infallibility. Yet, he was satisfied afterwards that the primacy of the pope within the Church had been strengthened.[83]

Blome was in regular contact with Veuillot in Rome and cemented a closer relationship with Bréda, who had come to defend Chambord's interests in the council's corridors.[84] The *Dornbirnien* was also there as a correspondent for *L'Univers* and *Le Monde*. As an experienced political agent, he infiltrated the salons and succeeded in winning over prominent prelates and aristocrats. After a while, with rather too much self-confidence, he could announce: 'My influence is increasing rather than decreasing ... I regularly pick up interesting information in my many conversations and to that extent I am kept informed about developments so that even bishops sometimes ask me for information about the council's progress.'[85] 'We, lay people, have our modest role to play and recently I have even been called *l'Evêque du dehors*.'[86] His relations with Veuillot and Blome of course also brought him into Monsignor Mermillod's circle.

Gaspard Mermillod (1824-1892) was auxiliary bishop of Lausanne from 1864, with his residence in Calvinist Geneva. He was a very charismatic and passionate man, and a well-known preacher in the French-speaking world.[87] An ardent ultramontane, he vigorously defended the temporal power of the papacy, especially because he saw it as a condition of its independence.[88] He

82 *Journal Blome*, entry for 9 May 1870, Gut Salzau, V.
83 Blome's diary breaks off between June 12 and 11 September, during which time he went on a business trip to Austria and Hungary. In his diary he does not express any final judgement on the outcome of the council. However, subsequent remarks make clear that he considered the infallibility statement to be a major victory. See Blome to Revertera, 2 March 1892, HAH, IV, 56, 32.
84 Bréda to Cramer, 2 Dec. 1869, NKDC, *Cramer*, 434, 12 a, II: 'Henry [Chambord] has authorized me to talk about him by name to the Holy Father, to Cardinal Antonelli, and to Father Schrader S.J. (...). If one talks of countries invaded and of kings expelled, one should cite as an example not only Italian sovereigns but also Henry.'
85 Bréda to Cramer, 20 March 1870, ibid.
86 Bréda to Cramer, 8 April 1870, ibid.
87 On Gaspard Mermillod (1824-1892) see: Comte, *Le cardinal Mermillod*; Jeantet, *Le cardinal Mermillod*; Massard, *L'Oeuvre sociale du cardinal Mermillod*. Louis Veuillot described him thus: 'Frail in appearance, youthful in spirit and visage, though still a young bishop, he has an important place in the Council. The Church may well not have a worker who exerts himself more.' (*Rome pendant le concile*, Paris, 1927, 149).
88 Mermillod to Dr. Dufresne, 1 March 1870 (cited by Charles Comte, *Le cardinal Mermillod*, 106).

Gaspard Mermillod. Photograph, J. Temporel, c. 1865.
[Leuven, KADOC]

was one of the main activists in the radical wing of the council's majority. This still relatively young prelate could in several respects be called 'modern' in that he was convinced the Church had to turn to the people and therefore had to use modern means of communication such as the press. He was also very sensitive to the social question.[89] He exercised a great influence on many prominent laymen and would involve a number of them in the press committee that he set up during the council at the Pope's behest.[90]

In the first weeks after the opening of the council, opponents of the infallibility declaration had already begun to manipulate public opinion in order to bring external pressure to bear on the talks. Several council fathers were found to have violated the duty of confidentiality and through friendly diplomats and others to have leaked classified information, which was later widely reported in the press.[91] The Pope therefore decided to release one council father in each language area from the obligation to maintain confidentiality and to give him permission to pass on information to the Catholic press. In the next stage he gave his approval for the establishment of a news agency under Mermillod's management that would work closely with the Jesuits of the *Civiltà Cattolica* and would pass on announcements in a systematic way to the Catholic newspapers, thereby challenging the press campaign of the opponents of the infallibility declaration.[92] The agency worked very zealously and met every week, but it was not very efficient. The apologetic messages sent out into the world were not sufficient to counter the rumour mill. However, a number of prominent laymen were brought together in this agency, which later would form the core of a large international network that would have a much broader impact. Among them were figures who are known to us, such as Blome, his 'lieutenant' Pergen and Bréda, as well as English nobles such as Charles de Barre-Bodenham esq. and Lord Rudolph Denbigh, the French count and publisher Edmond Lafond and the Roman duke, Scipione Salviati.[93] Most of them were deeply involved in the activities of the papal committees in their own countries.

The press agency conceived the idea of starting a society of militant lay people who would devote themselves consistently to 'the restoration of the social kingdom of Christ on earth', or in other words, the restoration of the social influence of the Church. On Friday, 25 February 1870, Mermillod celebrated Mass for them in the Mamertine Prison where the apostles Peter and

89   *Infra*, 252
90   Franco-Martina, *Appunti storici*, 228; Schatz, *Vaticanum I*, vol. II, 219-222; Hasler, *Pius IX*, 44-46; Vailhé, *Vie du P. Emmanuel d'Alzon*, vol. II, 532-536.
91   Franco, *Appunti storici*, entry for 3 Feb. 1870, 187-188. Count Tauffkirchen, the Bavarian Ambassador to the Holy See, was abreast of highly confidential information, which was subsequently circulated in the German press. Franco mentions that Blome came across it when he saw confidential council documents on the ambassador's desk.
92   Franco, *Appunti storici*, entries for 27 Feb. and 30 March, 228 and 264-267.
93   The next chapter offers extensive information on these figures.

Paul had been incarcerated according to tradition. He gave a speech in which he called on them 'to deepen their faith and to spread the teachings and commandments of Christ, who is a God not only for the sacristy but for the whole world'. Those present set up a society with the stated aim of 'bringing about the kingdom of Revelation and Redemption on both the scientific and socio-political levels'. They committed themselves to making every effort to restore the tie between religion and society, using the resources of the press, schools and organizations, in addition to an intense prayer life. A central committee, consisting of the founding members in Rome, would lead the organization and would be assisted by national committees.[94]

The most active 'Mamertins' such as Blome, Denbigh and Bréda, deliberated about possible strategies for pooling Catholic forces on an international scale, and orienting them in an ultramontane direction. Bréda very skilfully broached a project that he had already worked out with Cramer in the autumn of 1869 for starting a major international newspaper. Initially, he had thought of 'a paper that will support all the anti-centralist and anti-bureaucratic movements in Europe and that will defend the autonomy of the churches, families, municipalities, provinces, etc'.[95] Now he gave his plan a Catholic label, thereby winning over the Mamertins. Blome and Denbigh were willing to invest substantially[96] and they hoped for additional financial commitments from French sponsors and from Cramer, with whom Bréda had remained in contact.[97] The Dutch financier declared himself to be willing, but apparently he had not yet learned his lesson and once again tried to sell the idea of establishing a Catholic bank for the financial support of the planned newspaper. He even had the audacity to declare that 'there is not any risk when people have a little knowledge of human beings and business and keep far away from daring ventures'.[98] Blome however held back, noting earlier distasteful experiences with the business empire of Langrand-Dumonceau,[99] without his knowing anything about Cramer's involvement in the operations of the Belgian tycoon. Among the Mamertins only Bréda was in the know, and he apparently made

94 Lugmayer, 'Zur Vorgeschichte der sozialen Rundschreiben Leo XIII', 59-63. He cites from Blome's 'Geneviana' file, which was preserved for a long time by his daughter Carola but is now untraceable (see *infra*, 185 n18). Bréda's letters to Cramer (NKDC, *Cramer*, 434, 12 a, I) also provide interesting information about this meeting: 9, 26 and 27 Feb. 1870; *Journal Blome*, entry for 25 Feb. 1870, Gut Salzau, V.

95 Bréda to Cramer, 31 Dec. 1869, NKDC, *Cramer*, 434, 12 a, II.

96 Bréda to Cramer, 20 March 1870, NKDC, *Cramer*, 434, 12 a, II. Blome was willing to make 300,000 francs [1.26 million euro] available and for his part Denbigh pledged 100,000 francs. [420,000 euros]

97 Detailed information on these plans is to be found in: Bréda to Cramer, 13 and 20 Feb., 4 and 20 March, 8 and 13 April, 9 May and 8 July, ibid.; Cramer to Bréda, 22 Jan., 20 and 25 Feb., NKDC, *Cramer*, 24, I, 10, 25 and 26. On Cramer's plans for a Catholic bank, see Cramer to Bréda, 28 Feb. and 18 April 1870, NKDC, *Cramer*, 24, I, 33-41 and 61.

98 Cramer to Bréda, 1 March 1870, NKDC, *Cramer*, 24, I, 42.

99 Bréda to Cramer, 8 July 1870, NKDC, *Cramer*, 434, 12 a, II.

no mention of it. So Blome and his friends got the impression that Cramer was a solid partner who could help shape the planned newspaper. They all agreed that the new paper would be best located in Geneva, Mermillod's home, in neutral and centrally located Switzerland. They scheduled a meeting of the main interested parties, including Cramer, in Paris during the summer months, but the outbreak of the Franco-Prussian war on 19 July 1870 prevented this. Two months later, Rome was occupied by Italian troops and the temporal power of the pope came to an end. The long-awaited catastrophe seemed at hand. The question now was whether the Church would be willing and able to play the restorative role that Blome and his friends had assigned to it.

CATHOLIC DEFENCE

THE BLACK INTERNATIONAL

I n the early hours of Tuesday, 20 September 1870 Italian troops under General Raffaele Cadorna launched an attack on Rome. Their artillery bom-
barded the city wall between Porta Pia and Porta Salaria. At nine o'clock
in the morning a gap of thirty meters was forced open, and two columns of
infantry, followed by six battalions of *Bersaglieri* entered the city. A fierce gun
battle with the papal troops ensued, but it was mostly a token resistance: with
their 13,000 soldiers, they were no match for the 70,000 Italians. At ten o'clock
the white flag was hoisted over St. Peter's Basilica. Generals Cadorna and
Kanzler began to negotiate the terms of the capitulation, and after two hours
they signed an agreement at the Villa Albani. The papal troops were allowed
to retreat and they spent the night under the Bernini columns in St. Peter's
Square. The following day the foreigners among them were deported to the
port of Civitavecchia, to be repatriated a few days later. Thus, Rome came into
the hands of the Kingdom of Italy, and now became its actual capital.[1]

   This turn of events came as no surprise. Two weeks after the outbreak of
the Franco-Prussian War, the French expeditionary army departed from Rome,
leaving the military position of the *Patrimonium Petri* considerably weakened.
Still, it was the international situation that mainly gave cause for concern.
That the Italian government would use the war between the two great powers
to seize the crown jewel of Rome was to be expected. As a precautionary meas-

---

1   Miko, *Das Ende des Kirchenstaates*, vol. II; Caracciolo, *Roma capitale*, 68-74; Guenel, *La
    dernière guerre*, 129-146; Martina, *Pio IX*, vol. III, 233-247, Coltrinari and Trogu, 'Atanasio de
    Charrette', 72-92.

ure, it waited until after the Battle of Sedan and the proclamation of the republic in Paris to send an ultimatum to Pius IX requesting that the Eternal City
be transferred to Italy, arguing once again that the transfer was necessary in
order to restrain the revolutionary turmoil in the peninsula. The Pope refused
to believe in an imminent Italian attack and continued to put his trust in a
new intervention by the great powers. He rejected the ultimatum, upon which
the Italian troops invaded the *Patrimonium Petri* on September 11th. General
Kanzler declared a state of emergency in Rome, and recalled the papal troops
who were scattered all over the territory. On September 14th, the Pope decided to offer only symbolic resistance. Two days later the Italian army was at
the gates and a decisive attack loomed. Heated discussions flared up among
the Pope's advisers about the form that further resistance should take. Kanzler and the senior officers insisted on resistance in order to save the army's
honour, while Antonelli called for an immediate surrender. Finally, the Pope
opted for an intermediate solution: he offered to negotiate after a breach was
made in the city walls, and on September 20th that plan was followed.[2]

During the attack the Pope gathered the members of the diplomatic
corps around him and protested vehemently that the aggression was a violation of international law. After the surrender, the diplomats went to the Italian
headquarters to argue in favour of a conciliatory approach, but they did not
threaten foreign intervention. Otherwise, even before the invasion, the Italian
government had received reassuring signals from the great powers who were
concerned that the Franco-Prussian war would develop into a European-wide
conflict and perhaps even lead to revolutionary situations. An intervention in
favour of the Pope could trigger that process. European diplomats and a large
section of public opinion reacted with resignation and a certain fatalism to the
capture of the Eternal City. They reconciled themselves to a fact that had gradually become unavoidable, and few were dismayed that international conventions and the principle of legitimacy had once again been trampled on.[3]

A pressing question, which really preoccupied international diplomacy,
was whether the Pope and the Curia would remain in Rome after the surrender
or go into exile.[4] The Italian government was terrified of that eventuality, and
foreign diplomats had also expressed their concern as it could cause great unrest and agitation in the Catholic world. The decision lay with the Pope and his
closest advisers. On September 21st Pius IX began consultations with the most
influential cardinals in the Curia, although, surprisingly, he did not include
Antonelli and his circle in those deliberations. A large majority felt that the
position of the Pope in Rome was untenable and that serious consideration

2   Kertzer, *The Prisoner of the Vatican*, 50-58.
3   Fiorentino, *La questione romana intorno al 1870*, 65-71.
4   Valente, 'Pio IX, il Sacro Collegio e il Corpo diplomatico', 784-833; Ciampani, 'Alignments
     among the Cardinals', 195-230; Martina, *Pio IX*, vol. III, 247-254.

had to be given to finding a refuge, with Malta, Belgium, Tyrol and the Rhineland, in that order, being the preferred locations. The cardinals felt the Pope was the one who had to make the choice. He quickly decided to maintain the link between the papacy and the Eternal City. Antonelli agreed completely: in his view, by departing from Rome, the Holy See had more to lose than to gain, both politically and materially. His diplomatic action was limited for the time being to 'protesting and waiting'.[5] He also hoped that the upcoming peace negotiations between France and Prussia could be used to incite those countries to exert pressure on Italy in favour of the papal cause.[6] Pius IX then remained in Rome, within the walls of the Vatican, where the Italian government left him undisturbed. He would never again leave, and from now on he lived as 'the prisoner of the Vatican', which enhanced his martyr's halo and increased his already considerable popularity in the Catholic world.[7]

Abandoned by princes and governments, the Pope received massive support from Catholics all over the world. Shortly after the capture of Rome, more than fourteen thousand petitions were sent to the Vatican, with no fewer than some five million signatures.[8] Although this protest movement started spontaneously, it would soon be activated and coordinated by an international committee of lay people that would operate in close consultation with the Holy See. Gustav von Blome played a central role in that committee. He wanted to mobilize the Catholic people in order to restore the rights of the pope. In addition, he wanted to use the Roman question to establish a Christian social order once again in Europe. In particular, he sought to restore 'Christian' monarchies and governments in Catholic countries such as the Dual Monarchy, France, Spain and Italy. The mobilization of the Catholic masses could have a decisive effect here. During this period, at a turning point in his personal life and in European politics in general, Blome wrote a tract entitled *Wo is Europa's Zukunft? (Where is Europe's Future?)* In what was to be his main publication, he expressed his political and religious views in a clear and concise way. The publication was distributed in several languages and was highly praised by Pius IX.[9]

5 Pesci, *I primi anni di Roma capitale*, 18-25.
6 Fiorentino, 'Dalle Stanze del Vaticano', 303-310.
7 Kertzer, *The Prisoner of the Vatican*, 85-99.
8 Fiorentino, 'Dalle Stanze del Vaticano', 308; Lamberts, 'La mobilitazione cattolica internazionale', 339-348.
9 Blome to Cramer, 23 Feb. 1871, NKDC, *Cramer*, 434, 12 b, I; Cramer to Blome, 26 Feb. and 10 March 1871, NKDC, *Cramer*, 24, I, 478 and 509. Three thousand copies of the tract were distributed in the Netherlands.

The future of Europe

Impressed by the dramatic events of the summer of 1870, Blome wondered what the future of Europe would look like. Would it be one of German global supremacy, a united European workers' republic or would the nation states be regenerated by parliamentarianism?

Those influenced by contemporary racial theories believed in the irresistible rise of the Germanic race. However, there were no longer any pristine primeval races that could become the carriers of a new civilization. One could not rely on any one race to renew society or shepherd in a new cultural era.

Did the future then belong to socialism, which since 1864 had been organized in a Workers' International? The time had indeed come when workers were fiercely protesting against a hitherto unknown inequality that was a result of capitalism. In the footsteps of the liberals, they were demanding equality and fraternity. Undoubtedly they would soon take over the helm, with the aim of achieving working-class domination in a kind of Spartan state. Here should be noted that Blome especially was aware of political socialism, which had been manifesting itself in Germany since the 1860s, although elsewhere in Europe it still represented a minority among the workers, among whom apolitical anarchism in particular had taken hold. The breakthrough of revolutionary socialism was inevitable, according to Blome, but the victory would be short-lived. A Spartan state that negated freedom and property rights, the basic conditions for the spiritual and material progress of mankind, went against human nature and had no sustainable future.

This also was true of the liberal state, which wanted to establish the dominance of the intellectual and business classes. This kind of state strove above all for unlimited material progress, and to this end subjected its citizens to the blind and inhuman laws of capitalism. Liberals created an atomistic society in which the protective social bonds were destroyed. They were, moreover, proponents of a State without God in which the law, as an expression of the popular will, exercised a compelling moral force. Public opinion, which was manipulated via the press by wealthy groups, was a guide for thinking and acting in the liberal state. Such a system, which was based mainly on rationalism and materialism, could not offer Europe a sustainable future either.

Thus, neither racism nor socialism nor liberalism offered a reasonable prospect for Europe. A profound analysis of the existing situation against the background of past history could possibly throw light on what developments would be desirable. With regard to the evolution of international politics, Blome noted that the 'guaranteed legal status' in operation from the time of the European Concert had been replaced by a lack of respect for international law. The self-interest of the nation states increasingly took precedence. In domestic policies also, the common interest was no longer given priority because of the mounting struggle between political parties which, to make matters worse, caused considerable instability in the regimes. Particularly worrying, moreover, was that the breakthrough of liberal constitutionalism in most countries was accompanied by the strengthening of a centralized state authority which, with the aid of the bureaucracy, exercised ever more control over its subjects and intruded on their private lives. The ultimate illustration of this was the introduction of general military conscription on the Prussian model. The modern liberal state also threatened the Church, opposing its social influence, pushing it out of the fields of education and charitable work, and hindering its free development. In short, it gave everything to Caesar at the expense of God, and this was a disastrous development. According to Blome, religion had to permeate the whole of society, not only the lives of individuals but also natural communities and the State. That did not mean a return to medieval theocracy. The Church could intervene only indirectly in politics by making moral pronouncements; governments were free to heed, or not, the moral views of the Church, which did not possess any means of external coercion.

In Blome's view, Europe's future could only be assured by a restoration of Christian society. The horrors of the previous few months had to open people's eyes and destroy godless hubris. The disappointed people longed for peace, freedom, law and order, but these were not to be found anywhere outside the old – though at the same time eternally young – Church. The Catholic masses would begin to move, with their reaction to the capture of Rome functioning as a catalyst: '*Dieser Aufschrei ist das Lebenszeichen der Katholischen Welt.*' ('This cry is the Catholic world's sign of life.') The social reign of Christ would be restored, and Christian states would take the place of Byzantine despots or the police commissioners of a nonsensical popular sovereignty. The future of Europe would be dictated by the fundamental principles of the *Syllabus Errorum*.

This final statement was indeed very provocative and discredited the publication in the eyes of liberal Catholics such as Monsignor Dupanloup.[10] Still, it was not an illusion, this dream of a European society in which ethical principles would determine both international and domestic politics, where the power of the State would be restricted, and where protective social bonds would be maintained and given the necessary opportunities for expansion. It was Blome's conviction that the Church – more than any other body – could contribute to the realization of that dream. In his view, the terrible events of 1870 created the appropriate climate for this, and he would do his utmost to stimulate this development.

10   De Mun, *Ma vocation sociale*, 41-47.

The Geneva Committee

The events following the suspension of Vatican I ensured that the 'Mamertins' were scattered.[11] They had planned a meeting in Paris on September 11th to discuss the setting up of the proposed newspaper, but the Franco-Prussian War had thrown everything into disarray. After the outbreak of the conflict, Bréda hastily returned to France to contribute to the war effort. He was hyper-patriotic and felt that this was not the time anymore for international Christian politics; in the circumstances, he completely ruled out cooperation with German Catholics. During the summer months, the other 'Mamertins' returned to their homelands or, like Blome, fled in haste from Rome as soon as the attack on the city began. Cramer followed developments only from a distance and could devote himself to his favourite activity: hatching grand plans. He believed the need was so great now that the 'Mamertins' had to make a move. Failing to convince Bréda, he turned directly to Monsignor Mermillod in Geneva, and requested the launch of an international protest campaign against the capture of Rome. If possible, that campaign should also contribute to 'the creation of a partnership between all organizations that could be useful in revitalizing the Catholic world'. The proposed action would be best coordinated by an agency, the costs of which Cramer was willing to carry.

On October 3rd, Mermillod summoned the Dutch financier by telegram to Geneva. Four days later Cramer reported to the episcopal residence, where Monsignor Spalding, the Archbishop of Baltimore, was staying, en route from the council. Blome arrived an hour later, having gone on to Geneva after his flight from Rome. The four of them deliberated on the strategy they should adopt and decided to launch an 'Appeal to Catholics', asking them to protest on a mass scale against the loss of the Pope's temporal power.[12] Signatures for this document were collected by telegraph and were then sent to all the bishops, Catholic newspapers and political leaders. At the same time a meeting was planned in Geneva on October 23rd to discuss further measures and actions. Mermillod sent one of his priests to present the Pope with the agenda for the scheduled meeting. Cramer's input was essential for the launch of this action; as Blome would later testify, 'without your generous initiative nobody would have given the example and nothing would have happened'.[13]

11   Footnotes on the Geneva Committee and the Black International have been kept to a minimum. More detailed references to the sources are to be found in Lamberts, 'L'Internationale noire. Une organization secrète au service du Saint-Siège', 15-102. In the main, only additional sources are noted here.

12   *Appel aux catholiques*, 8 Oct. 1870, NKDC, *Cramer*, 456, 20 a: 'That Catholics rise up, therefore ... That they organize committees; that they increase the number of petitions, and that they protest to their respective governments. Secular authorities must take account of our rights and our freedom of conscience.'

13   Blome to Cramer, 17 Dec. 1872, NKDC, *Cramer*, 434, 12 b, II.

Some thirty prominent lay people accepted the invitation and convened on 23-24 October in Geneva under the chairmanship of Mermillod. The French and Germans together made up half of the group, a remarkable fact in a time of war. In his welcome speech the bishop explicitly made a link between the meeting and the 'Mamertins'. He called on those present to unite and act in defence of the church's rights and the restoration of the social reign of Christ.[14] The gathering decided to activate protests against the seizure of Rome – petitions, parliamentary interpellations, pilgrimages and other mass demonstrations – so as to put pressure on governments and force them to condemn the annexation of the city. In order to streamline the planned actions, they decided to set up a *Comité de défense catholique* (Catholic Defence Committee), with a bureau as the executive body. It would publish a *Correspondance de Genève/ Genfer Korrespondenz* in order to provide information to all Catholic newspapers about events in Rome and about activities in defence of the Holy See. The Catholic committees that were represented made 30,000 francs [126,000 euro] available for the operation of this bureau. They decided to give a further boost to Peter's Pence, in order to provide for the financial needs of the Curia and the universal Church. Finally, they drew up an 'Address to the Pope', in which they promised him their full support in the fight for the restoration of his temporal power. They stated explicitly: 'The kingdom of Peter guarantees the freedom of our consciences. It gives expression to the social reign of Christ and his dominion over the world.'[15]

Cramer, who had initiated the Geneva meeting, was sent as an envoy to Rome to deliver the 'Address' to the Pope. At the same time he was commissioned to find suitable correspondents for the *Correspondance de Genève*. Pius IX and Antonelli were elated about the help that was being offered by the Catholic committees. Indeed, the loss of the papacy's temporal power had resulted in the Vatican's diplomatic channels losing considerable influence. The bishops and the clergy, for their part, were obliged to act cautiously with their national governments; getting committees of lay people to mobilize the Catholic people seemed an appropriate way to exert pressure. In its address to the Pope, the Geneva Committee made the first move: 'You can count only on two powers: God and the people. The Catholic world is crying out to God and the faithful are on your side.'

In the previous weeks the Pope and his secretary of state had hardened their stance towards the 'aggressor'. In early October, following a plebiscite, Rome was annexed to the Kingdom of Italy. Chaos reigned in the city and there were regular outbursts of anticlericalism, which did not incline the Pope to be more accommodating. Nor did the expropriation of ecclesiastical buildings for the government's administration. Especially painful was the seizure of the

14 Lugmayer, 'Zur Vorgeschichte der sozialen Rundschreiben Leo XIII', 59-69.
15 The Geneva Committee to Pius IX, 23 Oct. 1870, NKDC, *Cramer*, 456, 20 a.

Quirinale – the papal palace in the city centre – and of the Collegio Romano, the prestigious Jesuit university. Even Antonelli opted for a policy of confrontation at this time. The atmosphere did not improve when on November 1st, in the encyclical *Respicientes*, Pius IX excommunicated all those who had participated in the usurpation of his temporal power.

In this tense climate the Pope eagerly accepted the help offered by the Catholic committees. He asked that the protests be extended and gave his approval to the setting up of the bureau in Geneva and to the planned periodical. Antonelli was on the same wavelength and declared himself ready to nominate a correspondent who would provide the *Correspondance de Genève* with confidential information from the Vatican. In addition, he kept some diplomatic irons in the fire in order to find the beginnings of a solution to the Roman question.

Meanwhile Mermillod had set up the bureau in Geneva that was to be responsible for coordinating the planned demonstrations and for publishing the *Correspondance*. Besides Blome, this bureau initially included the legitimist Count Charles de Nicolay and Paul de Malijay, the former aide-de-camp to General Kanzler. The initials of their first names, GCP, formed the code that would be used in the coming years to refer to the work of the Geneva Committee. Very quickly it became apparent that Malijay and Nicolay were lightweights and were not suitable for this work; in fact, from the beginning, Blome was the actual leader of the bureau and of the entire organization. As a former diplomat, he enjoyed the full confidence of the Holy See, and in addition had the necessary competence and capacity for work. Mermillod kept an eye on the undertaking from a distance. According to Blome, he was 'an unparalleled invigorating force, but not a leader or a steadfast guide'[16]. For a while Cramer considered settling in Geneva also, but his financial problems still demanded all his attention and did not permit him to leave the Netherlands. Once Blome became aware of Cramer's involvement in the bankruptcy of Langrand-Dumonceau, a crisis developed in his relationship with him.[17] Cramer, however, played down his share in the financial scandal, as we have already noted. He kept up a lively correspondence with Blome and in that way directed opera-

---

16   Blome to Cramer, 20 Dec. 1870, 21 Feb., 3 March and 21 Oct.1871, NKDC, *Cramer*, 434, 12 b, I.

17   Blome to Cramer, 17 Jan. 1871, ibid.: 'You presented yourself, and I have presented you to all our friends in all countries as the most reliable supporter of the movement. I said to each one individually: without him we will not accomplish much, but with him we will move mountains, his assistance is essential for us. He has the ideas, the talent to actualize them, the energy, the zeal, the necessary independence, he enjoys the consideration of all business men, etc. Imagine the deluge if this awful Langrand were to drag you down with him'; Id. to id., 7 April 1871, ibid.: 'You are too bound to the Catholic movement for it not to feel the inconveniences that bother you.'

tions from a respectful distance.[18] Both regretted that Bréda was not involved, but his anti-German attitude at the time made this completely impossible.

Blome carried out the work mainly on his own then, with the help of some subordinates. Much time was taken up with the editing of the *Correspondance*, which from 27 October 1870 appeared two to three times a week in German and French. Additionally, through circulars and private correspondence, he kickstarted Catholic agitation across all of Europe.[19] Of even greater importance were his contacts with the Vatican. Fortunately, here he could count on the help of Anton Pergen, who quickly made himself fully available; thanks to his confidential relationship with Pius IX and Antonelli, 'Toni' was the right person to take care of the Rome connection.

Initially, however, that connection did not function as desired. Antonelli did not immediately fulfill his promise to appoint a correspondent and in mid-November Pergen travelled to Rome to settle the matter. He got the Pope and the secretary of state to agree that a double line of communication with the Vatican would be opened. The bureau would regularly inform Pius IX about its activities via Monsignor Mercurelli, the papal secretary for political correspondence. The secretary of state on his part would give instructions to the bureau through 'X', a curial prelate proposed by Pergen himself who clearly belonged to his circle of friends. This 'X' remained unknown to virtually all members of the Geneva Committee. In the correspondence he was initially called the *intermédiaire* and later the *innominato*. He would supply the *Correspondance* in the coming years with reliable information and instructions from the secretariat of state.

The secrecy surrounding the *intermédiaire* ensured that the connection between the Geneva bureau and the secretariat of state could not be traced. In that way, the Vatican could manipulate Catholic opinion and put pressure on governments, without being subject to diplomatic or curial conventions.[20] The Geneva bureau, for its part, gained a lot of authority in the Catholic world because of the reliability of its Roman information, although it had to pay a price

---

18   Cramer's incoming and outgoing correspondence is the main source for the early history of the Geneva Committee. Furthermore, the records of Joseph de Hemptinne are also important for this episode. Blome's archives contained a 'Geneviana' file, which for many years was in the possession of his youngest daughter Carola, a canoness in the monastery of Nonnberg. She gave the file to Karl Lugmayer, after whose death it was transferred to the diocesan archives in Linz. On inquiry, it seemed not to be there (anymore). See Bader, ed., *Karl Lugmayer und sein Werk*, 210.

19   The '[very] confidential letters' were signed with the initials GCP. Five were written during the last months of 1870 and eighteen in the course of 1871.

20   [Czacki], 'Progetto per l'organizzazione della stampa', [April 1878], ASV, SS, *Spogli Czacki* en *Spogli Franchi*. See also the retrospective considerations of Cardinal Wladimir Czacki, [January] 1887, ASV, *Episcopi et Principes*, Pos. et Min., 142. The Holy See now applied a strategy that was previously used regularly by other European governments, notably by Napoleon III and Bismarck.

for this: it would become increasingly dependent on the Vatican, through the *intermédiaire*, and would become entangled in the web of curial power politics.

The *Correspondance* reported on the massive protests and large-scale petition campaigns in all the European countries and in North America. In mid-November 1870 Cramer noted with satisfaction: 'The agitation is increasing and is becoming more widespread. The *Correspondance* is contributing to this in an efficient way.'[21] In mid-February 1871 he wrote: 'The Geneva bureau has in everyone's eyes become the headquarters of the Catholic troops. It watches over everything, gives the orders and is the centralizing point that leads and manages.'[22] Cramer was clearly carried away by his enthusiasm. The Geneva Committee indeed gave a strong boost to the protest movement, but gradually a form of petition fatigue crept in.

A decree of 4 March 1871 led to the seizure of a growing number of monasteries in Rome, inflaming passions once again. Two months later a major campaign got underway against the Law of Guarantees of 13 May 1871, which was intended to regulate the position of the Pope and at the same time relations between Church and State in Italy. It guaranteed the complete independence of the Pope as spiritual head of the church, but took from him every temporal power and subjected him to Italian law.[23] As far as the regulation of the Church-State relationship in Italy was concerned, the government allowed some freedom to the Church, but still retained many regalistic measures, such as the *Exequatur* for the appointment of bishops and parish priests. The Curia argued that the position of the Pope concerned Catholics of all countries and could not be unilaterally regulated by Italy. In any case, what confidence could the Pope have in a government that had so often broken its promises? Moreover, Italian cabinets succeeded one another very quickly, and a new leadership team rarely felt bound by the commitments of its predecessor. Two days later, on May 15th, the Pope categorically rejected the Law of Guarantees in the encyclical *Ubi nos*. The secretariat of state urged the bishops to protest to their respective governments against this law and the Geneva Committee worked diligently to disseminate the request.

The Committee then launched yet another action. From early 1871 it sent deputations to the Vatican to assure the Pope of the support of the international Catholic community. The Belgians took the lead and were soon followed by other national deputations, including one from England led by the Duke of Norfolk and Lord Denbigh. The deputations of lay people to Rome had an

---

21 Cramer to Cardinal Pitra, 28 Nov. 1870, NKDC, *Cramer*, 24, I, 266; Cramer to Scherer, 11 Dec. 70, BCUF, *Scherer*.
22 Cramer to Blome, 13 Feb. 1871, NKDC, *Cramer*, 24, I, 442.
23 Vidotto, *Roma Contemporanea*, 33-43.

Johann Anton Pergen. Photograph.
[*Vienna, Österreichische Nationalbibliothek*]

undeniable effect: they proved to be an appropriate means of putting pressure on the Italian government to adopt a cautious policy towards the Holy See.[24]

The secret activities of the Geneva bureau soon attracted the attention of the political world, beginning with the publication of the encyclical *Respicientes* on 1 November 1870. This contained an implicit excommunication of the Italian king Vittorio Emanuele II. The Vatican gave the impression that the encyclical was intended only for the bishops, but through the *Correspondance de Genève* it found its way to a large number of Catholic newspapers in Italy and elsewhere. The seizure of these newspapers was only partially successful and the sensational news spread very quickly across the peninsula.[25] The approach pursued proved rewarding, and was afterwards repeated regularly.[26] In mid-February 1871, Blome noted with satisfaction: 'The diplomats are getting annoyed. Complaints about Geneva have been made to the Vatican, but it of course has responded that the prisoners [the Pope and his entourage] could not know about events on the other side of the Alps.'[27] The German ambassador to the Holy See, Harry Arnim, already knew enough about the Geneva Committee to be able to discern the link with the Curia. He saw it above all as a Jesuit maneuver, which was not a bad guess because Mermillod and his friends maintained very close contacts with that order.[28]

The national security services increasingly began to monitor the Geneva group. The Italians were the first, followed by the Germans, the Austrians and the Swiss. Blome and his friends soon realized that their correspondence was being intercepted, and so they regularly used couriers for their communications with the Vatican. The most confidential documents were entrusted to Pergen, who travelled to Rome very frequently. Blome had his headquarters in Geneva in the imposing Hotel Metropole, on the left bank of Lake Geneva, near the old town. He probably stayed there under a pseudonym, as Pergen certainly did when he later took up residence there as Antoine d'Aspang, a reference to his family's castle south of Vienna. In their correspondence with the Catholic committees outside of Italy, the members of the network threw up a smokescreen by frequently using pseudonyms that made their communications incomprehensible to the uninitiated reader. Terms like *le principal, le patron, qui de droit, Mathilde, ma soeur, le deuxième étage*, all referred to the Pope.[29] Antonelli was referred to as le *troisième étage* and *le commis*. Blome

24 Van den Branden de Reeth to Hemptinne, 18 April 1871, ADH, *Corr. 1870-72*. See also: Pesci, *I primi anni di Roma Capitale (1870-1878)*, 43-52.
25 Miko, *Das Ende des Kirchenstaates*, vol. III, 334-344. Letters from the Bavarian, French and Prussian envoys.
26 Pergen to Cramer, 30 May1871, NKDC, *Cramer*, 434, 12 c.
27 Blome to Cramer, 16 Feb. 1871, NKDC, *Cramer*, 434, 12 b, I.
28 Arnim to Bismarck, 25 Feb. 1871, cited by Miko, *Das Ende*, vol. IV, 67.
29 The papal apartments were then on the second floor of the main Vatican building, while those of Antonelli were on the third floor.

was given the suggestive names of *le tyran*, *l'autocrate* and *Jupiter*. As the foster father of the undertaking, Monsignor Mermillod was called *Joseph*, and Pergen was *le jeune ami* or *le cadet*. Rome was referred to as *Le Canton 16*, *Londres* or *là-bas* and Geneva as the more transparent *Calvinopolis*. Letters from Rome were *les photographies*. According as the committee acquired more enemies, the secrecy increased, a process that happened quickly enough, as will be seen later.

Violette

The main communication tool of the Geneva bureau was the *Correspondance de Genève/Genfer Correspondenz*, for which the pseudonym *Violette* was used. It was a *sui generis* organ, which did not have any subscribers, but was sent without charge every two or three days to approximately three hundred Catholic newspapers.[30] It supplied information about events in Rome and the Catholic movement in Europe, as well as contributions with a more doctrinaire slant. In this way, as a secret mouthpiece of the Vatican, it gave direction to the Catholic papers and made interesting materials available to them.[31] The editorials in the magazine were provided in principle by the Vatican, through the *intermédiaire*. He worked closely with Antonelli,[32] who appeared to have sufficient confidence in Blome's political skills.[33]

A major problem facing the *Correspondance* was finding staff.[34] The search for a suitable French-language journalist and a German counterpart was an arduous ordeal as potential candidates pulled out one by one, or else were deemed inadequate. The Catholic committees did make some assistants available, such as clerks and an office boy, but they were 'like bees swarming around the office'.[35] They were volunteers and replaced one another very quickly. The bottom line was that Blome was virtually solely responsible for the editorial work, which was not suitable for a man of his rank. As an Austrian aristocrat and a member of the *Herrenhaus*, journalism was indeed not

---

30   Lory, 'La 'Correspondance de Genève', 103.
31   [Pergen], *Réflexions d'un solitaire sur l'Œuvre de Genève*, [1871], NKDC, *Cramer*, 456, 20 a;
     Minutes of the annual meeting in Geneva, 29 Aug. 1872, ibid.
32   Pergen to Leo Thun, 12 Aug. 1871, SALD, *Thun-Hohenstein*, A 3 - XXI, E 513, 909-913. In this
     letter Pergen mentions that the editorials of GCP were usually prepared in Rome and that
     the editorial staff in Geneva could change little in them. See also Pergen to Cramer, 22 May
     1871 and 14 Aug. 1872, NKDC, *Cramer*, 434, 12 c.
33   Blome to Cramer, 23 March 1871, NKDC, *Cramer*, 12 b, I: '[Antonelli] has peremptorily de-
     clared that he would put a stop to all reports the day that neither Pergen nor I would be
     here anymore. He knows me, wishes to show me the confidence that he pleasantly refuses
     to give to others, and he makes me responsible for everything as long as I am here.'
34   Lamberts, 'La découverte du "quatrième pouvoir" par le Saint-Siège', 589-620.
35   Blome to Cramer, 25 Feb. 1872, NKDC, *Cramer*, 434, 12 b, I.

compatible with his position. Earlier in his career he had already contributed to Catholic newspapers, in Hamburg and in Vienna, but that work had always been done in the greatest secrecy. Even now he attached the greatest importance to his anonymity:

> Do you know what would happen if people were to find out that his Excellency, the Count lowers himself to write in a newspaper and that he even strikes up a chat with the printers? The Viennese salons would remain forever closed to him. 'Fie anyway! A scribbler! We do not receive such a person'; 'Yes, yes! I've always said that that Blome would come to a bad end. He was not like the others. That kind of eccentric always breaks his neck'; 'Bah! An editor! Would he also have become a Jew?' At the court: 'Wow! A privy councillor, a minister in disponibility! The emperor cannot any longer receive someone who is so compromised.'[36]

During this period Blome worked sixteen hours a day, without a break, and in the end the pressure was too much for him. Besides the editorial work, he also kept up a busy correspondence with the national committees in order to streamline the mobilization of Catholic opinion. He regularly complained about the shortage of competent employees: 'It is fair to say that all the employees in the Austrian diplomatic service, which usually comes in for so much criticism, are like eagles compared to the nonentities that the Catholic movement brings forth.'[37] His wife, Séphine Buol-Schauenstein, occasionally lent a hand, but in February 1871 she gave birth to her eighth child and was not available for some time. Blome wanted to give up at that point.[38] Pergen managed to dissuade him from doing so. He had just returned from Rome with the message that the Pope was full of praise for the work of the Geneva bureau and attached great importance to its continuing.

Fortunately, at the end of February 1871, a light glimmered on the horizon. Pergen brought in the lawyer Clemenz-Friedrich Eickholt, who assumed responsibility for the administration and would become a permanent fixture.[39] At the same time the French Jesuit Régis de Chazournes joined the team.[40]

---

36 Blome to Cramer, 28 March and 7 April 1871, NKDC, *Cramer*, 434, 12 b, I. Even in 1877 Blome still attached a lot of importance to his anonymity with regard to the *Correspondance* (Blome to Cramer, 7 Jan. 1877, NKDC, *Cramer*, 434, 12 b, II).

37 Blome to Cramer, 17 March 1871, NKDC, *Cramer*, 12 b, I.

38 Blome to Cramer, early Feb. 1871, NKDC, *Cramer*, 12 b, I: 'Let us never organize a Catholic movement any more. We lack manpower, we are too poor in intelligence, in dedication and in capital.'

39 Blome to Cramer, 23 Feb. 1871, NKDC, *Cramer*, 434, 12 b, I: 'The most distinguished member of the pontifical artillery, studied law at the University of Vienna, was raised in the Tyrol, and is consecrating his life to the service of the pope.'

40 On Régis de Chazournes (1832-1883) and his work at the *Correspondance*, see: Burnichon, *La compagnie de Jésus en France*, vol. IV, 405-407. He belonged to the Jesuit province of Lyon. On the province's theoretical orientation, see: Dumons, 'Jésuites lyonnais', 131-143.

His provincial had opposed his posting with tooth and nail because Jesuits had been forbidden to live in Switzerland since 1848. Moreover, the Geneva paper had not only a religious but also a political dimension, making the operation still riskier. Blome and Mermillod turned to the Jesuit Superior General, Beckx, and promised him that they would burden Chazournes only with secretarial work. Under this condition, he was allowed to leave for Calvinist Geneva, where he doffed his soutane and went around like a lay person. The agreement was that he would work at the *Correspondance* just for two months, but Blome threatened to stop the publication if the Jesuit were called back. Knowing how much importance the Pope attached to the undertaking, Beckx succumbed – once again – to the pressure. Within a short time, however, it became clear that Chazournes was not only doing secretarial work but was also playing an important part in editing the paper. Beckx then decided to bring him back from Geneva, after a seven-month stay.[41]

Meanwhile, Chazournes' work had given Blome the opportunity to catch his breath at his favourite spa town of Karlsbad. Pergen took on the role of interim director for four months. He maintained written contact with Blome and forged a relationship also with Cramer, who was still considered to be a mainstay of the enterprise. The 'cadet' got along well with Eickholt and became close friends with Chazournes. The editorial work was now almost routine. However, just one problem persisted in connection with foreign news: the information from Italy and especially from Rome came in without a hitch, but there was a shortage of foreign correspondents. This obliged Pergen to look through 80 to 100 newspapers every day, searching for information on developments in the Catholic world. Still, he would later testify: 'My campaign during the summer of 1871 was like a triumphal march. I could effortlessly weave a crown with the laurel leaves that others supplied.'[42]

Violette consisted of three sections: 'News from Rome', 'News about the Catholic movement' and 'Reflections'. The first section was very comprehensive in the initial months. Blome and Pergen had an extensive network in Rome that they could immediately call on for the *Correspondance*. They recruited informants from diplomatic and journalistic circles, among the prelates of the Curia and the Jesuits. Their paper quickly gained the reputation of being more accurate than influential Catholic newspapers like *L'Univers*.[43] The section on 'News about the Catholic movement' primarily included information about Germany and Austria, and to a lesser extent about France. The 'Reflections' section was the most important in terms of content. It included leading articles that dealt mainly with the Roman question, international politics and,

---

41 Beckx to Gaillard, 17 Feb., 22 and 25 May, 23 June 1871, ARSJ, *Reg. Lugd.*, V, 147, 153, 154 and 156.

42 Pergen to Cramer, 19 Aug. 1871 and 27 Oct. 1872, NKDC, *Cramer*, 434, 12 c.

43 Blome to Villermont, 22 Dec. 1871, ADV, II, G, 2; Blome to Hemptinne, 15 Feb. 1872, ADH, *Corr. 1870-72*, 204.

increasingly, the relation between Church and State. It was the *intermédiaire* who supplied most of the articles for this section, and Blome felt he had little leeway to amend these contributions.[44] Even more annoying was that he had to translate difficult chunks of scholastic philosophy of law from Latin, a task that cost him a lot of time.[45]

In its lead articles, the *Correspondance* defended the temporal power of the Pope with the usual arguments. It sharply criticised the non-intervention policy of the great powers and clung to the hope that eventually at least one government would come to the aid of the Pope, with others then following. The paper believed that the 'Italian Revolution' had an even more anti-religious character than that in France in 1789, and that it wanted to undermine not only the temporal but also the religious power of the Pope. That was certainly an exaggerated position. The *Correspondance* bestowed on the Italian king Vittorio Emanuele II some rather insulting epithets, such as 'king of thieves, bogus king, puppet king, liar', and called his government a tool of the freemasons, a collection of perjurers, thugs and cowards.[46] That was certainly not diplomatic language, but it did come from the secretariat of state.

In its 'Reflections' section the *Correspondance* also devoted considerable attention to France and Germany. It praised the conservative government that had come to power in France after the fall of the Empire and hoped that it would come to the Pope's aid, preferably together with Austria. When that prospect did not materialize, it adopted a more critical tone but continued to treat the French government with much goodwill. That was not the case with the German government. At the end of 1870 the periodical expressed the hope that Bismarck would not abandon the Pope and that he would put pressure on Italy, once peace with France was concluded. However, the opposite happened. Bismarck sought rapprochement with Italy and tried to isolate France as much as possible. On the domestic front, he came into conflict with the *Zentrum*, the newly formed Catholic party. His government was also ever more openly supportive of the schismatic movement of the Old Catholics who refused to recognize papal infallibility. At the end of July 1872, the *Correspondance* began a frontal attack on Bismarck because of his foreign and domestic policies.

From now on, the Dutch chancellor was the primary target of attacks by the *Correspondance*, thus further souring relations between the government and the Catholic Church in Germany. Aware of papal support for the periodical, Bismarck had the articles meticulously screened and used the most

---

44 Blome to Cramer, 3 March 1871, *Cramer*, 434, 12 b, I: 'The true editor is not in Geneva. Frankly, I am also annoyed at having nothing to do but correct – professional jealousy, yes?'; Blome to Cramer, 23 Nov. 1871, ibid.: 'I have begged that we be sent shorter articles, but in vain ...We do not have the time to rework these articles.'

45 Blome to Cramer, 23 Nov. 1871, NKDC, *Cramer*, 434, 12 b, I.

46 *CdG*, No. 139, 11 Sept. 1871.

compromising passages to raise doubts about the patriotism of the German bishops.[47] The result was that more and more prominent prelates, including the influential Bishop of Mainz, Wilhelm-Emmanuel von Ketteler, distanced themselves from the paper.

The periodical took a twofold approach with regard to Austria. On the one hand it expressed its appreciation for Francis Joseph I because of his sympathy for the papal cause, but it also accused him of being too weak to give Austria what it deserved: 'a thoroughly Catholic government that would defend the papacy abroad and protect ecclesiastical freedoms at home'.[48] On the other hand, the Beust government was lambasted: it sowed division in Cisleithania and conducted an antipapal policy in Italy. Beust was the paper's favourite scapegoat and Blome undoubtedly was complicit in this. The Saxon was given unflattering epithets such as 'the evil genius of the liberals', 'the concierge of the Italian freemasons', 'the knave of Italy'.[49] When he was dismissed in November 1871 the paper was jubilant.

In judging the various governments, the *Correspondance* was largely guided by their attitude to the Roman question. By mid-1871 it had become clear that foreign intervention in favour of the Pope was no longer to be expected. Nor could diplomacy offer any more help. All the Pope could now count on was the continuing protest of the Catholic people. That corresponded with a leitmotif of Blome's, who kept insisting vociferously that the Pope had to rely particularly on the faithful for the restoration of his rights and the establishment of a Christian social order.[50]

The Black International

Blome and his friends were until then completely preoccupied by the Roman question. However, the Commune uprising in Paris in the spring of 1871 made clear that revolutionary socialism constituted as serious a threat to the stability of society as the Franco-Prussian War and the demise of the Pope's temporal power. Not only the political and religious but also the social order was shaken; not only anticlerical liberalism and excessive nationalism, but also socialism presented significant risks to society and the Church. The Catholic people had to resist this and dedicate themselves to restoring the social influence of the Church, which at the same time would ensure a regeneration in so-

---

47 Goyau, *Bismarck et l'Eglise. Le Kulturkampf*, vol. I, 278.
48 *CdG*, No. 6, 14 Jan. 1871.
49 *CdG*, No. 24, 23 Feb. 1871; No. 34, 13 March 1871; No. 60, 3 May 1871.
50 Blome complained that the Holy See was still not making full use of the Catholic popular movements (Letter to a Roman prelate, 26 Feb. 1871, cited by Lugmayer, 'Zur Vorgeschichte der sozialen Rundschreiben Leo XIII', 65).

The Abbey of Einsiedeln. Photomechanical print, c. 1890.
[Washington, Library of Congress]

ciety. From that viewpoint, it seemed advisable to consolidate the operations of the Geneva Committee and to give it a broader and more sustainable base.

With that goal in mind, in late August 1871, Mermillod convened a closed meeting of prominent Catholics in the Benedectine abbey of Einsiedeln, in the alpine heart of the Swiss cantons.[51] Fifty people in all turned up, half of whom were French and German, as had been the case a year earlier also. Many of those present were active in papal or charitable societies. The Spanish and French included many legitimists. The majority were aristocrats: the princes Karl von Löwenstein and Karl von Isenburg-Birstein, the Duke of Norfolk and Duke Salviati, the Marquis Patrizi and some fifteen earls, besides nobles of lower rank. The middle-class participants came mainly from France, Germany, Belgium and Switzerland. The majestic, rural abbey of Einsiedeln, with its glorious past, was a suitable venue for this select company and guaranteed the secrecy of the meeting. Some information was leaked to the press, but the content of the discussions remained a matter of guesswork. A Swiss radical-liberal politician wrote, rather overconfidently: 'Whatever the dignitaries have decided, one thing is certain: their struggle against the modern *Zeitgeist* is hopeless, they are not capable of turning back the wheel of time, even for a second.'[52]

51   On the Abbey of Einsiedeln and this meeting: Kälin, *Schauplatz katholischer Frömmigkeit*, 140-147.
52   Alois Steinauer in the *Bund*, 16 Sept. 1871, cited in: Kälin, *Schauplatz*, 147.

The theme of the congress was 'the restoration of the social reign of Christ'.[53] One of the participants, Ignatius von Senestrey, the bishop of Regensburg, aptly expressed the objective in a prayer, which in the future would be referred to as 'the creed (or prayer) of Einsiedeln'. Some striking passages in this prayer to the Blessed Virgin speak for themselves:

> We acknowledge and confess that the kingdom of Jesus Christ includes not only every human being in particular but the whole world, and that all human society should be subject to Him. Because the Pope of Rome is the representative of Christ on earth, we submit the regulation of our whole lives, including our public and social behaviour, to his decisions and commands. We reject and abhor the evil principles and teachings of a false science that wants to banish the kingdom of Christ from human society and to bring in the pernicious omnipotence of the State ...[54]

This prayer was indeed more of a confession of faith than a supplication. It also implied a commitment to fight for the Church's independence from and supremacy over the State.

Those present wanted to join forces in order to bring about both a political and a social revitalization of society, and therefore determined to strengthen the organization, which had been founded just a year before. They decided that the bureau would henceforth be supplemented by a *Comité des Permanents*, in which there would be one representative from every country. These *Permanents*, together with other prominent lay people, would organize annual congresses, implement congress decisions and the instructions of the Holy See. They also had to supply the bureau in Geneva with regular bulletins about developments in their own countries. The congress participants promised to increase both the financial and editorial support for the *Correspondance*. They resolved to set up a telegraph agency and to improve the supply of information to Catholic dailies through a correspondence network. They discussed further ways of defending the Pope's temporal power. In addition, they wanted to strengthen Catholic organizations in view of the struggle against liberalism and State omnipotence and – a new element – the Socialist Workers' International. Following the Commune uprising, the conference participants had become well aware that the social question was of growing interest and demanded an adequate response from the Church. Afterwards their organization would regularly be called the 'Black International', as a

53   Menozzi, 'Regalità sociale di Cristo', 79-123; Id., *Sacro Cuore*, 107-132.
54   This translation is based on a Dutch translation of the prayer, which was approved by Monsignor Zwijsen, bishop of Den Bosch, on 22 Jan. 1872 (NKDC, *Cramer*, 456, 20 a).

counterpart to the 'Red Workers' International'.[55] Yet, it would direct its efforts primarily against liberalism, the present enemy, and only secondarily against socialism, the enemy of the future.

From now on, the *Permanents* would play a crucial role in the organization in addition to the Geneva bureau, and strengthen the connection with the Catholic committees in two ways. First, they sent information to Geneva every month about developments in their own countries. The non-confidential topics were suitable for publication in the *Correspondance*, while the confidential topics were synthesized in a report that was submitted to the secretariat of state and to all the *Permanents*. Second, the latter were expected to follow up congress decisions in their own countries. They also regularly received circulars with secret instructions from the Geneva bureau.[56] In this way the organization functioned alongside the ecclesiastical system in connecting the Holy See and the faithful, with a view to mobilizing Catholic opinion. The laity had to extend a helping hand to the clergy, who were increasingly being subjected to discriminatory laws in different countries and were being limited in their range of action. But, as Pergen stressed in his typical military jargon: 'The shepherds [bishops] must continue to be the generals, the committees to provide the officers, the people to supply the soldiers and the pope is the king.'[57]

The annual congresses of the Black International took place usually in August, in Geneva or its immediate surroundings. The meetings had a secretive, closed character and were attended by the *Permanents* as well as carefully selected representatives of the Catholic committees in their own countries. There were thirty to forty participants as a rule, with the largest delegations always coming from Germany and France, followed by the Swiss who were on home ground. The Belgians, Austrians and Italians normally put in an appearance also. The congresses offered an opportunity to exchange thoughts about the organization, strategies to be adopted and the development of the Catholic movement in the affiliated countries. Meetings lasted for three days and always followed the same pattern. Monsignor Mermillod as chair opened the proceedings with his trademark inspiring address, after which the *Permanents* delivered a report about developments in their respective countries. Then various commissions deliberated about acute problems: the Roman question, the press, education, the voluntary sector, social and political issues. In the final

55   *CdG.*, No. 185, 30 Nov. 1871: 'We are Black Internationalists, we are rebels'; La Tour du Pin to Pergen, 28 June 1872, HHSA, *Pergen*, II: '... the great Black International of which you are the promoter...'; Ravelet to Cramer, 17 Oct. 1871, NKDC, *Cramer*, 437, 13 d; Salviati to Pergen, 19 May 1874, HHSA, *Pergen*, II: 'I would prefer that the Black International were public also.'

56   The *'lettres très confidentielles'* were given a serial number. They dealt with the working of the organization, the annual meetings, the deputations to Rome and the activities that had to be undertaken in the different countries.

57   [Pergen], *Réflexions d'un solitaire sur l'Oeuvre de Genève*, [1871], *Cramer*, 456, 20 a.

session they presented their conclusions to the plenary gathering. As with all conferences, the contacts formed between the participants constituted the most valuable aspect of these meetings.

The first task of the restructured organization was to maintain the *Correspondance de Genève* and put it on a more solid footing. The financial allowance was increased by half and now stood at 60,000 francs [252,000 euros]. In the next few months, the agency made attempts to set up a telegraph service that would send brief, succinct messages from Rome via Geneva to interested Catholic newspapers. Such a service operated for several months in the spring of 1872, but then had to end its activities for lack of funds. Simultaneously the bureau worked on a grand plan to establish a Catholic news agency. Obviously Cramer was an enthusiastic supporter of this and was not slow to share his ideas about it. Nevertheless, it became clear very quickly that the International did not have the organizational strength and financial resources to set up an international press agency. Since this was too ambitious, the office then opted for a decentralized approach. The example of the *Correspondance française*, an agency that provided information and articles to some forty Catholic newspapers in France through a system of autography and telegraph, inspired the setting up of national correspondence networks. All these initiatives indicated that the organization attached great importance to promoting and influencing the Catholic press.[58]

Still it was the Roman question that topped the agenda. In Einsiedeln the congress delegates had noted that the Catholic protest movement was bogged down, and felt 'a new element was needed to keep the Catholic momentum going, but only the Vatican could take an appropriate initiative in that regard'. This wording was vague, but the delegation that was sent to report to Rome was given more concrete, verbal instructions. Remarkably, Bréda was part of this delegation; after the Commune uprising, he had gradually shifted his priorities and had hesitatingly sought a rapprochement with the Geneva group.[59] The delegation was to urge the Vatican to adopt a more resolute stance, so that it would be possible eventually to use the Roman question as leverage for profound social changes. Specifically, they proposed to the Holy See that the interrupted Vatican Council would continue outside of Italy, for example, in the Tyrol, and that the Pope would leave Rome on that occasion. The council had to formulate a Catholic alternative for the social chaos. The Pope's departure from Rome would galvanize Catholic mass movements, would likely bring about a regime change in Austria and would ease it away from its neutrality. Austria would then, with the help of other states, and especially France, restore the temporal power of the Pope. Moreover, the restoration of a Christian

58 Lamberts, 'Une organisation secrète', 75-78.
59 Bréda to Cramer, 7 May, 12 June 1871, 1 July and 4 Aug. 1872, NKDC, *Cramer*, 434, 12 a, III. Bréda also took part in the conference at Einsiedeln, after consulting with Blome.

state in the Dual Monarchy would also bring about the restoration of Christian monarchies in France and Spain.[60] The plan was partially inspired by the influential Bohemian politician Leo Thun-Hohenstein, who approached Emperor Francis Joseph I to ask if he would be prepared to extend his hospitality to the Pope.[61] It would soon become clear, however, that there was no enthusiasm in papal circles for the far-reaching ideas of the International, and Antonelli especially drew back from considering such extreme measures. In the winter of 1871 Monsignor Mermillod went to Rome to advocate in his turn the departure of the Pope, but his attempt failed as well.[62]

The Vatican thus appeared to be unwilling to take the lead in a political restoration movement, but clearly it had discovered the power of Catholic popular movements. That was certainly the case with Pius IX, who on receiving the Geneva delegation, remarked: 'The people are good and governments are bad. Do the kings then want the pope to become a republican?'[63] In January 1872, on receiving a larger international delegation, the Pope expressed his full agreement in an address in which he declared: 'The governments do not represent either the mind or the heart or the will of the Catholic people.'[64] These statements did not imply a preference for democracy, but did contain a rejection of the (patrician-) bourgeois governments and their anticlerical policies. The Vatican would in the coming years fully utilize the support of the Catholic masses to further secure its position in Italy, and to resist governments hostile to the Church. Here the Holy See strove primarily for religious goals, but in the long run the appeal to the people would inevitably acquire a political colouring and would drive the church in the direction of democracy.

For the moment there was little movement on the Roman question. Both parties stuck to their positions and over time consolidated the status quo. The Holy See continued to use the Geneva bureau to maintain international support and so continue to exert pressure on the Italian government. On the occasion of several papal jubilees, the International ensured that messages of congratulations were sent by telegraph to the Vatican. It also regularly organized international deputations to Rome, for example to protest against the transfer of the administration of the Italian government, or to raise objections to the abolition of yet more monasteries in the Eternal City. By sending these international deputations of lay people, the International wanted to influence public opinion, and demonstrate to the Italian government that the Pope could count on the continuing support of a large section of Europe's elite.

---

60 Report by Bréda, 18 Sept. 1871, ASV, *SS.*, *Spogli Rampolla*, I; Bréda to Leo Thun, 4 Oct. 1871, SALD, *Thun-Hohenstein*, A 3 - XXI, E 525, 979-985. See also the perspicacious analysis in Viaene, *The Roman Question*, 168-174.
61 Pergen to Leo Thun, 7 Nov. 1871, SALD, *Thun-Hohenstein*, A 3 - XXI, E 533, 1078-1081.
62 Blome to Cramer, 18 and 23 Nov. 1871, NKDC, *Cramer*, 434, 12 b, I.
63 GCP to the Permanents, *Très confidentiel* No. 9, 28 Sept. 1871, NKDC, *Cramer*, 456, 20 b, 5.
64 Cramer to Bréda, 26 Jan. 1872, NKDC, *Cramer*, 24, II, 43.

The nine muses

Besides the bureau, the *Permanents* from now on played an important role and the success of future operations would largely depend on them. In their own circle they were called the 'nine muses', as nine countries were represented on the committee. Some turned out to be pillars of strength, others were little more than dead weights. Since they had to act as links between the Catholic committees and the bureau in Geneva, it was important that they enjoyed sufficient prestige in their respective countries and could set things in motion.

That was certainly not the case with Jan Willem Cramer. However, as co-founder of the organization, he could not be passed over as *Permanent* for the Netherlands. From October 1870 he carried out a lively correspondence with Blome and from May 1871 with Pergen. That his financial troubles continued to haunt him was a problem. Moreover, as we have seen, he was a *persona non grata* among the Dutch bishops and therefore did not get the chance to be a liaison with Catholic organizations, which were well developed in the Netherlands thanks to a broad freedom of association. The bishops had developed a tight hierarchical system of government for their minority church, which left little room for input from prominent laymen. Least of all did they want to give a free hand to Cramer, who was known to be unpredictable and had an unsavoury reputation as a financier. They always put a stop to any of his attempts to launch petition movements or send deputations to Rome. Cramer appealed to Antonelli and the Pope several times to urge the Dutch bishops to be more zealous, but to no avail. The Vatican knew that it could count on the Dutch bishops in matters of vital importance, and that they were not waiting for Cramer in order to show their loyalty. So it was mainly as an informant and adviser that he would play a significant role in the International for another three years.[65]

The Belgian *Permanent*, the entrepreneur Joseph de Hemptinne from Ghent was of a completely different caliber.[66] He represented the most industrial and most 'liberal' country on the European continent. Even in Catholic circles, Belgians were open to political and economic liberalism, as had already been evident in the 1830s. However, after 1848, a new generation of laymen emerged who turned against the basic principles of political liberalism. As has been repeatedly noted, this was a pattern throughout Europe, but what was remarkable in the Belgian case was that these laymen were overwhelmingly from a bourgeois background. They were very active in the charitable conferences of the St. Vincent de Paul Society and later in the Peter's Pence

---

65   De Valk, 'A Struggle behind the Scenes', 387-408; De Coninck, *Een les uit Pruisen*, 345-352.
66   Lamberts, 'Joseph de Hemptinne: een kruisvaarder in redingote', 64-108; Id., 'De rol van Joseph de Hemptinne in de Zwarte Internationale', 1083-1102; De Maeyer, 'La Belgique. Un élève modèle de l'école ultramontaine', 365-377.

Joseph de Hemptinne. Photograph, C. D'hoy, 1863.
[Leuven, KADOC]

Association. Their main exponent was Joseph de Hemptinne, a wealthy indus-trialist, who provided generous support to many Catholic charities in which he was personally involved. Due largely to him, the diocese of Ghent, which in the 1830s had been a liberal Catholic bastion, now became the most im-portant ultramontane foothold in the country. The Belgian ultramontanes did not immediately question the liberal constitutional regime, but Hemptinne himself became increasingly doubtful about it, asking if Catholics could in all conscience swear an oath of loyalty to their liberal constitution. In this field, he was an autodidact, with little understanding of the subtle nuances of intellectuals, theologians and bishops to whom he presented his questions. As his activities became more international in scope and he came into more direct contact with papal circles, he realized that the Holy See and the Belgian bishops were not on the same wavelength. He therefore turned more and more to Rome for guidance and advice. Through the Peter's Pence Association he became involved with the Geneva Committee and he would become one of the most active *Permanents*. Unlike Cramer, he succeeded in mobilizing support for the papal cause in his own country. Moreover, in March 1871, with the explicit support of Pius IX, he set up a society of militant lay people that called themselves – appropriately enough – the Crusaders of St. Peter or *les Croisés de St-Pierre*. It was above all members of this core group who participated in the congresses of the Black International. They would contribute significantly to a strengthening of the ultramontane movement in their own country, with far-reaching consequences.

In Switzerland, where Catholics – as in the Netherlands – accounted for about forty percent of the population, the function of *Permanent* was taken by Theodore Scherer-Boccard (1816-1885), the chairman of the *Piusverein*, the most important Catholic lay organization in the Swiss Federation. In the German-speaking cantons, that association did not have much impact on Catholic conservative politicians, who, as in Belgium, had predominantly liberal Catholic sympathies. Ultramontanism had more success in working-class circles and was advancing in the French-speaking cantons such as Geneva and Fribourg. Because of considerable immigration, 51% of Calvinist Geneva was Catholic in 1870. Monsignor Mermillod was in charge of a powerful movement that was positively disposed to the Pope. He ensured close collaboration with the International and would regularly use its services whenever the Church in Switzerland was put on the defensive by anticlerical government measures.[67]

Gaining the support of major European countries such as the Dual Monarchy, Germany, France and Italy was especially important for the International. Austria-Hungary was not a problem. Contact with the nascent organizational Catholicism was arranged by Blome and Pergen who played a central role in the Geneva bureau. Eduard von Stillfried-Ratenicz, chairman of the *St. Michaelsbruderschaft* since 1865, also contributed to this. He became the first Austrian *Permanent*, but in 1873, for health reasons, he passed on the torch to Pergen, who in the meantime had gained enough experience to assume the leadership of the Catholic movement in Cisleithania. Another Austrian, who played a significant role in the Geneva Committee particularly in the early years, was the already mentioned Count Leo Thun-Hohenstein (1811-1888). He had been minister of education under the neo-absolutist regime and had played a major role in arranging the concordat with the Holy See (1855). Afterwards he became the undisputed leader of the federalist Bohemian nobility, who opposed the *Ausgleich* and demanded greater autonomy within the empire for the Czechs. His involvement in the Black International was such as to enhance its credibility in the ranks of the Catholic aristocracy. The same ap-

---

67   Altermatt, 'L'engagement des intellectuels catholiques suisses', 409-426.

plied to the younger princes Alfred and Aloys von und zu Liechtenstein, who in time would follow in his footsteps.[68]

Besides Austria, Germany's contribution was also of great importance. The Bavarian prince Karl von Löwenstein (1834-1921), chairman of the *Zentralkomitee der katholischen Vereine Deutschlands* and the driving force behind the annual *Katholikentage*, was closely involved in the creation of the Geneva Committee and also took part in the conference at Einsiedeln. A short time later, however, he distanced himself from the organization, under the influence of Bishop Ketteler who had difficulties with the *Correspondance* because of its sharp attacks on Bismarck.[69] Löwenstein then put an end to the support of the *Zentralkomitee* for the *Correspondance*.[70] After that, he would no longer participate in the activities of the organization, but various people in his immediate circle continued to cooperate, such as Baron Franz von Wambolt (1829-1908) from Hessen-Darmstadt, who was appointed *Permanent* for Germany at Einsiedeln.[71] He was one of the most active members for two years and in early 1873 even took over the leadership of the bureau for a few weeks. He, together with Löwenstein, would later play an important role in the rise of social Catholicism in Germany. In 1873 Wambolt was followed as *Permanent* by Prince Karl von Isenburg-Birstein (1838-1899), Löwenstein's brother-in-law and also a member of the *Zentralkomitee*. When Bismarck launched his *Kulturkampf* against the Church of Rome[72], Isenburg succeeded in getting the German Catholic committees more involved once again in the International. The Westphalian Baron Felix von Loë (1825-1896) also came more to the fore. In 1872 he became chairman of the *Mainzer Verein der deutschen Katholiken*, which was closely aligned with the goals of the Geneva committee and would soon become the largest popular organization in Germany. The *Verein* was fiercely opposed by Bismarck and it was disbanded in 1876, but Loë's role was not then ended, as will be mentioned later.[73] The German representatives in the International were on the right side of the Catholic *Zentrum* party, which had a more liberal Catholic orientation, but they moved in the same orbit.[74]

68 Lamberts, 'Political and Social Catholicism in Cisleithania', 299-318. On the princes of Liechtenstein, see *infra*, 252.

69 Blome to Cramer, 30 Oct. 1871, NKDC, *Cramer*, 434, 12 b, I; Blome to Hemptinne, 3 Nov. 1871, ADH, *Corr. 1871-72*, 168. See also Ketteler to Isenburg, 8 Dec. 1871, cited by Lugmayer, 'Zur Vorgeschichte der sozialen Rundschreiben Leo XIII', 64.

70 Siebertz, *Karl Fürst zu Löwenstein*, 289; note in SAWT-R, *Löwenstein*, Lit. D Nr. 675, 3.

71 On Franz von Wambolt (1829-1908), see Knoll, *Der soziale gedanke im modernen Katholizismus*, 112-115.

72 On the *Kulturkampf*, see infra, 230-232.

73 Félix von Loé (1825-1896) would still play a role in the 'Union of St. Peter' and the 'Maison Salmini' (see *infra*, 239). He would later become chairman of the 'Canisius-verein' (1879) and from 1882 of the 'Rheinische Bauernverein'. See *NDB*, XV, 1987, 13-14.

74 Becker, 'Eine katholische Adels-Internationale', 273-298; Ross, *The Failure of Bismarck's Kulturkampf*, 125-132.

The French contribution to the Geneva committee was also of great importance, but the successive *Permanents* were hardly representative figures.[75] The International used other channels to stay in contact with the main Catholic organizations, which were given greater leeway after the fall of the Empire. That was true for the conferences of the St. Vincent de Paul Society and above all for the *comités catholiques* (Catholic committees), which organized an annual congress every year from April 1872 on.[76] Various prominent figures from those committees took part in the meetings of the International. Moreover, contacts with the *Oeuvre des cercles catholiques d'ouvriers* (Society of Catholic Workers Circles) were of great importance for the future. The leading figures of that society, Albert de Mun and René de La Tour du Pin, came into contact at an early stage with the Geneva group. De Mun had a deep appreciation for Blome's tract, *Wo ist Europa's Zukunft* and for Mermillod's social views.[77] Still, it was mainly La Tour du Pin who, in time, would work actively for the International and would contribute to its social orientation. A striking fact is that almost all the International's French contacts had ties with legitimism.

Obviously, Italy could not be excluded from the work of the Geneva group. The bureau had a lot of informants in the ecclesiastical world, but had to look for influential figures in the Catholic organizations.[78] These organizations had started with some difficulty only in the 1860s and were still very fragmented. In the 1870s an umbrella organization known as *Opera dei Congressi* was established.[79] It worked closely with the clergy and took on the task of propagating Catholic principles in all spheres of life, with the aim of integrating the masses in a veritable *contre-société*. It would eventually succeed in doing this very well, and thus helped lay the basis for a well-organized civil society in Italy. For decades it would remain the most important Catholic organization, because the Curia forbade Catholics to participate in national politics. This *non expedit* was intended as a boycott of the new Italian state, but at the same time it hindered the involvement of Catholics in political life and the formation of a vigorous confessional party.[80] The actual leader of the *Opera dei Congressi* was Duke Scipione Salviati (1823-1892), who had taken part in the

---

75 The first French *Permanent* was Edmond Lafond, who had earned his spurs in the Peter's Pence Association and was already a member of the Mamertins. He would be replaced in 1873 by a close friend of Bréda's, the diplomat Adolphe d'Avril (1822-1904). He too was active in the international organization, but he didn't have strong ties either with French Catholic organizations. See Moulinet, 'Le Comité de Genève', 319-344.

76 Moulinet, *Laïcat catholique et société française*.

77 De Mun, *Ma vocation sociale*, 44-46; Molette, *Albert de Mun*, 14-15. See also *infra*, 266.

78 Canavero, 'Mobilisation du mouvement catholique en Italie', 345-360.

79 Multon, 'L'Opera dei Congressi', 29-44.

80 Ciampani, 'The Roman Curia', 198-204. This '*non expedit*' was already enacted in the 1860s for the annexed territories and after 1870 was extended to the whole country. Only after the First World War would a Catholic party, the *Partito Popolare Italiano* (the Italian People's Party), be established in Italy.

Scipione Salviati. Oil on canvas.
[*Migliarino-Pisa, Villa Salviati*]

congress at Einsiedeln and in 1873 became the Italian *Permanent*. Because of his important role in the International, he deserves special attention.

Salviati was in fact a member of the princely family of the Borghese, but he had inherited the ducal title and the name Salviati from Cardinal Gregorio Salviati, a relative on his mother's side. A very wealthy man, he owned palaces in Florence, Pisa and Rome, as well as vast estates in Migliarino, in the region of Pisa, where he usually lived. His family in Rome belonged to the 'black nobility' who had remained faithful to the Pope, and he was himself completely devoted to the papal cause. Thanks to his status, his extensive network and close relationship with the Pope, he soon become the éminence grise of the Catholic movement in Italy. He directed the annual conventions of the *Opera dei Congressi* in close consultation with the Vatican. In him the International had found an authoritative figure who could strengthen their bond with the increasingly active Catholic movement in Italy.[81]

81   Orfei, 'Notizie sul primo movimento cattolico', 101-109; Gambasin, *Il movimento sociale nell' Opera dei Congressi (1874-1904)*.

Spanish involvement in the activities of the International remained very limited. The Spanish *Permanent* was the publicist and literary figure, Gabino Tejado (1819-1891), who belonged to the neo-Catholic tendency within Carlism, meaning that he placed church interests above dynastic. He had close ties with the Catholic resistance movement which from 1868 challenged the secularization policy of successive liberal governments. But his activities were soon curtailed by the outbreak of a new Carlist uprising, as will be discussed later.[82] Because he opposed the coup, he was barred from the political leadership of Carlism. The civil war would significantly hamper his contacts with the Geneva Committee.

England was a case unto itself. There the Catholic minority was very heterogeneous and was still perceived as a strange element in British culture. The Black International found its audience, not so much among the many Irish immigrants but among the old Catholic families and a number of upperclass converts. The first English *Permanent* was Charles de la Barre Bodenham (1813-1883) from Hereford, who belonged to an old aristocratic Catholic family and had been one of the 'Mamertins'. However, he did not enjoy enough prestige to bring influential Catholic aristocrats along with him, or to win the cooperation of Monsignor Manning, the archbishop. The International therefore engaged other intermediaries besides Bodenham, thereby helping to establish the Catholic Union, which was chaired by Henry Fitzalan-Howard, Duke of Norfolk, the most prominent Catholic nobleman in the country. Explicit reference was made to the Geneva committee in the founding of this lay organization, which still exists. A board member, Thomas William Allies (1813-1903), an educator and a convert from the Oxford Movement, replaced Bodenham in 1875 as the English *Permanent*. In general, however, the interaction between the International and the British Catholic elite remained very limited.[83]

A failed restoration

After the congress of Einsiedeln Blome once again took charge of the bureau in Geneva, but he had growing doubts about the continuing usefulness of the venture. He was very disappointed in the wavering and, in his view, lukewarm stance of the Vatican. The events of 1870-1871 had awakened almost eschatological expectations in him, the hope that the mobilization of the Catholic masses would lead to a more Christian social order and even perhaps to a restoration of the Christian monarchies. These expectations were not met. In the course of 1872 he became convinced that in the circumstances it was bet-

---

82   Holt, *The Carlist Wars*, 246-259; Callahan, *Church, Politics and Society in Spain*, 248-278; Montero and Robles, 'Le mouvement catholique en Espagne', 427-446.

83   Heimann, 'English Catholic Particularism', 447-463.

ter '*de faire les morts*'('to play dead').[84] Indeed, from mid-1871 Antonelli had increasingly adopted a wait-and-see attitude, which was also evident in his opposition to the proposal that the council be continued outside of Rome so as to contribute to a restoration movement in Europe. For these reasons Blome wanted to retire.[85] A few years later, Pergen would testify:

> The *Correspondance de Genève* was the visible expression of the titanic struggle of one man [Blome] against the regrettable policy of the Antonelli faction. As long as that man kept the upper hand and could cherish the well-grounded hope of dislodging the cardinal from his passivity, the newspaper flourished and thrived. From the moment he had to acknowledge defeat, the newspaper, which called for action, became more colourless by the day and was doomed to disappear.[86]

Blome had still other reasons for giving up. He had been living with his family for more than a year in expensive hotel rooms and was looking for a permanent home. Moreover, he felt he got too little support from the other committee members.

The Pope's entourage resolutely opposed eliminating the Geneva bureau which offered a valuable addition to the diplomatic and ecclesiastical channels in manipulating public opinion. In March 1872 Pius IX sent a *breve* (brief) to the *Correspondance de Genève* that was so laudatory that even the Geneva team was surprised. The *Permanents*, with Cramer at their head, also tried to dissuade Blome from going through with his plans.[87] His reply was to be expected: the others took for granted that he would wear himself out for the job, but they did not provide him with the necessary resources to operate it in a proper way. If they wanted to maintain the bureau, they just had to provide a suitable replacement, and if they were not able to do that, they would be better off abandoning the cause.

Finding a replacement for Blome was certainly not a sinecure. In the intervening period, the *Correspondance* had made many enemies in both the political and ecclesiastical worlds, and skilled leadership was required to

84 Blome to Cramer, 2 Nov. 1872, NKDC, *Cramer*, 434, 12 b, II.
85 Blome to Cramer, 17 Dec. 1872, NKDC, *Cramer*, 434, 12 b, II: 'Me, I am withdrawing for the moment because I see that nobody wants to do anything serious, and that ... is the most powerful reason for my resolve'; Blome to Cramer, 1 Dec. 1872: 'The *Correspondance* is nothing more than an easy way out for the *commis* [Antonelli] and a revelation to the world of his weakness', ibid.
86 Pergen to Friedrich Thun, Dec. 1875, SALD, *Thun-Hohenstein*, A 3 - XIX, H 82, 19.
87 Cramer to Breda, 16 Feb. 1872, NKDC, *Cramer*, 24, II, 63; Cramer to Blome, 20 Feb. 1872, NKDC, *Cramer*, 24, II, 74: 'You have given an impetus to the worldwide movement; you have led the protests ... In the moment of truth that is coming, you will be the rallying point between the papacy on one side and the Catholic world on the other ... And nevertheless, you would abandon us!'

avoid all the pitfalls. The director had to be a man of authority, preferably with political and diplomatic experience, have the full confidence of the Holy See and enough financial resources at his disposal to enable him take on this un-paid function. Pergen was possibly eligible, but he was considered by many, including his mentor Blome, to be still too young and inexperienced. Cramer then pushed Bréda forward, praising the able pen and sharp insight of the *Dornbirnien*. However, Bréda was headstrong and impulsive, did not enjoy Antonelli's full confidence, and would have to be given financial compensa-tion. Blome and Cramer, who were still the central figures in the committee at this stage, finally came to a compromise. With Vatican approval, they en-trusted the leadership of the bureau for six months to the Pergen-Bréda duo, a partnership that had some chance of succeeding, as each complemented the other. Pergen was highly esteemed in the Vatican and was familiar, as none other, with the network that had been built up. Bréda had the necessary diplo-matic and journalistic talents; he had already stayed in Geneva for two weeks in January 1872 and had observed the activities of the bureau, so he knew what awaited him. It seemed a plausible solution, but still Blome was not entirely happy with it.[88]

Cooperation between Bréda and Pergen was hampered from the outset because Blome had promised Bréda in good faith that he and Pergen would act as co-directors, each performing different tasks but together deciding on the paper's direction. However, the people in the Vatican, Antonelli and his *in-termédiaire* seemed to think differently and relied mainly on Pergen, as quick-ly became obvious. Within a very short time after Bréda's arrival in Geneva, frictions surfaced. Problems arose about the handling of the correspondence with Rome. Bréda found the epistles of the *intermédiaire* too long and cumber-some; nor was he always happy with the content. The result was that he edited the texts far more extensively than Blome had, much to Rome's displeasure. Blome's occasional changes had been overlooked, but Bréda did not carry the same weight and was criticized severely. The complaints were sent to Pergen and through him they reached Bréda, leading to tensions between both direc-tors. Finally at the end of June, Pergen felt obliged to inform Bréda that on the authority of the Vatican, he was henceforth to be the sole director. Then the bombshell exploded. Bréda felt betrayed and decided that he would from then on cooperate in the work of the *Correspondance* only from the sidelines.

This was just not a conflict about competences but also about their vision on the Geneva organization.[89] Bréda thought that Pergen adopted an overly

88   Blome to Cramer, 4 March 1872, NKDC, *Cramer*, 434, 12 b, II: 'I cannot help feeling a secret terror, a premonition, if you like, that it will go wrong'; Id. to id., 12 March 1872, ibid.

89   Extensive documentation on this conflict is to be found in Pergen's archive (HHSA, *Pergen*, II, *corr. Bréda* and especially in the file '*pièces justificatives*') and in Cramer's archive (434, 12a and 24, II).

submissive attitude to Rome.[90] The 'cadet' was too much of a cardinal's man, an instrument in the hands of Antonelli and his *intermédiaire*. Bréda felt that the Geneva bureau had to take a more independent course, and had to be more than a subordinate agency of the Vatican. The secretary of state had apparently profited from Blome's leaving to bring the bureau more under his own control and, in Bréda's view, Pergen did not offer enough resistance.[91] From earlier history we know that the *Dornbirnien* was more of a politician than a churchman; he clearly did not want the Geneva operation, which had been initially founded by the Catholic committees, merely to serve Antonelli's policy of accommodation.

Much was at stake in this conflict. The Vatican had not initiated the Geneva undertaking, but papal support had ensured its unexpectedly rapid development. In such circumstances was it still possible to take a distance from the Holy See, and above all, was there a willingness to do so? The answers to these questions could only be given by Blome and Cramer, 'the two real founders of the organization'. Their response was identical: the agency had no reason to exist without the approval and support of the Curia; it could only be an auxiliary office of the Vatican. Cramer declared: 'We and our organization must be passive instruments in the hands of the *commis* [Antonelli].'[92] Blome reiterated this: 'The organization must remain absolutely dependent on the true centre.'[93] Still, he had a little more understanding for Bréda's position, as they were both more politically inclined.[94] Nevertheless, he considered that Bréda's wilfulness had put the Geneva committee in danger; there was no room for independent action by the laity against the ecclesiastical authorities.

The situation worsened when Bréda unexpectedly travelled to Rome at the beginning of July, at the urgent request of a curial cardinal.[95] During his stay he succeeded in discovering the identity of the *intermédiaire* and, to make matters worse, he disclosed this to third parties, thereby bringing the whole network into danger. In an interview with Antonelli he was almost equally tactless. The secretary of state was highly surprised by the unannounced visit and was bluntly told by Bréda that the Geneva bureau wanted more flexibility and autonomy. The *Dornbirnien* also visited Pius IX and got the impression that the Pope and his secretary of state were not on the same wavelength,

90 Bréda to Cramer, 22 June 1872, NKDC, *Cramer*, 434, 12 a, III: 'One is a *persona grata* in that area [the secretariat of state] only when one becomes a slave to it.'

91 Bréda to Cramer, 30 June, NKDC, *Cramer*, 434, 12 a, III: 'One restrained oneself under Blome because he inspires respect; advantage was taken of the present occasion.'

92 Cramer to Blome, 2 July 1872, NKDC, *Cramer*, 24, II, 154.

93 Blome to Cramer, 13 July 1872, NKDC, *Cramer*, 434, 12 b, II, I.

94 Blome to Cramer, 9 July 1872, NKDC, *Cramer*, 434, 12 b, II: 'He has so much talent, so much education and so much experience. Pergen speaks about him with unjustified contempt'; Blome to Cramer 13 July 1872, ibid.

95 Bréda was called to Rome by 'l'Angelo', most likely Cardinal Pitra (Bréda to Cramer, 2 July 1872, NKDC, *Cramer*, 434,12 a, III).

and that a two-track policy was being pursued in the Vatican. It was obvious to him that the agency had to follow the more radical, principled direction favoured by the Pope. Bréda might well be a stubborn and restless man, but he had assessed the situation well. Moreover, he got the impression that the *intermédiaire* was an ambitious and opportunistic prelate: 'He lacks seriousness and depth, blowing hot and cold by turns.'[96] According to him, the contact person often acted on his own, but Pergen denied this very emphatically: 'During my last trip to Rome, I became convinced that he submits every letter to the *commis,* before posting it.'[97] Bréda refused to be convinced and wondered if the bureau in Geneva should continue to blindly follow the Roman directives, considering that it was not clear who had actually formulated them.

Bréda returned to Geneva on July 19th, his actions having aroused alarm in Blome and Cramer. The question was whether they should blindly follow the Vatican, and if so, whether they would continue the line of the Pope or that of his secretary of state. The solution was to minimize the divide between Pius IX and Antonelli. Besides, Blome's opinion was clear: 'When the bureau was founded, *le principal* [Pius IX] urged us to follow the instructions of the *commis* [Antonelli]. Our obligations are clear and are well defined ... If the Pope no longer agrees with his secretary of state, then he must appoint another confidant.'[98] Blome and Cramer thus opted for a permanent, even stronger bond with the secretary of state. Bréda foresaw very astutely what a stranglehold this would be: 'The [Catholic] committees have been deprived of their organization by and for the convenience of the *intermédiaire*, for whom Pergen, in all honesty and without his being aware of it, is a docile instrument.'[99]

At that moment however, this was not the primary concern of those in charge of the organization. Bréda's actions in Rome had caused a lot of upset and had displeased even the Pope. Moreover, Pergen feared the indiscretion regarding the *intermédiaire* would complicate his cooperation and possibly even render it impossible: 'Aside from him, there is nobody in whom the *commis* and the *principal* have as much trust.'[100] The survival of the operation was in jeopardy. In mid-August Pergen travelled to Rome to try to iron out the differences. He was able to tell Antonelli that Blome and Cramer completely supported him and that Bréda, following his Roman escapade, had been completely sidelined. He returned just in time for the next congress of the International in Geneva (29-31 August) where he informed the *Permanents* that the

---

96 Bréda to Pergen 10 Aug. 1872, HHSA, *Pergen*, I, *Bréda, pièces justificatives.*
97 Pergen to Cramer, 14 Aug. 1872, NKDC, *Cramer*, 434, 12 c.
98 Blome to Pergen, 20 July 1872, HHSA, *Pergen*, I.
99 Bréda to Cramer, 28 July 1872, NKDC, *Cramer*, 434, 12 a, III.
100 Pergen to Cramer, 14 Aug. 1872, NKDC, *Cramer*, 434, 12, c.

Holy See wanted the agency to continue, notwithstanding all its woes, and that the leadership was from now on entrusted *de jure* to him.[101]

Bréda took no further part in the congress and broke off all contact with the Geneva bureau, and even with his old friend Cramer – at least for a short time. The Dutch *Permanent* had indeed adopted a remarkably tough stance in the recent conflict, whereas Blome, by contrast, had put much more effort into being a mediator. When Bréda later looked back on this turbulent episode, he concluded: 'Blome, despite his usual coolness and aloofness, treated me with great affection and I was very moved by it.'[102] Apparently, 'Jupiter' felt partly responsible for the debacle and also shared the Bréda's distrust of Antonelli. He even went a step further and declared to Cramer:

> You put all the blame on the *commis*. That is the opinion of the *Dornbirnien*. It is not mine. This kindness or, and let us not beat about the bush here, this weakness in applying principles that had been pushed forward so resolutely, is characteristic of him whom we do not name [Pius IX]. This is why nothing more can be expected from that side as long as he shall dwell among us ... There are times when one must be prepared *de se mettre en panne* ... The *Papa duro* will come in his own time. Our impatience will not bring us even one second closer to that time.[103]

Blome was and remained primarily a diplomat and a conservative statesman. He had hoped that the Church with the support of the Catholic masses would play a leading role in the restoration of the Christian monarchies. When the Vatican was not willing to do that, he withdrew from the International in which he had been such a central figure. He could no longer afford to continue working for the venture. In a passage replete with the metaphors typical of his epistolary style, he explained his decision to Cramer:

> In any case, I must reject the role you have assigned to me, that of a prompter in the wings. Like the old Prince Metternich, I see only two alternatives: to be either an actor on the stage or a spectator. When the major drama will be performed, which I thought was already on the programme, I will play a role that is commensurate with my abilities and I will, as always, stand my ground. As long as people are content with vaudeville, I will watch from the gallery. I will not appear on

---

101 Blome to Cramer, 17 Dec. 1872, NKDC, *Cramer*, 434, 12 b, II: 'The young officer [Pergen] comes invested with complete power. He is dedicated, he has been given the mission'; Cramer to Blome, 25 Dec. 1872, NKDC, *Cramer*, 24, II, 366: 'It is true that the young officer is invested with full power and that he is now the formal head of the organization.'
102 Bréda to Cramer, 20 April 1873, NKDC, *Cramer*, 434, R 12, A, III.
103 Blome to Cramer, 31 Dec. 1872, NKDC, *Cramer*, 434, 12 b, II; Id. to id., 25 Nov. 1873, ibid.: 'To act effectively, we need a *Papa duro* and a Christian monarch. Until the advent of these two great men, no effort will succeed. That is my conviction.'

the stage, because the minor roles of comedians or extras do not suit me. Neither will I be a prompter in the wings, because I would ruin everything if I were to come across a performance that did not match my temperament and my taste.[104]

From this text can be deduced that the former diplomat considered it beneath his dignity to be a messenger boy for the Curia, which in his view pursued an overly cautious and opaque policy, at least politically. Cramer scored a point when he later objected: 'Blome considers the Geneva Committee to be solely a war machine, when in fact the intention was to organize a Catholic undertaking.'[105] Pergen especially was deeply disappointed by Blome's decision and after his departure lamented:

That man whom I revered as a demigod, whom I loved like a second father, has disappointed me deeply. He still dreams only of *dolce far niente* ... You cannot imagine how much he has changed. That man, for whom nothing was serious enough, speaks only of ... doing nothing. He spends his days playing Offenbach and solving chess problems ... I have done my utmost to get him to understand that for its leaders, the Catholic movement is not an aviary, in and out of which they can fly, according to the impulses of the moment ... My words fell on deaf ears.[106]

Pergen had become involved in the diplomatic service as a military attaché and was much less of a statesman than Blome. His commitment was motivated more by his Catholicism than by politics, and he could not therefore understand how Blome could abandon ship at a time when opposition to the organization was growing and all hands were needed on deck. The 'cadet' gave absolute priority to Catholic action and he would remain fully engaged in it, both internationally and in Austria. A few years later he would confide to a prominent Austrian diplomat: 'My political convictions are rooted in my faith ... The Catholic movement is both a shield as well as a sword for my political views.'[107] With Blome it was the other way around: his social and political ideas largely determined his religious position.

In that context, it was significant that Pergen, unlike Blome or Bréda, had little sympathy for the French and Spanish legitimists. During this period the legitimists did not succeed in capitalizing on their momentum and they experienced a serious and, as it turned out, a definitive setback. It was quite symptomatic of the state of affairs that the Vatican did not come to their aid, indicating once again that the Holy See did not wish to play an instrumental

104 Blome to Cramer, 30 Dec. 1872, NKDC, *Cramer*, 434, 12 b, II.
105 Cramer to Pergen, 24 Jan. 1873, HHSA, *Pergen*, I.
106 Pergen to Cramer, 13 Nov. 1872, NKDC, *Cramer*, 434, 12 c.
107 Pergen to Friedrich Thun, 5 Feb. 1876, SALD, *Thun-Hohenstein*, A 3 - XIX.

role in the restoration of Christian monarchies and simply did not share the aims of conservative allies who were still trying to push through a restoration.

The fall of the Second Empire in France had created unexpected opportunities for the restoration of the Bourbon monarchy.[108] The constituent assembly, elected in February 1871, was almost a carbon copy of the armorial of the French nobility. It lifted the banishment of the Bourbons and thus paved the way for the accession of the Count of Chambord to the throne. However, in a solemn statement on 5 July 1871, he rejected both the principles of the French Revolution and the tricolour as the national flag. The tricolour symbolized a parliamentary monarchy based on popular sovereignty and he wanted to replace it with the traditional lily of the Bourbons. The repeated entreaties of the moderate monarchists had no effect. Chambord continued to consider a liberal monarchy to be a 'bastard of the revolution' and did not want to hear about any situation where '*le roi règne, mais ne gouverne pas*' ('the king reigns but does not govern'). His moderate supporters sighed: 'We had a beautiful dream and it has been shattered.' Finally, on 20 November 1873, a transitional regime was installed for a period of seven years, the so-called *Septennat*, which in the end would lead, not to the hoped-for restoration of the monarchy, but to the definitive establishment of the republic.

There was much sympathy in church circles for the legitimists. *L'Univers* resolutely chose Chambord's side. Vatican diplomacy also supported the restoration of the monarchy in France and expected the pretender to the throne to pursue a church-friendly policy. Nevertheless, it refused to identify the cause of the Church with that of the legitimists, and certainly not with Chambord's inflexible attitude. Pius IX urged him repeatedly to be more realistic, but in vain; when the restoration foundered on the rejection of the tricolour, he replied laconically: 'All this for a serviette.'[109]

The Holy See took an even greater distance from the Carlists in Spain, who started a new rebellion in April 1872 after they had become the victims of massive electoral fraud.[110] The situation was now more favourable for them than it had been the previous time. They directed their opposition against Amadeo, or King 'Macaroni', because he was seen as an Italian interloper. After his abdication in February 1873, a republic was proclaimed, and support for the insurgent Carlists grew. They acquired a strong position in the north of the country but failed to get a foothold in the larger cities. Their movement was primarily rural, regional and ultra-Catholic, but with leaders who were badly organized and hopelessly divided, they failed to force a breakthrough. In the meantime, moderate monarchists prepared for the return of the ousted

108 Bled, *Le Lys en Exil*, 219-280; Brown, 'Catholic-Legitimist Militancy', 233-254; Locke, *French Legitimists*, Princeton, 1974; Kale, *Legitimism*, 263-290.
109 Martina, *Pio IX*, vol. III, 354-364.
110 Holt, *The Carlist Wars*, 246-269; Callahan, *Church, Politics and Society*, 248-278.

Bourbon dynasty. Following a *pronunciamento* by the army, the minor son of the displaced Queen Isabella ascended the throne in January 1875, under the name Alfonso XII. That signalled the death knell of the Carlists, who gradually lost their support and finally gave up the battle in February 1876.

Carlism could count on a lot of sympathy among the lower clergy in Spain, but the bishops were more cautious. They welcomed the restoration of the monarchy in 1875 and were satisfied with the new constitution, which, while not restoring the former ecclesiastical privileges, largely confirmed the state's confessional character. The Spanish church learned to live with the moderate liberal regime of Alfonso XII and the Holy See encouraged that attitude.[111] Pius IX was not partial to the Carlists, though they were among the most ardent defenders of the restoration of his temporal power.[112] In his view, they confused religion and politics all too easily. In the Spanish case also, it was clear that the Vatican did not wish to pursue the ideal of the restoration of Christian monarchies. For the Church the actual form of government did not really matter; rather it sought to defend its freedom and influence within the existing political structures that were now somewhat liberalized. The Black International, now fully under Vatican control, was assigned its place in that strategy.

In the Vatican's grip

At the congress in Geneva in late August 1872, following the vicissitudes in the relationship between Pergen and Bréda, the *Permanents* rallied behind the 'cadet' and the Roman option.[113] Their refusal to continue financing the bureau and the *Correspondance* further increased the latter's dependence on the Vatican which now carried the financial burden of the venture almost exclusively, with the Pope himself apparently footing the bill.[114] In the first two years, the Catholic committees underwrote about two thirds of the annual budget, but in 1873 only the Belgian committee still gave a substantial contribution. The Vatican then assumed responsibility for more than eighty per cent of the ex-

---

111 Martina, *Pio IX*, vol. III, 335-342.
112 Marcella, 'La Spagna e la questione romana', 381-406.
113 Minutes of the annual meeting in Geneva, 29-31 Aug. 1872, NKDC, *Cramer*, 456, 20 a. From that year on the *Permanents* came together two days in advance to decide on the strategy to be followed.
114 The income and expenses of the CdG can be minutely reconstructed thanks to the information contained in the archives of Cramer, who was the treasurer of the operation (NKDC, Cramer, 456, 20 b, 3). According to Czacki, Antonelli was of the opinion that the Pope spent too much money on the paper. See Czacki's report, [May 1878], ASV, SS, *Spogli Franchi*, b 3: 'The Holy Father Pius IX took good care of it, by sending secret information through trustworthy persons, promoting it with various pontifical *brevi* (briefs) and, finally, by giving it financial subsidies.'

Pius IX and his household, with Giacomo Antonelli (third from the right), c. 1865. Photograph.
[*Leuven, KADOC*]

penditures, thereby bringing the International fully under the control of the Holy See. Blome baldly declared: 'In August, the creditors withdrew. Since then, the organization has changed completely in character, without people realizing it.'[115]

The fact that the Holy See now took over almost the entire financing of the *Correspondance de Genève* shows once again that the Pope and his immediate entourage attached great importance at the time to the venture. That is confirmed by the risks they took during the same period to enlarge its editorial staff. After Bréda's departure the editorial level of the publication had declined noticeably.[116] Pergen groaned under the work load and had hardly any skilled employees on whom he could rely. As usual, he described his campaign of late 1872 in military terms: 'I was being besieged by a regular army, while my garrison consisted of soldiers from the National Guard who were undisciplined and without any war experience. No dazzling action has added lustre to the defence of the fort. But I have persisted and have not capitulated.'[117] Still, if Rome wanted the publication to continue, its editorial staff needed to be urgently reinforced.

115 Blome to Cramer, 17 Dec. 1872, NKDC, *Cramer*, 434, 12 b, II.
116 Hemptinne to Villermont, 15 July 1872, ADV, II, A, 26; Mousty to Hemptinne, 31 July 1872, ADH, *Corr. 1870-72*, 238: 'In fact, the *Correspondance de Genève* has become very insignificant.'
117 Pergen to Cramer, 27 Oct. 1872, NKDC, *Cramer*, 434, 12 c.

Immediately after the congress in Geneva, Pergen asked Beckx, the Jesuit superior general in Rome, to put two fathers of the order at the disposal of the *Correspondence*: Régis de Chazournes, who had previously worked for the periodical, and a German colleague. Expecting strong resistance from Beckx, the 'cadet' immediately sent a copy of his request to the Pope, who sent Monsignor Mercurelli to put pressure on the Jesuit general. As anticipated, Beckx objected strenuously, pointing to the great dangers connected with Jesuit involvement in a paper that was so closely monitored by Bismarck's agents. He sought Antonelli's support, but the secretary of state as well as the Pope insisted that Pergen's request be granted. Eventually Beckx agreed and the French provincial was charged with making Chazournes available once again to the Geneva periodical.[118]

Pergen had to promise that he would make every effort to ensure the Jesuit's anonymity. He therefore decided that Chazournes would be based not in Geneva, as he had been the previous time, but in Thonon-les-Bains, on the French side of Lake Geneva. The Jesuit would be known there as 'Baron d'Arcy', the private tutor of a cousin.[119] His arrival filled Pergen with great joy as the two men had become close friends a year before. On 28 October 1872 Pergen travelled to Annecy, where the transformation of Chazournes into Baron d'Arcy was taking place. The cadet reported enthusiastically on this to Cramer, who had become one of his confidants after Blome left.[120] Chazournes' return lightened his load considerably.[121] But, because of the secrecy, every time he went to visit Chazournes, he had to take a boat ride of 90 minutes several times a week from the Hotel Metropole on the shores of the lake to the picturesque fishing village of Thonon-les-Bains.

Until the paper was discontinued, the French Jesuit would be a mainstay of the operation.[122] Pergen had also asked for the cooperation of a German Jesuit, but eventually gave up asking, to Beckx's great relief.[123] The 'cadet' did

118 Beckx to Gaillard, 23 Sept. 1872 (copy), ARSJ, *Reg. Lugd.*, V, 199; Beckx to Pergen, 10 Oct. 1872 (copy), ARSJ, *Ext. Saec. 1858-1879*, 422-423: 'To meet the wishes of the Holy Father and so as not to let you down, I am making this sacrifice, although, as I have already mentioned, it is very difficult for me and I foresee a lot of misery. Therefore I beg you with all urgency, dear friend, to do everything possible to free us from that danger, as soon as possible.'

119 Chazournes to Pergen, 30 Sept., 9 and 24 Oct. 1872, HHSA, *Pergen*, I.

120 Pergen to Cramer, 27 Oct. 1872, NKDC, *Cramer*, 434, 12 c.

121 Pergen to Cramer, 13 Nov. 1872, NKDC, *Cramer*, 434, 12 c: 'With regard to the leading articles, I only have to deliver him the manuscripts of the mysterious man [*l'intermédiaire*], to give him some directions regarding the political line and to reread his formulations.'

122 Chazournes to Beckx, 27 Jan. 1872, ARSJ, 1006, *Lugdunensis, 1872-82*. Chazournes described his way of life thus: 'I lead a serious, retiring life ... Apart from the contacts demanded by my function, I hardly see anybody ... I have with me a continual witness to my actions, one of my nephews whose presence explains and masks my presence here. My situation is perfectly accepted and altogether impenetrable.'

123 Pergen to Beckx, 29 Jan. and 16 Feb. 1873, ARSJ, 1006, *Lugdunensis, 1872-82*.

everything to keep the *Correspondance* going with the available resources and personnel. Again, he described his job in military terms: 'The Vatican is going to avoid the big fight. We must then prepare ourselves for a long siege.'[124] The *Correspondance* could still play an important role in defending the rights of the pope and in resisting anticlerical government measures in various European countries. In view of this, Pergen had to keep the International's network in operation, but in the end it became too much for him.

At the end of November 1872 matters came to a head and Pergen was direly in need of a rest. Blome then offered himself up for the last time and served as acting director for six weeks. Then 'Jupiter' retired for good.[125] He was deeply disappointed by the orientation given to the International by the Vatican, although he would later boast about his important contribution to its work.[126] In the meantime he bought a fairy-tale estate in Bellagio on Lake Como where he wanted to unwind and reflect on his future.[127]

After Blome's final departure, the *Correspondance* and the operation of the bureau went rapidly downhill. This was due not only to his leaving, but also to the fact that shortly afterwards Pergen himself had to retire permanently. He had already decided to withdraw in September 1873 for at least a year for family and financial reasons, but his father's unexpected death in late February hastened his departure. He left Geneva at full speed and after that would no longer function as director. Wambolt, the German *Permanent*, took over the leadership for six weeks. Meanwhile, key members of the Committee met in Rome in early March, on the occasion of a visit by an international deputation, and decided that the Geneva operation had to continue, at all costs. With the support of Pius IX and the bishop of Regensburg they found somebody who was prepared to take over the function of director for a longer period, the Bavarian ex-diplomat Ferdinand Hompesch.[128] The arrival of Wambolt and later of Hompesch meant that the formal leadership of the bureau came into German hands, whereas the Austrians, Blome and Pergen, had set the agenda until then. The Germans, however, were quick to realize that only

124 Pergen to Cramer, 1 Jan. 1873, NKDC, *Cramer*, 434, 12 c.
125 Pergen to Cramer, 1 Jan. 1873, NKDC, *Cramer*, 434, 12: 'The tyrant [Blome] arrived in a more than foul mood. He was more prone than the *Dornbirnien* [Bréda] to violent and unjust outbursts against the intermediary and his superiors. Moreover, he had ideas that were totally false regarding our personal rights in relation to the Geneva organization.' In July 1873 Pergen would try, in vain, to get Blome to participate in the annual meeting in Ferney (Pergen to Cramer, 18 July 1873, NKDC, *Cramer*, 434, 12 c).
126 Blome to Vogelsang, 21 Sept. 1883, cited by Klopp, 'Briefe des Graven Gustav von Blome', 199-200: 'By 1870 I had already brought about an international cooperation between prominent Catholics with annual meetings in 1870 in Geneva, then in Einsiedeln in 1871, again in Geneva in 1873, in Ferney in 1873, then in Bregenz, etc. The Vatican directly led this admirably functioning organization.'
127 See *infra*, 253-255.
128 On Hompesch-Bollheim (1824-1913), see B. Haunfelder. *Reichstagabgeordnete der Deutschen Zentrumspartei, 1871-1933*, Düsseldorf, 1999, 184.

Pergen continued to have the full confidence of the Vatican, something they resented.

Wambolt and Hompesch did not enjoy the respect given to Blome and Pergen, and the rapid change in management hastened the transformation of the work. Both in Rome and Geneva people had gradually begun to wonder if the *Correspondance* was still of much use. The periodical continued to devote a lot of attention to the Roman question both in its news and editorials, but the Vatican was evolving at an accelerated pace towards a political accommodation with the Italian 'usurper'. Changes were in the air. Moreover, the *Correspondance* faced increasing opposition from the German side, and as the *Kulturkampf* reached its height, Antonelli urged more restraint. Financing the publication had also become too big a burden for the Vatican.[129]

It was significant that the Holy See now took the lead, with the *intermédiaire* especially playing an important role. He informed Pergen that the *Correspondance* would be discontinued and that the organization would become directly dependent on the Curia. He negotiated this matter with the 'cadet' in person, without the knowledge of the bureau in Geneva; even Monsignor Mermillod remained in the dark. At the annual conference in Ferney, at the beginning of August 1873, the *Permanents* decided in good faith to consolidate the *Correspondance* and reinforce their committee with new representatives. Pergen was given the thankless task of advocating the decisions of the congress in Rome, but – as he had feared – his mission was in vain. The Vatican's decision to stop the *Correspondance* was irrevocable. At the beginning of October, the *intermédiaire* announced that the bureau in Geneva would be shut down along with the *Correspondance*. He himself would take over the coordination of the organization itself and would henceforth be called the *innominato*. In future he would supply the *Permanents* directly with the information that they had to send on to the Catholic press, still under the GCP signature. They, for their part, had to send him their monthly reports and other interesting news items. Through him they could also get in touch with '*qui de droit*', meaning the Pope, and the two-way traffic would henceforth go directly to Rome. The notion of a collective was hardly mentioned, the only hint of it being the retention of the annual meetings. The scope of these changes was clear. The entire organization was immediately put under the guardianship of the Holy See and in Rome it was the *innominato* who would henceforth be the key figure. Cramer's judgement on this development was very accurate: 'What Rome has imposed on us is pure absolutism. They would like the laity to give a helping hand, but to do so in a spirit of complete submissiveness.'[130]

The key figures of the committee were deeply disillusioned and the *Permanents* were in danger of losing contact with one another. At the last minute

129 Czacki's report on the establishment of an *Uffizio stampa* [April 1878], ASV, *SS, Spogli Franchi*, b 3.
130 Cramer to Pergen, 25 Oct. 1873, HHSA, *Pergen*, I.

Cramer succeeded in getting the Vatican to appoint a vice-chair who would maintain mutual relations and organize the annual congress. In this way, at least an organizational framework would be retained. As was to be expected, Pergen, '*l'enfant chéri*', was appointed vice-chair.[131] Mermillod continued to be the formal chairman.

Hompesch, the outgoing director, contended that the new organization created more possibilities for the *Permanents* than had the previous one, and that was true to some extent. They now had direct access to the Pope and his entourage, a prerogative that some would use extensively. However, with the abolition of the bureau in Geneva, a major focal point for their joint action disappeared. There was now hardly any counterweight to the control of the Curia. With the disappearance of the *Correspondance de Genève*, the International also lost its main means of exerting influence on the outside world.

The *innominato*

The *innominato* gave the *Permanents* the task of concluding an agreement with a limited number of newspapers, to which he could, through them, send his press releases. Those messages signed *Frédéric* could be published, with GCP acknowledged as the source, whereas the messages signed *Ferdinand* were confidential and had to be kept secret. The information intended for the newspapers would henceforth consist of instructions and no longer of complete articles. Clearly, news coverage in the future would largely depend on the input of the *innominato*.

Some of those around Pergen correctly foresaw that the Geneva operation would lose its efficacy. In the first months of 1874 the *innominato* sent his press releases with some regularity, but gradually did so less frequently. Apparently he still received monthly reports from some *Permanents*, but he no longer supplied a summary to others. As a result, mutual involvement decreased noticeably. Pergen watched all this with dismay, but felt completely hamstrung and could do little from faraway Vienna, although he did succeed in continuing the annual congresses.

Meanwhile some *Permanents*, in consultation with the *innominato*, were exceptionally active in the Catholic movement of their own countries. Such was the case with Joseph de Hemptinne, the Belgian *Permanent*. His archive reveals the main clues to the mysterious *innominato*. In the early years the Ghent industrialist pursued a relatively moderate course with his *Croisés de St-Pierre*.[132] This society of lay people, with the bishops' consent, studied is-

131 Hompesch to Hemptinne, 26 Nov. 1873, ADH, *La Croix;* Pergen to Friedrich Thun, 15 Dec. 1873, SALD, *Thun-Hohenstein*, A 3 - XIX, H 82,5.
132 Lamberts, 'Joseph de Hemptinne', 83-95.

sues of public and civil law that were important for the status of the Church. In addition, they were involved in press activities and in developing all sorts of Catholic charities and associations. On being awarded the title of Roman count by Pius IX at the end of 1873, Hemptinne's zeal grew and he felt encouraged by the Pope to do battle with the liberal Catholic government that was then in power in Belgium. This led to a clash with the bishops, who not without reason were afraid of a liberal takeover. The Ghent industrialist felt that he could not rely on the bishops in political and religious matters, and appealed to the Pope for guidance. This attitude resulted in a split among the *Croisés* in April 1874. The more moderate members, led by Leuven professor Charles Périn, went on to form a new lay association on the Viennese model, called the *Confrérie de St-Michel* (Brotherhood of St. Michael). As its rule of conduct, this fraternity pledged submission to the Pope's teachings and obedience to the bishops. It would exert an important influence on the confessionalization of the Catholic party and the development of social Catholicism in Belgium at the end of the century.

De Hemptinne decided to continue working with a small core of faithful who would obey him and the pope, would pledge not to implement 'bad' laws and were prepared to fight resolutely against liberal Catholicism. He got approval for the new statutes of the *Croisés* from his Roman correspondent, the *innominato,* alias *Ferdinand*. He also funded a radical ultramontane weekly newspaper, *La Croix*, which immediately caused uproar in ecclesiastical circles because it openly glorified medieval theocracy and especially showcased its dislike of the Belgian liberal constitution. The paper raised doubts about the admissibility of the oath of allegiance to the constitution, and urged Catholics not to participate in elections, arguing that believers could not in any way cooperate with a pernicious regime that was founded on wrong principles. This strategy would constitute a form of political suicide that could be disastrous for the survival of religious freedoms. The bishops would have preferred to ban the weekly, which they, in a clear allusion, described as 'a big cross', but they were afraid of a possible appeal to Rome. Finally, they advised their clergy not to read *La Croix*. In Rome *Ferdinand* and Monsignor Mercurelli defended the paper. It was investigated by a number of theologians and on May 21 the Pope rewarded it with a laudatory *breve* (brief), to the dismay of the Belgian bishops. Admittedly, *Ferdinand* urged moderation, requesting that issues such as the constitutional oath and the direct political power of the pope no longer be treated. The editors also were asked to show more respect for the bishops.

The results of this intervention were not immediately noticeable. In August 1874 the episcopate once more listed their grievances with *La Croix*: its laicism, lack of respect for the bishops, theocratic excesses, condemnation of the constitutional oath and incitement to abstention in the elections. This litany was sent to Pius IX in the hope that he would rein in the editors and Hemptinne. However, the Pope let it be known via Antonelli that no condemnation of *La Croix* would be forthcoming from him and that the editors had to be supervised rather than discouraged. The bishops then just learned to co-exist with *La Croix*, though most of them continued to work against it in a subtle way. For that reason it had a larger distribution abroad than in Belgium, and was especially popular in ultramontane and legitimist circles in France. It also found great favour with most members of the International, as we shall see later.

At the end of 1875 the *Croisés* showed how seriously they took their obedience to the Pope and their rejection of the laicizing legislation. On 3 October 1875, Pius IX in an address to Belgian pilgrims asked them to work hard for a change in the marriage laws of their country, and in particular to ensure the abolition of the constitutional requirement that the civil ceremony precede the religious one. The *Croisés* immediately sent a petition with this request to King Leopold II, to the dismay of the conservative government and the Catholic episcopate. The moderate ultramontanes were not in agreement either. Indeed, the petition could be regarded as an implicit request for constitutional reform, which in the circumstances could only lead to a curtailment of religious freedoms. The *Croisés*' petition did not have the slightest effect, but they did emerge from the confrontation as the moral victors, because Pius IX praised their initiative while rebuking some of the bishops.[133] De Hemptinne subsequently became known as 'the pope of Ghent'. When he began to spread his radical views in a series of small catechisms, he was not given an ecclesiastical 'imprimatur' in his own country, but the Pope personally wrote by hand in the first catechism: 'Your principles are correct. I bless your good will and pray to God that he will give light and strength to all who are called to defend these principles.'[134]

All these incidents show how Pius IX in the last years of his pontificate used the Black International as a parallel circuit to support radical ultramontanism, sometimes against local bishops. It should be added that the *innominato* regularly counselled Hemptinne to act moderately, and cautiously encouraged him to adopt a more pragmatic attitude towards the liberal, parliamentary regime in Belgium. Still, the prevailing tone in his advice and instructions was very anti-liberal and radically ultramontane. In bourgeois, industrialized Belgium it created a dissonant sound, even in Catholic circles. Pius IX and the *innominato* drove Joseph de Hemptinne in a direction that would land him on the periphery of the Catholic movement in his own country.

133 Lamberts, 'Une offensive de Pie IX', 50-78.
134 *Ferdinand* to Hemptinne, 21, 24 Jan. and 5 Feb. 1876, ADH, *corr. 1875-76*, 116, 117 and 121.

The surmise is that the *innominato* also directed Pergen's actions in Austria, but there are no traces of this in his huge archive because all the correspondence with the mysterious contact person has been destroyed, presumably intentionally. Pergen had been chair of the *St. Michaelsbruderschaft* since May 1873. He progressively put himself forward as the leader of the Catholic movement in Cisleithania and became recognized as such.[135] His actions brought him into conflict with Cardinal Rauscher, who was not happy with the lay movement taking autonomous initiatives. In March 1875, along with the *St. Michaelsbruderschaft*, he succeeded in organizing a mass demonstration in which many Catholic organizations from throughout the empire participated. From this grew the idea of organizing the first major *Katholikentag* in Austria, on the German model.[136] Rauscher's death, in late 1875, facilitated the plan, but the liberal government later put a stop to it. Freedom of assembly was still subject to many restrictions in Austria, and the government eagerly seized the opportunity to thwart the initiative.[137] In the end, mainly thanks to Pergen's efforts, the great Catholic congress still went ahead in Vienna, from 30 April to 3 May 1877.[138] It would give a definitive boost to Catholic organizations in Cisleithania.

The *innominato* was particularly involved in expanding the Catholic movement in Italy. Duke Scipione Salviati became *Permanent* in late 1873 and he immediately founded a *Consiglio di permanenza* in his own country. This council carried out its activities in secret in order to escape police surveillance. It discussed the congress decisions of the International and implemented them as much as was possible. Salviati invited the foreign *Permanents* to the main demonstrations of the Catholic movement in Italy, and asked their support for protests against anticlerical government measures. This *Consiglio* took over the actual leadership of the *Opera dei Congressi* and planned the annual congresses of the Catholic umbrella organization, in close consultation with the *innominato* and the Pope. Salviati consulted the Vatican in advance about the resolutions to be adopted, which were then wholeheartedly approved and endorsed. In addition, the duke, always with the agreement of

---

135   Pergen to Cramer, 27 Jan. 1874, NKDC, *Cramer*, 434, 12 c: 'A speech... that I gave at the beginning of October put me, despite myself, at the head of the movement in Austria'; Blome to Cramer, 10 Feb. 1874, NKDC, *Cramer*, 434, 12 b, II: 'Pergen is working wonders in Austria. I am very proud of him.'

136   Silberbauer, Österreichs Katholiken, 66-67.

137   Pergen to Cramer, 19 July 1876, NKDC, *Cramer*, 434, 12, c. On Pergen's decisive role in the organization of the *Katholikentag*, see Knoll, *Zur Tradition*, 119. Knoll cites a statement by Von Gagern: 'The *Katholikentag*, that's Toni Pergen.'

138   Leisching, 'Die römisch-katholische Kirche', 204-210; Silberbauer, Österreichs Katholiken, 66-68. Stillfried's letters in Pergen's archive (HHSA) include a lot of information about the organization of the first *Katholikentag*.

the *innominato,* gave direction to the Catholic press and political guidance to the Catholic movement.[139]

Whether the *innominato* also intervened in the development of the Catholic movement in other countries through the International's network is not clear. That seems unlikely, if one takes into account the profile of the relevant *Permanents* and their position in the Catholic organizations of their countries. Cramer, for example, was certainly not a confidant of *Ferdinand*. In fact, he gradually disappeared from view at this stage, having failed to gain the support of the Dutch bishops for the establishment of a national lay committee.[140]

Through the *innominato* the *Permanents* had a direct line to the Pope, which allowed them to lodge any possible complaints about those who hindered their efforts. If desired, they could quite easily denounce their opponents. However, that was only a side activity in the work of the International, and this constituted a major difference from *La Sapinière*, a secret anti-modernist network active during the pontificate of Pius X.[141] In the correspondence that has been recovered, there is some evidence of denunciations via the *innominato*, but – insofar as is known – only in a few cases did the Vatican follow up on these complaints. There was certainly not any witch-hunt.[142]

Not surprisingly, the secret contacts of some *Permanents* with papal circles helped disrupt their relations with the local clergy, as was more than clear in the case of Joseph de Hemptinne. Indeed, the Geneva group had to cope with the suspicion of the local church hierarchy from the beginning. That was especially the case in the Netherlands and in England, two countries with a pronounced clerical church structure, but in fact it was a general phenomenon. Several bishops distrusted Monsignor Mermillod, who functioned as a patron for the organization.[143] Others were disturbed by the political agenda of some *Permanents*. The problem however had a wider dimension. The centralization process in the church ran parallel with a process of clericalization. Gradually, the ecclesiastical framework was reinforced and the clergy

---

139 Canavero, 'Mobilisation du mouvement catholique', 350-359. A lot of information about Salviati's activities can be found in the records of Manna Roncadelli (UCSCM, ASMSCI) and in the documents of the 'Opera dei Congressi' in the 'Archivio del Seminario Patriarcale' in Venice.

140 De Valk, 'A Struggle behind the Scenes', 397-407.

141 Poulat, *Intégrisme et catholicisme intégral*; Id., *Catholicisme*, démocratie et socialisme.

142 Lamberts, 'Une organisation secrète', 56-57. The only complaints that were followed up related to the Bishop of Passau, the Catholic University of Louvain/Leuven and the Belgian Jesuit Carbonelle.

143 The inner circle of the committee of Geneva became more and more convinced that Mermillod's patronage brought not only benefits but also major drawbacks for the organization. See *inter alia*: Pergen to Cramer, 14 Jan. 1873, NKDC, *Cramer*, 434, 12 c: 'Without failing to appreciate the great qualities and high merits of the president of our general meetings, an experience of almost three years has proved to me beyond all measure that the patronage with which he honours our organization is one of the principal causes of the distrust or indifference that we meet with from the majority of his brothers.'

consolidated its dominant role in the church. However, the hierarchy had to acknowledge that the support of prominent laymen was necessary for the development of Catholic action, and especially of more politically and socially oriented activities. In countries like Germany and Switzerland the clergy was also subject to discriminatory laws and had to leave the defence of ecclesiastical rights largely to the laity.[144] The question was how much autonomy lay people should have. The ecclesiastical hierarchy did not want their freedom of action to be measured too broadly; in early 1874, for example, a GCP message pointed out that the first duty of the laity was 'to comply fully with the wishes of their bishops'.[145] The difficulty was in finding a balance between lay aspirations and clerical claims.

For the *Permanents* their relationship with the Church hierarchy was a particularly sore point. Their problem was that they could not legitimize themselves with the local bishops. The Vatican obstinately refused to give them an explicit mandate, with the result that they were all too easily considered by the bishops as schemers, meddling in ecclesiastical affairs. This hampered their actions considerably. Salviati, Cramer, Stillfried and Leo Thun insisted repeatedly that the secrecy be abandoned and that the secretariat of state inform the bishops about the existence of the organization.[146] The Italian *Consiglio* was emphatic about this, but the Pope and his entourage did not accede to the request.[147] They were not in favour of an obvious and coordinated action by the laity that would involve the Vatican.[148] Pius IX was not prepared to rally openly behind a militant lay movement, but he did use it to follow an intransigent course in a disguised way. The *innominato* was his main instrument for this.

After Blome had withdrawn, the *innominato* was increasingly the key figure in the network, the spider in the web as it were. Where he first had been an *intermédiaire* between the Vatican and the Geneva Committee, he was now 'the anonymous one', 'he who is not to be named'. Anybody even somewhat familiar with Italian literature of the time could not fail to make a connection with the mysterious *innominato* in Alessandro Manzoni's historical novel *I promessi sposi* (*The Betrothed*), the undisputed masterpiece of Italian Romanticism. This *innominato* was a dark, satanic figure who came to apprehend the error of his ways and went on to lead an exemplary life. To what extent was this also applicable to the *innominato* who moved in the entourage of Pius IX?

144 The *Correspondance de Genève* paid a lot of attention to the role of the laity in the Catholic movement. See: Lory, '*La Correspondance de Genève*', 108-117.
145 Cramer to Pergen, 12 Feb. 1874, HHSA, *Pergen*, I. On Pius IX's stance towards lay action, see Martina, *Pio IX*, vol. III, 277-282.
146 Salviati to Pergen, 2 March and 19 May 1874, HHSA, *Pergen*, II; Stillfried to Pergen, 15 June 1873, ibid.; Leo Thun to Pergen, 7 Aug. 1875, ibid.
147 Salviati to the Consiglieri di permanenza, 17 Feb. 1878, ASPV, *OC*, II: 'The "permanenza" has an unofficial mandate, but it does come from the pope.'
148 Salviati to Pergen, 19 May 1874, HHSA, *Pergen*, II.

The *innominato* did everything to keep his identity secret. Giacomo Martina, known for his classic study of Pius IX, combed the Vatican archives for decades and never found any trace of him. Until now, his letters have been found only in the archives of Hemptinne who was never certain about the identity of his mysterious correspondent, though he had his suspicions. However, when he communicated these to the *innominato*, the person in question denied them most emphatically.[149] Pergen of course knew, while Bréda and Salviati succeeded in discovering his identity. Comments in their correspondence offer a solution to the mystery.[150]

The *innominato* was almost certainly Wladimir Czacki (1835-1888), who in the early 1870s was private secretary to Pius IX. He came from a noble family with extensive holdings in Russian Poland.[151] As a young aristocrat he received a cosmopolitan education and spent time in Germany, France, Italy and elsewhere. Between 1852 and 1862 he lived mostly in France. In Paris he frequented artistic circles and published a few collections of his own poetry. He had close ties with Charles de Morny, the half brother of Napoleon III and a very powerful man in the empire. De Morny taught him to see the importance of the modern press and the way in which governments could use it to influence public opinion. In 1865 Czacki settled permanently in Rome, where he stayed in the palace of his aunt, Sofia Branicka, on the Piazza dei SS. Apostoli. She was married to Prince Livio Odescalchi III, and hosted a salon where Czacki met a large number of Polish *emigrés* and priests, leading curial prelates and prominent figures of the Roman Catholic and European nobility.[152] He became friendly with the Austrian military attaché Pergen and with the curial prelates Franchi and Nina, among others. He decided to become a priest and was ordained in 1868. Perhaps this turnabout in his life explains why he later called himself the *innominato*. Princess Odescalchi introduced him to Pius IX, who was very impressed with this cultivated aristocrat. Czacki, a linguistic genius, became the Pope's private secretary for foreign language correspondence. In a very short time he was also appointed a secret chamberlain, house prelate and papal adviser on Polish and Russian affairs.

In addition, Czacki worked as an unsalaried consultor in the secretariat of state and in the *Affari Straordinari* (Congregation for Extraordinary Ecclesiastical Affairs), which provided advice on key political and religious issues. He

---

149 *Ferdinand* to Hemptinne, 13 Nov. 1876, ADH, *corr. 1875-76*, 167; Czacki to Hemptinne, 4 Dec. 1877, ADH, *Corr. 1877-1889*: 'You speak to me … of an *innominato* who is no longer there. But I do not know what that means.'

150 Lamberts, 'L'Internationale noire', 51-53.

151 On Wladimir Czacki (1835-1888) see Soderini, 'Le cardinal Wladimir Czacki', 237-259; Godlewski, 'Czacki', *Polsi Slownik Biograficzny*, vol. IV, Krakau, 1938, 146-147; Weber, *Quellen und Studien*, 306-314; Id., 'Dans les couloirs du Vatican', 38-129; Viaene, 'A Brilliant Failure', 231-256.

152 Von Hutten-Czapski, *Sechzig Jahre Politik und Gesellschaft*, 12-15.

Wladimir Czacki. Photograph.
[*E. Soderini*, Il Pontificato di Leone XIII, *II. Milaan, 1934*]

regularly visited the Pope, who became very fond of him because of his easy conversation and entertaining company. Antonelli also admired him greatly. Czacki thus was the right person for the position of *intermédiaire* and, as already mentioned, was put forward for it by Pergen. Thus, the Polish prelate became the central figure in the international network, thereby advancing his ecclesiastical career. In late 1873 he became secretary of the Congregation for Studies and in 1876 consultor of the Congregation of the Holy Office. In March 1877, he would be appointed secretary of the *Affari Straordinari*, and from then on he had an important say in the international politics of the Vatican at the highest level.

Judgements of Czacki by those who came in contact with him varied greatly. In the Vatican, many were dismayed by his success in gaining the trust of the elderly Pius IX and accused him of abusing the Pope's physical deterioration to push through his own policies.[153] When he was appointed secretary of the *Affari Straordinari*, the Belgian ambassador to the Holy See described him as 'an intelligent and passionate man who does not shy away from intrigues'.[154] Initially, Salviati distrusted him, but his admiration grew perceptibly.[155] There are many indications that Czacki was a cunning and opportunistic figure.[156] He endorsed the radical ultramontane politics of Pius IX, but also maintained good contacts with prelates like Dupanloup[157] and Gioacchino Pecci, the future Pope Leo XIII whose conciliatory and pragmatic policy he would later resolutely support. Still, there are some constants in his career that bestow a kind of authenticity on his commitment to the International. He was convinced that the Holy See had to give direction to Catholic public opinion through an active press policy and believed that the church had to turn to the masses.[158] His work in the context of the International fitted in with that vision.

153 Monsignor de Neckere, a Belgian curial prelate, pointed out repeatedly that Czacki abused the declining health of Pius IX in order to carry out his own policies (Mgr. de Neckere to Mgr. Faict, Bishop of Bruges, 8 May 1882, cited in Huyghebaert, *Correspondance de Mgr F. de Neckere*, vol. II, 794). See also: Joseph Palomba, Austrian diplomat, to Pergen, 17 Oct. 1880, HHSA, *Pergen*, II: '[Pius IX] overcome by old age and the fatigue of a long reign, became the plaything of astute men who imposed their will on him.'

154 Reusens to d'Aspremont Lynden, 16 April 1877, AMBUZ, *Corresp. politique*, Légations, St-Siège, 15, 68.

155 Salviati to Pergen, 15 Dec. 1878, HHSA, *Pergen*, II; Id. to Paganuzzi, 14 May 1879, ASPV,*OC*, II: 'He is one of the most distinguished prelates known to me.'

156 Mgr. de Neckere to Mgr. de Montpellier, Bishop of Liege, April 1878, cited in Huyghebaert, *Correspondance de Mgr. F. de Neckere*, vol. II, 718-719: 'Czacki certainly does not have any principles, but he has a most developed genius for intrigue, stemming first from self-interest, and second from an innate taste for intrigue for its own sake'; La Tour du Pin to Pergen, 24 Sept. 1879, HHSA, *Pergen*, II: 'You told me rightly that in changing masters, he would become the opposite of what he used to be before.'

157 Czacki to Dupanloup, 13 Feb., 22 March, 20 April and 12 Nov. 1876, 29 March 1877, BNP, NAF, 24680.

158 See *infra*, 247.

The defence against Leviathan

From an ideological point of view, the Black International was completely opposed to liberalism, which it saw as leading automatically to socialism because of its materialistic orientation, its capitalist economic model that brought about great social excesses, its rationalistic faith in the perfectability of human beings and society, and its fight against the social influence of religion. It coupled the privatization of religion with the expansion of state power. The International declared that liberals perceived the modern nation state to be the sole sovereign power and that they considered churches to be private bodies subject to the State like all other organizations. The International opposed this and sought to maintain and, if necessary, recover the social influence of the Church, as was advocated in *Quanta Cura* and the *Syllabus of Errors*.

The *Permanents* made two attempts to give a positive interpretation to the negative wording of the *Syllabus* and charged a number of theologians with the task of coming up with a positively worded 'creed'. One of the two drafts has been preserved and includes 32 propositions. Dating from 1873, the text strenuously defends the autonomy of the church, and strongly emphasizes its supremacy over the State. In that respect, it has a purely theocratic approach and goes much further than Blome's tract of 1871. It also gives a sense of an excessive anti-statism. The former diplomats Blome and Pergen felt that the theocratic emphasis was highly exaggerated and that the powers of the State were overly curtailed. The initial intention was to submit the detailed texts to the Curia for approval, but the plan fell through, thanks mainly to opposition from Blome who still continued to exert some influence from the sidelines.[159]

In fact, Church-State relations were regularly on the agenda of the International's congresses. The aim was not only to secure the freedom of the Church, but also to secure its social influence through some form of cooperation with the State. At the meeting at Ferney in 1873, Salviati proposed to put together a 'Handbook of Christian public law' and to disseminate the principles of the *Syllabus* through popular catechisms, something Hemptinne would do later in Belgium. At that congress, the Ghent industrialist raised the question of the oath: could Catholics in conscience swear an oath of allegiance to liberal constitutions? The gathering favoured a restricted oath that did not contravene individual conscience and the rights of the Church.

An interesting issue raised at the same congress was that of increasing militarism, which was linked to the strengthening of the nation state. The committee called for the disbanding of standing armies, but the German *Permanent*, Prince Isenburg objected strenuously. The proposal was watered down to a desire 'to prevent the excessive growth of armies and to fight militarism'. International conflicts had to be primarily resolved by arbitration. Of particu-

159 Lamberts, 'Une organisation secrète', 65-72.

lar interest is that the meeting formally spoke out against universal military conscription: 'We must oppose this detestable development that threatens to bring back slavery once again.' This was a remarkable position, of a piece with the broader opposition to the omnipotence of the State.[160]

A veritable contest was going on at this time between the modern State and the Catholic Church, which was defending its autonomy and its traditional sphere of influence. The State was interfering more and more in the lives of citizens. With its all-embracing claims and demand for the total loyalty of its subjects, it naturally found itself in direct competition with the Church. The question was whether Church and State would divide up territories according to Montalembert's formula of 'a free Church in a free State'. The alternative was that one of the powers would be dominated by the other. A theocratic tendency within the Church was inclined to subordinate the State to the Church, while the regalistic tendency wanted the opposite. The old debate picked up again during this period.

On the liberal side a radical movement developed that was in some ways in keeping with regalism. It rejected the separation of Church and State and preached a form of 'state absolutism'. The State alone was responsible for justice, security and peace. It alone should draw up the framework for the freedom of the individual citizen; its mission was to make the individual spiritually free, and radical liberals would not tolerate churches or any other intermediate power thwarting this pursuit.[161] For them modernity meant more State and the gradual elimination of intermediate structures that came between the individual and the government.[162] For them the State was an agent of modernization. They believed that in order to bring about freedom, the principles of liberalism permitted coercion to be put on the Catholic Church, the strongest opponent of and threat to the individual's emancipation.[163] This reasoning led many liberals not only to push the Church out of public life, but also to subject it to the authority of the State. In the 1870s a veritable offensive was conducted against the Roman Church, which was branded as an anti-modern institute, and a *Kulturkampf* was waged against it, especially in countries where the nation state was linked to secularizing movements.[164]

The International devoted more and more attention at its congresses to the areas of conflict between Church and State. It took up arms against 'government oppression'. In several countries, it founded *comités du contentieux* (litigation committees) with eminent jurists who assisted the clergy in the legal

160 Minutes of the annual meeting in Ferney, 5-7 Aug. 1873, NKDC, *Cramer*, 456, 20 a.
161 Nipperdey, *Deutsche Geschichte (1866-1918)*, vol. II, 365.
162 Kitchen, *A History of Modern Germany*, 140-144.
163 Gross, *The War against Catholicism*, 246-250.
164 Borutta, *Antikatholizismus*.

defence of ecclesiastical rights.[165] With clockwork regularity, the members of the International were mobilized against the anticlerical measures of successive Italian governments,[166] which initially wanted to break the supremacy of the Church, safeguard the rights of non-churchgoers and expand the State's influence. From 1876 on, left-liberal governments went one step further and wanted to affirm the supremacy of the State over the Church, following the German and Swiss examples.

In Switzerland in the 1860s radical liberals had already turned against the Catholic Church, which they considered to be a foreign element in Swiss society because of its authoritarian structure of governance.[167] They wanted the Church to reflect the more democratic structure of the Protestant Church and so they aligned themselves with the Old Catholics who rejected the decisions of Vatican I. Both groups favoured strong State control over the Church. They wanted to expand the power of the federal government in the religious and cultural spheres and to democratize the structure of the Catholic Church's governance. The struggle was played out mainly in the cantons, especially in the diocese of Basle and in Geneva where the two parties came to a head-on clash. In February 1873 Mermillod was exiled because he had been appointed Apostolic Vicar without the knowledge of the government. The Geneva radicals then launched a legislative initiative aimed at creating a state church that would be independent of Rome. Catholics vehemently protested against this, resulting in the removal of most parish priests, the expulsion of the congregations and the expropriation of their property. The International paid a lot of attention to the *Kulturkampf* in Switzerland and launched several actions there in support of the Catholic clergy.

The conflict between liberals and Catholics died down in Switzerland after 1878. The introduction of forms of direct democracy gradually strengthened the position of Catholics in the mixed cantons, thereby weakening the anticlerical measures of radical governments. In Geneva, peace was achieved by eliminating the office of Apostolic Vicar. Mermillod was appointed bishop of Lausanne in March 1883 with headquarters in Fribourg. He was again allowed to enter Switzerland freely but had to stay away from Geneva. In all, the Swiss *Kulturkampf* resulted in the State tightening its grip on the Church to some degree, but the conflict also strengthened Catholic organizations, thereby ensuring sustainable protection for the Church.

---

165 Lamberts, 'Une organisation secrète', 85-86.
166 On the Italian government's measures against the Church, see Martina, *Pio IX*, III, 233-302; Fiorentino, *Dalle Stanze del Vaticano*, 303-319; Id., 'The Roman Question', 187-193; Vidotto, *Roma contemporanea*, 56-63; Papenheim, 'Roma o morte', 202-226.
167 On the *Kulturkampf* in Switzerland, see Lindt, *Protestanten. Katholiken. Kulturkampf*; Stadler, *Der Kulturkampf in der Schweiz*; Pfeiffer, *Der Kulturkampf in Genf (1864-1873)*; Bossard-Borner, 'Village Quarrels and National Controversies', 255-284.

Nowhere was the struggle between the Catholic Church and the State so sharp as in the new German empire, where in fact the concept of the *Kulturkampf* originated.[168] The conflict was fuelled by a latent anti-Catholicism, which was much stronger than the anti-Semitism present in most German territories and that in the 1850s became a lever for the revival of liberalism. After the victory over Austria, the liberals wanted to further consolidate unified Germany as a modern society, with a modern culture and morality. The core values in their philosophy were science and *Bildung*, the conditions most suitable for the progress and development of the individual, whereas the anti-modern position of Catholics who gave priority to authority, tradition and the old social bonds went completely against this. The *Syllabus* and the dogma of papal infallibility were perceived as a mockery of modern culture.

From now on the national liberals were Bismarck's allies. He went on the offensive against the Catholic Church primarily for political reasons, and took particular offense at the creation of the *Zentrum* party which, in his view, put Catholic special interests above the public interest. It was the incarnation of anti-national and centrifugal forces and presented a threat to the new government and its national foundations. Bismarck was especially annoyed by the federalist programme and democratic tendencies of the *Zentrum*. This party in fact opposed the authoritarianism of the chancellor, who defended the privileges of the Protestant elite. It wanted to give a political voice to a disadvantaged population group, and mobilized it to protest against the reigning establishment. It saw the Church as offering the best protection against the hegemony of the State, and it had links with an ultramontane network that also included Jesuits, clergy and the episcopate. Bismarck was afraid of a widely diffused Black International, of which the Geneva Committee was a component. He suspected this International of colluding with all the state's potential enemies and so decided to wage a preventive war against it. It was not his intention to wipe out the Catholic Church in Germany or to completely destroy its moral influence; ideally, he wanted to return to the system that had existed in Prussia before 1848 which provided for strict state supervision of the churches.

The *Staatskonservativer* Bismarck thus joined with the national liberals to counteract the *Zentrum* and the political orientation of the Church hierarchy. His support of the Old Catholics reinforced resistance on the Catholic

---

168 On the *Kulturkampf* in Germany, see Nipperdey, *Deutsche Geschichte (1866-1918)*, II, 364-382; Lerman, *Bismarck*, 176-184; Gross, *The War against Catholicism*, 240-292; Borutta, 'Enemies at the Gate', 227-254; Becker, 'Der Kulturkampf als ëuropäisches und Deutsches Phänomen', 422-446; Id., 'Il ruolo di Bismarck', 69-108; Schmidt-Volkmar, *Der Kulturkampf in Deutschland*; Ross, *The Failure of Bismarck's Kulturkampf*; Id., 'The Kulturkampf and the Limitations of Power', 669-688; Id., 'Enforcing the *Kulturkampf*', 456-482; Lill, *Der Kulturkampf*; Martin, *Der katholische Weg ins Reich*; De Coninck, *Een les uit Pruisen*, 117-158; Martina, *Pio IX*, vol. III, 369-410.

'Between Berlin and Rome'. A chess game between Bismarck and Pius IX. Caricature in Kladderadatsch, 1875. [*Berlin, Bildarchiv Preussischer Kulturbesitz*]

side. A first phase of the *Kulturkampf*, which took an acute form especially in Prussia, was designed to reduce the influence of the Church in society. This climaxed first in the anti-Jesuit law of 4 July 1872, which mobilized the entire population and led to a fierce parliamentary debate in the first session of the *Reichstag*. There were only two hundred Jesuits throughout the whole empire, but they were accused of opposing the unification of the country and of encouraging the establishment of the *Zentrum*. For those reasons they were expelled. In a second phase, with the May Laws of 1873, the government intervened in internal church matters. Resistance escalated as did the crackdown: many congregations were banned, almost two thousand priests were put in prison or expelled and a considerable amount of church property was confiscated. Around 1880 more than half of the Prussian episcopate was in exile or in prison, a quarter of the parishes had no priest and a third of all religious houses and congregations had been abolished. There was an almost systematic persecution of the Catholic Church in the new empire and especially in Prussia.

The Black International kept up its end in the opposition to the *Kulturkampf*. It urged the *Permanents* to arrange protest campaigns in their own countries against Prussian anti-Jesuit measures[169] and regularly repeated

169 Blome to Hemptinne, 13 Oct. 1871, ADH, *corr. 1870-72*, 163; Pergen to Cramer, 28 July 1872, NKDC, *Cramer*, 434, 12 c.

its efforts to organize protests when the *Kulturkampf* intensified. In 1875 it launched financial relief campaigns for the German clergy and gave its support to the establishment of training centres for German seminarians abroad.[170] It also had a direct connection with the *Mainzer Katholikenverein*, which was founded in 1872 to coordinate the Catholic opposition, but two years later was forced to disband.[171] One consequence of the sharp conflict between Church and State was that prominent German Catholics, who had taken a distance from the International in late 1871, once again began to make overtures.[172]

Bismarck and the National Liberals overplayed their hand. They overestimated the ability of the State to effectively push through the measures taken, and by the same token they underestimated Catholic resistance. The Old Catholics proved to be powerless allies for Bismarck. The conflict strengthened the ties between the clergy and the faithful, and achieved exactly what the Vatican had wanted to attain with the Vatican Council: a more unified and disciplined clergy under an infallible head. It intensified the confessionalization and politicization of the Catholic population which was pushed in a more ultramontane direction. Now, more than ever, they constituted a homogeneous group and they rallied massively behind the *Zentrum* to fight for their emancipation. In 1881 that party became the largest fraction in the *Reichstag*, and gradually would emerge as a crucial player in German politics. The national culture did not become homogenized; to the contrary, confessional tensions even increased, and for a long time the population would be split into two nations, one Protestant, the other Catholic. The *Kulturkampf* in fact brought the shortcomings of imperial Germany as an authoritarian State to light, and left the country more divided than ever before.

After 1878 the battle against the Catholic Church abated. Bismarck replaced the national liberals with conservative allies and launched a campaign against socialism, a confrontation that would be as disastrous as the *Kulturkampf*, which was formally ended around 1887. Other than predicted in 1872, Bismarck saw himself finally obliged to go the way of Canossa, although his defeat was not complete. The State had gained some ground over the Church, which for its part had forged closer ties with its faithful. As in Switzerland the Catholic organizations were strengthened and would form a buffer against the power of the State.

In Austria the confrontation was much less sharp than in Germany or Switzerland, although the liberals there also demanded full sovereignty for

---

170 Baudon to Hemptinne, 28 and 30 Oct.1875, ADH, *corr. 1875-76*, 62 and 65; A. de Robiano to Hemptinne, 19 Jan. 1876, ADH, *corr. 1875-76*, 115; von Loë to Hemptinne, 20 Feb. 1876, ADH, *corr. 1875-76*, 127.

171 GCP to the *Permanents*, 7 Oct. 1872 and 1 Feb. 1873, NKDC, *Cramer*, 456, 20b, 4; GCP to the *Permanents*, 10 Feb. 1876, NKDC, *Cramer*, 455, 20a.

172 Pergen to Friedrich Thun, 23 Aug. and 7 Sept. 1875, SALD, *Thun-Hohenstein*, A 3 - XIX, H 82, 12 and 13.

the State.[173] As already mentioned in the second chapter, they wanted to extend its responsibilities into the registration of civil status, education and welfare. After Vatican I, they felt even more obliged to defend the rights of the State. At the council, the Church had indeed extended its claims to power and invested the power it claimed in the Pope. For that reason, in late August 1870, the liberal government felt entitled to terminate the concordat, which had been negotiated in a different context. However, thanks to the emperor, the ecclesiastical legislation that was later promulgated was very moderate, and all in all, the Church retained a privileged status.[174] A fierce *Kulturkampf* then never developed in Austria, unlike in Germany. One result of this was that Austrian Catholics would be less anti-statist than the German, and this would have an impact on their position in social matters, as we shall see later. Even so, the anticlerical policies of the liberal governments also led to a strengthening of Catholic structures in Cisleithania.

'The period of despair'

Even after the Geneva bureau and the *Correspondance* had been closed down, the Black International still retained some importance thanks to the bilateral contacts between the *innominato* and some *Permanents*, as well as the annual congresses. With the explicit approval of the Pope, Pergen convened a new annual meeting in Ferney (20-22 August 1874). The attendees devoted singular attention to the defence of the Church's rights against 'state tyranny' and decided to strengthen the *comités du contentieux*. Encouraged by the meeting, Pergen was able to carry out his work as vice-president in a more dynamic way.[175] He had recently married but had not even taken the time to go on honeymoon. His young wife helped him with his extensive correspondence. He resumed the practice of drawing up a monthly summary of the reports he received and sending it to all the *Permanents*.[176] There was also a certain revival of activity among the latter, but efforts in the Vatican dwindled apace.[177]

---

173 On Church-State relations in Austria in the 1870s, see Martina, *Pio IX*, vol. III, 411-434; Cole, 'The Counter-Reformation's Last Stand: Austria', 285-312; Bled, *Les fondements du conservatisme autrichien*, 108-118; Leisching, 'Die römisch-katholische Kirche in Cisleithanien', 125-155; Rumpler, *Eine Chance*, 426-438.

174 Pfleger, *Gab es einen Kulturkampf in Österreich?*; Höbelt, *Franz Joseph I*, 71-76.

175 Pergen to Friedrich Thun, 9 Nov. 1874, SALD, *Thun-Hohenstein*, A 3 - XIX, H 82, 6.

176 Pergen to Cramer, 19 Oct. and 20 Nov. 1874, 28 March 1875, NKDC, *Cramer*, 434, 12 c. In the first three months of 1875, he wrote 330 letters in support of the actions of the International and Catholic organizations in Austria.

177 Salviati to Pergen, 3 Nov. 1874, HHSA, *Pergen*, II.

In April 1875 a big international delegation was sent to Rome where Antonelli counselled 'calmness and moderation'.[178] This advice only reinforced the despondency felt by more and more *Permanents*. Pergen and Salviati agreed they had to persevere with the Geneva undertaking for the services that it could render later.[179] There was still some commitment among the lower ranks, but leadership from the Vatican was lacking in this *Periode der Ratlosigkeit* ('period of despair') as Pergen called it.[180] The advanced age of Pius IX (83 years) and of his secretary of state Antonelli (69 years) probably also helped foster this gloom.

The survival of the organization depended mainly on Pergen's continuing efforts. He reconciled himself to the fact that its activities had been scaled back, but wrote: 'There is no reason to surrender the garrison of a besieged fortress, if the command for a sortie is not given.'[181] In the meantime, the *Permanents* had to focus primarily on the development of the Catholic movement in their own countries, for which they could get inspiration from the exchange of ideas at the annual congresses. With the approval of the *innominato*, Pergen continued to organize the annual congresses in Bregenz (1875) and Annecy (1876), which yielded fruitful discussions. The participants paid increasing attention to the social question, and reached innovative insights in that area, as will be evident later. They also agreed to attend one another's meetings more often, and to circulate the resolutions of those national meetings internationally.

The *Permanents* still regarded the disappearance of the *Correspondance de Genève* as a great loss. They therefore decided at their congress in Bregenz to start an international periodical which, because of the wide press freedom in England, would be distributed from London. This *Correspondance anglaise* would be drawn up by the editorial staff of the Belgian weekly *La Croix*. Pergen did not believe in the feasibility of the plan, but since it had received the blessing of the *innominato*, he did his utmost to implement it.[182] In the end, the *Permanents* failed to raise sufficient funds, and some also had reservations about the radical views of the *La Croix* editors. The plan did not go through in its original form, but at the congress in Annecy the *Permanents* decided to try a variation: the editors of *La Croix* would in the future send around autographic circulars. This system was put into operation, with the *innominato* and some *Permanents* providing information for the circulars on a regular basis. Plans

178 Cramer to Bodenham, 26 April 1875, NKDC, *Cramer*, 24, IV, 94.
179 Salviati to Pergen, 13 July 1875, HHSA, *Pergen*, II; Leo Thun to Pergen, 7 Aug. 1875, HHSA, *Pergen*, II.
180 Pergen to Cramer, 28 March 1875, NKDC, *Cramer*, 434, 12, C: 'This sad era which the good Father Schrader S.J. has so well characterized with the words: "People did not want that *Sturm und Drang* period, but they had to endure the *Leidens* period."'
181 Pergen to Friedrich Thun, 26 July 1875, SALD, *Thun-Hohenstein*, A 3 - XIX, H 82, 11.
182 Pergen to Friedrich Thun, Dec. 1875, SALD, *Thun-Hohenstein*, A 3 - XIX, H 82, 19.

were made for a German and even an English edition of the 'Belgian auto-graph', indicating that the International continued to attach great importance to the press as a way of influencing public opinion.[183] However, unexpected developments in the Vatican in late 1876 put a stop to all these schemes.

Shortly after the Congress of Annecy a significant shift took place in Rome on the death of Cardinal Antonelli on 6 November 1876, which caused a lot of commotion among the active members of the International. Blome, who had not always agreed with the secretary of state, took the view that he had been a man of great significance.[184] The pressing question was now whether his de-parture would have any repercussions on the organization. It was not imme-diately obvious that anything would change. In a letter of November 13th the *innominato* informed Hemptinne that he would continue with his correspond-ence.[185] He also apparently supplied further information to the autographic department of *La Croix*. In late November Pergen sent around another impor-tant circular, in which he called on the *Permanent*s to continue their protests against the anticlerical measures of the left-liberal government in Italy.[186]

A month later, disaster hit. Without warning, the *innominato*, alias *Ferdi-nand*, informed the *Permanent*s that he was withdrawing and that the network would be discontinued. He proposed organizing a new information system, but remained very vague about it. In fact, it was a death blow for the Interna-tional and the *Permanent*s understood it as such. In his farewell letter the *in-nominato* again stressed that his incognito had to be preserved into the future: 'In the past I was the only one who was aware of the secret underpinning our work ... You have been very tactful in respecting the silence that was imposed on me ... I would like to point out that this embargo will continue.'[187]

The message completely surprised the *Permanent*s as well as the inner circle. According to Salviati, the decision was 'hasty and indecent'. The *in-nominato* could have mustered a little more respect for the *Permanent*s who had devoted so much time and effort to the organization.[188] De Hemptinne, who had maintained a very close relationship with *Ferdinand*, was especially shocked. Indeed, he was the only one, besides Pergen, to receive a separate

183 Lamberts, 'Une organisation secrète', 78-80.
184 Blome to Cramer, 14 Dec. 1876, NKDC, *Cramer*, 434, 12 b, II. See also Luigi d'Ondes Reggio to Vito d'Ondes Reggio, 5 April 1878, cited De Rosa, *Storia del movimento cattolico in Italia*, vol. I, 231.
185 *Ferdinand* to De Hemptinne, 13 Nov. 1876, ADH, *corr. 1875-76*, 167.
186 De Hemptinne to Pergen, 1 Dec. 1876, HHSA, *Pergen*, I.
187 *Ferdinand* to the *Permanent*s, 25 Dec. 1876, NKDC, *Cramer*, 455, 20 a.
188 Salviati to Pergen, 8 Jan. 1877, HHSA, *Pergen*, II.

farewell letter.[189] He regretted not so much the disappearance of the organization itself as the fact that his direct access to the Pope was cut off.[190]

The reasons why the International was so abruptly disbanded are a matter of conjecture and apparently had as much to do with the position of the *innominato* as with the death of Antonelli and the choice of Cardinal Simeoni as his successor. Contrary to expectations, Giovanni Simeoni, the papal nuncio in Madrid and not Alessandro Franchi, a close friend of Czacki's, was appointed secretary of state. At the time of his appointment, Simeoni was not aware of the existence of the Black International.[191] Shortly after taking office, he decided that the influencing of the press would henceforth be done through the nuncios, a decision that to some extent signalled a return to an earlier policy.[192] This measure offered Czacki the chance to be rid of a burden that, given his increasing workload and shaky health, had become ever more oppressive. Moreover, in late December he may have been promised that he would be made secretary of the thoroughly reformed *Affari Straordinari*, which meant that from then on he would help shape the policy of the Holy See in an official capacity. He continued to strongly support the idea of Rome exerting influence on the Catholic press, but apparently he could not or did not want to act as an informer or *intermédiaire* any longer. That the disbanding of the existing information network also put an immediate end to the mutual contacts and annual conferences appeared at the time to be of secondary importance in the Vatican. The way in which the Black International was abolished made clear the extent to which it had become dependent on the *innominato*, while at the same time highlighting the lack of importance attached to it in papal circles at that time.

Officially, the organization no longer existed. The *Permanents* had lost their mandates, there were no more monthly reports, no network of correspondents, no annual congresses. The *Permanents* could possibly still maintain their personal contacts 'in anticipation of the moment when we will again reach out to one another to defend the sacred cause'.[193] Indeed, some of them did that, like Pergen who continued to correspond with Salviati and Hemptinne. The latter had in fact insisted on this: 'Let us keep our connections and

189 *Ferdinand* to De Hemptinne, 30 Dec. 1876, ADH, *corr. 1875-76*, 173: 'Count P[ergen] himself will communicate this to all the *Permanents*. For my part I am not writing to anybody except you. Why? ... It is a fact that our relations have been too friendly, fraternal and mutually beneficial to break off these relations without shaking your hand, without saying the most profound *adieu* from the depths of my soul to you.'

190 De Hemptinne to Pergen, 31 Dec. 1876, HHSA, *Pergen*, I: 'The removal of the means of corresponding with Rome cripples me.'

191 This can be deduced from a letter from Salviati to Pergen, 6 Dec. 1877, HHSA, *Pergen*, II. On Giovanni Simeoni (1816-1892), see: *Enciclopedia cattolica*, vol. XI, 1953, 628.

192 Simeoni to S. Vannuttelli, nuncio in Brussels, 6 Jan. 1877, ASV, *NB*, envelope 47, pos. 40. See also the contribution by Viaene, *A Brilliant Failure*, 240.

193 Pergen to Friedrich Thun, 28 Dec. 1876, SALD, *Thun-Hohenstein*, A 3 - XIX, H 82, 18.

our bonds of friendship and at a moment willed by Providence we will again take up the weapons that our chief [Pius IX] has ordered us to lay down.'[194]

In 1877, the leaders of the disbanded International pursued the same course as before, but no longer in consultation with the *innominato*. On the advice of the Pope and his entourage, Hemptinne continued publishing *La Croix*, but was urged 'to show understanding for the persons while being relentlessly harsh on the errors'.[195] In Austria, as has already been mentioned, Pergen succeeded in arranging a Catholic congress that was remarkably successful. In Italy Salviati maintained his *Consiglio di permanenza* as a shadow cabinet of the *Opera dei Congressi*, which organized a major congress in Bergamo.[196]

A new direction

On the dissolution of the International the *innominato* had proposed reorganizing the press network, but no further mention was made of this in the first months of 1877. Simeoni, the new secretary of state, had yet to settle into the job before a new path could be decided. He was in many ways 'the opposite of his predecessor' and soon adopted a more combative stance on the Roman question, in reaction to a number of anticlerical measures by the new left-liberal government in Italy. The *zelanti* appeared to have assumed the initiative. In April Pergen indicated to his friends that there was some movement on the GCP issue.[197]

A new campaign for the restoration of the temporal power of the Pope pushed for the support of the Catholic masses, who once more had to step up the pressure on governments and parliaments.[198] This meant a return to the strategy that had been followed between 1870 and 1873. People from many sides looked to Pergen. According to Mermillod, not one mobilization plan would have the approval of Pius IX if Pergen were not involved. The 'cadet' decided to go to Rome in mid-September to advocate a revival of the organization 'that so relentlessly and so inconveniently has been deprived of life'.[199] While there he succeeded in convincing the *innominato*, Wladimir Czacki, of the desirability of reviving the international lay organization.

As secretary of the *Affari Straordinari* and a confidant of the Pope, Czacki made an important contribution to the foreign policy of the Holy See. He aimed at creating an alliance between Great Britain and Catholic France, or

194 Hemptinne to Pergen, 31 Dec. 1877, HHSA, *Pergen*, I.
195 Derély, editor of *La Croix*, to Hemptinne, [beginning of 1877], ADH, *corr. 1877-1889*.
196 Canavero, 'Mobilisation du mouvement catholique en Italie', 355.
197 On this episode see: Lamberts, 'Une organisation secrète', 86-92.
198 Viaene, 'Question d'Orient', 400-401.
199 Pergen to de Hemptinne, 10 Sept. 1877, ADH, *corr. 1877-1889*.

preferably Austria, so as to instigate some movement once again on the Roman question. In order to bring London and Vienna together, he called on former members of the Black International such as Lord Denbigh, Bréda and Hompesch. Blome was also indirectly involved, but he was very critical, and rightly so, of the grand plans that were on the table.[200]

Czacki believed that an orchestrated Catholic press campaign could be of great help in winning over public support for the alliance in the countries concerned. He did not want to use Catholic opinion any longer to wage war against the international order, but rather to give the Vatican a place within that system.[201] He made an offer to Pergen to settle permanently in the Vatican so he could lead a Catholic news agency from there, but the 'cadet' rejected the offer, on the advice of various people, including Marquis René de La Tour du Pin with whom he was very friendly.[202]

Finally, the decision was made to resurrect the Black International once more. Pergen was authorized to bring together some trusted confidants and work out a plan for reorganization. The Vatican was prepared 'to preserve the spirit of the earlier organization, but the form has to change completely. People there do not want to have anything to do with our former chairman [Mermillod] or with any dead weights.' Pergen was also able to report that he had ensured in advance that 'without acquiring an official character, the restructured organization shall be freed from the obligation to maintain secrecy in its relationships with the centre [Rome].'[203] On 25 November 1877, he convened a meeting in Innsbruck with Salviati, Hemptinne, La Tour du Pin and with Felix von Loë who had become a leading figure in the ultramontane wing of the German lay movement. The five participants were explicitly asked by the Pope 'to consider the reorganization of GCP, the usefulness of which has been fully recognized since its dissolution'.[204]

The report of the meeting stated:

> We the undersigned, have jointly considered the possibilities of replacing the organization that was founded in 1870 under the patronage of Monsignor Mermillod in Geneva. The spirit and purpose of that foundation found expression in the so-called 'prayer of Einsiedeln'. It existed until late last year and exerted a beneficial influence on the Catholic movement and especially the good press.

200 Viaene, 'Question d'Orient', 409 and 413.
201 Id., 'A Brilliant Failure', 241-242; Id., 'Question d'Orient', 405-413.
202 La Tour du Pin to Pergen, 17 and 22 Sept 1877, HHSA, *Pergen*, II: 'My friend ... living in exile is nothing when one is young and not constrained by personal or business ties. But once commitment has pushed its roots into a native soil, it is too late to graft it elsewhere; it will not turn green and will die without taking hold again.'
203 Pergen to Hemptinne, 16 Oct.1877, ADH, *corr. 1877-1889*.
204 Hemptinne to his son, Dom Hildebrand O.S.B., 9 Jan. 1878, ADH, *Hildebrand*.

The report referred not only to past history, but also to papal support and to a recent *breve*, addressed to the congress of the *Opera dei Congressi* in Bergamo, in which the Pope had explicitly legitimized the Catholic lay movement and the Catholic congresses. The participants decided to set up a Union of St. Peter, the members of which would 'use all appropriate means to pass on the Holy See's instructions to the good press and the leaders of the Catholic movement in their countries'. They would receive these instructions directly from the secretariat of state, and, for their part, would deliver a monthly report to the Vatican on developments in their own countries. From their midst they would choose a secretary, whose task would be to promote mutual contacts and ensure that branches of the Union would be set up in as many countries as possible. This liaison would organize a congress at least once a year, chaired by a bishop or other ecclesiastical dignitary, thereby strengthening the link with the church hierarchy. Thus the secrecy was ended, as was also evident from the fact that the names of the correspondents would henceforth be given to the papal nuncios. Moreover, a national committee could be formed in every member country so that the Union could reach a wider audience.[205]

An analysis of this text makes clear that those present wanted to revive not only the press network but also the International with its contacts, its reporting and its annual congresses. What was particularly important was that an *innominato* no longer acted as *intermédiaire*, but rather that there was direct contact with the secretariat of state. The local church hierarchy also became more involved in the organization. If this proposal were to be accepted in Rome, the Black International would rise from the ashes and would then be able to function in more favourable circumstances than heretofore. The new climate that had emerged in the previous year appeared to make this possible: the shifts in international politics, the election of a left-liberal cabinet in Italy and the heavy defeat of the right in the French parliamentary elections of October 14th, with the resulting far-reaching consequences. The Church was pushed further onto the defensive in European politics and in that context a renewed appeal to the Catholic people was considered.

Salviati was the one who had to defend the plan for re-organization in Rome where he negotiated with Czacki and Simeoni. The latter seemed to be very sympathetic,[206] but the actual settlement of the case depended on Czacki, who still had privileged access to the Pope. He, however, was overloaded with

---

205 'Procès-verbal d'association au service du St-Siège', 25 Nov. 1877, ADH, *corr. 1877-1889*.
206 Salviati to Pergen, 12 and 14 Dec. 1877, HHSA, *Pergen*, II. Several passages of Salviati's letters are written in code, which has been deciphered by Professor Bart Preneel of KU Leuven.

Rome 14/12 77

Mon cher Comte,

N'ayant pas vu de réponse, je crains que vous ne soyez occupé de la santé de votre femme; s'il en est malheureusement ainsi veuillez me le dire ne fut-ce que pas deux mots.

gazaksedzehcygcorijjcynyapkzjxbcay pkciiaahvygzxek

Nous avons ici très beau temps quoique nous soyons au mois de décembre.

En hâte, mais de cœur
tout à vous
S

P.S. Je vous adresse cette lettre à Vienne, ma précédente je vous l'avais adressée à Aspang

Letter by Salviati to Pergen, 14 Dec. 1877, with a cryptogram.
[Vienna, Haus-, Hof- und Staatsarchiv, Pergen Archives]

work and kept deferring the matter.[207] Moreover, Pius IX's health had become worrying, further jeopardizing the reorganization; nevertheless, in late January Czacki was still very optimistic about the plan's prospects.[208] A few weeks later the inevitable happened: Pius IX died on 7 February 1878, after the longest pontificate in church history. The Union of St. Peter was buried with him.

The Vatican now focused all its attention on the conclave and the election of a successor, but there was great confusion about the procedure to be followed. The main question was whether the cardinals would meet in full freedom in Rome or whether it would not be better to organize the conclave outside of Italy.[209] In an apostolic constitution issued on 21 August 1871, Pius IX had laid down that the cardinals had to pronounce on the matter after his death. He had clarified the guidelines in 1874 and again for the last time in 1877. The latest amendments were prepared by a committee, with Czacki as secretary. Remarkably, the leading cardinals had not dared to speak to the Pope about the appropriate adjustments and had instead turned to Czacki who seemed to have more influence on the aging head of the church than anybody else. After the death of Antonelli he had also helped with the rehabilitation of the archbishop of Perugia, Cardinal Giaocchino Pecci, who had been sidelined for decades and was now again to be included in the Curia.

Just one day after the death of the Pope, on February 8th, the cardinals present in Rome came together to study the three apostolic constitutions about the election of a new pope and to decide where the conclave would be held. A large majority opted for a conclave venue outside of Italy. However, the vice-dean of the College of Cardinals, Camillo di Pietro, insisted on postponing the decision until there was more clarity about the attitude of the Italian government. It quickly made clear that it would respect the cardinals' choice and would not exert any pressure. The foreign powers also seemed to have a preference for organizing the conclave in Rome. The following day, on February 9th, a new vote was taken in the College of Cardinals, and a large majority now agreed that the conclave would take place in the Eternal City, and would begin on February 18th. On that day 61 of the 64 cardinals who were entitled to vote were present, including 23 non-Italians.

The uncompromising policy of Pius IX had led to an estrangement between the Holy See and the great powers, but nevertheless they followed the election of the Pope with great attention. The infallibility declaration and the increase in his powers had made the position of the Pope even more important than before. The foreign governments – led by the Italian – had in previous

---

207 Salviati to Pergen, 27 Dec. 1877, HHSA, *Pergen*, II: 'The greatest difficulty is in the character of the In[nominato], who wants to do everything himself and is overwhelmed by work. To me he is like those theatrical choruses that keep repeating *corriamo* ("let us run") for a quarter of an hour and don't move.'

208 Salviati to Pergen, 23 Jan. 1878, HHSA, *Pergen*, II.

209 Martina, *Pio IX*, vol. III, 504-514.

years pushed forward their own candidates, but the long pontificate of Pius IX ensured that several *papabili* had died by now. Most governments wanted a more moderate pope, who would pursue a policy of accommodation with modern society. They put their hopes on Pecci, but they could exert only indirect influence on the College of Cardinals. As a Catholic great power, France held a veto in reserve against the election of Bilio, the architect of the *Syllabus Errorum*.[210]

The outside world was counting on a long conclave.[211] Two directions were evident within the College of Cardinals: the *zelanti* or *intransigenti* had a preference for Bilio, though he himself was not keen on the job, while the *transigenti* favoured Pecci, who was already 68 years old and would probably be a transitional pope. After the first round of voting, Pecci was well in the lead, but Bilio and Franchi were also in the running. In the second round the archbishop of Perugia made some gains, but not enough for the required two-thirds majority. Franchi, who had a 'liberal' reputation, knew he had no real chance and stepped down in favour of Pecci, thereby giving him his votes.[212] The next morning, on February 20th, the matter was clinched. Pecci was elected and took the name Leo XIII. He expressed gratitude to Franchi and immediately appointed him secretary of state.[213] The inseparable duo of Franchi (state secretariat) - Czacki (*Affari Straordinari*) now had a decisive voice in Vatican policy, especially as the new Pope was kept far away from curial politics for a long time and still had to settle into his new office.

Over time, however, Leo XIII would become primarily a 'political' pope. He was also more than a transitional pope because he lived until 20 July 1903.[214] From 1843 to 1846 he had been nuncio in Brussels, a diplomatic experience he was proud of and that had a great influence on him. In Belgium he had seen how the Church could thrive within the structure of a liberal state, and at the same time had witnessed the social consequences of industrial capitalism. He was later pushed aside and appointed archbishop of Perugia, a position that he filled for more than thirty years. During his secluded life he led a studious existence and he became a fervent advocate of a revival of the scholastic phi-

---

210 Fiorentino, 'Il conclave di Leone XIII', 159-194; Kertzer, *Prisoner of the Vatican*, 137-158.
211 Soderini, *Il Pontificato di Leone XIII*, vol. I, 21-80; Ciampani, 'The Roman Curia', 210-218; Id., 'Un cardinale Barnabita', 362-369.
212 On Alessandro Franchi (1819-1878), nuncio in Madrid, prefect of 'Propaganda Fide' from 1874 and secretary of state in 1878, see: *DHGE*, XVIII, 1977, kol. 576-581.
213 Weber, *Kardinäle und Prälaten*, 342-356 and 730; Id., *Quellen und Studien*, 137-141. See also the chronicle of Paul Vasili [Juliette Adam], *Roma Umbertina*, 83-86.
214 The literature on Leo XIII is very extensive. Some older biographies contain a lot of interesting information: Soderini, *Il Pontificato di Leone XIII*; De T'Serclaes, *Le Pape Léon XIII*; Hayward, *Léon XIII*. See also more recent studies: Launay, *La papauté à l'aube du XXe siècle*; Chadwick, *A History of the Popes*, 273-303; Schwaiger, *Papsttum und Päpste*, 45-104; Viaene, ed., *The Papacy and the New World Order*; Levillain and Ticchi, eds., *Le Pontificat de Léon XIII*.

losophy of Thomas Aquinas.[215] In one of his first encyclicals *Aeterni Patris* (4 August 1879), he would impose neo-Thomism as a guiding philosophy on the church.[216]

Much more than his predecessor, Leo XIII would emerge as an 'intellectual' Pope and a teacher of the Church. He published numerous encyclicals, especially on ethical and political issues, and he aimed for fruitful contact between the Church and modern culture. On the political level, he wanted to take more account of contemporary state structures. Like Pius IX, he saw the Church as a *societas perfecta*, but he had more respect for the autonomy of the State. For him, all forms of government were acceptable, though he did have an implicit preference for a monarchist regime. Leo XIII soon put an end to the crusade against political liberalism, and encouraged Catholics to use the available political tools to defend Church interests. In particular, he supported the formation and development of Catholic parties that would be mostly led by liberal Catholics.

The new Pope strove for better relations with the great powers. He especially sought out solutions to the *Kulturkampf* in Germany and Switzerland, but unlike Pius IX, here he relied primarily on diplomacy. He could do so because the mobilization of the Catholic people by his predecessor had garnered broad support for the papacy. Personally he attached much more importance to good relations with the powerful than to the sympathy of the masses. The pilgrimages and the delegations to Rome then dwindled visibly.[217] In addition, the new Pope had a very clericalist attitude: prominent lay people could, in his view, play only a subordinate, secondary role in the church and he would build the Roman church into an institution of clerical power. An organization like the Union of St. Peter could therefore not expect to get much support from him.

The new Pope's attitude to the Roman question was of the greatest importance in assessing his policy.[218] Just as much as his predecessor, he held on to his temporal power as a guarantee of the Holy See's independence. In order to settle the Roman question, he aimed at better relations with the Quirinal

215 The medieval philosopher Thomas Aquinas (1225-1274) linked Christian doctrine with elements of Aristotelianism. He argued that there was no fundamental contradiction between nature and grace, faith and reason. His philosophical and theological system (neo-Thomism) experienced a revival in church circles in the last quarter of the nineteenth century.

216 Aubert, 'Aspects divers du néo-thomisme', 133-248; 'L'enciclica *Aeterni Patris*. Il centenario (1879-1979)', *Scripta Theologica*, 11 (1979) 425-824; Thibault, *Savoir et pouvoir*.

217 Hemptinne to Dom Hildebrand, 28 March 1880, ADH, *Hildebrand*: 'The revenues from Peter's Pence are seriously diminishing everywhere ... Leo XIII seeks to rely on politicians who give nothing and is somewhat abandoning the *hommes d'oeuvres* who do give'; the same to his daughter-in-law Ida de Meeûs, 24 Oct. 1880, ADH, *Varia*: 'The movement towards Rome is slowing down and the Pope is being forgotten.'

218 Schwaiger, *Papstum*, 61-64; Chadwick, *History of the Popes*, 290-295; Kertzer, *Prisoner of the Vatican*, 198-213.

and especially with the great powers, in the hope that they would pressure the Italian government into making concessions. For that, he had to take advantage of the changing coalitions between the powers and he regularly felt obliged to pursue other paths. Initially, he relied mainly on the conservative empires of Germany and Austria, but from 1887 he put his trust in Catholic, albeit republican, France.[219] The problem was that this diplomatic jousting had repercussions for relations with the Catholic population in the countries concerned, and that political and pastoral objectives sometimes collided with each other. Relations between the Vatican and the Quirinal also had their ups and downs. Radical anticlerical politicians regularly torpedoed efforts at rapprochement that had been laboriously worked out.[220] On such occasions the Vatican repeatedly threatened that the Pope and the Curia would leave Rome.[221] In other instances, pressure from radical ultramontane organizations such as the *Opera dei Congressi* prevented the Pope from being too indulgent towards the left-liberal governments.[222]

It quickly became clear that Leo XIII would follow a more flexible course, which the members of the fledgling Union of St. Peter quickly realized. Czacki, despite his busy schedule, had not forgotten them. In April 1878 he asked his friend Franchi, the new secretary of state, to set up a press network that would build on what was left of the work of Geneva. In the text of the report submitted, he explicitly mentioned the meeting in Innsbruck and the agreements that were made there. What was remarkable was that he considered only the 'press network' and made no further mention of a lay organization with mutual contacts, reports and annual meetings.[223] In May Salviati thus reported to Pergen: 'Regarding the *innominato* with whom you corresponded: I know that his plans have been approved in principle. I say *his* because we cannot definitely say *our*. What we proposed in November has been put aside.'[224] In his new proposal, Czacki above all kept in mind what could be attained with Leo XIII, but in the past he had already shown that he was especially interested in an effective press policy. The new Pope quickly gave his fiat to a plan for

---

219 Prudhomme, 'Léon XIII et le nouvel ordre international', 203-216; Trincia, *Il nucleo tedesco*; Viaene, ed., *The Papacy and the New World Order*, 103-210.

220 So, there were some violent incidents on the transfer of Pius IX's coffin from St. Peter's Basilica to the church of San Lorenzo (13 July 1881) and on the unveiling of the statue of Giordani Bruno on the Campo dei Fiori (9 June 1889). See Kertzer, *Prisoner of the Vatican*, 179-197 and 258-271.

221 Ticchi, 'Ubi Roma, ibi Papa', 355-400.

222 Kertzer, *Prisoner of the Vatican*, 179-213.

223 A draft of this very detailed report, which was drawn up in April 1878, is located in ASV, *SS, Spogli Czacki* and a later version in ASV, *SS, Spogli Franchi*, b 3.

224 Salviati to Pergen, 14 May 1878, HHSA, *Pergen*, II.

setting up an *Uffizio stampa*, and on 1 June 1878 Franchi brought the establishment of this agency to the attention of the nuncios.[225]

The new press network was an improved version of GCP.[226] It had a staff of seven employees who served directly under Czacki, the secretary of the *Affari Straordinari*, and who sent useful information to the affiliated newspapers. More general news items or instructions were sent to the members of the directorate, which consisted mainly of the founders of the Union of St. Peter.[227] Only Hemptinne was no longer a member. He had not received either any sympathy from Leo XIII for his radical actions against the constitutional regime in Belgium, or any support for the further publication of *La Croix*,[228] decisions which he magnanimously overlooked. He was replaced on the committee by the Belgian Prince Eugène de Caraman-Chimay, who would prove to be quite inactive.[229] The members of the directorate had to determine whether the affiliated newspapers had taken up the information submitted and had followed the guidelines. They were also expected to supply the Vatican regularly with information on the development of the Catholic movement in their own countries. The *Uffizio* was called in code the 'Salmini House', after its correspondence address in Rome, while the messages and communications were signed with the letters S.P.L.L, referring to Salviati, Pergen, Loë and La Tour du Pin. The press network was still shrouded in an atmosphere of secrecy, but contacts with the Vatican no longer went through a mysterious *innominato*. There was now a clear link with the *Affari Straordinari* and the secretariat of state, and the nuncios were kept informed about events, thereby obviating tensions with the church hierarchy.[230]

The launch of the *Uffizio* was delayed by the unexpected death of secretary of state Franchi in late July 1878. Rumours circulated that he had been poisoned because of his overly 'liberal' orientation. The Italian government ordered an investigation and concluded that the poisoning accusation was unfounded.[231] Franchi was succeeded by Nina, another friend of Czacki's. Salviati, who was very familiar with the curial administration, noted: 'It is clear that the *innominato* is still in control: he created Franchi and now Nina is his creature.'[232]

---

225 Franchi to Serafino Vannutelli, nuncio in Brussels, 1 June 1878, ASV, *NB*, XLVIII, 31. See above all Viaene, *A Brilliant Failure*, 244-247.
226 Lamberts, 'Une organisation secrète', 92-95.
227 La Tour du Pin to Pergen, 28 May 1878, HHSA, *Pergen*, II.
228 Lamberts, 'Joseph de Hemptinne', 100-101.
229 Eugène de Caraman-Chimay (1834-1881) was chair of the 'Fédération belge des oeuvres catholiques' from 1876 on. In a letter to Caraman dated 8 Aug. 1878, Salviati carefully explained the working of the 'Salmini House'. A copy of this letter is to be found in Pergen's archive (HHSA, *Pergen*, II).
230 Viaene, 'A Brilliant Failure', 244-247; Id., 'Wagging the Dog', 326-331.
231 Fiorentino, 'Il conclave di Leone XIII', 172.
232 Salviati to Pergen, 12 Aug. 1878, HHSA, *Pergen*, II.

By mid-October 1879 the *Uffizio* was well underway. It was notably efficient in Italy, thanks to Salviati's extensive network.[233] In Austria Pergen appealed to the good offices of the counts Friedrich Thun and Franz Kuefstein, among others. The Salmini House operated on a regular basis until the autumn of 1880 and would experience another short revival the year after. It pushed for a conciliatory policy in Germany and Italy, as well as in Belgium and France, where in the 1880s liberal governments were pursuing an anticlerical policy. This did not please the members of the Uffizio's directorate, who increasingly felt they were being used as a tool and a cover for political changes with which they did not agree. Pergen in particular became discouraged.[234] Initially he had seen the press network as part of a broader effort to promote greater unity among Catholics, and along with Salviati, still cherished the hope that it would gradually lead to a stronger organization with many branches. Nothing came of this. Moreover, the committee members were assigned only an executive task within the press network. Pergen pulled out very quickly and though Salviati for a while showed a little more loyalty to Leo XIII, in early 1882 he too was overcome by a sense of despondency.[235] In the same year the Salmini House was finally shut down. Over the next few years the Vatican would try to influence public opinion through its own press organs and with '*bollettini*' that were sent to the nuncios by the secretariat of state.[236]

In the meantime, Wladimir Czacki, the initiator of the agency, disappeared temporarily from the scene in Rome. In August 1879 he became nuncio in Paris, a top posting in the papal diplomatic service. While in France he loyally carried out the papal policy of accommodation.[237] He insisted that the bishops and prominent Catholics had to come to an agreement with the (anticlerical) republic. In a very short time he got into a disagreement with the radical ultramontanes, who still supported *L'Univers* and who accused him of playing up to the Church's enemies. Overcome by their scorn, he returned to Rome after three years. On the intercession of the French government, he received a cardinal's hat on 25 September 1882. However, the Francophile Czacki did not subsequently quite fit in with the new papal policy which, under the influence of his rival Luigi Galimberti, was focused more on Germany and Austria. He

233 Extensive information on the working of the Italian section of the *Uffizio stampa* is to be found in the records of Luigi Manna Roncadelli, Salviati's 'lieutenant' ('Archivio per la storia del movimento sociale cattolico in Italia', Milan).

234 Pergen to Friedrich Thun, 1 Dec. 1878, SALD, *Thun-Hohenstein*, A 3 - XIX, H 65, 5. Franz Kuefstein encouraged him not to give up (4 Dec. 1878, HHSA, *Pergen*, I).

235 Salviati to Pergen, 31 Jan. 1882, HHSA, *Pergen*, II.

236 Viaene, 'Wagging the Dog', 331-346.

237 Marchasson, *La diplomatie romaine et la République française*; Ignesti, *Francia e Santa Sede*, 327: 'He was a faithful interpreter of Pope Leo's political and pastoral directives'; Weber, *Quellen und Studien*, 306-314; Crispolti, *Corone e Porpore*, 131-139.

was also too much of a 'conciliarist', a proponent of reconciliation with Italy.[238] The *innominato* who, in agreement with Pius IX, had recommended a radical ultramontane course to Hemptinne, had undoubtedly come a long way. Nevertheless, as has already been mentioned, one constant in his position was his continuing belief that the Church had to turn to the people. More than anyone, he impressed on the Pope that the Church could only maintain its influence in the world by taking advantage of social and democratic tendencies.[239]

Czacki also retained his interest in an efficient press policy. Following the demise of the Salmini House, the Vatican's press initiatives lacked direction. An impasse around 1887 led the Pope to set up two separate committees to study the problem of the press, and Czacki became the chief spokesman for one of them. Remarkably, he again opted for the 1878 formula of an *Uffizio stampa* that would operate via a parallel network of prominent Catholic lay people. He seemed to look back with a certain pride and nostalgia on the glory days of the Geneva committee, but this time *transigent* employees had to be chosen. The other committee was of the opinion that the press had to serve the apostolate more than diplomacy, and that it should be left in the hands of the local bishops. Initially Leo XIII saw the advantages in the establishment of a new press network, but the new secretary of state, Mariano Rampolla,[240] who took office on 2 June 1887, finally opted for a different approach. He refrained from again relying on a secret network of prominent laymen, preferring to follow an eclectic course in influencing the international press.[241] He turned the international policy of the Holy See in a pro-French direction. That again offered possibilities for Czacki, but then he died unexpectedly on 8 March 1888, at the age of 54. Reactions to his death were very mixed, although those of the leaders of the former Black International are not known.[242] Their paths had diverged too much.

What finally, on balance, had the Black International achieved? It failed to bring about a more Christian political order, such as diplomats and politicians like Blome, Bréda and Leo Thun had desired. That, however, had been

---

238 Prudhomme, 'Léon XIII et la curie romaine', 29-48; Jankowiak, 'La Curie romaine au temps de Léon XIII', 69-100.

239 Weber, 'Dans les couloirs du Vatican', 95-115.

240 On Mariano Rampolla del Tindaro (1843-1913), nuncio in Madrid from 1882 to 1887 and afterwards secretary of state until 1903, see: *Enciclopedia Cattolica*, X, 1953, col. 51-518.

241 Viaene, 'Wagging the Dog', 331-346.

242 Malijay to De Mun, [1888], CARAN, *De Mun*, AP 378, 13-IX: 'There was no regret for him in the Vatican ... In Rome his salon was the centre for gossip *par excellence* and would have become a dangerous place at the time of a conclave.' In contrast, there were more positive testimonials: Cardinal Gibbons, Archbishop of Baltimore to Baldassare Odescalchi, 27 March 1888, Archivio Odescalchi, XXXVII, C, 2: 'I admired his genius and the urbanity of his life'; Giulio Tosti to id., 20 March 1888, ibid. Edoardo Soderini, confidant and later biographer of Leo XIII, portrayed him shortly after his death with much sympathy and appreciation: Soderini, 'Le cardinal Vladimiro Czacki', 237-259.

only a secondary aim of the organization. It primarily aimed to coordinate the protests against the annexation of the *Patrimonium Petri* and simultaneously secure the international position of the Pope. It succeeded in giving the popular agitation of 1870-1871 a much broader character than it had in 1859-1860. It expanded the movement into Germany, Austria and Italy, created a strong international coordinating body, and it developed a wide repertoire of protest actions, including processions, petitions, mass demonstrations and especially national and international deputations. The mobilization of the Catholic masses could not reverse the annexation of Rome, but it did protect the autonomy and international status of the Holy See in an effective way. After the final collapse of the Papal States, Catholic opinion had become the papacy's chief line of defence. For that reason, Pius IX and his circle attached much importance to the functioning of the International in the early years.[243]

The press was the perfect tool to launch and maintain the mobilization of the people. In this area too the International played a significant role. The Holy See had hitherto only occasionally attempted to influence the Catholic press, but the launch of the *Correspondance de Genève* reversed that trend. The periodical was certainly not a journalistic showpiece, but it had a wide international distribution. The importance that the Pope attached to it can be deduced from his personal, risky interventions for its funding and staffing. The press network set up by the International, which worked very well for three years, continued to appeal to Czacki, as evidenced by the working of the *Uffizio stampa* (1878-1882) and the proposals for readjusting press policy in 1887.

The work of the International fitted in with the policy of Pius IX. He put greater confidence in the Catholic people than in diplomacy, and he was willing to involve prominent Catholic lay people who were committed to the preservation of the social influence of the Church. In the last decade of his pontificate his anti-liberal approach became even more radical, and through the International – using the *innominato* as an instrument – he covertly supported the radical ultramontane movement within the Church. In close consultation with the papacy, the *Permanents* contributed in several countries to the development of a militant Catholic movement. They were motivated by a desire for restoration, but they used modern techniques of mobilization. The Catholic organizations they founded or inspired would in the coming decades constitute an important basis for religious political parties that would pragmatically defend the rights and liberties of the Church within the framework of the liberal constitutional State. Thanks in part to the Christian popular movements and parties, the State acquired another dimension. Catholic opposition to state omnipotence contributed significantly to the formation of a state-free area, within which the Church and its organizational network could flourish

243 Ciampani, 'The Roman Curia', 226.

in freedom. Thus was the Leviathan held at bay. It would be contained even more by the social stance of the Catholic Church, which was partly inspired by the leading members of the Black International.

SOCIAL DEFENCE

THE FRIBOURG UNION

At the end of August 1874 the Black International held its annual meeting for the second time in the French village of Ferney, about seven kilometers to the north of Geneva. Voltaire had spent the last twenty years of his life in this delightful spot, with its view of Mont Blanc and the Jura Mountains. But it was not to honour the author of *Candide* that the members of the International descended there. Since February 1873 Ferney had been the refuge of Monsignor Mermillod who from that base could easily stay in contact with his clergy in Geneva. In the summer of that year, the International had gathered there for the first time, on the eve of its reorganization. Some thirty members of the network – mainly Austrian, French and Belgian – all met there again in 1874. This time their attention was focused primarily on defending ecclesiastical rights against government actions in various countries, but the social question was also put on the agenda for discussion.

On Thursday afternoon August 24th, the committee in charge of social and economic issues met under the chairmanship of René Marquis de La Tour du Pin, who would soon emerge as the main theorist of the *Oeuvre des Cercles catholiques d'Ouvriers* (Society of Catholic Worker Circles) in France. A fierce discussion ensued about the principles that should form the basis of the social order. La Tour du Pin felt that charitable work would help eliminate the main social problems and the majority agreed, noting in their report that 'Catholic charity can be sufficient to resolve the labour problem.'[1] Two young gray-suited aristocrats, who were clearly incensed by and disagreed with the

---

1   Minutes of the annual meeting at Ferney, 20-21 Aug. 1874, NKDC, *Cramer*, 455, 20, a, 2.

turn in the debate, stood up and left before the end of the discussion. They were the Austrian princes Alfred and Aloys von und zu Liechtenstein. They believed that charity and philanthropy no longer sufficed as a solution to the social question and that the principle of justice had to form the basis of the social order.[2] There was a world of difference between the two approaches: establishing a just society demanded structural reform, which was not necessary for the practice of charity. In retrospect, this confrontation marked an important turning point. A year later, at the Congress of Bregenz in 1875, the balance would tilt towards the principle of justice and La Tour du Pin would also gradually come to support socioeconomic structural changes.

It is striking that the ultramontanes, who dominated the Black International, displayed a greater social sensitivity than the liberal Catholics. They were more opposed to individualism and attached greater importance to the natural social ties that surrounded and protected the socially weak. More than liberal Catholics, they gave a boost to social Catholicism, which initially had a pronounced paternalistic slant, but later would come under more emancipatory and democratic influences.[3]

The International had already devoted a lot of attention to the social question at the Congress of Einsiedeln, some months after the Paris Commune uprising. Here they had been influenced by Mermillod, who as a celebrated preacher in the 1860s had already taken a conspicuous stance on social issues. In 1868 he had given a controversial sermon to the *beau monde* in Sainte-Clotilde in Paris: 'There are not two Gospels, one for your idleness and another to bless the chains of the poor.' During Vatican I he was involved in the drafting of a statement of principles on the social question. He later gave his full support to the *Oeuvre des Cercles catholiques d'Ouvriers* (Society of Catholic Worker Circles). On 14 April 1872, again in Sainte-Clotilde, he gave a sermon on the social question that had even more resonance than the previous one. He was the first prelate to raise social issues in such a clear way in French Catholic circles. In his view, the labour question could be solved by a mixture of charitable action and self-help by workers' organizations.[4]

Participants in the congress at Einsiedeln considered the main means of counteracting the Socialist International to include a greater social commitment by the clergy, founding Christian workers' organizations, convening popular conferences, developing a popular press, as well as restoring 'Christian public law' whereby the church's position would be strengthened.[5] At

2   Rollet, *Action sociale des catholiques en France (1871-1901)*, vol. I, 108; Talmy, *René de la Tour du Pin*, 11.
3   Mayeur, 'Catholicisme intransigeant, catholicisme social, démocratie chrétienne', 483-499.
4   Comte, *Le cardinal Mermillod*, 193-200; Molette, *Albert de Mun*, 19; Chenaux, 'Les origines de l'Union de Fribourg', 263-265.
5   Minutes of the annual meeting in Einsiedeln, 31 Aug.-3 Sept. 1871, NKDC, *Cramer*, 455, 20, a, 2; minutes of the annual meeting in Geneva, 29-31 Aug. 1872, ibid.

subsequent conferences much attention was given to Catholic youth groups and the Society of Catholic Worker Circles. Protective labour legislation for women and children was also discussed, but the majority was not persuaded.[6] In 1875, at the Congress of Bregenz, the committee on Christian economy decisively opted for a structural approach to social issues, accepted the principle of state intervention in social matters and insisted on regulating women's and children's labour. The committee also pointed to the excesses of financial capitalism and demanded that measures be taken against illicit profits. De Hemptinne, a cotton industrialist, had difficulty with some of those recommendations. For him charitable work and raising the moral consciousness of the working class were appropriate solutions to the social question. However, his view was not shared by a large majority who pushed forward the principle of justice and aimed at introducing structural measures. During the closing session, the gathering endorsed the recommendations of the committee. It was not without significance that almost half of the thirty-two attendees were Austrian and German aristocrats. The Liechtenstein brothers also joined in. These social aristocrats were very critical of capitalism and increasingly came under the influence of corporatist ideas. That was also true of Blome, who no longer participated in the congresses of the International, but still maintained frequent contact with its leading figures.

An Arcadian existence

From April 1872 on Blome again travelled throughout Europe, trying to catch his breath after one and a half years of hard work in Geneva. He had to look after his own affairs as a matter of urgency, while at the same trying to find a permanent residence, not an easy quest.[7] He found nothing to his liking in Vienna; nor was there a single residence in the surrounding area that could tempt him. Friends, whom he asked for advice, were told that anywhere French cuisine was available would be acceptable.[8] Finally, his attention was drawn to the Villa Giulia in the northern Italian city of Bellagio, where Lake Como and the Ramo di Lecco come together. This stately villa had been built in the eighteenth century in neo-classical style and was surrounded by a lush Italian garden and a vast olive grove. It was located on the banks of the Ramo di Lecco, but was linked to Lake Como by the *Viale della Villa Giulia*, a strip of land that was a kilometer long and thirty metres wide. It was the only residence in Bel-

---

6 Minutes of the annual meeting in Geneva, 29-31 Aug. 1872, NKDC, *Cramer*, 455, 20, a, 2.
7 Pergen to Cramer, 27 Oct. 1872, NKDC, *Cramer*, 434, 12 c: 'The long silence of Bl[ome] should not surprise you. I know the reason for it. He has been wandering around half of Europe looking for a stone (in the shape of an architectural monument) where he can rest his head and shelter his family. He is still looking.'
8 Blome to Revertera, Sept. 1872, HAH, IV, 56.

The Villa Giulia in Bellagio. Photograph, Bosetti.
[*O. Hintze,* Geschichte des uradeligen Geschlechtes der Herren und Grafen Blome, *Hamburg, 1929*]

lagio with a view of the two lakes surrounding the city. The extensive estate of nearly fifteen acres had been purchased in 1851 by the Belgian King Leopold I.[9] After his death in 1865 it came into the possession of his second son, the Count of Flanders, who almost immediately sold it on. Through a middleman it then came into the possession of Blome, who used his wife's fortune for the purchase. The northern Italian lakes were very popular at that time, and because of their mild climate they were known as idyllic places to stay. That was certainly true of Lake Como, which in a special way combined the charms of south and north, surrounded by lush Mediterranean vegetation that bordered on the bottom slopes of the Alps. The region was close to France, Switzerland, Germany and Austria and was a transit area to the heart of Italy. That certainly pleased Blome, and over the next few years his villa would be a meeting place for many prominent Catholics from neighbouring countries.

For now, he needed rest and repose above all. He was 43 years old when he took up residence in the Villa Giulia, and it was the first time in his life that he had a permanent residence. At that time he had six children, three sons and three daughters, between two and thirteen years of age. Now, finally, he was able to make time for his family, with whom he fully enjoyed the pleasures of country life. At the end of 1873 he had another daughter and gave her the

9   Deneckere, *Leopold I,* 347.

name 'Giulia', in honour of the place where he, as he said himself, had so far spent the happiest year of his life:

> I am so perfectly contented here that I consider it like a fatal lapse of my youth that I ever became involved in politics. My vocation is that of a work-shy country gentleman. The study to which I should devote myself is botany. That would have been much better than stuffing my head with the fantasies of international law. What delusions! My camellias, my azaleas, my rhododendrons: these constitute pure reality.[10]

Pergen reported to Cramer: 'As far as Romeo [Blome] is concerned, I only know that he is hopelessly in love with his Giulia and he does nothing else but run after butterflies, pluck camellias and make life difficult for his gardener.' He sighed: 'Oh Capua, Capua! How many Hannibals will be lulled to sleep by your pleasures.'[11]

Blome then seemed to have found the key to happiness, but he would soon come to know that perfect happiness is not of this world. A few years later he was confronted with all kinds of health problems: stomach complaints, measles, lumbago.[12] At the end of 1876 he even nearly died of typhoid.[13] He regularly sought a cure in spas, but they did not offer an adequate remedy for all of his ills.

He also had to deal with considerable financial hardship. The spectacular collapse of the Vienna Stock Exchange on 9 May 1873 ushered in a prolonged, global recession. The crash was caused by overproduction in the agricultural and industrial sectors, but it was precipitated by an overheating in the credit sector, a pattern that would be repeated in the coming decades with clockwork regularity. The unbridled expansion of credit and of property and stock market speculation in the previous years, known as the *Gründerzeit* in German-speaking countries, led to the economic system imploding. The crash and its after-effects reinforced opposition to capitalism in many circles, and in Austria led to an upsurge of anti-Semitism. Jewish bankers, after all, played a leading role in the Viennese financial world. Anti-Semitism was a widespread phenomenon among the main victims of the crisis: intellectuals, tradesmen, small shopkeepers, farmers and industrial workers. Also hard hit by the collapse of the stock market were many aristocrats, who had been tempted into making speculative transactions or had entrusted a portion of their assets in good faith to banks that now - sometimes fraudulenty - went under. Old moral and social prejudices against business, the banks and the stock market were

10 Blome to Cramer, 1 Jan. 1874, NKDC, *Cramer*, 434, 12 b, II.
11 Pergen to Cramer, 20 Jan. and 1 May 1873, NKDC, *Cramer*, 434, 12 c.
12 Blome to Revertera, 21 May and 1 June 1875, Jan. 1878, 30 May and 28 Nov. 1879, HAH, IV, 56.
13 Bréda to Cramer, 4 Jan. 1877, NKDC, *Cramer*, 434, R 12 a, III.

stirred up once again and Jewish bankers were especially identified as the culprits.[14]

Like so many other aristocrats, Blome was also hit by the Viennese stock market crash, which affected both his public funds and the income from his property.[15] To make matters worse, he had allowed himself be persuaded by Cramer, his good friend and comrade, to invest a substantial portion of his assets in risky new investments. The Dutch financier had shrewdly managed to gain the trust of his wealthy friends within the Black International who, though aware by now of his earlier financial problems, had been convinced by him that he was an innocent victim of Langrand-Dumonceau's manipulations. His intentions had been good, but 'an unjust world will judge people not by their intentions but by the consequences of their actions'.[16] At the beginning of 1873, Cramer again brought up his old plans for impoldering the Zuiderzee.[17] During that period also he committed himself to a plan by Henry Amy, a Belgian-American banker from New York and friend of Langrand-Dumonceau, to establish a Franco-American company in Paris in order to attract European capital for major infrastructure projects in the United States, where a spectacular economic expansion had got underway after the Civil War. Amy was chairman of the *Catholic Union* in New York and the enthusiastic recommendation he received from church circles there[18] helped to get Cramer on board. Even more enticing for Cramer was the prospect that he could make up for his big losses of the previous years. He again looked to Paul Bréda, who was once more in dire need of money, and charged him with organizing the company's headquarters in Paris. The Dutch businessman also succeeded in persuading some friends in the Geneva committee with 'Catholic' arguments to invest in the planned venture. So, he succeeded in snaring Lord Denbigh,[19] as well as Bodenham who was already burdened by large debts.[20] Against the advice of various friends, Blome also allowed himself to be roped in, because of his blind confidence in Cramer's judgement.[21] He himself knew little about

---

14 Rumpler, *Eine Chance*, 463-466.
15 Blome to Cramer, 13 June 1876 and 7 May 1877, NKDC, *Cramer*, 434, 12 b, II.
16 Pergen to Friedrich Thun, 7 Sept. 1875, SALD, *Thun-Hohenstein*, A 3 - XIX, H 82, 13.
17 Cramer to Pergen, 10 May 1873, HHSA, *Pergen*, I: The plans were deemed to be feasible and Cramer was in the seventh heaven: 'So here I am then on the way to becoming a benefactor of the Netherlands!'
18 Cramer to Bodenham, 12 Dec. 1873, NKDC, *Cramer*, 24, III, 669-673.
19 Cramer to Denbigh, 20 April 1875, NKDC, *Cramer*, 24, IV, 93.
20 Cramer to Bodenham, 12 Dec. 1873, NKDC, *Cramer*, 24, III, 669-673; Lady Bodenham, 15 Dec. 1873, NKDC, *Cramer*, 437, 13, k: 'You know well that there is nobody in whom he [Bodenham] has a more blind confidence'; Cramer to Bodenham, 16 Dec. 1873, NKDC, *Cramer*, 24, III, 678.
21 Blome to Cramer, 7 May 1877, NKDC, *Cramer*, 434, 12 b, II.

financial operations[22] and he had already called on the expertise of the Dutch financier to invest 'in strong Dutch securities'. Cramer's previous history should have spurred him to greater caution, but the close cooperation of the previous years had created a strong bond of trust. In order to participate in the Franco-American company, Blome sold part of his Dutch securities at a loss and also diverted capital from an inalienable inheritance that should have been invested in the most secure way. In addition, he bought bonds in the Denver & Rio Grande Railway Company for 450,000 euros and shares in the Central Colorado Improvement Company for 1.3 million euros.[23] These were companies owned by General William Jackson Palmer, who played a major role in the opening up of the Far West.

The Franco-American partnership was short-lived. In February 1875 Cramer could still proudly boast that it had thirty-six delegates and nearly a thousand agents, 'all men of our denomination, spread across all the French departments'. However, only a few months later failure appeared inevitable as too little capital had come in, due to the prolonged economic crisis. In October Cramer had to go into liquidation. At about the same time he felt forced to shelve his plans for impoldering the Zuiderzee. In fact he was at rock-bottom, but his friends had also been severely affected. Bodenham did not know which way to turn anymore, and Blome was also licking his wounds.[24] In June 1876 he had to confess that for the first time in his life he had serious concerns about his private assets. He had already been hit by the crisis in the Viennese banks and now he shared in Cramer's adversity also. But, the worst was yet to come. The economic crisis also hit the USA and in the spring of 1877 Denver stopped paying out bond dividends and the market value of Colorado tumbled. Blome, in a panic, started to sell and suffered heavy losses.[25] Cramer's son Henry, who gradually took over his father's financial affairs, even had the audacity to advise him, via Bréda, that he should rely in future on the services of a financial expert for managing his assets.[26] The Cramers were right in insisting that Denver and Colorado in fact were still healthy companies and that there was no real reason for panic.[27] Nonetheless, this episode put a definitive

---

22 Bréda to Cramer, 8 April 1870, NKDC, *Cramer*, 434, 12 a, 2: 'He does not have the first idea about financial matters.'

23 Cramer to Blome, 22 March 1874 and 1 June 1877, NKDC, *Cramer*, 24, IV, 21 en 550.

24 Lady Bodenham to Cramer, 22 Nov. 1875 and 30 June 1876, NKDC, *Cramer*, 437, 13, k.

25 Blome to Cramer, 7 May 1877, NKDC, *Cramer*, 434, 12 b, II: 'Oh, cursed be the day that you took Mr Amy to be a heavenly messenger telling you to undertake a Christian and salutary endeavour. He was the agent of arrant overseas scoundrels speculating on the credulity of good Catholics in Europe.' Blome to Henry Cramer, 23 May 1877, ibid.: 'And these Americans introduced themselves as good Catholics ... We were drawn into the trap by the prospect of doing a useful deed for the Church!'

26 Henry Cramer to Bréda, 12 May 1877, NKDC, *Cramer*, 24, IV, 492.

27 Cramer to Bréda, 12 May 1877, NKDC, *Cramer*, 24, IV, 489.

end to the intriguing relationship between the feudal seigneur Blome and the inveterate dreamer and apprentice magician, Jan Willem Cramer.

In the meantime, Blome's life took a new direction. During this period he worked on his political memoirs which, though never published, have been used extensively in the early chapters of this book. More important was the fact that once again he had his large library at his disposal in Bellagio, and from then on he devoted himself to an intense study of social problems. He was already widely read on the political and religious level, but now he set about expanding his socioeconomic knowledge, thereby gradually acquiring the reputation of being the most learned and educated aristocrat in the Dual Monarchy.[28]

As a conservative statesman Blome was extremely disappointed because the events of 1870-1871 had not led to a restoration of a Christian political order and ethical international politics. However, the clock could no longer be turned back. Metternich's world had perished forever and international politics would henceforth be dictated exclusively by the interests of the nation states. Moreover, the liberal parliamentary system had penetrated into most countries and even had some impact on the empires of Germany and Austria. Despite his firm principles, Blome was too pragmatic to pursue a chimera against his better judgement and to cling to a form of government that apparently belonged to the past. Still, the fight against liberalism was not lost. Socioconomic developments offered opportunities to break through the individualism of the liberals, give the constitutional state a more social dimension and bring about a more articulated society.

Blome now directed his attack against economic liberalism, which in that period proved particularly vulnerable. Gradually the social debit side of the liberal economy had become visible: unbridled industrial capitalism had caused great social misery in the factory towns and paved the way for revolutionary socialism, which was preparing to take over political power. The big threat to order and stability in society no longer came from the bourgeoisie but from the troubled working masses. In 1876 Blome wrote: 'We are experiencing the greatest social debacle since the beginning of our era ... Nothing would surprise me more than to see Karl Marx come to power one of these days, resulting in all the socialist theories being implemented.'[29] He later added: 'Only Marx and his associates have a clear vision. Their victory is only a matter of time.'[30] As was already evident from his tract, *Wo ist die Zukunft* (1871), Blome was resolute in his opposition to Marxist socialism, but he equally condemned the social excesses of economic liberalism. His anti-socialism went hand-in-hand with a social reformism.

28 Vasili [Juliette Adam], *La société de Vienne*, 202: 'a retired diplomat, the most learned man of the Austrian aristocracy'.
29 Blome to Cramer, 22 June 1876, NKDC, *Cramer*, 434, 12 b, II.
30 Blome to Revertera, 2 Feb. 1878, HAH, IV, 56.

Blome's stand against liberal capitalism was partially motivated by a class reflex. Capitalism, after all, mainly served the interests of the bourgeoisie, adversely affected landownership and disrupted the traditional rural economy. However, Blome had not always been a rabid opponent of capitalism; in the 1850s, the classical liberal theorist Frédéric Bastiat had been one of his favourite authors, and he had been a supporter of international free trade.[31] But he had begun to regret the aggressive individualism that disrupted traditional social bonds and subjected defenceless people to the blind laws of the market. He also resented the fact that industrialists were not in the least concerned about the fate of their factory workers. As a big landowner, he placed himself in a tradition of solidarity with the rural population for whom he felt responsible. He became convinced that the liberal economy had to give way to a more social economy, and he would become a strong supporter of corporative formulas as a way of creating a more supportive and harmonious society.

Obviously Blome was of the opinion that the Church had to play an important role in this social recovery. Its ethical principles were applicable not only to the individual lives of the faithful, but also to the social order. Its social ethics had to go beyond individual charity, which sometimes was little more than a fig leaf for the collective egoism of the propertied classes, and had to put the emphasis on social justice. There was also a tactical consideration at play here that was meant to push the Church towards greater social involvement. It had been abandoned by most political rulers, was fiercely opposed by the anticlerical bourgeoisie and could retain the support of the people only if it paid attention to their needs.

Blome found a theoretical basis for his social Catholic ideas in medieval Thomism, which was itself influenced by Aristotelianism and which was undergoing a revival, thanks especially to the Jesuits and the Dominicans.[32] Wilhelm Emmanuel von Ketteler, the bishop of Mainz, who in the 1860s was the first church leader to develop a more or less coherent social doctrine, had already appealed to Aristotelianism and Thomism.[33] In line with these philosophical systems, he stressed that man was preeminently a social being and that forming associations was an obvious and natural given. The Bishop also pointed to the dignity of all human beings who were entitled to just treatment in all situations, including work. If necessary, state intervention, through protective labour legislation, should put a stop to the exploitation of the workers in modern large-scale industry. In previous years Blome had clashed repeatedly with Ketteler, who had been highly critical of the Black International.

---

31 Blome to Pons, 6 June and 13 Aug. 1855, LASH, 126.15, 615.
32 Zagar, 'Aquinas and the Social Teaching of the Church', 826-855; Aubert, 'Aspects divers du néo-thomisme', 133-248; Thibault, *Savoir et pouvoir*.
33 On the social views of Mgr. Ketteler, see Petersen, *Wilhelm Emmanuel von Ketteler*; Iserloh, *Wilhelm Emmanuel von Ketteler*; De Gasperi, *I tempi e gli uomini*, 8-16; Misner, *Social Catholicism in Europe*, 136-144; Joblin, 'Doctrine et action sociale', 100-105.

However, he had a deep appreciation for the social ideas of the bishop of Mainz, as had some other Austrian aristocrats who, along with Blome, would play an important role in the Social Catholic movement in Austria.

The social aristocrats

The social issue was first openly discussed in Austria on the Catholic side[34] by Prince Aloys Liechtenstein (1846-1920), at a meeting of the *Katholisch-Patriotisches Volksverein für Niederösterreich* on 18 May 1875.[35] He urged Catholics to study the social question and pleaded for a recognition of occupational organizations and for protective labour legislation. Blome was very pleased with the speech.[36]

As a young diplomat Aloys Liechtenstein had spent two years in London, where he was struck by the appalling poverty among the workers and had come under the influence of the Christian socialists. At the end of 1873 he left the diplomatic service in order to immerse himself in sociopolitical affairs. The following year, he participated for the first time at the annual meeting of the Black International where, as mentioned above, he made his presence felt. At the meeting in Bregenz (1875), he played a major role in the shift towards the adoption of a structural approach to the social question. During the Austrian *Katholikentag* in 1877 he would directly attack the excesses of financial capitalism, earning himself the nickname of 'the red prince'. Shortly after, he was elected a member of the *Abgeordnetenhaus*. All told, he would be more important as a political activist than as a social theorist.

Liechtenstein's social views were particularly indebted to Ketteler, and even more to Baron Karl von Vogelsang (1818-1890), who would become the leading social Catholic publicist in the Dual Monarchy.[37] Vogelsang's biography reveals a number of similarities with that of Blome, a partial explanation for the close collaboration that developed between them. Vogelsang came from Prussia, where he had been opposed to the constitutional reforms of 1848. He

34   On the early development of social Catholicism in Austria (Cisleithania), see Wandruzska, 'Il cattolicesimo politico e sociale', 151-178; Weinzierl-Fischer, 'Aus den Anfängen', 475-486; Bled, *Les fondements du conservatisme autrichien*, 289-342; Grandner, 'Conservative Social Politics in Austria', 77-107; Silberbauer, Österreichs Katholiken und die Arbeiterfrage, 61-92; Knoll, *Zur tradition der christlichsozialen partei*, 96-149.

35   On Aloys von Liechtenstein, see Erika Weinzierl, 'Aloys Prinz Liechtenstein (1846-1920)', *Grösse Österreicher*, 96-113; Banauch, *Prinz Aloys von und zu Liechtenstein*; Schöpfer, *Klar und Fest*, 124-130.

36   Blome to Revertera, 21 May and 1 June 1875, HAH, IV, 56.

37   On Karl von Vogelsang (1818-1890), see Von Klopp, *Leben und Wirken des Sozialpolitikers Karl Freiherr von Vogelsang*; Allmayer Beck, *Vogelsang. Vom Feudalismus zur Volksbewegung*; Bader, *Karl von Vogelsang*; Id., 'Christliche Sozialreform im Sinne von Karl von Vogelsang', 153-162.

Karl von Vogelsang. Print, I. Eigner.
[*Vienna, Österreichische Nationalbibliothek*]

converted to Catholicism soon after, which he – like Blome – saw as a bastion against the spirit of revolution. Over time, he settled in the Dual Monarchy and at the end of 1875 he was given the editorial leadership in Vienna of the *Vaterland*, the organ of the Bohemian feudal nobility. He would give the paper a more pronounced social Catholic orientation.

He was a major supporter of corporatism that aimed to transcend individualism by assigning an important role to the professional associations, not only in social but also in economic life. The system also met with wide support outside the Catholic world and included the philosopher Hegel and later the sociologist Durkheim among its major theorists. It struck a key in Catholic circles because of its moral undertone and its confidence in organically developed social relations.[38]

Vogelsang developed his corporate vision of society on the basis of a conviction that human beings contributed to society mainly through their work. He was a proponent of mixed professional associations, to which both employers and workers would belong. These associations would become the regulatory organs of the economy, as well as offer social protection to their members. By providing a form of political representation based on interest groups, they also offered an alternative to the liberal parliamentary system, which at that time only represented capital. The State had become an instrument in the hands of the propertied class and this situation had to change; the political representative institutions should instead reflect the different interests in social and economic life. In fact, the main task of the State was to establish a just society, and in anticipation of the transition to a corporative social order, it had to enact protective labour legislation. Vogelsang was therefore an advocate of state intervention in social matters, but at the same time he opposed the State's omnipotence. A temporary strengthening of the role of the State in the social sphere could be reconciled with opposition to the Leviathan. It was only in anticipation of the recovery of the binding forces in society – with professional associations to the fore – that the State was called to restore solidarity among people. This position thus clearly differed from state socialism, which was gathering strength during that period.

Vogelsang was not content merely with a *Sozialpolitik*; he also worked zealously for *Sozialreform*, a thorough transformation of capitalism into a system in which social relationships and associations and not profit-seeking individuals would be paramount. These intermediate structures could simultaneously form a buffer against the omnipotence of the State. Vogelsang denounced not only the social excesses of industrialization, but also its disastrous impact on the environment and nature, and in this he was one of the precursors of the ecological movement. His system had a social character, but at the same time it was quite patronizing as it was embedded in the concept

---

38 Black, *Guilds and Civil Society*, 202-210 and 220-236.

of a 'social monarchy' and still assigned an important role to the traditional elites.

From the moment that Vogelsang took over the editorship of the *Vaterland*, he became a focus for like-minded social aristocrats. The year 1875 can therefore in many ways be seen as a turning point for the launch of the Social Catholic movement in Austria. In November Aloys Liechtenstein made contact with Vogelsang, who in turn on December 10th paid an introductory visit to Blome, which marked the beginning of a long and deep friendship.[39] The occupant of the Villa Giulia would in the next few years regularly – though anonymously – contribute to the *Vaterland* and would assist Vogelsang in word and deed whenever his social ideas brought him into conflict with Leo Thun-Hohenstein, the leader of the Bohemian nobility, who was the actual director of the newspaper.

At this time Blome was already deeply involved in socioeconomic issues.[40] He was familiar with the work of Karl Marx and maintained close contact with the French sociologist, Frédéric Le Play (1806-1882), whose collected works he had in his library.[41] Le Play was highly esteemed in France as a pioneer of empirical social research.[42] His approach would find many supporters in social Catholic circles, until well into the twentieth century. Catholic reformers were attracted by the key position given to religion, property and the family in his theories about social reform. He also supported setting up corporations because they reinforced social harmony and thus could contribute to a peaceful and at the same time lasting solution to the social question. However, it was true that Le Play saw economic liberalism as an achievement and was not in favour of social intervention by the State; on that level social Catholics like Blome would take distance from him.

During this period Blome renewed his friendship with Friedrich Revertera, whom he had come to know in 1856 at the Austrian embassy in Paris.[43] The two friends, who were coevals, held similar sociopolitical views. From 1864 to 1867 Revertera was Austrian ambassador in St. Petersburg, and just like Blome had left the diplomatic service on Beust's appointment. As a result of the stock market crisis, he lost almost all his wealth due to the fraudulent

---

39 Klopp, *Vogelsang*, 96: 'One can say that of all the friends Vogelsang had, few have stationed themselves as closely to his side as Blome.' Most of Blome's letters to Vogelsang have been published by Wiard Klopp and have been an important resource for this chapter. See Klopp, 'Briefe des Grafen Gustav Blome', 134-302.

40 Stillfried to Pergen, 13 June 1874, HHSA, *Pergen*, II.

41 Le Play to Leo Thun, 24 March 1875, SALD, *Thun-Hohenstein*, A 3 - XXI, E 713, 1-4.

42 On Frédéric Le Play (1806-1882), see Savoye and Cardoni, eds., *Frédéric Le Play*; Bregon de Lavergnée, ed., 'Le Play et le monde catholique', 3-250.

43 On Friedrich Revertera (1827-1904), see Slapnicka, 'Friedrich Graf Revertera-Salandra', 83-96.

bankruptcy of two banks to which he had entrusted his assets. This naturally reinforced his anti-liberal and anti-capitalist stance.[44]

At the end of 1877, Blome and Revertera took the initiative to start a social periodical intended to give an impetus to the study of the social question in Catholic circles, and they asked Vogelsang to be its editor.[45] He expressed his willingness, on condition that the publication would defend the ecclesiastical and political (federalist) programme of the *Vaterland*, which for its part would sharpen its social position. In this way, the unity between the Bohemian feudal lords and the German social aristocrats was preserved. The periodical appeared monthly from the beginning of 1879 and after some time came to be known as the *Monatsschrift für christliche Sozialreform*. It offered an excellent forum of discussion for Austrian social aristocrats and would also be widely distributed abroad.[46]

The social aristocrats' attraction to corporatist formulas was reinforced by the fact that the Dual Monarchy in many ways still had a pre-capitalist economy. The old professional bodies had survived there for a long time and only in 1859 did parliament allow the right to a free choice of occupation. Corporatism was still a reality that only had to be reactivated. The social aristocrats were given the opportunity to do this when a conservative government came to power in 1879. The German liberals then lost their ascendency in Austrian politics, as was the general pattern across Europe, with liberals being beaten back almost everywhere, except in France and Spain. Their economic model was discredited because of the prolonged recession, and the process of democratization had also undermined their political dominance. Anti-liberal popular movements, both conservative and socialist, gained momentum.

In Austria, Eduard von Taaffe (1830-1895) was entrusted with the leadership of a government that relied on the German conservatives and the Slavic sections of the population. The Czech deputies resumed their participation in parliamentary debates. Taaffe's government, which was to remain in power until 1893, fought the economic crisis by once more giving the government a guiding role in the economy. It also drew up a social policy in order to meet the demands of tradesmen and farmers, and to counter the growing social unrest among the workers.[47]

In a first phase the conservative government worked particularly on developing protective labour legislation. The circle around the *Monatsschrift*,

---

44 Blome's extensive correspondence with Revertera is one of the main sources of information for the reconstruction of his later life [HAH, IV, 56].
45 Allmeyer-Beck, *Vogelsang*, 67.
46 On the *Monatsschrift*, see the already cited works by Bled, Silberbauer, Knoll and Klopp.
47 On the development of social legislation in Austria, see Ruppe, 'Die ersten sozialen Reformen in Österreich', *Neue Ordnung*, 1 (1925) 90-99, 118-128 and 149-152; Allmeyer Beck, *Vogelsang*, 84-92; Silberbauer, Österreich Katholiken, 92-97; Grandner, 'Conservative Social Politics in Austria', 77-107.

which defended the rights of productive labour against the financial powers, exerted a strong influence here. In the *Abgeordnetenhaus* Egbert Belcredi (1816-1894) and Aloys Liechtenstein played a central role in the legislative work, while in the *Herrenhaus* Blome stood out. He had kept himself far removed from all political activity under the successive liberal governments, but with the access of the Taaffe government and the prospect of major social reforms, he had resumed his place once again in the upper house. In 1882-1883 a bill came up for discussion that would give a legal status as well as a greater involvement in economic policies to craft associations. Blome was very pleased about this '*Neubelebung der Genossenschaften*'. He immediately pushed for the introduction of legislation in favour of factory workers and in May 1884 the debate on an *Arbeiterschutzgesetz* began. The bill was fiercely defended by Blome in the *Herrenhaus* and was passed, with some adjustments. The final piece of legislation forbade both child labour and night work for women, and introduced a general limitation in the number of working hours.

In a second phase, in 1887-1888, the focus was on social insurance. A draft law provided for accident insurance for industrial workers who, together with the factory owners, would deposit the necessary contributions and manage the funds, under the supervision of regional authorities. Blome was again the main champion of the bill in the *Herrenhaus*. Later, compulsory health insurance was introduced for all low-skilled workers, excluding those in the agricultural sector. Again it was the workers and employers who would pay the required dues and would manage the funds, supervised by the district authorities. Interestingly, state intervention in the insurance industry was much less advanced than in Germany, where in the same period a more statist social security system had been set up by Bismarck in order to cut the socialists off at the pass.

Around 1890 Austria had the most coherent social legislation on the European continent, at a time when socialism, which was not yet a strong political force, was exerting only indirect pressure on policy. A distinctive feature of the legislation was that the corporative character of the economy was strengthened, and cooperation between employers and workers was encouraged. Yet the corporatists could not fully realize their vision: geographically-based bodies hampered the development of an insurance system based on occupation. Still, some of the excesses of capitalism had already been addressed by state intervention in social issues and by the creation of professional associations. That solution served as a model for other social Catholics.

An international network

The group around the *Monatsschrift* became a reference point for social Catholics in other countries, primarily France, where the *Oeuvre des Cercles catholiques d'Ouvriers* (Society of Catholic Worker Circles) was the most important exponent of social Catholicism.[48] The organization wanted to encourage and channel the social involvement of the ruling classes. Besides attracting socially minded aristocrats and bourgeois, it also reached out to tradesmen and shop assistants in the big cities. The driving forces of the *Oeuvre* were the cavalry officers Albert de Mun[49] and René de la Tour du Pin,[50] who had come into contact at an early stage with the Black International. La Tour du Pin, who was deeply interested in ideological issues, especially kept in close touch with the leaders of the International. He forged a deep friendship with Pergen who was a few years younger than he and with whom, as an officer, he had much in common. In February 1877 he became military attache to the French embassy in Vienna, a position he would hold until March 1881. He then stepped up his contacts with Pergen, who brought him in as French liaison in the Union of St. Peter and later in the Salmini House. La Tour du Pin was a convinced legitimist and he took advantage of his stay in Vienna to regularly visit the Count of Chambord, who lived in neighbouring Frohsdorf. Remarkably, he never succeeded in bringing Pergen into contact with the French pretender to the throne.[51] In Vienna he sought out not only Pergen's company, but also that of the Liechtenstein brothers and of Blome during his sporadic sojourns in the capital. Through his legitimist background he came under the influence of corporatist ideas, which were further reinforced by the Austrian social aristocrats.[52]

Albert de Mun would later characterize his friend as 'somebody who was steeped in ancestral traditions ... a feudal lord of Count Blome's school.'[53] Indeed, La Tour du Pin greatly admired Blome, especially for his intelligence

---

48 On the history of the early origins of social Catholicism in France, see Duroselle, *Les débuts du catholicisme social en France*; Maugenest, *Le mouvement social catholique en France au XXe siècle*; Rollet, *L'action sociale des catholiques en France*, vol. I, 14-186; Levillain *et al.*, 'Noblesse et catholicisme social', 5-55.

49 On Albert de Mun (1841-1914), see especially Levillain, *Albert de Mun*; Molette, *Albert de Mun*.

50 On René de La Tour du Pin Chambly (1834-1924), see Rivain, *La Tour du Pin précurseur*; Talmy, *Aux sources du catholicisme social*; idem, *René de la Tour du Pin*; Millon, *René de la Tour et la philosophie sociale du catholicisme*; Murat, *La Tour du Pin et son temps*.

51 La Tour du Pin to Pergen, 12 Jan. 1900, HHSA, *Pergen*, II.

52 Kale, *Legitimism*, 180.

53 Talmy, *René de la Tour du Pin*, 15.

René de La Tour du Pin. Photograph.
[*E. Bossan de Garagnol*, Le colonel de La-Tour-du-Pin d'après lui-même, *Paris, 1934*]

and erudition, and would later even call him a '*surhomme*'.[54] Blome endorsed his conviction that there was a great need for theoretical reflection on the social question in Catholic circles. Sometimes the Austrian ex-diplomat took part in the annual meetings of the *Oeuvre* in Paris and did not fail to make a big impression.[55] At the end of 1881 La Tour du Pin would call on Blome's authority for a corporatist programme to be accepted by the *Oeuvre*. He learned from the Austrian social aristocrats that the new social order had to be based on justice and that the State had to play a role in this.

In the circles of the *Oeuvre* Paul de Bréda surfaced again and was entrusted with various assignments by La Tour du Pin.[56] So the *Dornbirnien* wrote a report in 1879 on the corporative organization of labour in the industrial world. In early 1881 he drew up a memorandum for Leo XIII in the name of the *Oeuvre*, in which he pleaded for social intervention by the State and for international labour legislation. In another memorandum to the Pope, La Tour du Pin himself urged the Church to develop a social doctrine as Catholics were in need of guidance in this area, and mentioned Thomism as a possible basis for a universal social teaching. The two memoranda were submitted to Mermillod, who maintained close ties with the *Oeuvre* and was at that time staying in Rome where he had regular contact with the Pope. Thus, from 1881 the *Oeuvre* wanted to force papal intervention in the social sphere. In his writings Bréda pointed out explicitly that the Church could enhance its credit among the working classes by taking a bold stance on the social question. For now, however, Leo XIII had other priorities, smoothing out conflicts between Church and State in the major European countries.

Meanwhile, the research continued, both in France and in Austria. The Vienna group's work was further strengthened by the collaboration of Franz von Kuefstein (1841-1918), also a former officer and a relative of Pergen's wife.[57] In 1872 he married Princess Maria della Pace Odescalchi, a daughter of Sofia Branicka. From 1875 he was involved in the activities of the Black International

---

54 La Tour du Pin, 'Le Comte de Blome', 311: 'Truly it seems that the school which talks of the "surhomme" has known him and has found in him the type it sought.' Blome is repeatedly mentioned in La Tour du Pin's letters to Pergen (HHSA, *Pergen*, II). See 20 June 1877: 'le Maître'; 21 Oct. 1877; 30 Oct. 1878; 28 Nov. 1878: 'I am your disciple and that of the tyrant *Comasque*.'

55 This, for example, was the case in May 1878. See Albert de Mun to Roquefeuil, 20 June 1878, cited in Molette, *Albert de Mun*, 166.

56 On the basis of information supplied by Lorin and La Tour du Pin, Georges Goyau would characterize Bréda in 1892, one year after his death, as follows: 'Heavily indebted, always broke, mistresses; borrowed a lot of money from Lorin. Christian socialist and noble bohemian.' (*Journal Goyau*, BNF, *Div. Man. Occid.*, NAF 27218).

57 On Franz von Kuefstein (1841-1918), see Hartmut Lohmann, art. 'Kuefstein' in: *Biographisch-Bibliographisches Kirchenlexicon*, vol. IV, 1992, col. 745-747. Goyau later characterized him thus: 'Kuefstein, a very chic representative of the Austrian feudal nobility, more a socialist than a democrat.' (*Journal Goyau*, Dec. 1892, BNF, *Div. Man. Occid.*, NAF 27218).

and, as an autodidact, increasingly concentrated on studying socioeconomic issues. He worked closely with Pergen, who was also deeply interested in the social question.

From 1880 on, Kuefstein spent the winter months in Rome and thus was able to establish a link between the Austrian social aristocrats and the Roman milieu.[58] With the Pope's support he initiated the setting up of the *Circolo Romano degli Studi sociali ed economici* (Roman Circle for Social and Economic Studies) in which especially theologians and philosophers participated alongside lawyers and social-minded aristocrats. They produced papers on labour, property ownership and profit sharing. Above all, they wanted to adjust the capitalist system and did not immediately move in the direction of a *Sozialreform*.

In the same period, the study of the social issue was also raised by prominent German Catholics. In the 1870s, because of the *Kulturkampf*, they had given absolute priority to the political and religious struggle, but around 1880 the realization dawned that the social question deserved all their attention. Again it was mainly aristocrats who took the initiative to give a more scientific basis to Catholic social commitment.[59] The initial impetus came from Prince Karl von Löwenstein, who had been involved in the foundation of the Black International.[60] On the *Katholikentag* of 1882, as chairman of the *Zentralkomitee der katholischen Vereine,* he proposed starting a study group that would provide a social programme for German Catholics. To this end, he brought together a number of politicians, dignitaries, theologians and journalists at his castle in Haid (Bohemia) in June 1883 and a month later in Salzburg.[61] A *Freie Vereinigung katholischer Sozialpolitiker* (Free Association of Catholic Social Politicians) was set up. Löwenstein also got Austrian social Catholics like Vogelsang and Blome involved in the initiative.[62] The Haid theses advocated

---

58 On the *Circolo Romano*, in addition to the cited works by Knoll and Sorgenfrei, see: De Gasperi, *I tempi e gli uomini*, 127-144; Kuefstein, *Vorgeschichte der Enzyklik 'Rerum Novarum'*; Casella, *Cattolici a Roma dopo l'Unità d'Italia*.

59 A lot of information on this is to be found in Blome's letters to Vogelsang, which, as noted earlier, have been published by Wiard Klopp. Further information is to be found in the archive of Prince Karl von Löwenstein, which is preserved in the Staatsarchiv Wertheim, Rosenberg section (SAWT-R).

60 On Karl von Löwenstein, see Siebertz, *Karl Fürst zu Löwenstein*; Reytier, 'Karl Heinrich zu Löwenstein', 48-60.

61 On this meeting and on the *Freie Vereinigung* to which Georg Ratzinger (1844-1899), a grand-uncle of Pope Benedict XVI, belonged, see De Gasperi, *I tempi e gli uomini*, 33-34; Lugmayer, *Grundrisse zur neuen Gesellschaft*; Weiss, *Lebensweg und Lebenswerk*, 354-355; Klopp, *Vogelsang*, 231-245; Allmeyer Beck, *Vogelsang*, 93-94; Misner, *Social Catholicism*, 181-189; Novotny, *Die Vorarbeiter der Enzyklika Rerum Novarum*, 41-101; Bled, *Les fondements*, 330-334; Silberbauer, Österreichs Katholiken, 111-116.

62 Blome took part in these meetings at Vogelsang's behest. He thought they would offer the possibility of developing an international social programme (Blome to Vogelsang, 19 Sept. 1883 in: Klopp, *Briefe*, 195).

a class-based defence of interests with a corporative slant. A fierce debate ensued about making corporations compulsory and about a possible ban on usury, two propositions that Vogelsang vehemently defended but were not endorsed by the majority of the gathering. At Haid and Salzburg a corporative programme was set up, which in the end would have only limited influence on the social policy of German Catholics. Ludwig Windthorst, the leader of the *Zentrum*, was afraid that a programme directed towards *Sozialreform* would threaten the unity among Catholics. Particularly in the western, more industrialized areas of the empire, Catholics had a more positive attitude towards industrial and financial capitalism, following the example of their Belgian neighbours. Most of the German social Catholics wrongly accused Vogelsang of being a 'state socialist', because his corporative system provided for broad state intervention, at least temporarily. They simply were terrified of the increasing power of the State which they saw as an enemy. Blome poured oil on troubled waters and called for the Germans to be allowed go their own way.[63]

Though Vogelsang pulled out, Blome continued to participate in the activities of the *Freie Vereinigung*. The study of the social question and intricate chess games were the ingredients for a princely life for the resident of the Villa Giulia during this period.[64] At the successive annual meetings he always played an important role in the debates.[65] At the meeting in Regensburg, in October 1886, he presented two important reports, which deserve more attention.[66]

The first report dealt with the 'reorganization of society through the formation of occupational associations'. It was based on the conclusion that society had become destabilized by individualism, and that there was an urgent need to organize all citizens according to their interests and social functions. This was not about resurrecting the old estates, but encouraging and further developing the still existing occupational associations. No general pattern could be laid down for this: local conditions would determine whether these associations were best established on a voluntary basis or by legal regulation. Blome was a proponent of mixed occupational associations to which both owners and workers belonged, but he pointed out that they should be organized in such a way that the workers and small tradesmen would be fully recognized and valued. He also supported a form of special interest representation on a political level. Thus, universal suffrage would benefit the different occupational categories. How exactly the occupational associations could determine the political life of a nation was, however, something for the future. Real life just evolved in many ways, and pluriformity in society was as much a postulate of morality as a prerequisite for the effectiveness of institutions.

63   Blome to Vogelsang, 20 Aug. and 29 Sept. 1883 in: Klopp, *Briefe*, 185-188 and 195.
64   Blome to Revertera, 22 May 1882, HAH, IV, 56.
65   At the annual meetings in Mainz (12-15 Aug. 1887) and Prague (12-14 Aug. 1888).
66   Blome's reports, 12 Jan. and 15 Feb. 1887, SAWT-R, *Löwenstein*, Lit. D Nr. 675, I, 25.

A second report dealt with professional associations in large-scale industries. Blome admitted that it would be much harder to bring employers and workers to cooperate in large-scale industries where labour and capital formed two separate categories. However, though that distinction was a reality, it did not necessarily have to lead to a hostile relationship. By being given moral and material benefits they now lacked, workers could become interested in the development and survival of the enterprise in which they worked. Blome developed an idea of Bréda's that called for the establishment of a 'business patrimonium', a common fund that could be used for social insurance, workers' housing and public schools. Unfortunately, the difficult economic climate at that time hardly favoured such initiatives. Rather, the economic crisis had the effect of exacerbating polarization and even furthering a class struggle between employers and workers which, in Blome's view, social Catholics should take into consideration. If they could not realize the corporative formulas at the micro level, at least at the macro level they had to try to bring about social dialogue through consultative bodies. These basic texts indicate that Blome favoured a flexible, pragmatic application of corporative ideas and did not want to fall into the doctrinarianism that he imputed to the liberals. This would be a leitmotif in his stance on the social question.

From 1888 on, the *Freie Vereinigung* became less active, and two years later it was officially disbanded. German social Catholics appeared less and less interested in theoretical discussions and gave priority to finding a solution for concrete social problems. However, they did take from corporatism the ideal of a harmonious, centre-oriented society. The concrete realization of such a social model became the objective of the Fribourg Union, which in the mid-1880s brought together study groups of social Catholics from different European countries with the intention of designing, insofar as was possible, a coherent social programme.

The Fribourg Union

It was René de La Tour du Pin who took the initiative to bring together the most important representatives of these study groups. After his return from Vienna in 1881, he resigned from the army and retired to the family estate in Arrancy where he took care of his elderly parents. That limited his freedom of movement but did not prevent him from continuing to play a leading role in the *Oeuvre*. In the spring of 1884 he contacted several kindred spirits, including

Kuefstein and Pergen, to persuade them to join an international partnership.[67] Inspired by the Black International, he appealed to Monsignor Mermillod, who also maintained good relations with the *Oeuvre* and had played a role in the *Circolo Romano* during his stay in Rome. As mentioned earlier, the Swiss prelate had been appointed bishop of Lausanne and Geneva in March 1883, with his residence in Fribourg. La Tour du Pin asked him to be patron of the undertaking he wanted to launch. The bishop took some time to be persuaded and finally convened a preparatory meeting in his episcopal palace on 18 October 1884.

Besides Mermillod and La Tour du Pin, three representatives of the aforementioned study circles attended this meeting: Louis Milcent for the *Oeuvre*, Löwenstein for the *Freie Vereinigung* and Kuefstein for the *Circolo Romano*. The Belgian economist Charles Périn also happened to be present, but kept his distance as he was not in favour of a *Sozialreform*. The Austrians were conspicuously absent, although this did not mean that they were ignored, and in the following years they would, together with the French, put their undeniable mark on the initiative. It was a coincidence that in late 1884 Pergen was prevented from participating because of his wife's prolonged illness and that Blome, whose father died at this time, was fully taken up with settling inheritance matters and taking over the family estate in Salzau. Later, La Tour du Pin pointed repeatedly to the important contribution of his Austrian friends to the initiative. To Pergen he spoke of 'this modest attempt to push ahead with your Geneva work', 'the international conference of Fribourg, for which you should cherish fatherly feelings, because I only took the initiative, having borrowed both the idea and the practice from you' and 'we are now working closely together again, in an area where you have been, and will always remain, my guide and master'.[68] La Tour du Pin had kept in constant contact with Blome after his return from Vienna.[69] In the spring of 1885 he visited him in Venice so as to work out a strategy and was particularly pleased that the 'master' had responded enthusiastically.[70] From then on he included him among the founders of the Union.[71]

The planned organization was called the *Union catholique d'études économiques et sociales* (Catholic Union for Economic and Social Studies)

67 On the Fribourg Union, see: Lugmayer, 'Zur Erinnerung an die Freiburger Vereinigung', 196-232; Duthoit, 'L'Union de Fribourg', 20-48 ; Massard, *L'œuvre sociale du cardinal Mermillod*; Sorgenfrei, *Die geistesgeschichtlichen Hintergründe*, 57-64 ; Philippe Chenaux, 'Les origines de l'Union de Fribourg', 255-266; Mattioli, 'Die Union de Fribourg', 15-32; Misner, *Social Catholicism*, 202-208.
68 La Tour du Pin to Pergen, 30 March and 8 Dec. 1885, 11 July 1887, HHSA, *Pergen*, II.
69 Blome to Vogelsang, 7 March 1883 in: Klopp, *Briefe*,166.
70 La Tour du Pin's report, 15 March 1885, HHSA, Pergen, II; Id. to Pergen, 30 March 1885: 'The Master, [Blome], seems to have been reawakened also.'
71 La Tour du Pin to Pergen, 23 Sept. 85 and 11 July 1887, HHSA, *Pergen*, II.

and would serve primarily as a think tank. It differed in that respect from the Black International, of which it nonetheless wanted to be a continuation. The International had been a fighting machine, used by the Vatican in its struggle against political liberalism. The new organization wanted to prepare the ground for a coherent social doctrine that would counter economic liberalism. As a former officer, La Tour du Pin expressed the difference in military terms: 'The Geneva Committee was in the end the offensive action of a rearguard, whereas the movement to which we are contributing is in the vanguard.'[72] The Union also had much looser ties with the Vatican. It mainly consisted of people who had been disappointed by Leo XIII's policy in the first years of his pontificate. Gradually, a rapprochement came about as the Pope came increasingly to share the social concerns of the Union. In the encyclical *Humanum Genus* (20 April 1884) he had already openly called for a restoration of Christian corporations as a way to combat social misery. In mid-March 1885 during an audience with French industrialists who were linked with the *Oeuvre*, he made clear that the social question was on his agenda and he explicitly announced a forthcoming encyclical about 'Christian social order'.[73] The social aspirations of Leo XIII and of the Union would increasingly parallel one another.

In October 1884 the founders of the Union proposed a general plan that included three topics: the organization of labour, the issue of ownership, and the role of professional organizations, all of which they wanted to examine from an international perspective. They immediately asked the existing study circles to put the issue of international labour legislation on their agenda as soon as possible. The intention was that in addition to the Geneva Convention for war victims, a Fribourg Convention for workers would be developed to protect the social victims of modern industry.

The first annual meeting of the Union took place in Fribourg from 21 to 23 October 1885. Statutes were drawn up which provided for the establishment of an executive committee with three members per country. The leadership was to be in the hands of a bureau with a president (Mermillod)[74], a vice president (Blome), an administrative secretary (La Tour du Pin) and a secretary of studies (Kuefstein). Prince Löwenstein became honorary chairman, but he would rarely attend the meetings. Mermillod mainly played the role of host and orator, and was also expected to take care of contact with the Vatican.

The actual pivotal figure was Blome. The prominent role he would play in the Fribourg Union can be explained by the great prestige he had acquired as a former top diplomat and especially as the driving force of the Black In-

72 La Tour du Pin to Luigi Manna Roncadelli, 26 June 1885, UCSCM, ASMSC, *Roncadelli*, 2/25/189.
73 La Tour du Pin's report, 15 March 1885, HHSA, *Pergen*, II.
74 La Tour du Pin to Pergen, 22 May 1885, HHSA, *Pergen*, II: 'Our old *Leiter* (if I may put it like that), Mgr. Mermillod.' Albert de Mun was also critical of Mermillod (Levillain, *De Mun*, 940).

ternational. Later he had become an important link in the circle around the *Monatsschrift*. His efforts in the Austrian *Herrenhaus* for the development of social legislation also had put him in the spotlight. Moreover, he had carried out considerable research in the previous decade on socioeconomic problems and was a very active member of the *Freie Vereinigung*. His extensive international contacts and his knowledge of languages made him the obvious mediator between the various national movements. Alcide De Gasperi would later rightly characterize him as '*un bel tipo d'europeo*'.[75] At a time when nationalism was making inroads in Catholic circles, pitting Germans and French especially against each other, a figure like Blome, with his impressive political and social record, was able to streamline the work of the Union. His old friendship with Monsignor Mermillod, which was repeatedly referred to during the hearings, also destined him to play a leading role in the Union.[76]

La Tour du Pin, who was not a gifted speaker, stayed modestly in the background during the proceedings, but in fact he was the guiding force. During the last annual meeting Blome commented on his contribution: 'He is the true founder of the Union; he conceived the idea and set up the organization.'[77] Franz Kuefstein, as secretary of studies, also played an important role. Despite repeated requests, Pergen never attended a meeting, but he followed the negotiations from the sidelines and was once part of a delegation to the Vatican. Vogelsang himself never joined the Fribourg Union, notwithstanding Blome's many exhortations, but his ideas still exerted a great influence on the whole endeavor.[78]

The research was carried out in a thorough fashion. At the annual conferences discussions were held in various committees on the basis of voluminous reports that were prepared and sent in advance to the participants. This way of working was in striking contrast with that of the Black International. The discussions in the committee meetings took up most of the available time. Prior to those discussions, a preliminary general meeting was held in which an overview was given of the Union's work and of the social developments in the member countries. During a final general assembly the reports and reso-

---

75 De Gasperi, *I tempi e gli uomini*, 93.
76 La Tour du Pin in *Association catholique*, 10 Aug. 1903: 'The unrivalled guidance of Count de Blome'; Id. to Pergen, 21 March 1886, HHSA, *Pergen*, II: 'Blome, the most eminent of our eminences'; Id. to id., 9 Aug. 1886, ibid.: 'our effective director and undisputed master, Count Blome'; Albert de Mun: 'His merit as much as his rank made Count Blome a natural president for the small assembly of Fribourg' (article by De Mun in *L'Écho de Paris*, 1912, cited in Massard, *L'œuvre sociale*, 106); Mermillod: 'We know how much he [Blome] guides the phalanxes on the battlefield of diplomacy as on that of dedication and of sacrifice' (6th annual meeting of the Union, 5 Oct. 1890, SAWT-R, *Löwenstein*, Lit D, Nr. 675, I, 27).
77 Annual meeting 7 Oct. 1891, SAWT-R, *Löwenstein*, Lit D, Nr. . 675, I, 27.
78 Blome to Vogelsang, 24 Aug. 1885 and 17 Sept. 1886 in: Klopp, *Briefe*, 242 and 253; Id. to id., 28 July and 12 Sept. 1888 (LASH, 126, 15, 624). Vogelsang argued that his lack of knowledge of French was an insurmountable obstacle to his participation in the meetings.

lutions of the various committees were discussed and approved. The work of the Union remained secret and the importance of this secrecy was repeatedly stressed.[79] Only after considerable time would the resolutions be published.[80]

In the course of its short history (1884-1891) the Union would involve 86 people in its work. The Swiss formed the largest group (25), most of whom were *hommes d'oeuvres* and took only a minor part in the debates. The most active members were the French (21), the Austrians (15) and the Germans (8). The Italians (10) and especially the Belgians (5) kept more in the background. In contrast to the Black International, the Union did not have any representatives from the Netherlands and Great Britain. This time also, in a remarkable change, a number of clerics, especially regulars, participated in the study group. Almost all the attendees were 'social reformers'. They were decidedly anti-liberal and strove for a community-based society. Still some, such as the French geographer Henri Lorin and the Swiss politician Gaspard Decurtins, were more pronouncedly democratic and believed that democratic along with social reforms were necessary.

At the first annual meeting, from 21 to 23 October 1885, Mermillod outlined the historical background of the initiative. He explicitly referred to the Black International, which had fiercely resisted the tendency to banish religion from public life. Now, the Church had to let its moral influence be felt in the social question, in order to reconnect with the working class. 'When the people do not come to the Church, the Church must go to the people.'

In a memorandum the members of the Union asked for the Pope's moral support for their activities.[81] When an answer was not immediately forthcoming, Blome became incensed and made his further cooperation dependent on the Pope's explicit approval, which he considered necessary for the creditworthiness of the Union in Catholic circles.[82] Without papal support the activities of the international study group would have little effect. Finally, the Pope communicated his support to Mermillod, on condition that the required obedience was given to the church leaders.[83]

At the October 1886 meeting, Blome pointed out that the Church needed to develop a coherent social doctrine. In his view, there were two obstacles that had to be avoided here: liberalism and idolatry of the State. Governments had a role to play in the social sphere, but the creation of associations and the political representation of interest groups should provide a salutary counterweight. Both at this meeting and at that of October 1887 the first in-depth studies were discussed. A report was sent to the Pope each time, in which the

---

79 Intervention by Mermillod at the annual meetings, 13 Oct. 1886 and 12 Oct. 1887, SAWT-R, *Löwenstein*, Lit D, nr. 675, I, 27.
80 First in 1893, and reissued in 1903. See also *infra*, 291.
81 Address to Leo XIII, 14 Jan. 1886, SAWT-R, *Löwenstein*, Lit D, Nr. 675, I, 27.
82 Blome to Albert de Mun, 7 Sept. 1886, CARAN, AP 378, 13, IX, 26.
83 Leo XIII to Mermillod, 12 April 1886, SAWT-R, *Löwenstein*, Lit D, Nr. 675, I, 27.

congress participants insisted on an intervention in favour of international labour legislation.[84]

During an audience with Leo XIII on 30 January 1888, as part of the celebration of the fiftieth anniversary of his ordination, a delegation from the Fribourg Union was given the opportunity to explain its work in detail. It emphatically requested that a social encyclical be worked out.[85] Mermillod later sent a detailed memorandum to the Pope, with a summary of the studies that had been carried out till then. This audience received considerable attention in curial circles and made clear that the Pope had begun to give priority to the social question. This encouraged the members of the Union, who got the feeling that they had understood the signs of the times. As Blome put it: 'The seeds we sow will again grow and bear fruit. Our role is to bring closer the day when ... God will have free play.'[86]

A society marked by solidarity

From the beginning, the members of the Union made clear that they wanted to base their research on the central ideas of Thomistic philosophy. Their views were quite varied, yet sufficiently similar to constitute a fairly coherent programme. Their starting point was that the general well-being should be the main objective of sociopolitical organization, and the principle of justice should constitute its moral foundation. Contemporary capitalism was grossly deficient in this respect. The Union was highly critical of the modern money economy where capital was given an absolute priority over labour, which was seen as a mere commodity, leading to the unjust treatment of workers. Capitalism also created an excessive concentration of economic resources and wealth, and a resulting blatant social inequality. There had to be a more equitable distribution between the proceeds of capital and of labour. Private property also carried social obligations.[87] Workers were entitled to a minimum wage that would allow them and their families to lead decent lives. Moreover, they should also be given a share of the profits.

84 Minutes of the annual meetings of 10-13 Oct. 1886 and 9-11 Oct. 1887, SAWT-R, *Löwenstein*, Lit. D Nr. 675, I, 27.

85 Report of the audience with Leo XIII, 30 Jan. 1888, SAWT-R, *Löwenstein*, Lit. D Nr. 675, I, 27. The delegation consisted of Union members who happened to be in Rome for the jubilee celebrations and included Löwenstein, Pergen, Kuefstein, Medolago, Soderini, Lorin and Mermillod.

86 Blome's address during the annual meeting, 7 Oct. 1888, SAWT-R, *Löwenstein*, Lit. D Nr. 675, I, 27.

87 Minutes of the annual meeting on 12 Oct. 1887, SAWT-R, *Löwenstein*, Lit. D Nr. 675, I, 27; minutes of the annual meeting 10 Oct. 1888, ibid.

The Union members felt that such social objectives could be best achieved in a corporative system that relied on mixed occupational associations where workers and employers together organized production and determined working conditions. They particularly emphasized that the workers within those associations should be given a real say.[88] They expected the State to encourage the formation of corporations and eventually even to make them mandatory. From 1888 on, they were willing to agree to separate associations for employers and workers, as long as they would enter into dialogue with each other at a higher level in order to achieve greater social harmony.

The Union was of the view that (mixed) occupational associations should, in the long term, be represented politically. Some form of interest representation was more in line with social reality than either liberal parliaments, which were elected by individual, manipulable voters, or governments which relied on big capital. Participation in political life would be best channeled through occupational associations, which would at the same time provide a buffer against the omnipotence of the State.

Since establishing a truly corporative regime would require a long time, social state intervention was required, at least temporarily, through the introduction of protective labour legislation and compulsory social security.[89] In order to avoid unfair competition between the different national economies, it was also desirable that international labour legislation, inspired by ethical principles, be worked out. Some reports noted with regret that international politics was no longer guided by moral principles and expressed sharp criticism of power politics, the arms race and advancing imperialism.[90]

In the short term, the members of the Union thus strove for social intervention by the state in order to get rid of the worst social excesses of the capitalist economy. In the long term they wanted to create a corporative regime, in which a large number of competences in the socioeconomic sphere would be given over to (mixed) occupational associations. The State should then withdraw into the background and play only a supplementary role. This corporatism aimed at creating a structural link between civil society and the State, through a form of interest representation, among other means. The macro elements of this system would prove sufficiently elastic to absorb the increasing pressure of the democratic forces.

The Union's programme could hardly be called conservative. La Tour du Pin had already written to Pergen in 1881: 'We are not conservatives, but reformers. There is no human species for which a conservative has less sympathy because they awaken his conscience and put his wisdom into question.'[91]

88 Annual meeting 7 Oct. 1891, report by Depoin, BCUF, H 3562, 4.
89 Report by Kuefstein, 8 Oct. 1890, sixth annual meeting, BCUF, H 3562, 4.
90 Report by d'Avril, 10 Oct. 1886, SAWT-R, *Löwenstein*, Lit. D Nr. 675, I, 27.
91 La Tour du Pin to Pergen, 20 Dec. 1881, HHSA, *Pergen*, II.

Albert de Mun. Photograph, 1891.
[*Leuven, KADOC*]

The concept of *Sozialreform* made clear that these social Catholics did not want the existing socioeconomic system to continue. Rather, they wanted a new system where social entities and not individuals would be the main constituent parts.

Blome's views obviously corresponded with the programme outlined, as is also evident from the reports that he had drawn up for the *Freie Vereinigung*. Still, his personal views are worth clarifying in the light of an official address that he gave in Vienna on 10 December 1888, on the occasion of Vogelsang's 70th birthday celebrations.[92] In that speech he struck a fierce anti-liberal and anti-capitalist note, but he wondered especially how an *'Ordnung der Dinge'*

92   Blome's address, 10 Dec. 1888, Gut Salzau, XII.

could be reconstructed. What was essential in his view was that civil society, which thus far was not adequately organized, would provide a counterbalance to big capital. The forming of associations was the answer to liberal individualism, and this he had already learned from Metternich. Not the old estates, but modern professional associations had to form the basic cells of future society. In the first place they would defend their occupational interests, but at the same time would give their members more self-confidence, professional pride and respect for the law – in short, promote all the social virtues. What form these professional organizations would exactly take had to be determined by the natural course of events. At least at the macro level, a corporative transformation of society was the appropriate means of promoting social peace and bringing about a harmony of interests. A system of interest representation on a political level would help to achieve this also, but here too there was space for great diversity. Liberalism did not want order, socialism did not want variety. Of utmost importance was the creation of associations that would emanate, as much as possible, from the people themselves.

Blome's views were less stringent than those of Vogelsang. The latter held fast to the idea of mixed occupational associations, while Blome gradually came to accept that the setting up of separate workers' unions in large industries was inevitable.[93] They probably would encourage class divisions, but that problem had to be taken care of by creating consultative bodies at a higher level. Blome also left open the question whether the State should impose a corporative regime. As a general principle, he considered that the initiative for forming associations should come, insofar as was possible, from the people themselves, whereas Vogelsang felt that the State should make corporations compulsory. He also insisted on the need for a rapid introduction of some form of representation of interests, while Blome felt this could happen only in the long term and in a variety of ways.

However, these differences in emphasis did not prevent Blome from continuing to work very closely with Vogelsang. As already mentioned, he supported him in the clashes with the Bohemian nobility over the *Vaterland*'s policy. That did not mean that he always agreed with the paper's positions. So, for example, he warned that the newspaper should not take an overly explicit anti-Semitic stance and insisted that it continue to be the mouthpiece of all Catholics.[94] Such differences of opinion, however, did not endanger his good

93   In 1887 he sided with Cardinal Manning's defence of the American *Knights of Labor*, secret workers' associations that opposed the monopolists (Blome to Revertera, 6 April 1887, HAH, IV, 56). See also his report for the *Freie Vereinigung*,15 Feb. 1887, Sawt-R, Löwenstein, Lit. D Nr. 675, I, 25.

94   Blome to Vogelsang, 15 Feb. 1889, LASH, 126, 15, 624. Blome had already spoken out in 1883 against a fusion with an anti-Semitic periodical (Blome to Vogelsang, Dec. 1883, cited in Klopp, *Vogelsang*, 275).

relations with Vogelsang whose sudden death, on 8 November 1890, affected him deeply.

Blome's flexible and pragmatic position on the social question also became apparent in the spring of 1886 when he was dragged by Albert de Mun into a dispute with La Tour du Pin. The latter had taken over the editorship of *L'Association catholique*, the ideological journal of the *Oeuvre*. This periodical had published an article that was branded by the rank and file as 'socialist' because it awarded a disproportionate influence on social issues to the State and put severe limitations on private property. De Mun asked for advice on this delicate question from a number of bishops and cardinals as well as from Blome, once again highlighting the great prestige the latter enjoyed among French social Catholics. While most prelates felt that *L'Association catholique* had to be the mouthpiece of the *Oeuvre* and that the article in question should be denounced, Blome advocated that the periodical leave room for divergent views. Between liberalism and socialism, after all, was a wide spectrum. In his view, the article in question could not be accused of socialist and certainly not Communist tendencies. Moreover, the credit and ownership issues should not be a cause of much concern for the moment as they would indeed be resolved in the future in a way that could not be foreseen. The first priority now was to reorganize society. For the time being social Catholics should concern themselves mainly with social legislation, the creation of associations and the representation of interests, about which they had quite clear ideas. Above all they should not go the way of liberals who worked out abstract models for everything.[95] Blome thus proved to be a proponent of open debate and he did not want to be pinned down to concrete formulas for social reform. At the same time, he stated his priorities: creating professional associations, drawing up social legislation and implementing some form of political interest representation. He highly appreciated the political struggle for those objectives that De Mun led in the French National Assembly.[96]

The first harvest

At the end of the 1880s the social Catholics had their first noteworthy success. To begin with, they dominated the second *Katholikentag* held in Vienna in April 1889.[97] Pergen, who had again gradually come to the fore in the Catholic movement, played a central role in the preparations for this mass gathering, just as he had twelve years before. The circle around Vogelsang and the

---

95 Blome to De Mun, 8 May 1886, CARAN, AP 378, 13, IX, 25.
96 Blome to De Mun, 21 July 1889, CARAN, AP 378, 13, IX,26: 'On this occasion, I feel the need to reiterate how much I am your sincerely devoted admirer.'
97 Klopp, *Vogelsang*, 345-348; Alfred Missong, *Gustav Graf Blome: zu seinem 30. Todestag*, radio address 24 Aug. 1936, Gut Salzau, IX, 4.

Monatsschrift drew up the social programme. To Blome fell the great honour of serving as general president of the *Katholikentag*, which would be the starting point for the Christian social movement in Austria. The populist politician Karl Lueger presented himself for the first time as a Catholic leader and Prince Aloys Liechtenstein gave a remarkable programmatic speech, which was praised even by the socialists. The two men, who would later assume the leadership of the Christian Social Party, were in the spotlight on this *Katholikentag*. The social aristocrats and the Christian Socials found themselves agreeing on a common anti-liberal approach. It was more than symbolic that Blome, who was then sixty years old, was asked as éminence grise to give his patronage to the event.

During this period Blome profiled himself on the international front as 'the doyen of the social Catholics in Europe', an honorary title awarded him by La Tour du Pin.[98] From 7 to 10 September 1890 he acted as chairman of the international section of the third Social Congress of Liège.[99] When four years earlier Belgian Catholics had again resumed the tradition of the Mechlin congresses of the 1860s, their initiative called on the reserves of social Catholics in other countries, given their reputation for being very open to economic liberalism. This was even the case with the Leuven professor Charles Périn, who had long been the intellectual leader of Belgian ultramontanism. He accepted the liberal economy with the profit motive as its driving force. He looked for a solution to the social problem in moral progress and in the creation of a spirit of Christian charity among employers and workers. Périn was not averse to workers' associations, but they had to emerge voluntarily and be supervised by the employers. He opposed a corporative regime that would regulate both labour and the economy and that would be implemented with the help of the State.[100] At the same time he was a staunch opponent of any kind of social state intervention. He exercised great influence not only in Belgium but also in France and became the main spokesman of the so-called School of Angers, which turned ever more vehemently against the state interventionism of the Fribourg Union.[101]

98 La Tour du Pin, 'Le Comte de Blome', 309.
99 On the social congresses of Liège, see: Rezsohazy, *Origines et formation du catholicisme social en Belgique*, 103-114; Gerard, ed., *Histoire du mouvement ouvrier chrétien en Belgique*, vol. I, 64-78; Van Isacker, *Averechtse democratie*, 56-67; De Gasperi, *I tempi e gli uomini*, 87-112; De Maeyer, *Arthur Verhaegen*, 220-229; Defourny, *Les congrès catholiques en Belgique*, 147-251.
100 Périn, *Le socialisme chrétien*. On Charles Périn (1815-1905), see the note by Armand Louant in *Biographie Nationale*, 30 (1959) 665-670; Brants, *Charles Périn. Notice sur sa vie et ses travaux* ; Simon, *L'hypothèse libérale en Belgique*.
101 La Tour du Pin to Milcent, 7 Oct. 1882, cited in Jarlot, 'La genèse du catholicisme social', 340: 'Your last report finishes with this line: "Our system is summed up in two words: *patronage* and *association*." I have replaced this by: *patronage*, *association* and *legislation*, because these three words truly constitute the corporative regime. This is what distinguishes us from Périn.'

A majority of the Belgian Catholics, who in 1886 initiated an international congress on the social question in Liège, espoused the ultramontane tendency. For the members of the Fribourg Union this was not exactly reassuring and they assumed that Périn's spirit would dominate the proceedings. However, at that particular congress, under the influence of a social revolt that engulfed the Liège and Hainaut industrial basins in the spring of 1886, a cautious plea was made in favour of social state intervention. At the first annual meeting of the Union, De Mun reported very favourably on the Liège congress.[102] Mermillod, who had also attended the meeting, agreed and even invited the main Belgian organizers, including Leuven professor Joris Helleputte, to Fribourg.[103] During the annual meeting of 1887 Blome sang the praises of the second Liège congress, which had taken place shortly before, but he himself had not bothered to attend; indeed, international participation in the first Liège congresses remained very limited.[104]

That was not the case in 1890, when Blome explicitly asked the members of the Union to be present at Liège. As La Tour du Pin put it: 'At his command, we have rallied as enthusiastic soldiers in great numbers around our commander.'[105] The result was as expected. Thanks to the support of the members of the Union, the third Liège congress came out strongly in favour of social state intervention and international labour legislation. At the same time it stressed that the government should only play a complementary role with regard to private initiatives and social associations. The main task of the State, after all, was to protect the natural rights and achievements of individual citizens and social groups.

With regard to establishing occupational associations, the Liège gatherings had spoken out previously in favour of corporative formulas. Helleputte especially emerged as a staunch supporter of mixed associations in Belgium and, with his considerable organizational talent, would introduce them into the agricultural and craft sectors. Following Blome and the Union, the Liège congress of 1890 left space alongside the corporations for independent workers' associations, specifically trade unions, and for that reason it became an important reference point for the first Christian Democratic movements. The leader of the Ghent social Catholics, the 'red baron' Arthur Verhaegen, would continue along that path and help found an autonomous Christian Workers' Movement in Belgium. At the Liège congress of 7 September 1890 he gave an important speech that was largely in agreement with the blueprint of the Fri-

---

102 De Mun called the congress 'the most important public manifestation of social Catholicism that has been held in the French-speaking world' (Congress 1886, session of 10 Oct., SAWT-R, *Löwenstein*, Lit. D Nr. 675, I, 27).
103 De Maeyer and Van Molle, eds., *Joris Helleputte*, vol. I.
104 Defourny, *Les congres catholiques*, 152.
105 Annual meeting of the Union in 1890, session of 5 Oct., BCUF, H 3562, 4.

bourg Union.[106] He sketched the broad outlines of a macro corporative model that for long would inspire Christian popular movements in Belgium and would help adjust the liberal model of society on both the socioeconomic and political levels.[107] By introducing a form of political representation of interests, a broadly developed civil society would become the dominant factor within the Belgian parliamentary state.

At the annual meeting of the Fribourg Union in October 1890 great satisfaction was expressed with the previous congress in Liège and especially with the positions that had been taken in favour of social legislation.[108] The Union had still further reasons to be pleased: Mermillod had shortly before been named a curial cardinal, an honour that could be interpreted as a mark of appreciation for its work. Blome complimented the new cardinal warmly.[109] However, Mermillod was already physically and mentally exhausted and would die in Rome on 23 February 1892.[110]

In 1890, the Union also took credit for the fact that with the International Labour Conference in Berlin, the first step had finally been taken towards enacting international labour legislation.[111] The desire that international agreements be concluded in this area had for long been expressed by many people, including the English industrialist and early socialist Robert Owen, the Alsatian Daniel Legrand and the Belgian criminologist Eduard Ducpétiaux. In the late 1870s the idea was taken up by the social aristocrats, and was a central thread in the activities of the Fribourg Union, which repeatedly asked the Holy See to support it. In 1885 Albert de Mun filed a motion in favour of an international initiative in the French Assembly. During the annual meeting of the Union in October 1887, Gaspard Decurtins,[112] who represented the Grisons canton in the Swiss Federal Council, promised that he too would take such an initiative, and together with the Geneva radical, Georges Favon, he put forward a motion that Switzerland would organize an international labour conference. This was unanimously approved by the Federal Council and the

---

106 De Maeyer, *Arthur Verhaegen*, 220-229.

107 Lamberts, 'De ontwikkeling van de sociaal-katholieke ideologie in België', 53-63.

108 Annual meeting of the Union in 1890, session of 5 Oct., BCUF, H 3562, 4.

109 Mermillod returned the compliments of Blome, whom he described as 'a brave soldier, or better, a captain ... I congratulate the Union on the results achieved through the energetic leadership of Count Blome.' (Annual meeting of the Union, session of 5 Oct. 1890, BCUF, H 3562, 4).

110 Blome to Revertera, 8 June 1890, HAH, IV, 56.

111 Massard, *L'oeuvre sociale du cardinal Mermillod*, 235-258; Defourny, *Les congrès catholiques*, 232-235.

112 In a letter to his brother in October 1886, Louis Milcent characterized Gaspard Decurtins (1855-1916) thus: 'Like one of the mountain men of old, tall, full of verve and simplicity, with a marvellous eloquence and a knowledge that none of us can match – a knowledge of St. Thomas as well as of Karl Marx. At the same time, not very *au courant* with our refined civilization, which he disdains and ignores.' (cited by Ch. Molette, *Albert de Mun*, 212). On Decurtins, see also: Fry, *Kaspar Decurtins*.

Swiss government began sending out invitations to a conference in Berne on 5 May 1890. However, the new German emperor Wilhelm II himself took over and convened an international labour conference in Berlin on 15 March 1890. The decisions of this conference remained very vague and were limited mainly to wishful thinking, but it was important that the issue was officially raised for the first time at an international forum. During the annual meeting of the Union in October 1890 Blome paid careful attention to the Berlin conference, and pointed to the pioneering work of Decurtins and De Mun in this area. He noted that neither had been delegates at the conference, but 'there is nothing more delightful than to make preparations for triumphs in which one does not participate'.

Afterwards, Decurtins would continue his efforts. He was behind a non-governmental conference held in Zurich in 1897, where the establishment of an International Labour Office was proposed. A similar conference was held in Brussels, with the Duke d'Ursel, a former member of the Union, as honorary chairman. There the decision was made to set up an *Association internationale pour la protection légale des travailleurs* and an *Office International du Travail*. The international organization established its headquarters in Switzerland (Basle) and began operations in 1901. Thanks to its preparatory work and the support of the Swiss government, biennial international conferences would be organized from 1906 onwards, where the first binding international agreements were signed. After World War I, these preparations would lead to the establishment of the International Labour Organization, as an ancillary organization of the League of Nations.

Rerum Novarum

The greatest success that the Union could boast of was the publication of the papal encyclical *Rerum Novarum*.[113] As mentioned earlier, Leo XIII's attention in the first years of his pontificate was focused mainly on settling the problems of the *Kulturkampf* and questions of doctrine, but from the mid-1880s it was clear that he wanted to become involved in the social debate. At the end of 1887 he sought the advice of Albert de Mun,[114] who subsequently consulted Blome.

---

113 On *Rerum Novarum*, its preparation, content and impact, see Kuefstein, *Vorgeschichte der Enzyklik 'Rerum Novarum'*; De Gasperi, *I tempi e gli uomini*, 127-144; Antonazzi, *L'Enciclica 'Rerum Novarum'*; Boutry, *'Rerum Novarum'*; Mayeur, 'La question sociale', 489-497; Levillain, 'L'écho des écoles du catholicisme social', 107-131; Joblin, 'Doctrine et action sociale', 89-113; Sorgenfrei, 'Die geistesgeschichtlichen Hintergründe'; Bedouelle, 'De l'influence réelle de l'Union de Fribourg', 241-254; Mayeur, 'Aux origines de l'enseignement social de l'Eglise', 11-33; Misner, *Social Catholicism*, 213-222; Dorr, *Option for the Poor*, 11-20; Krier, *Catholic Social Teaching*, 11-28; Mattioli, 'Die Union de Fribourg', 15-32.

114 Molette, *Albert de Mun*, 212.

The Austrian social aristocrat comprehensively set out his expectations of the proposed encyclical.[115] In his view, it was of paramount importance that modern pauperism, which resulted from economic liberalism and led to socialism, should be indicted. Moralizing the lower classes was not a sufficient remedy. Structural reforms to counteract individualism were necessary; a social legislation, inspired by Christian principles, had to bring about once again a harmonious and peaceful society. In that process, the State, whose task it was to look after the welfare of its subjects and to make justice prevail, had a vital role to play. The encyclical had to remind governments and parliaments of their duties as well as advocate international labour laws. It also had to recommend corporative occupational associations and structural changes.

As has been already mentioned, after its audience on 30 January 1888, the Fribourg Union provided the Pope with a synthesis of its research. Meanwhile, several workers' pilgrimages to Rome, organized by the *Oeuvre*, kept up the pressure. Church leaders in the Anglo-Saxon world also pushed for the Holy See to take a stance. Cardinals Manning in Britain and Gibbons in the US especially took up the cause of the working class, which included many members of their congregations, urging the Church to speak out – on moral grounds – against the exploitation of workers. An important external factor was the spectacular rise of political socialism, which came increasingly under the influence of revolutionary and atheistic Marxism and in 1889 took the initiative to found the Second Workers' International.

The encyclical *Rerum Novarum* finally appeared, after long preparation, on 15 May 1891. It would be the most important papal encyclical in modern church history. It confirmed the Catholic Church's turn towards the people, and laid the foundation for a social teaching which – to this day – gives it great moral influence throughout the world.

The encyclical was based on Thomism, which itself was profoundly influenced by Aristotelianism. It put particular emphasis on the dignity of the human person, who was defined as a social being. It sharply criticized the existing economic order because it led to a misunderstanding and exploitation of workers, but it did not totally reject the liberal capitalist system and its emphasis on private ownership. However, the excesses of capitalism had to be resisted and the economic system had to be adjusted in a more socially equitable direction. Workers had a right to a decent, fair wage and humane working conditions. They should be able to organize themselves in associations, whether mixed or not, in order to defend their interests in a spirit of class collaboration and not of class struggle. Social associations could play a key role in resolving social tensions. The State also had an important role to play, but only secondarily. Historically and ontologically, natural social bonds preceded the State and placed restrictions on its role and mandate.

115   Blome to de Mun, 17 Nov. 1887, CARAN, AP 378, 13, IX, 26.

A well-functioning society should recognize and provide opportunities for the different actors in its midst. The State's main task was to protect the natural rights of individual citizens and social groups; it existed for the citizens and their social entities, not vice versa. It was not an end but only a means for the fulfillment of human beings who, both in their own right and as social beings, possessed inalienable rights prior to becoming partners in a political community. Social connections were autonomous forces whose origins and functions were derived from natural law, which preceded positive law. They could and should play an essential role in social reforms. The encyclical therefore opted for building a society from below and took a clear stance against the modern Leviathan.

Nevertheless, Leo XIII developed a positive vision of the State at the same time. In the Catholic tradition, the State remained the most important social bond.[116] It was a natural and necessary given, with a positive goal and an indispensable function. Above all, it had to promote the common good. It could develop three types of activities: create the conditions for individual action, complement its efforts and complete the tasks which it could not possibly achieve.[117] By exercising its direct power, it protected private property in the socioeconomic sphere, but had to use its indirect power to reconcile the use of that property with the common good. Through careful social legislation it could contribute to improving the working and living conditions of the socially vulnerable and to promoting social justice, but its intervention should be proportionate and should be restricted to combatting abuse. The State always had to strive for a careful balance between the common good and the autonomy of individuals and social entities.

The encyclical turned against liberalism and to an even greater extent against socialism. In opposition to both ideologies, it stated that the disarray in society had above all a moral and religious cause: the denial of God and his laws by society. According to the Pope, only religion had the power to fundamentally solve social problems. At the same time, Leo XIII criticized statism, both that of the liberals and of the socialists. He dismissed socialist notions like class struggle and collectivism, while accusing liberalism of exaggerated individualism, a disregard of social obligations and a denial of social justice. Among his recommendations for the future were a plea for a just wage, the defence of the interests of the lower classes through creating associations, and enlightened social intervention by the State. The Church here set itself up as a defender of social human rights before it showed the same concern for individual human rights.

---

116 According to the Dutch Calvinist principle of 'sphere sovereignty', the State was put on the same level as other spheres or sectors of life.

117 The Jesuit Luigi Taparelli d'Azeglio (1793-1862) especially influenced the theory of the state formulated in the encyclical. See Millon-Delsol, *L'Etat subsidiaire*, 131-136.

Leo XIII. Photograph, J. David, c. 1890.
[Leuven, KADOC]

The social teaching developed by *Rerum Novarum* also contained the seeds of the modern principle of subsidiarity, which forty years later would be explicitly mentioned in Pius XI's encyclical, *Quadragesimo Anno* (1931).[118] Ketteler had already used the concept of 'subsidiary law' to regulate the relations between the different levels of society and the State, in which he strongly emphasized the autonomy of social groups. Like Ketteler, Leo XIII expected the solution of social problems to come in the first place from grassroots groups and the lower administrative authorities. Competences had be allocated responsibly between the different social and political levels. Thanks above all to the agency of Christian Democracy, the heir to the Catholic social movements, the principle of subsidiarity would after the Second World War be put into practice in the European integration process.[119]

What influence did the Fribourg Union have on the encyclical *Rerum Novarum*? In older historiography, this was strongly emphasized. Such was the case for instance with Alcide De Gasperi, who in the interwar period devoted an extensive study to the forerunners of *Rerum Novarum*.[120] More recent historians paint a more nuanced picture: they point out that Leo XIII did not question the basic principles of economic liberalism and did not speak out in favour of a *Sozialreform*, the implementation of a corporative regime. Rather he opted for *Sozialpolitik*: getting rid of the excesses of the capitalist system through cautious social legislation.[121] The encyclical *Quadragesimo Anno* (1931), which was promulgated during the Great Depression, would go much further in that regard. Thus *Rerum Novarum* certainly did not opt for the corporative model of Vogelsang or La Tour du Pin. However, the expectations that Blome had formulated in 1887 were largely met. The Pope did not limit himself to moral considerations but called for structural interventions. In opting for social intervention by the State, he followed the Fribourg Union and not the School of Angers, as he also did in advocating well-organized interest groups that would play an intermediary role in society. He did not exclusively favour a

---

118 'It is wrong to entrust to a higher authority that which can be achieved by lower organizations. The State should only intervene when necessary and even then in such a way that it does not absorb or destroy smaller entities. It is an important principle of *subsidiarity* that the State cannot assign to itself functions belonging to a lower level as the State would then put too much of a burden on itself. It must be aware that an appropriate allocation of tasks to different associations – applying the principle of the "subsidiary function" – will be beneficial for its own social authority and efficiency.'

119 On the subsidiarity principle as a constitutional principle of the European Union, see *infra*, 317.

120 De Gasperi, *I tempi e gli uomini*, 135-144. The first edition of this study was published in 1932 under the pseudonym M. Zanatta. The author had been secretary-general of the Italian People's Party/Partito Popolare Italiano, and in order to withdraw from fascism, had sought refuge in the Vatican, where he led a studious life. Between 1945 and 1953 he would lead the first postwar Italian government and play an important role in the European integration process. See Canavero, *Alcide De Gasperi*, 51-52; *infra*, 316.

121 Misner, *Social Catholicism*, 214-218; Mattioli, 'Die Union de Fribourg', 28-32.

corporative form of association but left an opening for the creation of separate trade unions. Both Blome and the Union had preceded him in this. All this allows us to conclude that the Union's ideas were reflected to a large extent in the encyclical, for which it had been a useful think-tank. Interestingly, this international study circle, which included mainly social aristocrats among its members, operated in such a way that the Church did not lose its historic engagement with the people.

In early October 1891, at the next annual meeting of the Fribourg Union, Blome struck a euphoric note:

> The most important event of the past year has been the promulgation of the encyclical *Rerum Novarum*. The Pope's pronouncement ushers in a new social era, to be compared with what the historical dates of 1814 and 1848 meant for the political history of peoples. We are particularly delighted to find confirmation in this encyclical of positions that we have taken since the foundation of our work. *Roma locuta*. What we found to be just, what we had proposed, is now defined by the highest authority. *Causa finita*.

Yet, in Blome's view, the work was not completely finished. The Pope had indeed summarized all the ills, but had not passed on all the remedies. The usefulness and even the necessity of creating associations had been established. Guidelines had been issued regarding the terms of legitimate social state intervention. The encyclical, however, had confined itself to pointing to voracious usury as an elusive Proteus.[122] The Union had to consider this more fully in the future; if the credit regime were not changed, other means of action would not be sufficient to avert social danger. After having devoted its attention for a long time to the issue of labour, the Union now had to scrutinize that of credit. The task now was 'to contain voracious usury, and to assign money a less important place in the economy'.[123] Capitalism had to be fought at its very core. Five years before, Blome, unlike Vogelsang, had still not given any priority to this topic, but now he apparently found the time to be ripe.

During the same annual meeting, the credit issue was cautiously brought up for discussion, along with the question of wages, and a renewed plea was made for sharing profits with workers. The committee that had discussed the corporative issue spoke in favour of a free choice of occupation and the right to join professional associations, whether mixed or not, that would be legally recognized and subject internally to democratic rules. Once again the com-

---

122 Proteus is a character in Greek mythology, a sea god that had the power to assume all sorts of shapes.
123 Minutes of the annual meeting in 1891, sitting of 7 Oct., BCUF, H 3562, 4. 'Contain voracious usury, put money back in its place.'

plaint was made that political economy had lost all ties with morality. The economy as such had an impact on international politics, and in that context the arms race and imperialism were once more criticized. All this shows that the Union certainly did not take any clear-cut conservative positions, either economic or sociopolitical.

The annual meeting of 1891 would be the last one. Was this due to the death of Cardinal Mermillod a few months later? He certainly had been an important unifying figure, but his theoretical and academic contributions had been very limited. His death was indeed a significant factor, but the main reason for the winding-up of the Union probably lay with La Tour du Pin, who thus far had been the driving force behind the organization. At that time he lost the support of the *Oeuvre* for his tight corporative programme. Much more consistent and more rigid than Blome, he was a proponent of mandatory corporative associations, and of a fully developed system of political representation based on interest groups. This led to tensions with the more pragmatic Albert de Mun. The periodical *L'Association catholique*, which was a mouthpiece for the corporative stance of La Tour du Pin, had already separated from the *Oeuvre* in 1890. Tensions however persisted and in 1892 there was a final break between the two '*frères-ennemis*'.[124] De Mun then reconciled himself to the encyclical *Au milieu des sollicitudes* (20 February 1892), in which Leo XIII urged French Catholics to participate in a *Ralliement* with the Republic and asked them to work for the Church's interests within the existing regime. This papal intervention was perceived as a slap in the face by the legitimists, who continued to dream of a restoration of the monarchy. La Tour du Pin was not willing to agree to the *Ralliement*. He remained an ardent monarchist, and at the same time an avowed adversary of democracy, supporting social action for the people but not by the people.[125]

Similar ideological tensions emerged in different countries and prevented further international meetings from being held. La Tour du Pin could no longer identify himself with the *Oeuvre* and tensions between the social aristocrats and the Christian Socials deepened in Austria also. The two groups supporting the Union, the French and the Austrian, were therefore paralyzed, probably the main reason why no further meetings took place. An additional reason was that the nationalist reflex was strengthening in Catholic circles also, and this did not have a beneficial impact on their international collaboration. Finally, with the promulgation of *Rerum Novarum* the institutional

---

124 See the correspondence between Lorin, La Tour du Pin and De Mun in the latter's archive: CARAN, AP 378, 14.

125 Goyau characterized La Tour du Pin in February 1893 (BNF, NAF, 27218) in this way: 'He says that in order to succeed the social movement must (in his view) keep an aristocratic character, that the formula must be "dedication to the people". Some people are trying to steer this movement towards democracy, and that could perhaps be much better, but in my view, that would be like throwing pearls to swine.'

Church had taken over the reins and prominent (aristocratic) lay people were increasingly sidelined.

Still, two years later, an attempt was made to pick up the thread again. On 17 April 1893 some members of the Union, including Prince Löwenstein, gathered at Kuefstein's house in Rome, on the occasion of a papal jubilee. Those present spoke out in favour of continuing the Union, although in different venues. They immediately scheduled a meeting in Zurich, on the periphery of an international workers' congress, but in all probability nothing came of it. One tangible result of the meeting in Rome was that the earlier resolutions of the Union were bundled together and published. Now that the Union had earned its credentials with the publication of *Rerum Novarum*, it no longer seemed necessary to maintain the secrecy of its past operations. Ten years later, in 1903, a futile attempt was again made to re-establish the Union, suggesting that its disappearance was still perceived as a loss in some circles.[126]

After World War I, the Union would rise from its ashes as the Union of Mechlin (1921-1960). The new organization, which was under the protection of Cardinal Mercier, was originally a Franco-Belgian affair mainly, but over time it gathered recruits from eleven countries, with Germany being the notable absentee. Unlike its predecessor, it brought together mostly clerics and university professors. Describing itself as an 'international study group for social issues', it wanted, inter alia, to undertake studies on financial capitalism, but in a decade in which the banks and stock exchanges were experiencing a phenomenal growth, a fundamental critique of the credit system never materialized.[127] Nevertheless, the Union did exert a significant influence with the publication of the *Code social de Malines*, which was first issued in 1927 and subsequently went through several reprints and translations. This code in fact expressed the fundamental principles of the Fribourg Union. It put the emphasis on the social function of property, called for the strengthening of intermediary structures and made a plea for social state intervention. It would be very influential in Italy, where it served as the inspiration for the *Codice de Camaldoli* (July 1943), which in the period after World War II would become the basic socioeconomic document of Christian Democracy in the peninsula.

---

126 Réunion intime internationale des catholiques sociaux à Fribourg, 20-22 Oct. 1903, Invitation, BCUF, H 3562, 4. The initiative for this was taken by the former Italian members, Stanislao Medolago Albini and Giuseppe Toniolo. They planned a meeting in Fribourg from 20 to 22 October 1903, but it is not clear whether this conference actually took place and what its possible results were. The resolutions of the Union were re-published: Rivière, *Réimpressions des thèses de l'Union de Fribourg*.

127 Eugène Duthoit, *Le Code social de Malines et ses origines*, Gut Salzau, XII, 3; Van Molle, 'Croissance économique et éthique catholique', 317-336; De Maeyer, 'Katholische Soziallehre', 112-114 and 117.

This episode makes clear that the Fribourg Union still continued to be a reference point in social Catholic circles throughout the 20th century.[128]

The early stages of Christian Democracy

For the social Catholics, the encyclical *Rerum Novarum* was a charter that could now serve as a guideline for the future. It would inspire many popular organizations aimed at the emancipation of the Catholic lower classes – peasants, craftsmen, industrial workers and the petty bourgeoisie. In an increasing number of countries these social organizations created a platform for confessional, interclassist parties.

The encyclical formulated a number of basic principles, but different interpretations emerged. A major division soon arose in social Catholic ranks, such as in France, where the more 'liberal' School of Angers opposed the corporative tendencies of the *Oeuvre*. As mentioned already, rumblings also were felt in the *Oeuvre* itself between De Mun and La Tour du Pin. The *Ralliement* further sharpened the differences of opinion. Along with many other legitimists, La Tour du Pin withdrew from Catholic organizations. For them, accepting the Republic implied a choice for democracy, whereas *Abbés-démocrates*, like Jules Lemire, decisively made that choice, and the first Christian trade unions also revealed a democratic orientation. La Tour du Pin stuck to an elitist vision of society and advocated a closed and tightly organized corporatism as a component of a Christian state. He also moved more and more in a nationalist direction and would later come to sympathize with the *Action Française*, a radical right-wing, monarchist and nationalist movement that adopted some of his social ideas.[129]

Though the corporative ideas were undoubtedly patronizing, they did not lead automatically to authoritarian views on the State. That was shown, for example, in the position of Henri Lorin (1866-1932), who had been a very active member of the Fribourg Union. This *polytechnicien* and geographer came from an affluent patrician and legitimist family.[130] His salon in the Faubourg Saint-Honoré in Paris and his castle in Maule became important meeting places for Catholic intellectuals and social Catholics. Through his uncle Édouard Lefebvre de Béhaine, who was French ambassador to the Holy See from 1883 to 1896, he became friendly with secretary of state Rampolla, and was able to get easy access to the Pope himself. Lorin was very close to La Tour du Pin, but at the same time he was a great admirer of De Mun, for whom he frequently

---

128 De Maeyer, 'Katholische Soziallehre und Christliche Arbeiterorganisationen', 110-119; Dau, *Il Codice di Camaldoli*.
129 Prévotat, *Les catholiques et l'Action française*, 81-84.
130 Pinon, 'Henri Lorin', 187-197; Grondeux, *Georges Goyau*, 63-76.

served as a liaison in Rome.[131] In May and June 1891 he made every effort to prevent a final rupture between the two friends. Yet, his political views differed radically from those of La Tour du Pin. He advocated reconciliation with the Republic and democracy.

In the spring of 1892 Lorin became acquainted in Rome with Georges Goyau (1869-1939), who was then working on a doctorate in history at the *École française de Rome* and later would become a renowned essayist and member of the *Académie française*.[132] A busy correspondence between the two ensued, which has been partially preserved and which throws an interesting light on the French and even the international social Catholic milieu during this period. Lorin introduced Goyau to Vatican circles and subsequently used him regularly as an intermediary in his dealings with the Curia. The two soulmates both turned against state absolutism, which in their view dated back to Roman law.[133] They felt that the Church had to exert a lasting influence on social life and should be given the necessary freedom to do so. In the field of political economy, they advocated a moderate corporatism that eventually would replace the liberal market economy. Their correspondence reveals their sympathy with the burgeoning Christian democratic movement in several European countries.[134] They followed with interest and approval the sociopolitical actions of Decurtins in Switzerland, and paid even more attention to developments in Belgium where an autonomous Christian Workers' Movement was slowly getting underway.[135] Progressive priests like Pottier and Daens were at loggerheads with conservative politicians who called in the Vatican to force them into line, but Lorin and Goyau made as much use as they could of their Roman contacts to thwart these manoeuvers.[136] They also sympathized with the progressive wing within the US episcopate.

Curiously enough, Lorin continued to maintain good relations with La Tour du Pin. In August 1895 he wrote to Goyau: 'We preach his programme because we are his disciples, but we go further than he does.'[137] He himself stuck

---

131   Lorin to De Mun, 29 May 1891, CARAN, AP 378, 14, XI, 30.

132   Grondeux, *Georges Goyau*.

133   Id., 89-90: 'Anti-liberalism and anti-absolutism are linked in Goyau's doctrine ... He is Roman in the idea that the papacy is an antidote, a power counterbalancing all absolutisms, the source of all equilibrium.'

134   Lorin to Goyau, 21 April 1894, BNF, NAF, 16818, 46-50; Id. to id., Spring 1894, BNF, NAF, 16818, 39-43: 'In orienting the Church towards the side of the people, the Pope has made it a power for the future.'

135   Note by Goyau, Spring 1893, BNF, NAF, 27218: 'Belgium, at this moment, is holding out for Christian socialism.'; Lorin to Goyau, 23 Aug. 1894 and 1 July 1895, BNF, NAF, 16818, 58-59 and 89-94.

136   Lorin to Goyau, 27 Aug. and 19 Sept. 1895 BNF, NAF, 27218, 101 and 110-111.

137   Lorin to Goyau, Aug. 1895, BNF, NAF, 16818, 102-104. The correspondence between Lorin and Goyau shows that in 1904 the former still had a very confidential relationship with La Tour du Pin.

to his democratic choices. In 1904, together with Marius Gonin he launched the 'Social Weeks' in France, that is, social gatherings for Catholic militants and *hommes d'oeuvres,* which were also replicated on a large scale outside of France.[138] He continued as chairman of these meetings until 1919. During the interwar period he served for ten years in the National Assembly as a deputy for a smaller social Republican faction.

This dyed-in-the-wool democrat, who never gave up his corporatist ideas, maintained very cordial relations with Blome. He stayed repeatedly at his estate in Bellagio or received him in his Paris salon. He urged his young friend Goyau to make the acquaintance of the former Austrian diplomat.[139] One of the main reasons why Lorin could still get along well with Blome was that the latter had apparently tempered his dislike for democracy. In the spring of 1893 Goyau noted in his diary: 'La Tour du Pin has remained conservative, unlike De Mun, Blome and others.'

Blome's pragmatic attitude to democratic developments gradually led to his taking a greater distance from La Tour du Pin, although he still harboured a deep appreciation for the French marquis:

> I consider La Tour du Pin in general to be more important and more prescient than De Mun in social issues. The former's direction is more purposeful, clearer, and more energetic than that of the second ... I have always seen La Tour du Pin as the Moses and De Mun as the Aaron of the movement.[140]

For a long time Blome assumed that La Tour du Pin would become reconciled to the *Ralliement,* but that proved not to be the case. For his part, the French marquis wrote to Prince Löwenstein in early 1893 that for him Blome still remained his '*chef de file*' on several levels.[141] Later, contact between the two dwindled. At the beginning of 1898 La Tour du Pin wrote to Pergen: 'With Blome I maintain rather courteous relations. He has a good head, but as far as I am concerned, he attaches too little importance to tradition.'[142] The fact that Blome mitigated his aristocratic position presumably played a role in this judgement.

---

138 Durand, ed., *Les Semaines sociales de France (1904-2004).*
139 Lorin stayed in the Villa Giulia in Bellagio for a month in 1892 and 1895. His high regard for Blome is evident from the following passage in a letter to Goyau: 'Blome is staying in Paris for two days. He admires you greatly. *That means something!*' (Lorin to Goyau, 6 June 1897, BNF, NAF, 16818, 183-184).
140 Blome to Revertera, 25 Dec. 1892 and 2 Jan. 1893, HAH, IV, 56.
141 La Tour du Pin to Löwenstein, 13 Jan. 1893, SAWT-R, *Löwenstein,* Lit. D Nr. 675, I, 146.
142 La Tour du Pin to Pergen, 16 Jan. 1898, HHSA, *Pergen,* II. The separation between the two is also evident in a letter to Pergen 12 Jan. 1900, ibid.

The relationship between La Tour du Pin and Anton Pergen, by contrast, remained very friendly, although it was limited to epistolary contacts. An excerpt from a letter to Pergen at the beginning of 1898 speaks volumes: 'The end of the text I sent you yesterday shows to what degree I have remained your pupil – your pupil and so much more, because you have enriched my heart even more than my intellect.'[143] Like La Tour du Pin, Pergen did not pursue the democratic direction. In Austria he took a distance from the Christian Socials and became the leader of the more conservative social Catholics. He supported the circles that in 1895 attempted to provoke the Vatican to condemn the Christian Social Party.[144] In this matter he was on a different wavelength than Blome, his former role model.

Blome's attitude towards the advance of democracy can only be reconstructed indirectly. He made no public statements about it, and did not express any clear opinions in the limited correspondence of his that has been preserved from this period. His position on developments in Austria is the most illuminating.[145] At the *Katholikentag* of 1889, the social programme of the *Freie Vereinigung* and the Fribourg Union was adopted almost completely. At the suggestion of Vogelsang and the moral theologian Franz Martin Schindler, the activities of the social committee of the congress were subsequently continued in the so-called *Enten-Abende*,[146] which Blome sometimes attended. Almost all shades of the anti-liberal reform movements took part, but the orientation of the Christian Socials came increasingly to dominate. The *Enten-Abende* would continue to be held until 1899, operating as a kind of school for the Christian Social Movement. The 1889 *Katholikentag* also led to the founding of the *Leo-Gesellschaft* which was conceived as a Catholic academy that would pay close attention to social problems. Blome was the first president of the *Gesellschaftswissenschaft* section. Franz Schindler became secretary-general and after the death of Vogelsang would take his place as the representative theorist of social Catholicism in Austria.

Meanwhile, the anti-liberal forces also formed a political alliance. In the autumn of 1887 the *Vereinigte Christen* (United Christians) was started, a strange amalgam of democrats and clergy, German and Austrian patriots,

---

143 La Tour du Pin to Pergen, 16 Jan. 1898, HHSA, *Pergen*, II; see also 12 Jan. 1900, ibid.: 'So many things we have experienced and survived. From this good and saintly Pope Pius IX who loved you so much, up to all the illusions that one harbours about his eminent but less sympathetic successor [Leo XIII].' In a letter of 16 Jan. 1898 he was very critical of papal policy: 'Rome's social guidance has failed while its political guidance has thrown all organizations and all ranks into confusion.' (ibid.).

144 Bled, 'Les correspondants français du comte Pergen', 1-8.

145 Geehr, *Karl Lueger. Mayor of Fin de Siècle Vienna*; Boyer, *Political Radicalism in Late Imperial Vienna*; Wandruszka, 'Il cattolicesimo politico e sociale nell' Austria-Ungheria', 151-178; Banauch, *Prinz Aloys von und zu Liechtenstein*, 25-95; Silberbauer, Österreichs katholiken und die Arbeiterfrage, 121-180.

146 The meetings were held in the *Zur goldenen Ente Hotel* from 29 Jan. 1889.

aristocrats, tradesmen, farmers and workers. The German-national, pan-Germanic tendency was soon excluded. The *Vereinigte Christen* launched its programme on 20 February 1889, which in addition to an anti-liberal and corporative approach also had a strong anti-Semitic bias. Within the movement, the Christian Socials quickly got the upper hand, especially after the talented populist politician Karl Lueger came on board. Prince Aloys Liechtenstein also joined, to the dismay of his aristocratic friends. The Christian Social Party (1891) received remarkably strong support from the lower clergy. In the cities it recruited mainly among the anti-Semitic lower middle class and in rural areas among the peasantry. The traditional Catholic elites and the upper clergy had difficulty with this turn of events. They reproached the Christian Socials for their vehement anti-Semitism, their democratic stance and their stress on the social aspect rather than the religious. In 1895 they appealed to the Vatican to prevent the further spread of the movement in Catholic ranks, but to the dismay of conservative social Catholics, the Holy See took the side of the Christian Socials. While the Daensist movement in Belgium could not rely on the sympathy of the Vatican, the Christian Socials escaped denunciation. They were merely advised to mitigate their anti-Semitism and to pay due deference to the church hierarchy.

In 1895 the Christian Socials achieved a great electoral success in Vienna, but the Emperor held up the appointment of Lueger as mayor of the capital for two years. The big breakthrough came in 1897 following new electoral reforms. The introduction of direct universal suffrage in 1907 caused a complete rift. Conservative social Catholics were forced to reconcile with the Christian Socials and together they formed the *Christlichsoziale Reichspartei*, which along with Social Democracy would become the main political formation in Cisleithania.

Blome's reaction to these developments is revealed in his correspondence, sparse though it is. In December 1890 he wrote that he had some understanding for the *Vereinigte Christen*, but added that he had more sympathy for the group he encountered in the Fribourg Union. In March 1891 he complained about the shortsightedness of the court and the government in their dealings with the Christian Socials. In October 1892 he declared that he regarded anti-Semites as valuable allies, even if some of them did not fully espouse positive Christian principles.[147] Some time later, in March 1894, he made clear that he felt more sympathy for Lueger than for the Bohemian feudal lords, who were pure individualists and like the liberals principally wanted to protect the moneyed interests.[148] He thought the refusal to appoint Lueger as mayor of Vienna

147 Blome to Revertera, 21 Dec. 1890, 22 Jan. and 13 March 1891, Oct. 1892, HAH, IV, 56.
148 Blome to Revertera, 10 March 1894, HAH, IV, 56.

was a serious mistake.[149] With the electoral breakthrough of the Christian Social Party in 1897, he was overcome with euphoria:

> The principles for which I have fought and suffered all my life are now making a breakthrough, even though I am banned from the arena and can only look on from the gods. In 1868 I found myself in the midst of the hustle and bustle of battle, but now I cannot even attend the victory party.[150]

Indeed, Blome had campaigned all his life for an alliance between conservatism and the Catholic popular movements in order to contain liberalism. The liberals were now, both politically and economically, on the way back, a return largely helped along by the fact that the Catholic popular organizations had gained power.

Blome identified rather easily with the Christian Social Party because, in comparison to the *Zentrum* in Germany, it was more socially oriented and less influenced by liberal Catholicism.[151] The fact that he now sympathized with democratic popular movements did not mean that he in principle supported the parliamentary system and the notion of popular sovereignty. According to him, a parliamentary government in multinational Austria was nonsense. He was not averse to the people's involvement in government, but it had to be channeled through social and regional bodies; if not, the forces aiming at the disintegration of the State would prevail in the long run. It is striking that at the end of his life he had a growing appreciation for the English constitutional system, which in his view had found a good balance between tradition and change.[152]

An intriguing aspect in the development of the Christian Social Party was its anti-Semitism, which became one of its distinguishing characteristics.[153] Anti-Jewish feelings were rampant at the time in the whole Anglo-Saxon and European world. They were given political expression in Austria, in Germany where the concept of anti-Semitism was born in 1879, and in France where the Dreyfus affair at the end of the century acted as a catalyst. Jews were mostly associated with modernity and thus served as a convenient scapegoat for all its ills.

---

149 Blome to Revertera, 29 March 1896, HAH, IV, 56.
150 Blome to Revertera, 15 March 1897, HAH, IV, 56.
151 Mayeur, *Des partis catholiques*, 72.
152 Lorin to Goyau, July 1899, BNF, NAF, 16818.
153 Pauley, *From Prejudice to Persecution*; Hellwing, *Der konfessionnelle Antisemitismus im 19. Jahrhundert in Österreich*; Pulzer, *Die Entstehung des politischen Antisemitismus*; Blaschke, *Katholizismus und Antisemitismus im deutschen Kaiserreich*; Nipperdey, *Deutsche Geschichte, 1866-1918*, vol. 2, 289-310.

That was also the case in Austria where anti-Jewish feelings had traditionally been nourished by religious sentiments, but gradually they came to be reinforced by economic factors also. Jews had indeed achieved a strong position in the banking sector as well as in the industrial and financial world.[154] They also exerted a strong influence in the media and had close ties with liberal leaders. They were held accountable by the conservatives for the liberal constitutional reforms and the agitation against the Concordat. The banking crisis of 1873 further fanned anti-Jewish sentiments. The victims of the subsequent economic depression pointed to Jewish bankers and industrialists as the main culprits. Vogelsang and many social aristocrats, who associated them also with rationalism, individualism and liberalism, went on the attack against them. Anti-Semitism was even stronger among the lower middle class, small shopkeepers and tradesmen, while industrial workers were not immune either.

From the 1880s anti-Semitism became more than a mere sentiment or religious prejudice. It became a political programme and a stimulus for political action. Lueger would combine the populist anti-capitalism and anti-Semitism of the small tradesmen with the social and religious programme of Vogelsang. It became the formula for the success of the Christian Socials, who put great emphasis on the Jewish question, but saw it primarily as a social and not a religious affair. In 1891 the Austrian bishops spoke out formally against anti-Semitism, but they did not succeed in turning the tide. With the decline of liberalism, the Jews lost their main political support. They gradually became politically homeless, although that did not prevent them from experiencing considerable economic, cultural and scientific success in Vienna. In any case, the Emperor protected their interests. Incidentally, Lueger's anti-Semitism turned out to be mainly an instrument or tactic to win political power, although his actions ensured that anti-Semitism became an accepted and even respectable social phenomenon. It should be noted that the anti-Jewish position of the Christian Socials did not have a racist slant. This was very different in Germany, where the conservative-national opposition to the Jews gradually took on an ethnic-racist character.

Blome, who sympathized with the Christian Socials mainly for religious and social reasons, shared their anti-Semitism to some extent. He also tended to associate Jews with liberalism, anticlericalism and big business. Even though he repeatedly urged Vogelsang to keep a distance from anti-Semitism, that did not stop him, especially around 1890 with the emergence of the Chris-

---

154 Jews had contributed significantly to the wool industry in Bohemia and Moravia, the silk industry in Hungary and to the steel industry and the railways. They also owned many factories around Vienna, and held a very strong position in the banking sector there. In Vienna in 1857 there were only 6,217 Jews, in 1880 there were 72,588 (10% of the population), and by 1890 numbers had risen to 118,495.

tian Social Party, from sporadically giving expression to anti-Semitic views in his own correspondence.[155] Indeed, he saw Jews as fervent opponents of the social Catholic reform programme that he advocated.[156] Still, he expressed his appreciation of a number of Jewish people who were among his acquaintances.[157] His nuanced position was possibly partly determined by the fact that Metternich, his great model, had been a benevolent patron of the Jewish community in Vienna.

The hermit of Bellagio

Until the early 1890s Blome played a significant role in the international social Catholic movement, the highpoints of which were his involvement in the Austrian *Katholikentag* in 1889 and the Congress of Liège in 1890. He also had reasons to be satisfied about the encyclical *Rerum Novarum* and the breakthrough of the Christian Socials in Austria. While he was rather disappointed with the results achieved in the first phase of his public life, he could look back with satisfaction on the second period. His firmness of principle, for which he had sacrificed his diplomatic career, turned out to have borne fruit in the end.

This principled approach remained his hallmark. In 1892 he wrote:

> Diplomats ... are always inclined to regard moderation as the essence and principles as merely the form of things, while the reverse should be the case ... With moderation Napoleon and Bismarck would never have achieved their successes ... The correct line is: *fortiter in re, suaviter in modo* ... Our old Prince Metternich also applied this maxim and he, I think, was not a bad diplomat.

A little later he added:

> I do not in any way agree that duty can be fulfilled only by being in opposition. Nonetheless, it is true that for every human being there is a limit beyond which he cannot go and that limit is different for each of us depending on one's principles and opportunities for action.[158]

---

155 Blome to Vogelsang, 11 March 1890, LASH, 126, 15, 624: 'Anti-Semitism has become fashionable'; Blome to Revertera, 6 July 1891, HAH, IV, 56: 'Believe me now for but once in my life: anti-Semites are a hundred times more decent and honest than the protectors of the Semites.'
156 Blome to Revertera, 13 March 1891, HAH, IV, 56.
157 Blome to his son Hans, 28 May 1905, LASH, abt. 126.15, 641.
158 Blome to Revertera, 2 March and 19 Oct. 1892, HAH, IV, 56.

His own principles were fixed beacons by which he had oriented his life, taking account of concrete circumstances as they arose.

Blome's starting point had been that order, peace and stability in society were threatened by revolutionary movements, which were inspired by liberalism and later by socialism. As a result, international law as well as the socio-political order were under threat. Amid the ensuing chaos, there was only one unshakeable bulwark, the centuries-old Church of Rome. It had to be able to exercise its beneficial influence in order to save society. Its ethical principles had to inspire international politics, which was increasingly becoming the plaything of the power politics of the nation states. It should be able to maintain its authority and influence over the modern State, which had become an instrument in the hands of its enemies. Blome had hoped for a restoration of the Christian monarchies, beginning with Austria. He had previously counted on the shocking events of 1870-1871 and on the help of the Holy See, but once it became clear that the Papacy was taking a distance from legitimism and that the fight appeared hopeless, he was pragmatic enough to abandon his stubborn opposition to a cautious liberalization of state structures. As evidenced by his later attitude towards the Christian Socials, he was prepared to accept that the available political means should be used to defend the Church's interests and at the same time to safeguard the social order. That did not stop him from continuing his opposition to the basic principles of liberalism, which, in his view, led irrevocably to socialism.

In the 1870s, as a result of the economic crisis and the impoverishment of the proletariat, it became obvious that liberalism was especially vulnerable on the socioeconomic level. Blome would henceforth target capitalism primarily. Through an in-depth study of the social mechanisms, he wanted to contribute to a corporative structure and to a centre-oriented society based on solidarity and the principle of justice. Again, he looked to the Church to find a way of introducing such a system, and in fact got a more positive response from it for his social ideas than for his political legitimist aspirations. He was also sufficiently pragmatic in his approach to social problems. Over time, he came to accept the creation of autonomous workers' associations and even went quite a way himself in the direction of democracy. What was essential for him was that individualism would be destroyed and that social harmony be achieved through a combination of forming associations and social state intervention. In this way, a more articulated, multi-layered society would develop at the same time. As hoped and expected, the Church was willing to work towards this, thereby enabling it to exert a stabilizing influence on society, as he always had envisioned.

Blome then was willing to apply his principles in a pragmatic way, but 'principles are the essence of things and moderation can only be the form'. He was not inclined to compromise his principles much – for him, the limit was

Gustav von Blome. Photograph, 1903.
[*O. Hintze,* Geschichte des uradeligen Geschlechtes der Herren und Grafen Blome, *Hamburg, 1929*]

quickly reached. His firmness of principle had not made his life easy. It had spurred him to abandon his diplomatic career and break with Viennese society and the political establishment in Austria. It had even alienated him from the Roman Curia with which he had such close contacts between 1868 and 1872. After he retired to Bellagio, there is little evidence of any direct relations between him and the Vatican. He was disillusioned by Pius IX's indecision and looked forward to a *Papa duro*. Leo XIII certainly did not meet that expectation, although Blome did express his loyalty to the new Pope. As mentioned earlier, he attached the greatest importance to the Pope's support for the Fribourg Union, but he never went to see him in the Vatican.[159] In 1888 Mermillod declared that both Leo XIII and Pius IX had repeatedly praised Blome's unparalleled dedication to the church,[160] but as far as Leo XIII was concerned there is no mention of this in the available documentation.

Some people considered Blome to be rather headstrong at times.[161] His forceful personality and his iron will commanded widespread respect but also kept people at a distance. His manner also contributed to this. He was rather cold, aloof and not emotionally demonstrative, as Louis de Pons had already noticed. He was a strict and demanding father to his children. His two oldest sons did not turn out well. Because of their isolation in Bellagio, he was obliged to send them to boarding school and therefore could not monitor their upbringing as he would have liked. Arnold (1861-1926) neglected his studies and began to live a dissolute life, leading his father to break off relations with him. Louis (1865-1928), who was named after De Pons, did not fare much better. He joined a novitiate for a short time, left, hung around the university in Vienna, spent some time in the USA and on his return ran up a mountain of debts which his father had to pay.[162] Blome put all his hope then on his third and youngest son Hans (1867-1945), who was very sportive and opted for a military career in the cavalry. Though his career was not trouble-free, his father followed it with great attention and showered him with good advice.[163] The

159 Blome clearly favoured Pius IX over Leo XIII (Blome to Revertera, 19 Feb. 1892, HAH, IV, 56). Nevertheless, he had great praise for the encyclical *Longinqua Oceani*, which was directed to American Catholics (Blome to Revertera, HAH, IV, 56). In 1896 Blome declared once again: there is just one unshakeable throne, that of the pope (Blome to Revertera, 29 March 1896, HAH, IV, 56).

160 Minutes of the annual meeting in 1888, session of 10 Oct., SAWT-R, *Löwenstein*, Lit. D Nr. 675, I, 27.

161 Salviati to Manna Roncadelli, 15 Aug. 1878, UCSCM, ASMSC, Milaan, *Roncadelli*, 1/5/40.

162 Blome to Hans, 16 Feb. 1892 and 3 Feb. 1897, BCUF, LA 47, 1; Id. to id., 1 Dec. 1899, ibid.: 'If it is painful for a father to have to be ashamed of his sons, it is doubly bitter for him not even to receive from them the affection that accompanied his fatherly love for them since their earliest childhood. You only live, after all, by the heart.'

163 Blome to his son Hans, 27 July 1894, BCUF, LA 47, 1; Id. to id., 22 Aug. 1894, ibid.: 'With the biceps one can bring down perhaps a steer; with moral force one governs men.'; Id. to id., 1 Nov. 1894, ibid.: 'Strive to become an athlete of the spirit and of science.'

opportunity for a respectable career came in 1897 when Hans became chamberlain to Duke Ludwig Viktor, the youngest brother of the Emperor.

Blome's five daughters also caused him headaches. The seclusion in Bellagio hampered their *entrée dans le monde*. When finances would allow, Séphine Buol would go with them in the winter to Vienna to make them *salonfähig*, socially acceptable, and to help them find suitors. Three of them, Clémentine (Tinne), Marie and Carola would finally enter a convent, Anna made a love marriage with an impoverished officer and Giulia would marry an aristocratic widower at the age of thirty. It is clear that Blome had less success as a paterfamilias than in his public life.

Two surviving series of letters form the main source of our information about Blome's last years. The occupant of the Villa Giulia, who once called himself an '*animal scribax*', carried on a very lively correspondence throughout his life, but, after a painstaking search, only about a thousand letters have been found. For this period, we have his correspondence with his favourite son Hans, who became his support at the end of his life. A second set of letters was addressed to his close friend Friedrich Revertera, which contain interesting political as well as personal information. Indeed, following his financial setbacks and a long period out in the cold, Revertera had once again become politically active during the Taaffe government. In 1885 he was appointed a member of the *Herrenhaus* and at the end of 1888 he became ambassador to the Holy See, a position he held until 1901. He did not quite follow the same course as Blome and would keep his distance from the Christian Socials, but that did not affect their friendship in any way. Revertera visited Blome several times in Bellagio and they met occasionally in Austria. Their shared passion for chess strengthened their personal bond even more.

The correspondence with Hans Blome and Revertera sheds light on the impoverishment that the occupant of the Villa Giulia gradually came to experience. His financial situation had already gone downhill in the late 1870s, and in April 1882 he described himself as 'a poverty-stricken nobleman'. His problems increased after the death of his father in 1884. He was disadvantaged by Otto's will, which was very favourable to his half-sister. As heir of the Salzau fiefdom, he also had to pay off a mountain of debt that his father had run up in building his new castle; in fact, Gustav never finished off this huge residence and rarely stayed there. Income from his lands decreased during the acute agrarian crisis, which persisted until the mid-1890s. The Hagymàdfalva (Zwiebeldorf) domain at Grosswardein in Hungary, which he had inherited from his father, consisted of fertile land, but there were constant problems with the tenants and the stewards. The Montpreis estate, which he had bought at the end of his diplomatic career, was even less profitable and in 1900 he was forced to sell it. He had to live mainly off the income from the family estate in Salzau and from the vineyards and olive groves he owned in Bellagio. He complained constantly at this time about lack of money, which limited his spending on the education and placement of his children. Moreover, the lack of money kept him and his family stuck in Villa Giulia.

After some time therefore he considered selling the villa. Doing so would allow him to seek a home in Vienna and again play a more active role in the Catholic movement and political life in Austria, an attractive prospect now with the accession of the Taaffe government and the introduction of comprehensive social legislation. A move to Vienna would also benefit the social prospects of his younger daughters. Blome found it increasingly difficult to condemn his wife and children to staying in the countryside during the winter. As early as 1885 he was actively seeking a buyer for the Villa Giulia, which was actually owned by his wife Séphine. In 1889 he hoped to be able to sell the property for the tidy sum of five million euros to the Russian Grand Duchess Ekaterina, but the deal fell through. He also called on his friend Revertera to find a buyer in Rome, but without any success. In 1893 and 1894 he himself repeatedly travelled to London and Paris, to find candidates for his bucolic domain, but the French were not interested in Italian property and the English had lost their predilection for the Italian lakes. Blome failed to sell the Villa Giulia, where he once thought he had discovered an earthly paradise, and was thus condemned to live out his future years in what he gradually came to see as a wretched place.[164]

Overcome by loneliness, the occupant of the Villa Giulia increasingly felt he was '*un oublié, un isolé*'. In 1889 he called himself a '*villano*', a country yokel, withering away in rural solitude. He saw his horizons slowly contracting and kept up with developments in the world only through the newspapers to which he subscribed. In the summer of 1893 he wrote to Revertera: 'No sound from the outside world penetrates my seclusion. Political and social ideas have been extinguished in me.' He compared himself with the Old Testament figure Job: 'Job's fate is mine. In the land of Hus, I have nothing else to do but look in vain for someone to liberate me from the Villa.' ' It is a terrible fate to have to waste my remaining time here, surrounded by *Wiensüchtige* (Vienna-longing) women and cut off from all contact with the outside world, to be, as it were, buried alive.'[165] 'Always the same misery, with no prospect of salvation except through death. Nothing gives me pleasure, not even a game of chess.'[166]

164 Information about this is to be found above all in the correspondence with Revertera (HAH, IV, 56). See especially the letters of 24 March 1885, 9 and 28 Nov. 1887, 4 Nov. 1889, 5 Feb. 1890, 5 Dec. 1891, 12 Sept. and 1 Oct. 1892, 2 and 27 Jan., 18 Feb., 2 April, 11 July, 22 Nov., 27 Dec. 1893, 2 and 28 Feb. 1895.
165 Blome to Revertera, 28 Feb. 1895, HAH, IV, 56.
166 Blome to Revertera, 24 Dec. 1889, 18 Jan. 1892, 28 Aug. 1893, 7 Sept. 1894, 28 Feb. and 8 Dec. 1895 HAH, IV, 56.

He repeatedly referred to himself as 'the hermit of Bellagio' or the 'hermit of Lake Como'.[167]

Blome certainly had grounds for complaint. Material and family cares continued to haunt him and his isolation in Bellagio prevented him from leading an active political life. The latter must be put in perspective however. The role of the social aristocrats was virtually played out in Austrian politics; even in the social Catholic movement, clergy and popular leaders had taken control and their international orientation faded. In this new context there was little room for a figure like Blome.

If the material concerns of the hermit of Bellagio were real, especially in comparison with his earlier prosperity, nonetheless they were not such as to change his life radically. The Lake Como estate retained many of its charms. After the purchase of the villa at the end of 1872, the interior was restored and partly renovated, and large gardens were laid out. The flower garden became a particular attraction and drew large numbers of tourists on Sundays and holidays.[168] Sometimes these visitors could also use the private beach and the boats docked at the pier by Lake Como. From March to October, the children went on many trips and cruises.[169] Blome himself took little part in these and also avoided the company of tourists.[170] He spent most of his time reading and studying in his extensive library. Chess was his great passion, but he rarely found competitors who could measure up to his skill. There was a magnificent tennis court that was used a lot especially in the 1890s. A large staff maintained the domain, even when the family was abroad, with a French butler, Lemarchand, managing the personnel and the house.[171]

Visits from friends and acquaintances provided a welcome respite, and visits by Revertera were particularly welcome: not only did he bring political news from his activities as a diplomat in Rome but he was also a worthy chess partner.[172] Other friends and acquaintances from his diplomatic and 'Catholic' career also found their way to the villa. Prominent social Catholics such as Kuefstein, La Tour du Pin and Lorin stayed there repeatedly. Insofar as can be determined, Pergen strangely never visited Bellagio, all indications being that 'Jupiter' and the 'cadet' had become progressively estranged. In the late 1890s, the flow of visitors gradually tapered off.

Blome himself continued to travel a great deal. In the early 1880s he spent at least a few weeks in Vienna during the winter, usually with his family. In the

167 Blome to Revertera, 13 March 1896 and 5 March 1897, HAH, IV, 56.
168 Blome to Hans, 21 May 1888, BCUF, LA 47, 1.
169 Blome to Revertera, 12 Sept. 1892, HAH, IV, 56; Id. to his son Hans, 22 Sept. 1896, BCUF, LA 47, 1.
170 Blome to Hans, 22 Dec. 1901, BCUF, LA 47, 1: 'I like a life of routine and happily pass up the company of strangers.'
171 Blome to Revertera, 6 Sept. 1892, HAH, IV, 56.
172 Revertera visited the villa in Oct. 1893, Oct. 1894, Dec. 1896 and Dec. 1903.

spring he stayed in Venice and in the summer he stopped off in the resort of Gmunden. After 1885 these vacations became the exception, although he regularly visited a spa for health reasons, usually without his family.[173] From 1884 on he travelled every summer to Salzau, to look after his ancestral domain. He devoted the necessary attention to this, modernized the farming operation and provided decent housing and social services for its tenants.[174] Before the trip to Salzau he usually visited his domain in Montpreis. In addition, in the second half of the 1880s there were the various social congresses, which he regarded as 'true oases in the dreary desert of my existence'.[175] In the next decade the pace and duration of his trips gradually lessened, but Paris and of course Vienna were still regularly on the programme, and he also frequently stayed in London, which he came to value as *la métropole par excellence*.[176] When he stayed in those cities, he frequented elite clubs, where he sometimes came in contact with Austrian diplomats.

Around the turn of the century Blome's complaints about his family and material adversity tapered off. The economic situation had improved gradually and that apparently had a positive impact on his financial situation. On the family front he could take heart from the career and marriage of his youngest son, with whom he kept in frequent correspondence.[177] After a long search for a wealthy American heiress, Hans eventually married the Romanian princess Martha Stirbey (1877-1925), a granddaughter of Barbo Demeter Stirbey, who had been Prince of Wallachia between 1848 and 1856.[178] After a while he settled in Vienna, where he and his wife held a salon that soon acquired a good reputation. He was also included in court circles. Gustav, who had always kept his distance from that milieu, apparently got some satisfaction from it at the end of his life. Family adversity was also mitigated by the marriage of his daughters Anna and Giulia, who appeared to have happy lives.[179]

Blome now seemed reconciled to the monotony of life at the Villa Giulia. In January 1905, in the middle of winter, he wrote: 'Mama and I are throwing

173 He mostly went to the spa in Karlsbad (1885, 1888, 1889, 1890, 1892, 1893, 1896 and 1898), and a few times to Gastein (1891).
174 Biczo, 'Graf Gustav Blome', 80-85.
175 Blome to Revertera, 11 Nov. 1887, HAH, IV, 56.
176 He travelled to Paris in March 1888, Nov. 1888, May 1889, Feb. 1890, March 1893, April 1894, June 1897, July 1899, and May 1905. He travelled to London in March 1888, Feb. 1890, March 1893, April 1894, May 1896, April 1901 and March 1905, mostly for business, and later for medical reasons. London came to suit him more and more (Blome to his son Hans, 23 May 1905, BCUF, LA 47, 3).
177 He advised him in his efforts to win over a rich American heiress. 'You are poor, you do not have a legacy of any size awaiting you, and you are not in a situation of earning money through work. Therefore, you need a rich woman.' (Blome to Hans, 30 Nov. 1900, BCUF, LA 47, 1).
178 Blome to Hans, 1 June 1901, BCUF, LA 47, 1. He suggested to his son that he should be open about his less than rosy financial situation (30 June 1901, ibid.).
179 Blome to Hans, 15 June 1905, BCUF, LA 47, 3.

snowballs at each other. Great fun.' However, he sounded less excited when his wife Séphine was absent for several months and he was staying on the estate alone with his youngest daughter Carola: 'The little one and I have our rooms on two different floors, in the two outer wings of the house. We meet only at meals, when four staff serve us at the table. Such an existence lacks all charm.'[180] Old age, 'with its procession of infirmities', also began to take its toll. 'My discomforts are reducing my share of the physical well-being of humanity.'[181] In his last years he found solace for his ailments in the spa town of Wiesbaden, and this pleased him considerably. He could even indulge in chess in the *kurhaus*, and at 76 he still proved to be a formidable match for younger opponents; as he said himself, he had a big advantage over them, namely 'the renowned school of Vienna'.[182] In another spa town, Bad Kissingen, he died the following year, on 24 August 1906, at the age of 77. He was buried in the local cemetery.

Gustav von Blome, eight of whose children reached adulthood, was not blessed with many descendants. Through the male line, he had only one grandchild, Josephine, the only daughter of Hans. She would marry Count Christian Thun-Hohenstein and thus the Salzau domain would eventually come into the possession of a family with whom Gustav during his active career had maintained frequent contact. He had travelled a long way with these Bohemian feudal lords, but in cautiously taking the road to democracy, he had gone further than they had. Even his close friends Pergen and Revertera had not gone as far.

This is even more true of La Tour du Pin, who, as already noted, had gradually taken a nationalist and authoritarian direction and ended up in the slipstream of the *Action Française*. He would later become a '*maître à penser*' of the Vichy regime, which collaborated with Nazi Germany. Curiously enough, at the same time he influenced the social ideas of Charles de Gaulle. Though no longer on the same wavelength as Blome, he nevertheless wrote a heartfelt obituary for him.[183] He particularly highlighted the social achievements of the 'doyen of the social Catholics in Europe'. He called him, flatteringly, a successor to Joseph de Maistre and Louis de Bonald, with more depth than the former and a broader vision than the latter. He portrayed him as follows:

> An imposing, stately and grand figure, a paragon of masculine elegance ... He exuded strength and energy ... His gifts were so outstanding that they were almost formidable ... He spoke and wrote gracefully and perfectly all the languages a diplomat should master; his letters in French, in particular, were written in beautiful language and a compelling style

---

180 Blome to Hans, 18 Jan. and 29 Sept. 1905, BCUF, LA 47, 3.
181 Blome to Revertera, 3 Dec. 1903, HAH, IV, 56.
182 Blome to Hans, 19 and 27 Aug. 1905, BCUF, LA 47, 3.
183 La Tour du Pin, 'Le Comte de Blome', 309-312.

> ... His irresistible logic was accompanied by a brilliant eloquence ... He
> was very well-read and was an unerring guide in sociopolitical matters
> ... He never insisted on his own opinion, he was a good listener and
> he kept himself in the background like an accomplished diplomat, the
> better to observe and give discreet leadership ... He was indeed born to
> lead and was, to the highest degree, a *conducteur d'hommes.*

While the genre of the obituary certainly lent itself to exaggeration and to somewhat overplaying Blome's qualities, his personality was accurately described. Louis de Pons had already assessed it well when Blome was still a young man.

After his death, Blome was highly praised in the Austrian Catholic press. The liberal papers on their part reproached him for his role in marginalizing liberalism in Austrian society,[184] a charge he would certainly have interpreted as praise. He was not forgotten completely during the interwar years. The crisis of capitalism in the wake of the Great Depression of the 1930s revived interest in corporatism in social Catholic circles, as was clearly evident in the encyclical *Quadragesimo Anno* (1931). In that context – and especially in Austria – occasional reference was made to Blome's important contribution to developing ideas about corporatism. However, the problem was that the fascist regimes of the 1930s developed a form of state corporatism. In their system, corporations became instruments in the hands of a totalitarian State instead of a buffer against the State, as the social Catholics had envisioned. This would later have an impact on the assessment of this anti-capitalist, socioeconomic model. The publicists who paid attention to Blome's opinions and achievements, quite rightly did not associate them with the state corporatism of fascism. In fact, the most prominent among them were convinced anti-fascists, including the Austrian publicists, Alfred Missong[185] and Karl Lugmayer.[186] This was especially true of Alcide De Gasperi, who would give shape to post-war democratic Italy.[187] One of the constants in Blome's position had been his resistance to State

---

184 Biczo, 'Graf Gustav Blome', 79.
185 Alfred Missong, *Gustav Graf Blome, zu seinem 30. Todestag*, a radio address 24 Aug.1936,
     Gut Salzau, IX, 4. Alfred Missong (1902-1965) opposed the *Anschluss*, fled to Switzerland
     and Hungary and after the war was one of the co-founders and the party ideologue of the
     Christian Democratic ÖVP and a strong supporter of European integration.
186 Bader, ed., *Karl Lugmayer und sein Werk*. Karl Lugmayer (1892-1972) published several ar-
     ticles about the circle around Blome in the journal *Neue Ordnung*. He had strong ties with
     the Christian Workers' Movement, opposed the *Anschluss* and was placed under Gestapo
     supervision, though this did not prevent him from joining the political opposition. After
     the war, he contributed significantly to drawing up the programme of the ÖVP and he held
     various political mandates for that party.
187 De Gasperi, *I tempi e gli uomini*. In this study, the later Italian prime minister regularly
     mentions Blome whom he portrays with great sympathy.

omnipotence, which meant he could hardly be associated with the right-wing totalitarian systems that dominated the political scene in interwar Europe.

The road to state totalitarianism was opened up by the First World War. That war in itself could be called a logical result of international politics that had taken shape since the 1860s. It resulted in a total war between the major nation states, with the deployment of mass armies and large-scale industrial resources. The Great War led to a collapse of the bourgeois civilization of the nineteenth century, which was characterized by a strong belief in reason and science, material and moral progress, and the liberal constitutional state. All these achievements were now under threat. The war gave an impetus to extreme ideologies – Bolshevism on the left and Fascism on the right – which relied on State omnipotence to implement their social and political vision. The Leviathan was unleashed. All attempts to restrain it, by protecting individual freedoms or strengthening the social fabric, had failed. Eventually, the totalitarian regimes would be toppled, and after World War II the Leviathan would be pushed back behind the boundaries that had already been drawn in the nineteenth century.

EPILOGUE
ADENAUER IN CADENABBIA

As night fell on Tuesday, 19 April 1966, Konrad Adenauer was sitting on the eastern terrace of the Villa Collina in Cadenabbia, overlooking Lake Como.[1] It was his favourite after-dinner spot. The day before, Oskar Kokoschka, who had been painting a portrait of the former West German chancellor over the previous three weeks, had taken his leave. Both old men had made small talk, chatting mostly about politics. 'The great men had a great time together.' Kokoschka painted this 'unyielding, almost ruthless man' in varied soft colours. In the *Bundestag*, where the portrait would be hung, they had other memories of *der Alte*. The portrait, which is on loan, now adorns the office of Angela Merkel, the current German chancellor, who admires Adenauer deeply.

On April 18th the historian Golo Mann, son of Thomas Mann, had also paid a visit. Observing the aged ex-chancellor, he was struck by the similarities with the last portraits of Metternich: the porcelain delicacy of advanced age, the vague distant look. Both Kokoschka and Golo Mann were impressed by their meeting with Adenauer, who two and a half years earlier, at the age of 87, had resigned as chancellor, a position he had held for fourteen years. Adenauer then focused on writing the second volume of his memoirs with the help of his trusted secretary, Anneliese Poppinga. That volume covered the period 1952-1955, during which time his policy had finally taken shape. The writing of the first volume had gone rather slowly at first, but he gradually came to

---

1   On Konrad Adenauer (1876-1967), see Schwarz, *Konrad Adenauer*; Morsey, 'Konrad Adenauer (1876-1967)', 186-201; Williams, *Adenauer*.

enjoy the activity. He alternated work on the memoirs with long walks in the large park of the Villa Collina, discussions with guests and visitors, short trips in the familiar surroundings and playing *boccia*, a ball game to which he had become addicted years before.

Cadenabbia on Lake Como had been Adenauer's favourite holiday destination since 1957, the year he had won his greatest electoral victory.[2] Before that he used to go on holiday to Switzerland or the Black Forest, but now for health reasons he looked for a resort with a milder climate. His foreign minister, Heinrich von Brentano, whose family came from northern Italy, had drawn his attention to the peaceful village of Cadenabbia, on the western shore of Lake Como. Adenauer went along with the suggestion straight away as he had long felt drawn to Italy. In the early 1950s he had also forged close relationships with Italian Christian Democratic politicians such as Alcide De Gasperi, Fanfani and Segni. In the spring of 1957 he rented the Villa Rosa in the centre of Cadenabbia, but he later set his eyes on the quieter Villa Collina. As the name suggests, the villa was on a hillside fifty meters above the lake. It was surrounded by a big park, with valuable old cedars, pine trees, chestnut trees, cypresses and a large green beech tree. Terraced orchards of peach, lemon, apple and pear trees stretched up the slope on the side of the lake. A Mediterranean landscape unfolded on the east side of the villa, while on the west side lay an Alpine terrain with mountains, forests and meadows. The chancellor, who loved gardening, was fascinated by the atmosphere, the landscape and the vegetation of this ravishing place and would henceforth spend all his holidays there.

From the summer of 1959 the Villa Collina was the *Urlaubresidenz* and was occasionally also the *Ersatz-Kanzleramt*. Adenauer had consultations here in a casual atmosphere with his closest associates and with domestic and foreign politicians. He had in the meantime acquired the image of '*der grosse alte Mann des Westens*' and not only had a decisive say in West German politics, but also played an important role in the European integration process. Communications were frequent between the Villa Collina, the Quirinale in Rome and the Elysée Palace in Paris. In 1958, Adenauer made preparations there for his first meeting with Charles de Gaulle, who had come to power in France shortly before. Five years later, important decisions were taken in connection with the Franco-German friendship treaty, which for decades would remain the cornerstone of the European integration policy. In the summer of 1963 Adenauer stayed at the Villa Collina for the last time as chancellor. He would later return there as a private individual, accompanied by a limited staff, to concentrate on writing his memoirs.

Adenauer had every reason to look back with great satisfaction on his political career and achievements. To begin with, there was the reconciliation

2   Buchstab, *Konrad Adenauer in Cadenabbia*.

Adenauer's portrait by Kokoschka in the study of Angela Merkel. Photograph, Andreas Rentz, 2006.
[*Getty Images*]

with France, the age-old enemy of Germany. The rivalry between the two su-
perpowers, which had brought war and devastation to Europe several times in
the nineteenth and twentieth centuries, was settled remarkably quickly after
World War II, in what was an extraordinary achievement. This feat was made
possible by transcending nationalism as well as by the European integration
process, which was hastened by the Cold War. Moreover, after the collapse of
Nazi Germany, Adenaeur had managed in no time to give the German Federal
Republic an honourable place among the western democracies. In this too he
was helped by the Cold War, but his success was also due to the values and
ideas for which he stood.

Adenauer came from Cologne and became politically active in 1906, the
year in which Blome died. He was strongly influenced by the traditions of the
Zentrum, and specifically by its liberal democratic stance, its orientation to
the West and its rejection of authoritarian, militaristic Prussia. From 1917 to
1933 he held the office of mayor of Cologne. After the Nazis seized power, he
was sidelined and was interned for several months at the end of 1944. Once
the war was over he became politically active again and he set himself up as
the leader of the Christian Democratic Union (CDU), an interfaith centre-right
party that, at his instigation, entered into an alliance with the Christian-Social
Union (CSU) in Bavaria. The new party would soon acquire a strong position
in the western regions, which later made up the Federal Republic of Germany. It benefited from the moral and religious revival that took place after the
war, and even more from the discrediting of the extreme right. It also took
advantage of the Cold War, which fueled anti-communism. Led by Adenauer
the CDU/CSU gradually strengthened its electoral position from 31% in 1949 to
50.2% in 1957, thereby acquiring a dominant position in West German politics.
Adenauer aimed at integrating the Federal Republic as a full sovereign state in
a community of free democracies, and subordinated a possible reunification
of Germany to this. His policy aimed from the outset at cooperation between
the western European countries, with a Franco-German entente as its cornerstone. The social democratic SPD on the other hand, the main opponent of the
Christian Democrats, saw more merit in a neutral Germany that would form a
buffer between the two power blocs in Europe.

Adenauer's choice of a western-oriented policy was determined by his
Rhineland origins and even more by his Christian Democratic position. He
was an authoritative exponent of Christian Democracy, which in the 1950s
became the main political force on the western European continent.[3] The
Christian Democratic parties were the heirs of the confessional parties that

3   On post-war Christian Democracy, see Lamberts, ed., *Christian Democracy in the Europe-
     an Union*; Hanley, ed., *Christian Democracy in Europe*; Gehler and Kaiser, eds., *Christian
     Democracy in Europe Since 1945*; Kselman and Buttigieg, *European Christian Democracy*;
     Kaiser, *Christian Democracy and the Origins of European Union*.

had come into being at the end of the nineteenth century. In Italy also, where the *non expedit* had gradually fallen into disuse, a vigorous *Partito Popolare* emerged after 1918. Thanks to their social programme, which went back to *Rerum Novarum*, the confessional parties gradually became people's parties. In the interwar years most of these were sandwiched between liberal, conservative and extreme-right parties on the one hand and socialist and communist formations on the other. In Germany and Italy they were swept away by the fascist regimes. After the war then a totally new situation emerged. The defeat of fascism and the important contribution of the Soviet Union to the Allied victory led to a strengthening of the socialist and communist parties. The discrediting of fascism and of the conservative formations that had collaborated with it created a political vacuum on the right. The Christian Democrats were able to fill that vacuum thanks to their significant involvement in the resistance movements in several countries, which had given them the required democratic credibility. In the meantime, influenced by the events of the war, they had come to attach more importance to individual human rights. Christian Democracy succeeded in making a breakthrough even in secularized France where the *Mouvement Républicain Populaire / MRP* (Popular Republican Movement) brought about a final reconciliation between Catholics and the republic. However, after 1958 it would be overshadowed by Gaullism, which had a more nationalist and, in some respects, Bonapartist character. In the other core countries of the future European Union, Christian Democracy continued to play an important political role until the end of the century, though it had already begun to decline in the 1970s.

The Christian Democrats were of the opinion that Christian ethical principles should govern politics, both national and international. Human accountability before God erected a barrier against the deification of the State.[4] The State should primarily be at the service of the human person, respecting his/her dignity and guaranteeing his/her rights, and it should establish a just and peaceful society. On that level, the nation states had failed miserably. Their brutal power politics had led to two devastating world wars and had bled Europe dry. As a matter of urgency, a new international order had to be set up that would transcend nationalism and be based on ethical principles. To some extent, this meant a return to the politics of Metternich and the European Concert, although, in fact, the proposed cooperation between the participating states went even further and acquired democratic legitimacy. It also offered more latitude to the smaller states. For now however, it developed only in western Europe and was at times depicted, somewhat nostalgically, as a revival of the old Carolingian Empire, a concept dear to Adenauer. The new international order pursued by the Christian Democrats was obviously much closer to the thinking of Metternich than that of Bismarck.

---

4   Buchstab, 'Konrad Adenauer in: Wertgrundlagen und Politikverständnis', 279-294.

Adenauer got support for his European policy from political allies like Schuman in France and Alcide De Gasperi in Italy.[5] The latter, in particular, staunchly supported the creation of supranational institutions, not only in the economic but also in the political and military spheres. The West German chancellor himself favoured confederal solutions, which could be worked out in a flexible and pragmatic way. Still, he supported the plans of Monnet and Schuman for the creation of the European Coal and Steel Community (ECSC), with supranational authority. Later he allowed himself be persuaded by De Gasperi into attempting to set up a European Defence Community and even a European Political Community, but this failed. He then put his weight behind the Spaak Committee's proposals, which would lead to the Treaties of Rome and the establishment of the European Economic Community (EEC). Thus, European integration was finally launched. When Charles de Gaulle came to power in 1958, it seemed that the clock would be turned back, but on his first visit Adenauer – to his relief – was already able to see that the new French president was prepared, under certain conditions, to strengthen the EEC and continue its cooperation with the Federal Republic. From the spring of 1962 especially, the two statesmen coordinated their respective European policies. This would lead a year later to the Franco-German friendship treaty, which was the culmination of the chancellor's *Westpolitik*.

In countries where Christian Democrats were able to leave their mark on policy – particularly in West Germany, Italy, the Benelux countries and to a lesser extent France – they developed a community structure that was clearly different from the more liberal US model. With their personalist vision based on neo-Thomism, they laid great emphasis on the development of human persons in their natural social bonds, such as the family, trade associations and local communities. In general they assigned an important role to an organized civil society and attributed only a supplementary role to the State. In this they differed from the Social Democrats, who also supported an extensive network of organizations but were inclined to rely more on the state apparatus in order to achieve their objectives. The Christian Democrats opted instead for 'neo-corporative' formulas. They delegated important socioeconomic competences to organized interest groups and involved them in political decision-making. To encourage greater social harmony, they set up a consultation system with 'trilateral negotiations' between employers, workers and government. Overall, they attempted to connect the free market with social justice, which had to be brought about through a harmonious interplay between the State and social organizations. This form of 'social capitalism' would later become known

5   Chenaux, *Une Europe Vaticane?*; Gehler and Kaiser, 'Transnationalism and Early European Integration', 773-798; Cau, *L'Europa di De Gasperi e Adenauer*; Di Maio, *Alcide De Gasperi und Konrad Adenauer*.

as the 'Rhineland Model'.[6] In so far as was possible, the Christian Democrats tried to apply their social and political ideas on the European level also.

The principle of subsidiarity, which would become a key concept in the European Union, comes up at this juncture.[7] It calls for building up power from below in a diverse society that consists of several spheres and levels of authority. As a general principle, political and social functions are to be carried out on the lowest level possible. The higher authorities must respect the scope and autonomy of lower administrative bodies and social structures. They must especially encourage the lower levels to take initiatives, provide them with the necessary assistance and resources, and coordinate their actions. Only when a lower body proves inadequate does the higher authority have the right and even the duty to intervene; in that case, it does not replace the subordinate level but merely supplements it. The subsidiarity principle can be invoked for opposite ends: in a negative way to limit the powers of a higher authority or in a positive way to reinforce them. Additionally, it may be given both a territorial and a social application. Its concern is not with the form of government, but with the role of the political authorities and the distribution of their competences in conjunction with the social actors. In this way it functions mainly as a general norm, without prescribing concrete solutions. It connects, in fact, in many ways with the central issues of this book.

In those states where they could influence policy the Christian Democrats put the principle of subsidiarity into practice with both a social and geographical application. They also did much to introduce it into the European institutions; ultimately, following a long process, it was enshrined in the treaties of Maastricht (1991), Amsterdam (1997) and Lisbon (2007). On the European level it was in fact interpreted mostly in a negative way in order to limit the power of the Union, and priority was given to its being applied geographically in order to protect the lower administrative levels. Nevertheless, the social Catholic understanding of the principle was not completely lost. European policy certainly takes account of intermediary structures and civil organizations, as is reflected in its systematic dialogue with organized interest groups and its structural relationship with the main components of civil society. The social order that came about in post-war Europe differed fundamentally then from the nineteenth-century liberal model, which had advocated a centralized unitary state that was legitimized and supported by individual citizens and did not have any structural links with civil society.

After the Second World War the place of the churches in organized society was also acknowledged. Thanks to its tight hierarchical structure and the support of its faithful, the Catholic Church, which has received considerable

6   Lamberts, ed., *Christian Democracy*, 293-374; van Kersbergen, *Social Capitalism*.
7   Endo, 'The Principle of Subsidiarity', 553-652; Millon-Delsol, *L'état subsidiaire*; Id., *Le principe de subsidiarité*; Waschkuhn, *Was ist Subsidiarität?*; Foellesdal, 'Subsidiarity', 231-259; Lamberts, 'Historical Reflections on the Principle of Subsidiarity', 27-34.

attention in this book, succeeded in maintaining a great deal of autonomy, in spite of the *Kulturkampf*. In the interwar period, however, it was beleaguered both in Germany and Italy by totalitarianism and its sociopolitical organizations were discontinued, but it managed to retain its value system, its religious structures and a large field of operations. Moreover, it should be noted that the international status of the Holy See was regulated at this time. The Roman question was resolved by the Lateran Treaty of 11 February 1929, in which the Papacy finally acknowledged the Kingdom of Italy with Rome as its capital. In return, the Vatican was recognized as a sovereign State, thereby guaranteeing the independence of the pope as head of the universal Church, which the defenders of his temporal power had always envisioned. For the Holy See, the Lateran Treaty offered a better arrangement than the 1871 Law of Guarantees, but the fact that the agreement was worked out with Mussolini's fascist government cast a lasting shadow over it.[8] However, the settlement made clear that even totalitarian regimes could not ignore the strongly organized Catholic Church and were obliged to take it into consideration.

The postwar climate of freedom benefitted all the churches in western Europe. Their rights and freedoms were guaranteed by new constitutions in Italy, West Germany and France, thanks mainly to the Christian Democrats. Religious and sociocultural associations could henceforth develop freely. Christian education and the charitable sector also received the opportunities they needed for development. All this now allowed the Christian Democratic parties to profile themselves less as religious parties primarily defending the Church's interests. Within the Catholic Church itself, a revival of liberal Catholic ideas led to an acceptance of religious pluralism and a greater respect for the autonomy of the political order. Nevertheless, the Christian Democratic parties would still call on a Christian worldview, and they continued to defend Christian values in society.[9] This was also true of Adenauer, who did not explicitly profile himself as a devout Catholic, but whose religious beliefs nevertheless acted as a compass for his political activities.[10]

When *der Alte* in the evening of his life, sitting on the eastern terrace of the Villa Collina in Cadenabbia, recalled his political career and his achievements, his eyes would have wandered naturally over Lake Como, and the view of the magnificent tourist resort of Bellagio. On the right side of the panorama unfolding before him was the Villa Melzi, with its imposing neoclassical architecture and its world famous English garden. To the right of the villa was a jetty, the terminus of the *Vialone di Villa Giulia,* which cut through the middle of the peninsula and led to the villa on the *Ramo di Lecco* where Blome had spent

8   Mayeur et al., eds., *Histoire du Christianisme*, vol. 12, *Guerres mondiales et totalitarismes (1914-1958)*, 11-346; Chiron, *Pie XI (1857-1939)*, 217-240.
9   Lamberts, ed., *Christian Democracy,* 375-446.
10   Buchstab, *Konrad Adenauer. Wertgrundlagen*, 284; Hehl, ed., *Adenauer und die Kirchen*; Arnolds, 'Konrad Adenauers Programma', 225-226.

Adenauer looks at Lake Como from Villa Collina.
[*Berlin, Bildarchiv Preussischer Kultarbeitz /© bpk, Ulmar Pabel*]

the last thirty years of his life. Adenauer probably never realized that from his holiday perch he had a view of a branch of the estate of a German-Austrian statesman who had helped lay the basis of the policy that he himself had shaped. In fact, he probably did not know anything about Blome. The memory of the Austrian diplomat had indeed gradually faded away; he was completely forgotten in Bellagio, as the Villa Giulia had been sold shortly after his death and had gone through several owners after that. Adenauer probably saw the *Vialone* as merely leading to a distant horizon and it did not call up any historical memories for him.

Moreover, the West German ex-chancellor did not resemble Blome either in personality or profile. Adenauer was first and foremost a bold, sometimes even ruthless politician, who very skillfully made use of the instruments of parliamentary democracy. He was more of a tactician, with a moderate interest in theoretical and ideological issues. Blome, on the other hand, with his aristocratic background, had little affinity with modern mass politics. He could barely muster appreciation for electoral and parliamentary strategies, valuing instead ideology and long-term planning. His religious fervour, which was significantly influenced by sociopolitical considerations, was more intense than that of Adenauer.

The differences between the two were obvious, but the aims and achievements of the German chancellor were, in a number of respects, in line with Blome's aspirations and efforts. In his pamphlet *Wo ist Europe's Zukunft* (1871) he had formulated the dream of a European society in which ethical principles would determine both international and domestic politics, state power would be curtailed, the church's freedom of action be guaranteed, and protective social ties would be given the necessary opportunities for development.

European integration was also continuous with the ideas of Blome, the *bel tipo d'europeo*. That integration was made possible by Franco-German cooperation, which both in its social contacts and in its public activities had become a fixture. Blome would certainly have been very pleased that the power politics of nation states had been replaced by an international policy that, inspired by ethical principles, strove for a supranational order, focused on peace and security.

Blome would also have noted with satisfaction that the Leviathan was curtailed, not only within the international order but even so within states. From now on the State was to serve the welfare of its citizens. The legal status of the churches was secured. A network of intermediary structures offering support to citizens provided a further buffer against state power. The State and social organizations complemented each other in an atmosphere of understanding. That situation was due in part to the concept that Blome had envisioned. Unlike Bismarck, who had forged an alliance between conservatism and nationalism, he had opted for a merger between conservatism and Christian popular movements, which later culminated in Christian Democracy. Trends, which were defended by the Prussian ultra-conservatives, the Austrian romantic-conservatives and at a later stage by the social aristocrats, were reinforced by the struggle of the Catholic Church for a state-free area. Thanks in part to Blome and his allies, at the end of the nineteenth century, Catholics developed a coherent social teaching that opted resolutely for a 'social' containment of state power.

However, the Leviathan was not curtailed in postwar Europe solely by the social fabric or by organized civil society. The opposing liberal strategy also played a significant role. Though liberalism in Europe in the interbellum period was overrun as a political movement by anti-liberal mass movements, its ideas were not lost. After World War II, in reaction to both communist and fascist totalitarianism, the liberal, constitutional state underwent a revival. The widespread influence of the United States in western Europe also contributed to this. Liberal constitutional principles were now widely shared by other democratic movements. The State was expected more than ever to steadfastly safeguard the inalienable rights and freedoms of its subjects. Liberal and social strategies to curb the power of the State became intertwined. As had always been advocated by liberals, state power in post-war society was limited not only by the social fabric but also by the legal status of individual citizens. Blome had been less amenable to this argument, but Adenauer was different. He saw himself in the liberal Catholic tradition of the *Zentrum* and was more open to liberal democratic ideas. He connected those ideas with the legacy of social Catholicism and so united in his policies both the 'liberal' and 'social' efforts to limit state power.[11] It was a synthesis that typified the post-war European social model. At the end of the twentieth century it would come under ever more pressure from growing individualism, neoliberal tendencies in the economy – emanating especially from the Anglo-Saxon world – and increasing secularization in the spheres of philosophy and religion.

11   Arnolds, 'Konrad Adenauers Programm', 219-226 and 248-256.

BIBLIOGRAPHY

ABBREVIATIONS

AAM	Mechlin, Archiepiscopal archives
ACR	Rome, Archivio della Congregazione della Resurrezione
ADB	Marke-Kortrijk, Archives de Béthune
ADH	Afsnee, Archives de Hemptinne
ADV	Boussu-en-Fagne, Archives de Villermont
AEF	Fribourg, Archives de l'Etat
AEM	Mons, Archives de l'Etat
ALV	Ghent, Archives Lammens-Verhaegen
AMBUZ	Brussels, Archives of the Ministry of Foreign Affairs
ANB	Rome, ASV, Archivio della Nunziatura di Bruxelles
ARSJ	Rome, Archivum Romanum Societatis Jesu
ASMSCI	Milan, Archivio per la storia del movimento sociale cattolico in Italia
ASPV, OC	Venice, Archivio del Seminario Patriarcale, Archivio 'Opera dei Congressi'
ASV	Archivio Segreto del Vaticano
BAG	Ghent, Diocesan Archives
BCUF	Fribourg, Bibliothèque cantonnale et universitaire
BNF, NAF	Paris, Bibliothèque nationale de France, Division des manuscrits occidentaux, Nouvelles acquisitions françaises
CARAN	Paris, Archives nationales
HAH	Helfenberg, Herrschaftsarchiv
HHSA	Vienna, Haus- Hof- und Staatsarchiv
LASH	Schleswig. Schleswig-Holsteines Landesarchiv
NAP	Prague, Nationalarchiv
NKDC	Nijmegen, Katholiek Documentatiecentrum
SALD	Litomerice-Decin, Staatsarchiv
SAE	Einsiedeln, Stiftsarchiv
SS	Rome, ASV, Segreteria di Stato
SAWT-R	Wertheim, Staatsarchiv - Abteilung Rosenberg
UCSCM	Milan, Università cattolica del Sacro Cuore

ARCHIVES

Austria

HELFENBERG, *Archiv Schloss Helfenberg* (HAH)
Familienakten des Grafen Revertera
  IV: Nachlass des Grafen Friedrich Revertera: Schachtel 47-58

VIENNA, *Haus- Hof- und Staatsarchiv* (HHSA)
Nachlass Johann Anton Pergen: busta I: A-K, busta II: L-Z

Belgium

AFSNEE, *Archives de Hemptinne* (ADH)
Correspondence 1870-1889, GCP, *La Croix*, Dom Hildebrand

BOUSSU-EN-FAGNE, *Archives de Villermont* (ADV)
Correspondence with Hemptinne (II, A, 26) and Blome (II,G,2)

BRUSSELS, *Archives of the Ministry of Foreign Affairs* (AMBUZ)
Correspondance politique, Légations, St-Siège, vols. 14-15

GHENT, *Diocesan Archives* (BAG)
Records of Henri-François Bracq

GHENT, *Archief Lammens-Verhaegen* (ALV)
Records of Jules Lammens

MARKE-KORTRIJK, *Archief de Béthune* (ADB)
Records of Jean-Baptiste Béthune

MECHELEN, *Archiepiscopal Archives* (AAM)
Records of Victor Dechamps

MONS, *Archives de l'Etat* (AEM)
Records of Charles Périn: correspondence with Czacki (103), Hemptinne (180) and Mercurelli (244)

Czech Republic

LITOMERICE-DECIN, *Staatsarchiv* (SALD)
Nachlass Leo Thun-Hohenstein (A 3 – XXI)
Nachlass Friedrich Thun-Hohenstein (A 3 – XIX, especially H 65, 82 and 85)

PRAGUE, *Nationalarchiv* (NAP)
Familienarchiv Metternich, Acta Richardiana: nr. 160 (Blome)

France

PARIS, *Archives nationales* (CARAN)
Fonds du Séminaire de Saint-Sulpice: AB XIX, 510-529
Fonds Dupanloup: AB XIX, 522-529
    524b: Politique intérieure [4], politique extérieure [5], Etats Pontificaux [6], Conciles et Congrès [7]
    524 c: Presse: *Univers, Correspondance de Rome* (1856-1876) [8]
    525: Correspondance reçue par Mgr Dupanloup [et alia]
Fonds Albert de Mun: AP, 378, liasses IX-XI, dossiers 25-30

PARIS, *Bibliothèque nationale de France, division des Manuscrits Occidentaux, Nouvelles acquisitions françaises* (BNF, NAF)
Fonds Henri Lorin: 16818 (1893-1902) and 16819 (1903-1914)
Fonds Georges Goyau: 27186-27230, especially *Cahiers* (27217- 27219) and *Journal* (27218)
Fonds Louis Veuillot: 24634
Fonds Dupanloup:
    24680: correspondence with Czacki
    24698: correspondence with Mermillod
    24711- 24715: records of Dupanloup

Germany

REGENSBURG, *Diozesänarchiv*
Nachlass Bischof Senestrey (1858-1906)

SALZAU, *Archiv Gut Salzau*
Nachlass Gustav von Blome (1829-1906)

I. *Souvenirs de ma carrière politique* (1829- 7 Nov. 1860), 241 p.
II. *Souvenirs de ma carrière politique* (1861- Oct. 1868), 267 p. Annex: *Mémoire sur les phases administratives de l'Autriche de 1848 à 1870*
III. *Curieux épisode de ma vie* (1862)
IV. *Nicolas I et la Russie après ses trente années de Règne* (1855)
V. *Journal* (14 Nov. 1867- 19 Sept. 1870)
IX. Diplomatic records and drafts of articles
5. *Récit de ma conversion au catholicisme*
X. *Histoire contemporaine*
XI. Press cuttings
XII. Speeches and addresses

SCHLESWIG, *Schleswig-Holsteines Landesarchiv* (LASH)
Nachlass Gustav von Blome (SLA, Abt. 126.15)
    Nrs 613 - 616: Briefwechsel zwischen Comte de Pons und Graf Gustav von Blome
    Nr 617: Briefwechsel zwischen Fürstin Catherine Bagration, geb. Gräfin Skavronska, und ihrem Enkelsohn Graf Gustav v. Blome (1852-1857)
    Nr 620: Ernennungen und dienstliche Schreiben an Graf Gustav v. Blome der in österreichischen Diensten steht (1852-1882)
    Nr 622: Niederschrift von Graf Gustav v. Blome 'Historique des négocations qui aboutirent à la Convention de Gastein. Ma campagne diplomatique de l'été 1865' mit Nachträgen, Telegramm-wechsel während der Verhandlungen und Abschriften von verschiedenen Erlassen, Depeschen und Briefe (1865)
    Nr 624: Briefe an Freiherrn Carl von Vogelsang (1879-1890)
    Nr 631- 642: Briefe von Graf Hans von Blome an seine Eltern, vor allem an seinen Vater

WERTHEIM, *Staatsarchiv, Abteilung Rosenberg* (SAWT-R)
Nachlass Fürst Karl Heinrich zu Löwenstein-Wertheim-Rosenberg: Lit. D 675, I en 675, II

Italy

MILAN, *Università cattolica del Sacro Cuore, Archivio per la storia del movimento sociale cattolico in Italia* (UCSCM, ASMSCI)
Cartelle Luigi Manna Roncadelli: *Cart. I, fasc. 7, 9, 13 en 16*

ROME, *Archivio della Civiltà Cattolica*
Cartelle Carlo Maria Curci S.J.

ROME, *Archivio della Congregazione della Resurrezione* (ACR)
Carteggio Czacki - Semenenko

ROME, *Archivio Odescalchi*
Condoglianzi Czacki (XXXVII, C, 2)

ROME, *Archivum Romanum Societatis Jesu* (AR SJ)
Nuova Compagnia (1814-). Externi saeculares (1858-1879); Provincia Lugdunensis: Epistolae (1005-1007), Registri (t.V); Provincia Belgica. Epistolae, 1004 (1872-1883); Registri Cardinales et Praelati. I (1857-1876); Registri Curia Romana a die 14 Mart 1855 ad diem 20 Oct. 1880

VENETIE, *Archivio del Seminario Patriarcale* (ASPV, OC)
Archivio Opera dei Congressi

Switzerland

EINSIEDELN, *Stiftsarchiv* (SAE)
Diarium R.P. Adelrici Diezinger, archivarii monasterii Einsidlensis, 1871, pp. 140-151
Klostergeschichte III: Abbot Konrad Tanner bis Abbot Thomas Bossart

FRIBOURG, *Archives de l'Etat* (AEF)
Archives de la famille Schorderet

FRIBOURG, *Bibliothèque cantonnale et universitaire* (BCUF)
Correspondance entre Jean et Gustav von Blome: LA 47 (1-6)
Documentation concernant l'Union de Fribourg (H 3562, 4)

The Netherlands

NIJMEGEN, *Katholiek Documentatiecentrum* (NKDC)
Records of Jan Willem Cramer
   434-437: foreign correspondence (especially 12 a: Breda, 12 b: Blome, 12 c: Pergen, 13 k: Hemptinne)
   440: copies of letters sent by Cramer (1878-1883)
   455-456: *Correspondance de Genève*
   Volumes with copied letters, 1869-1877 (nr. 24) and a catalogue of letters (nr. 25 a)

Vatican City

Archivio Segreto del Vaticano (ASV, SS, ANB)
Segreteria di Stato
   rubr. 256: Bruxelles nunzio
   rubr. 270: Paesi Bassi e Belgio, ministro
Segreteria di Stato, Fondo Spogli: Bilio, Franchi, Czacki, Rampolla
Segreteria dei Brevi ai Principi, Posit. et Minut.

Archivio Particolare Pio IX

LITERATURE

Allmayer Beck, J. *Vogelsang. Vom Feudalismus zur Volksbewegung.* Vienna, 1952.
Altermatt, U. 'L'engagement des intellectuels catholiques suisses au sein de l'Internationale noire' in: E. Lamberts, ed. *The Black International.* Leuven, 2002, 409-426.
Ameil, G., Nathan, I. and Soutou, H., eds. *Le congrès de Paris (1856). Un événement fondateur.* Brussels-Bern, 2009.
Amicabile, A. *La Commune de Paris.* Paris, 2009.
Antonazzi, G. *L'Enciclica 'Rerum Novarum': testo autentico dai documenti originali e relatzioni preparatorie.* Rome, 1957.
Arnolds, W. 'Konrad Adenauers Programm und die CDU. Eine Skizze'. *Analecta Coloniensia*, 5 (2005), 217-278.
Atkin, N. and Tallett, F. *Priests, Prelates and People. A History of European Catholicism since 1750.* Oxford, 2003.
Aubert, R. 'L'intervention de Montalembert au congrès de Malines en 1863'. *Collectanea Mecliniensia*, 35 (1950), 525-551.
Aubert, R. 'Aspects divers du néo-thomisme sous le pontificat de Léon XIII' in: *Aspetti della cultura cattolica nell'eta di Leone XIII.* Rome, 1961, 133-248.
Aubert, R. *Le Pontificat de Pie IX (1846-1878).* Paris, 1963³.
Aubert, R. *Vatican I.* Paris, 1964.
Aubert, R., ed. *Correspondance entre Charles de Montalembert et Adolphe Dechamps, 1838-1870.* Leuven, 1993.

Bacht, H. 'Ein verschollenes Tagebuch zum Ersten Vaticanum. Eine Suchanzeige'. *Theologie und Philosophie. Vierteljahrsschrift*, 48 (1973), 371-397.
Bader, E. *Karl von Vogelsang. Die geistige Grundlegung der christlichen Sozialreform.* Vienna, 1990.

Bader, E. 'Christliche Sozialreform im Sinne von Karl von Vogelsang' in: R. Lill and U. Zellenberg, eds. *Konservatismus in Österreich. Graz, 1999, 153-162.*

Bader, E., ed. *Karl Lugmayer und sein Werk. Seine politisch-soziale Bedeutung und Aktualität.* Berlin, 2007.

Banauch, M. *Prinz Aloys von und zu Liechtenstein.* Vienna, 1997.

Bank, J. 'De Duitse herkomst van een katholieke elite in Amsterdam' in: L. Lucassen, ed. *Amsterdammer worden. Migranten, hun organisaties en inburgering, 1600-2000.* Amsterdam, 2004, 111-126.

Becker, W. 'Der Kulturkampf als ëuropäisches und Deutsches Phänomen'. *Historisches Jahrbuch,* 101 (1981), 422-446.

Becker, W., ed. *Die Minderheit als Mitte. Die Deutsche Zentrumspartei in der Innenpolitik des Reiches 1871-1933.* Paderborn, 1986.

Becker, W. 'Il ruolo di Bismarck nell' esplosione, nell' inasprimento e nella composizione del Kulturkampf prussiano' in: R. Lill, ed. *Il Kulturkampf in Italia e nei paesi di lingua tedesca.* Bologna, 1992, 69-108.

Becker, W. 'Die Enzyklika "Rerum Novarum" und die Sozialpolitik des deutschen Katholizismus' in: *'Rerum Novarum'. Ecriture, contenu et réception d'une encyclique.* Rome, 1997, 389-409.

Becker, W. 'Eine katholische Adels-Internationale. Die deutschen Teilnehmer an der Genfer Komitee (1870-1876)' in: E. Lamberts, ed. *The Black International.* Leuven, 2002, 273-298.

Bedouelle, G. 'De l'influence réelle de l'Union de Fribourg sur l'encyclique "Rerum novarum"' in: *'Rerum Novarum'. Ecriture, contenu et réception d'une encyclique.* Rome, 1997, 241-254.

Beekelaer, G.A.M. *Rond grondwetsherziening en herstel der hiërarchie. De Hollandse katholieke jongeren (1847-1852).* Hilversum, 1964.

Benedikt, H., ed. *Geschichte der Republik Österreichs.* Vienna, 1954.

Bergeron, L., Furet, F. and Koselleck, R. *Das Zeitalter der europaischen Revolution, 1789-1848.* Hamburg, 1969.

Berglar, B. *Metternich: Kutscher Europas, Artz der Revolutionen.* Göttingen, 1973.

Bertier de Sauvigny, G. de. *Metternich.* Paris, 1986.

Biczo, A. 'Graf Gustav Blome, ein österreichischer Sozialreformer'. *Jahrbuch der Vereinigung Katholischer Edelleute in Österreich,* 1930, 75-79.

Bismarck, Otto von. *Gedanken und Erinnerungen.* Vol. II. Stuttgart, 1898.

Blackbourn, D. 'Progress and Piety: Liberalism, Catholicism and the State in Imperial Germany'. *History Workshop Journal,* 26 (1988), 56-78.

Blackbourn, D. *The Long Nineteenth Century (The Fontana History of Germany).* London, 1997.

Blaschke, O. *Katholizismus und Antisemitismus im deutschen Kaiserreich.* Göttingen, 1997.

Bled, J.P. *Les fondements du conservatisme autrichien, 1859-1879.* Paris, 1988.

Bled, J.P. 'Les correspondants français du comte Pergen'. *Les Etudes Danubiennes,* 5 (1989), 1-8.

Bled, J.P. *Le Lys en exil.* Paris, 1992.

Blome, Gustav von. 'Zeitgemässe Betrachtungen. Vortrag, gehalten im Wiener gesellingen Vereine (Ressource)'. *Katholische Stimmen aus Österreich,* 1 (1868), 1-25.

Blome, Gustav von. *Wo ist Europa's Zukunft?* Freiburg im Breisgau, 1871.

Borutta, M. 'Enemies at the gate: the Moabit Klostersturm and the *Kulturkampf:* Germany' in: C. Clark and W. Kaiser, eds. *Culture Wars.* Cambridge, 2003, 227-254.

Borutta, M. *Antikatholizismus. Deutschland und Italien im Zeitalter der europäischen Kulturkämpfe.* Göttingen, 2010.

Bossard-Borner, H. 'Village Quarrels and National Controversies: Switzerland' in: C. Clark and W. Kaiser, eds. *Culture Wars.* Cambridge, 2003, 255-284.

Botos, M. 'La postérité de l'Union de Fribourg dans la mémoire catholique'. *Schweizerische Zeitschrift für Religions- und Kulturgeschichte,* 100 (2006), 305-314.

Boutry, Ph. 'L'Eglise et la civilisation moderne de Pie IX à Pie X' in: *Le deuxième Concile du Vatican (1959-1965). Actes du Colloque de l'Ecole française de Rome (Rome, 28-30 May 1986).* Rome, 1989, 47-63.

Boutry, Ph., ed. *'Rerum Novarum'. Ecriture, contenu et réception d'une encyclique.* Rome, 1997.

Boyer, W. *Political Radicalism in Late Imperial Vienna. Origins of the Christian Social Movement, 1848-1897.* Chicago, 1981.

Brants, V. *Charles Périn. Notice sur sa vie et ses travaux.* Leuven, 1906.

Brejon de Lavergnée, M., ed. 'Le Play et le monde catholique'. *Les Etudes sociales,* 149-150 (2009), 3-250.

Bridge, R. and Bullen, R. *The Great Powers and the European States System, 1814-1914.* London, 20052.

Brose, E.D. *German History, 1789-1871. From Holy Empire to Bismarckean Reich.* Providence, 1997.

Brown, M.L. 'Catholic-Legitimist Militancy in the Early Years of the Third French Republic'. *Catholic Historical Review*, 60 (1974), 233-254.

Brown, M.L. *Louis Veuillot, French Ultramontane Catholic Journalist and Layman*. Durham (NC), 1977.

Buchstab, G. *Konrad Adenauer in Cadenabbia*. Düsseldorf, 2001.

Buchstab, G. 'Konrad Adenauer. Wertgrundlagen und Politikverständnis' in: E. Gieseking et al., eds. *Zum Ideologieproblem in der Geschichte. Herbert Hömig zum 65. Geburtstag*. Lauf an der Penitz, 2006, 279-294.

Burckhardt, C.J. *Briefe des Staatskanzlers Fürsten Metternich-Winneburg an Buol-Schauenstein (1852-1859)*. Munich-Berlin, 1934.

Burnichon, J. *La compagnie de Jésus en France. Histoire d'un siècle (1814-1914)*. 4 vols. Paris, 1914-1922.

Callahan, W.J. *Church, Politics and Society in Spain (1750-1874)*. Cambridge (Mass), 1984.

Canavero, A. 'Mobilisation du mouvement catholique en Italie dans les années 1870' in: E. Lamberts, ed. *The Black International*. Leuven, 2002, 345-360.

Canavero, A. *Alcide De Gasperi. Cristiano, democratico, Europeo*. Soveria Mannelli, 2003.

Caracciolo, A. *Roma capitale. Dal Risorgimento alla crisi delle Stato liberale*. Rome, 1999.

Carle, P.L. 'Un projet de décret sur la misère ouvrière à Vatican I, précurseur de *Rerum Novarum*. *Pio IX*, 22 (1993), 181-184.

Casella, M. *Cattolici a Roma dopo l'Unità d'Italia (1869-1900)*, Battipaglia, 2011.

Cattaneo, B. *Montalembert. Un catholique en politique*. Chambray-les-Tours, 1990.

Cau, M., ed. *L'Europa di De Gasperi e Adenauer. La sfida della ricostruzione (1945-1951)*. Bologna, 2011.

Chadwick, O. *A History of the Popes*. Oxford, 1998.

Chenaux, Ph. *Une Europe Vaticane? Entre le plan Marshall et les traités de Rome*. Brussels, 1990.

Chenaux, Ph. 'Les origines de l'Union de Fribourg' in: '*Rerum Novarum*'. *Ecriture, contenu et réception d'une encyclique*. Rome, 1997, 255-266.

Chenaux, Ph. *L'Eglise catholique et le communisme (1917-1989), de Lénine à Jean-Paul II*. Paris, 2009.

Christophe, P. *Le Concile Vatican I*. Paris, 2000.

Christophe, P. and Minnerath, R. *Le Syllabus de Pie IX*. Paris, 2000.

Ciampani, A. 'The Roman Curia. Alignments among the Cardinals in the Vatican after the Unification of Italy' in: E. Lamberts, ed. *The Black International*. Leuven, 2002, 195-230.

Ciampani, A. 'Da Pio IX a Leone XIII: il dibattito nella Curia Romana dopo l'unità d'Italia' in: A. Ciampani and C. M. Fiorentino, eds. *La moralità dello storico. Indagine storica e libertà di ricerca. Saggi in onore di Fausto Fonzi*. Rome, 2004, 55-90.

Ciampani, A. 'Un cardinale Barnabita nel governo della Chiesa Cattolica durante I primi tempi del Regno d'Italia: Luigi Bilio'. *Barnabiti Studi. Rivista di ricerche storiche dei Chierici Regolari di S. Paolo (Barnabiti)*, 28 (2011), 333-374.

Ciampani, A. 'Il dibattito sulle origini di un partito cattolico in Italia e l'Unione Romana per le elezioni amministrative'. *Archivio della Società romana di storia patria*, 134 (2011), 81-126.

Clark, C. and Kaiser W., eds. *Culture Wars. Secular-Catholic Conflict in Nineteenth-Century Europe*. Cambridge, 2003.

Cole, L. 'The Counter-Reformation's last stand: Austria' in: C. Clark and W. Kaiser, eds. *Culture Wars*. Cambridge, 2003, 285-312.

Coltrinari, M. and Trogu, A. 'Atanasio de Charette, ultimo crociato di Pio IX'. *Pio IX*, 24 (1995), 72-92.

Comte, Ch. *Le cardinal Mermillod d'après sa correspondance*. Paris-Geneva, 1924.

Coppa, F.J. *Cardinal Giacomo Antonelli and Papal Politics in European Affairs*. Albany, 1990.

Corsini, U. and Repgen, K., eds. *Konrad Adenauer e Alcide De Gasperi. Due esperienze di rifondazione della democrazia*. Bologna, 1984.

Corti, E.C. *Metternich und die Frauen*. 2 vols. Vienna, 1947-1949.

Craig, G.A. *The Battle of Königgrätz*. Philadelphia, 1964.

Crispolti, F. *Corone e Porpore. Ricordi personali*. Milan, 1937.

Dau, M., ed. *Il codice di Camaldoni*, Rome, 2015.

Davis, J.A. *Italy in the Nineteenth Century*. Oxford, 2000.

de Changy, Hugues. *Le mouvement légitimiste sous la Monarchie de Juillet (1833-1848)*. Rennes, 2004.

de Coninck, P. *Een les uit Pruisen. Nederland en de Kulturkampf, 1870-1878*. Hilversum, 2005.

Defives de Saint-Martin. *Pro Petri Sede*. 3 vols. Mechlin, 1899-1912.

Defourny, M. *Les congrès catholiques en Belgique*. Leuven, 1908.

De Gasperi, Alcide. *I tempi e gli uomini che prepararono Rerum Novarum*. Milan, 1945³ [First edition published under the pseudonym M. Zanatta, Milan, 1931].

De Maeyer, J. *Arthur Verhaegen (1847-1917). De rode baron*. Leuven, 1994.

De Maeyer, J. 'La Belgique. Un élève modèle de l'école ultramontaine' in: E. Lamberts, ed. *The Black International*. Leuven, 2002, 361-386.

De Maeyer, J. 'Katholische Soziallehre und Christliche Arbeiterorganisationen in Belgien von der Freiburger Union (1884-1888) zur Union von Mechelen (1921-1960)' in: C. Hiepel and M. Ruff, eds. *Christliche Arbeiterbewegung in Europa, 1850-1950*. Stuttgart, 2003, 99-119.

De Maeyer, J. and Van Molle, L., eds. *Joris Helleputte, architect en politicus (1852-1925)*. 2 vols. Leuven, 1998.

Deneckere, G. *Leopold I, de eerste koning van Europa*. Antwerp, 2011.

De Rosa, G. *Storia del movimento cattolico in Italia*. Vol. I: *Dalla Restaurazione all'Eta Giolittiana*. Bari, 1966.

Derré, J.R. *Lamennais, ses amis et le mouvement des idées à l'époque romantique (1824-1834)*. Paris, 1962.

Derré, J.R. *Metternich et Lamennais*. Paris, 1964.

De Ruggiero, G. *The History of European Liberalism*, London, 1981.

De Sédouy, J.A. *Le Congrès de Vienne*. Paris, 2003.

Desmond, S. *Metternich, der erste Europäer*. Zürich, 1933.

De Valk, J.P. 'A Struggle behind the Scenes' in: E. Lamberts, ed. *The Black International*. Leuven, 2002, 387-408.

de Villepin, D. *Le soleil noir de la puissance (1796-1807)*. Paris, 2007.

di Maio, T. *Alcide De Gasperi und Konrad Adenauer. Zwischen Überwindung der Vergangenheit und europäischem Integrationsprozess (1945-1954)*. Frankfurt am Main, 2014.

Dorr, D. *Option for the Poor. A Hundred Years of Vatican Social Teaching*. Dublin-New York,19922.

Dufresne, Cl. *Morny: le roi du Second Empire*. Paris, 1993.

Dumons, B. 'Jésuites lyonnais et le catholicisme intransigeant' in: E. Fouilloux and B. Hours, eds. *Les jésuites à Lyon, XVIe-XXe siècle*. Lyon, 2005, 131-143.

Dumons, B. and Multon B., eds. *"Blancs" et contre-révolutionnaires. Espaces*, réseaux, *cultures et mémoires (fin XVIIIe-début XXe siècles): France, Italie, Espagne, Portugal*. Rome, 2011.

Dumont, J.N., ed. *Montalembert et ses contemporains*. Paris, 2012.

Durand, J.D. 'Christliche Demokratie und europäische Integration'. *Historisch-politische Mitteilungen*, 1 (1994), 155-182.

Durand, J.D. *L'Europe de la démocratie chrétienne*. Brussels, 1995.

Durand, J.D., ed. *Les Semaines sociales de France (1904-2004)*. Lyon, 2006.

Durand, J.D., ed. *Le 'Nouvelles Equipes Internationales'. Un movimento cristiano per una nuova Europa*. Rome, 2007.

Duroselle, J.B. *Les débuts du catholicisme social en France (1822-1870)*. Paris, 1951.

Duthoit, E. 'L'Union de Fribourg' in: *Catholicisme et Vie internationale.[Festschrift aus dem Anlass des 100. Geburtstages Kardinal Mermillods]*. Freiburg, 1924, 20-48.

Elrod, R.B. 'Realpolitik or Concert Diplomacy: the Debate over Austrian Foreign Policy in the 1860s'. *Austrian History Yearbook*, 17 (1981), 84-97.

Endo, K. 'The Principle of Subsidiarity: From Johannes Althusius to Jacques Delors'. *Hokkaido Law Review*, 43 (1994), 553-652.

Engel-Janosi, F. *Graf Rechberg. Vier Kapitel zu Seiner und Österreichs Geschichte*. Munich, 1927.

Engel-Janosi, F. *Der Freiherr von Hübner, 1811-1892: Eine Gestalt aus dem Österreich Kaiser Franz Josephs*. Innsbruck, 1933.

Eyck, E. *Bismarck*. Zürich, 1943.

Falconi, C. *Il Cardinale Antonelli. Vita e carriera del Richelieu italiano nelle Chiesa di Pio IX*. Milan, 1983.

Feuchtwanger, E.J. *Bismarck*. London, 2002.

Finley, J.C. *The Liberal who Failed [Montalembert]*. Washington DC, 1968.

Fiorentino, C.M. 'Dalle Stanze del Vaticano: il venti settembre e la protesta della S. Sede, 1870-1871'. *Archivum Historiae Pontificiae*, 28 (1990), 285-290.

Fiorentino, C.M. *Chiesa e Stato a Roma negli anni della Destra storica, 1870-1876. Il trasferimento della capitale e la soppressione delle corporazioni religiose*. Rome, 1996.

Fiorentino, C.M. 'Il conclave di Leone XIII ed alcuni momenti del suo pontificato nelle lettere del conte Ladislao Kulczycki a Cesare Correnti'. *Rassegna Storica del Risorgimento*, 84 (1997), 159-194.

Fiorentino, C.M. *La questione romana intorno al 1870. Studi e documenti*. Rome, 1997.

Fiorentino, C.M. 'The Roman Question. The Political and Social Transformations in the Early Years of Rome, Capital of the Kingdom of Italy' in: E. Lamberts, ed. *The Black International*. Leuven, 2002, 179-194.

Fleckenstein, G. and Schmiedl, J., eds. *Ultramontanismus. Tendenzen der Forschung*. Paderborn, 2005.

Foellesdal, A. 'Subsidiarity'. *Journal of Political Philosophy*, 6 (1998), 231-259.

Franco, F. *Les Croisés de Saint-Pierre*. 2 vols. Brussels, 1872.

Franco, G.G. *Appunti storici sopra il Concilio Vaticano*. Rome, 1972.

Fry, K. *Kaspar Decurtins. Der Löwe von Truns 1855-1916*. 2 vols. Zurich, 1949-1952.

Gadille, J., ed. *Les catholiques libéraux au 19e siècle. Actes du colloque international d'histoire religieuse de Grenoble des 30 septembre - 3 octobre 1971*. Grenoble, 1974.

Gall, L. *Bismarck, the White Revolutionary*. 2 vols. London, 1990.

Gambasin, A. *Il movimento sociale nell'Opera dei Congressi (1874-1904). Contributo per la storia del cattolicesimo sociale in Italia*. Rome, 1958.

Gambasin, A. 'Il rinnovamento cattolico italiano e i movimenti cattolici stranieri' in: *Il movimento cattolico e la societa italiana in cento anni di storia*. Rome, 1976, 197-237.

Garbari, M., ed. *Alcide De Gasperi e la storiografia internazionale. Un bilancio*. Trento, 2005.

Gatz, E. 'Das erste Vatikanische Konzil und die soziale Frage'. *Annuarium Historiae Conciliorum*, 3 (1971), 156-173.

Geehr, R.S. *Karl Lueger. Mayor of Fin de Siècle Vienna*. Detroit, 1990.

Gehler, M. and Kaiser, W. 'Transnationalism and Early European Integration: the Nouvelles Equipes Internationales and the Geneva Circle, 1947-1957'. *The Historical Journal*, 44 (2001), 773-798.

Gehler, M. and Kaiser, W., eds. *Christian Democracy in Europe Since 1945*. London, 2004.

Gerard, E., ed. *Histoire du mouvement ouvrier chrétien en Belgique*. 2 vols. Leuven, 1994.

Goddeeris, J. *De pauselijke zouaven: met opgave van de vrijwilligers uit West-Vlaanderen*. Handzame, 1978.

Godechot, J. *Les révolutions (1770-1799)*. Paris, 1963.

Gould, R.V. *Insurgent Identities: Class, Community and Protest in Paris from 1848 to the Commune*. Chicago, 1995.

Goyau, G. *Bismarck et l'Eglise. Le Kulturkampf*. 2 vols. Paris, 1911.

Grandner, M. 'Conservative Social Politics in Austria, 1880-1890'. *Austrian History Yearbook*, 27 (1996), 77-107.

Grondeux, J. *Georges Goyau, un intellectuel catholique sous la Troisième République (1869-1939)*. Rome, 2008.

Gross, M. *The War against Catholicism. Liberalism and the Anti-Catholic Imagination in Nineteenth-Century Germany*. Ann Arbor, 2005.

Guenel, J. *La dernière guerre du pape. Les zouaves pontificaux au secours du Saint-Siège (1860-1870)*. Rennes, 1998.

Haag, H. *Les droits de la cité (1833-1836). Les catholiques-démocrates et la défense de nos franchises communales (1833-1836)*. Brussels, 1946.

Haag, H. *Les origines du catholicisme libéral en Belgique (1789-1839)*. Leuven, 1950.

Hanley, D., ed. *Christian Democracy in Europe. A Comparative Perspective*, London, 1994.

Harbour, W.R. *The Foundation of Conservative Thought*, New York, 1982.

Hasler, A.B. *Pius IX (1846-1878). Päpstliche Unfehlbarkeit und 1. Vatikanisches Konzil. Dogmatisierung und Durchsetzung einer Ideologie*, Stuttgart, 1977.

Hayman, E. *Pauline de Metternich*. Paris, 1991.

Hayward, F. *Léon XIII*. Paris, 1937.

Hearder, H. *Italy in the Age of the Risorgimento (1790-1870)*. London, 1983.

Hehl, U. von, ed., *Adenauer und die Kirchen*, Bonn, 1999.

Heimann, M. 'English Catholic Particularism in Piety and Politics' in: E. Lamberts, ed. *The Black International*. Leuven, 2002, 447-463.

Heimann, M. 'Catholic Revivalism in Worship and Devotion' in: S. Gilley and B. Stanley, eds. *World Christianities c.1815-c.1914*. Cambridge, 2006, 70-83.

Heitzer, H. *Der Volksverein für das katholische Deutschland im Kaiserreich, 1890-1918*. Mainz, 1979.

Hellwing, I.M. *Der konfessionelle Antisemitismus im 19. Jahrhundert in Österreich*. Vienna, 1972.

Hershan, St.H. *The Naked Angel*. London, 1977.

Hintze, O. *Geschichte des uradeligen Geschlechtes der Herren und Grafen Blome*. Hamburg, 1929.

Höbelt, L. 'Bismarcks widerwilliger Widerpart: Alexander Mensdorff (1813-1871)' in: G. Kohl and C. Neschwara, eds. *Festschrift für Wilhelm Brauneder*. Vienna, 2008, 167-180.

Höbelt, L. *Franz Joseph I. Der Kaiser und sein Reich*. Vienna, 2009.

Hoffman, J. and Graham, P. eds., *Introduction to Political Theory*, New York, 2005.

Holt, E. *The Carlist Wars in Spain*. London, 1967.

Honderich, T. *Conservatism*. Oxford, 1991.

Horaist, B. *La dévotion au Pape et les catholiques français sous le pontificat de Pie IX (1646-1878)*. Rome, 1995.

Howard, M. *The Franco-Prussian War. The German Invasion of France, 1870-1871*. London, 2001.

Hübner, J.A. von. *Neun Jahre der Erinnerung eines österreichischen Botschafters in Paris under dem zweiten Kaiserreich, 1851-1859*. Berlin, 1904.

Hutten-Czapski, B. von. *Sechzig Jahre Politik und Gesellschaft*. 2 vols. Berlin, 1936

Huyghebaert, N. *Correspondance de Mgr F. de Neckere, recteur de San Giuliano à Rome de 1851 à 1903*, 2 vols. Louvain-la-Neuve, 2001.

Ignesti, G. *Francia e Santa Sede tra Pio IX e Leone XIII*. Rome, 1988.

Iserloh, E. *Wilhelm Emmanuel von Ketteler (1811-1877)*. Paderborn, 1999.

Jacquemyns, G. *Langrand-Dumonceau, promoteur d'une puissance financière catholique*. 5 vols. Brussels, 1960-1965.

Jankowiak, F. 'La Curie romaine au temps de Léon XIII' in: V. Viaene, ed. *The Papacy and the New World Order*. Leuven, 2005, 69-100.

Jarlot, G. 'La genèse du catholicisme social d'après les lettres de La Tour du Pin à Louis Milcent' in: *Mélanges Jean Brethe de la Gressaye*. Bordeaux, 1967, 331-345.

Jeantet, L. *Le cardinal Mermillod*. Paris, 1906.

Joblin, J. 'Doctrine et action sociale': réflexion sur l'évolution du mouvement social chrétien avant et après 'Rerum Novarum' in: *Rerum Novarum, Laborem Exercens. 2000. Symposium*. Rome, 1982, 89-113.

Joblin, J. 'Dimension historique du discours social de l'Eglise'. *Gregorianum*, 91 (2010), 326-342.

Jürgensen, K. *Lamennais und die Gestaltung des Belgischen Staates*. Wiesbaden, 1963.

Kaiser, W. *Christian Democracy and the Origins of European Union*. Cambridge, 2007.

Kale, S.D. *Legitimism and the Reconstruction of French Society*. Baton Rouge, 1992.

Kälin, K. *Schauplatz katholischer Frömmigkeit. Wahlfahrt nach Einsiedeln von 1864 bis 1914*. Fribourg, 2005.

Kenny, M.E. 'The Correspondant. Catholic Liberalism in the Cultural Press in XIXth-century France'. *American Benedictine Review*, 38 (1987), 243-260.

Kermina, F. *Les dames de Courlande. Égéries russes au XIXe siècle*. Paris, 2012.

Kertzer, D. *The Prisoner of the Vatican*. Boston, 2004.

Kissinger, H. *A World Restored. Metternich, Castlereagh and the Problems of Peace, 1812-1822*. London, 2000.

Kitchen, M. *A History of Modern Germany (1800-2000)*, Malden, 2006.

Klein, G. *Der Volksverein für das katholische Deutschland, 1890-1933. Geschichte, Bedeutung, Untergang*. Paderborn, 1996.

Klieber, R. 'Geld und Soldaten für den bedrängten "Papst-König"' in: H. Paarhammer and A. Rinnenthaler, eds. *Österreich und der H. Stuhl*. Frankfurt-am-Main, 2001, 65-122.

Klieber, R. 'Solidaraktionen österreichischer Katholiken im Kampf um den Kirchenstaat (1859-1870)'. *Römische Historische Mitteilungen*, 43 (2001), 653-679.

Klinger, H.B. *Salzau. Geschichte eines ostholsteinischen Gutes*. Neumünster, 2002.

Klopp, Wiard von. 'Briefe des Grafen Gustav Blome an den Freiherrn Karl von Vogelsang'. *Jahrbuch der Leogesellschaft, 33 (1928), 134-302*.

Klopp, Wiard von. *Leben und Wirken des Sozialpolitikers Karl Freiherr von Vogelsang*. Vienna, 1930.

Knoll, A. *Der soziale Gedanke im modernen Katholizismus*. Vienna, 1932.

Knoll, R. *Zur tradition der christlichsozialen partei. Ihre früh- und enwicklungsgeschichte bis zu der Reichsratwahlen 1907*. Vienna, 1973.

Köhn, J. *Beobachter des Vatikanum I. Die römischen Tagebücher des P. Georg Ulber O.S.B.* Regensburg, 2000.

Kraus, K. *Politisches Gleichgewicht und Europagedanke bei Metternich*. Frankfurt-am-Main, 1993.

Kriechbaumer R., Bussjäger, P., eds. *Das Februarpatent 1861*. Vienna, 2011.

Krier, M.L. *Catholic Social Teaching & Movements*. Mystic (CT), 20022.

Kroll T., *La rivolta del Patriziato: il liberalismo della nobiltà nella Toscana del Risorgimento*, Firenze, 2005.

Kronenbitter, G. 'Friedrich von Ghentz und Metternich' in: R. Lill and U. Zellenberg, eds. *Konservatismus in Österreich*. Graz, 1999, 71-87.

Kselman, Th. and Buttigieg, J.A. *European Christian Democracy. Historical Legacies and Comparative Perspectives.* Notre Dame, 2003.

Kuefstein, Franz von. *Vorgeschichte der Enzyklik 'Rerum Novarum' vom 15. Mai 1891.* St-Pölten, 1916.

Lamberts, E. *Kerk en liberalisme in het bisdom Gent (1821-1857). Bijdrage tot de studie van het liberaal-katholicisme en het ultramontanisme.* Leuven, 1972.

Lamberts, E. 'Joseph de Hemptinne: een kruisvaarder in redingote' in: E. Lamberts, ed. *De kruistocht tegen het liberalisme.* Leuven, 1984, 64-109.

Lamberts, E., ed. *De kruistocht tegen het liberalisme. Facetten van het ultramontanisme in België in de 19e eeuw.* Leuven, 1984.

Lamberts, E. 'Une offensive de Pie IX et des ultramontains radicaux contre la législation matrimoniale en Belgique (1875)'. *Revue d'histoire ecclésiastique*, 79 (1984), 50-78.

Lamberts, E., ed. *Une époque en mutation. Le catholicisme social dans le Nord-Ouest de l'Europe. (1890-1910).* Leuven, 1992.

Lamberts, E. 'De ontwikkeling van de sociaal-katholieke ideologie in België' in: E. Lamberts, ed. *Une époque en mutation,* Leuven, 1992, 49-63.

Lamberts, E., ed. *Christian Democracy in the European Union (1945-1995).* Leuven, 1997.

Lamberts, E. 'De rol van Joseph de Hemptinne in de Zwarte Internationale' in: J. Art and L. François, eds. *Docendo discimus. Liber Amicorum Romain van Eenoo.* Ghent, 1999, 1083-1102.

Lamberts, E., ed. *The Black International. L'Internationale noire (1870-1878). The Holy See and Militant Catholicism in Europe. Le Saint-Siège et le Catholicisme militant en Europe.* Leuven, 2002.

Lamberts, E. 'La découverte du "quatrième pouvoir" par le Saint-Siège' in: C. Bosshart-Pfluger et al., eds. *Nation und Nationalismus in Europa.* Stuttgart-Vienna, 2002, 589-620.

Lamberts, E. 'L'Internationale noire. Une organisation secrète au service du Saint-Siège' in: E. Lamberts, ed. *The Black International.* Leuven, 2002, 15-101.

Lamberts, E. 'Political and Social Catholicism in Cisleithania [Austria], 1867-1889' in: E. Lamberts, ed. *The Black International.* Leuven, 2002, 299-318.

Lamberts, E. 'Catholic Congresses as Amplifiers of International Catholic Opinion' in: V. Viaene, ed. *The Papacy and the New World Order.* Leuven, 2005, 213-224.

Lamberts, E. 'A Peculiar Heir of Metternich: Gustav von Blome (1829-1906). An Intermediary between Conservatism and Socio-Political Catholicism' in: B. Löffler and K. Ruppert, eds. *Religiöse Prägung und politische Ordnung in der Neuzeit. Festschrift für Winfried Becker.* Cologne, 2006, 193-220.

Lamberts, E. 'Historical Reflections on the Principle of Subsidiarity in the European Union' in: J. Loisen and F. De Ville, eds. *Subsidiarity and Multi-level governance.* Brussels, 2012, 27-34.

Lamberts, E. 'La mobilitazione cattolica internazionale per il Papato negli anni Settanta dell'Ottocento' in: A. Ciampani, ed. *L'Unità d'Italia in Europa.* Rome, 2013, 339-348.

Lange, U., ed. *Geschichte Schleswig-Holsteins.* Neumünster, 2003.

Langlois C. and Sorel, C., eds. *Le catholicisme en congrès (XIXe-XXe siècle).* Lyon, 2009.

La Tour du Pin, R. de. 'Le Comte de Blome'. *L'Association catholique. Revue du mouvement catholique social*, 62 (1906), 309-312.

Latreille, A., ed. *Charles de Montalembert. Catholicisme et liberté. Correspondance inédite avec le Père Lacordaire, Mgr de Mérode et A. de Falloux, 1852-1870.* Paris, 1970.

Launay, M. *La papauté à l'aube du XXe siècle: Léon XIII et Pie X (1878-1914).* Paris, 1998.

Lecler, J. *L'Eglise et la souveraineté de l'Etat.* Paris 1944.

Le Guillou, L. *L'évolution de la pensée religieuse de F. de Lamennais.* Paris, 1966.

Leisching, P. 'Die römisch-katholische Kirche in Cisleithanien' in: A. Wandruszka and P. Urbanitsch, eds. *Die Habsburgermonarchie.* Vol. IV. Vienna, 1985, 1-247.

Lerman, K. *Bismarck.* London, 2004.

Levillain, Ph. *Albert de Mun. Catholicisme français, catholicisme romain, du Syllabus au Ralliement.* Rome, 1983.

Levillain, Ph. 'L'écho des écoles du catholicisme social dans l'encyclique "Rerum Novarum"' in: *'Rerum Novarum'. Ecriture, contenu et réception d'une encyclique*, Rome, 1997, 107-131.

Levillain, Ph. and de Villeneuve, F. 'Noblesse et catholicisme social de la Restauration à la Première Guerre mondiale'. *Bulletin spécial de l'Association de la noblesse française*, (1992), 5-55.

Levillain, Ph. and Ticchi, J.M., eds. *Le Pontificat de Léon XIII: renaissance du Saint-Siège?* Rome, 2006.

Lieven, D. *The Aristocracy in Europe (1815-1914).* London, 1992.

Lill, R. *Der Kulturkampf*. Paderborn, 1997.

Lindt, A. *Protestanten. Katholiken. Kulturkampf. Studien zur Kirchen- und Geistesgeschichte des neunzehnen Jahrhunderts*. Zürich, 1963.

Locke, R.R. *French Legitimists and the Politics of Moral Order in the Early Third Republic*. Princeton, 1974.

Lory, J. 'La 'Correspondance de Genève' (1870-1873). Un organe de presse singulier' in: E. Lamberts, ed. *The Black International*. Leuven, 2002, 103-134.

Lugmayer, K. 'Zur Vorgeschichte der sozialen Rundschreiben Leo XIII'. *Neue Ordnung*, 1 (1925), 59-69.

Lugmayer, K. *Grundrisse zur neuen Gesellschaft. Berufsständische Bedarfswirtschaft nach Vorgängern und Zeitgenossen*. Vienna, 1927.

Lugmayer, K. 'Zur Erinnerung an die Freiburger Vereinigung'. *Jahrbuch der österreichischen Leo-Gesellschaft*, 1927, 196-232.

Mansel, Ph. *Paris, capitale de l'Europe (1814-1852)*. Paris, 2003.

Mara, La [Ida Maria Lipsius]. *Marie von Mouchanoff-Kalergis geb. gräfin Nesselrode in Briefen an Ihre Tochter: ein Leben-und Charakterbild*. Leipzig, 1907.

Marcella, A. 'La Spagna e la questione romana: i pellegrinaggi carlisti a Roma (1876-1882)'. *Rassegna storica del Risorgimento*, 89 (2002), 381-406.

Marchasson, Y. *La diplomatie romaine et la République française à la recherche d'une conciliation, 1879-1880*. Paris, 1974.

Martin, J. 'Pie IX et Mgr de Mérode'. *Pio IX*, 4 (1975), 3-27.

Martin, M. *Der katholische Weg ins Reich. Der Weg des deutschen Katholizismus vom Kulturkampf hin zur staatstragenden Kraft*. Frankfurt, 1998.

Martin-Fugier, A. *La vie élégante ou la formation du Tout-Paris (1815-1848)*. Paris, 1990.

Martina, G. *Pio IX (1846-1878)*. 3 vols. Rome, 1974-1990.

Martina, G. 'La confutazione di Luigi Bilio ai discorsi di Montalembert a Malines nell'agosto 1863. Un passo decisivo verso il Sillabo. Un momento significativo nella storia della tolleranza' in: T. Heydenreich, ed. *Pius IX. und der Kirchenstaat*. Erlangen, 1995, 55-69.

Martina, G. 'Verso il Sillabo. Il parere del barnabita Luigi Bilio al discorso di Montalembert a Malines nell'agosto 1863'. *Archivum Historiae Pontificiae*, 36 (1998), 137-181.

Martina, G. 'L'Eglise, la société moderne et les droits de l'homme: du Syllabus à Dignitatis Humanae'. *Revue d'histoire ecclésiastique*, 95 (2000), 595-612.

Martinich, A.P. *Hobbes: A Biography*. Cambridge, 1999.

Massard, C. *L'Oeuvre sociale du cardinal Mermillod. L'Union de Fribourg*. Leuven, 1914.

Mattioli, A. 'Die Union de Fribourg oder die gegenrevolutionären Würzeln der katholische Soziallehre' in: A. Mattioli and G. Wanner, eds. *Katholizismus und 'soziale Frage'. Ursprünge und Auswurkungen der Enzyklika 'Rerum novarum' in Deutschland*. Zurich, 1995, 15-32.

Maugenest, D. *Le mouvement social catholique en France au XXe s*. Paris, 1990.

Mayeur, J.M. 'Catholicisme intransigeant, catholicisme social, démocratie chrétienne'. *Annales*, 27 (1972), 483-499.

Mayeur, J.M. *Des partis catholiques à la démocratie chrétienne, XIXe-XXe siècles*. Paris, 1980.

Mayeur, J.M. 'Aux origines de l'enseignement social de l'Eglise'. *Revue de l'Institut catholique de Paris*, 1984, 11-33.

Mayeur, J.M. *Catholicisme social et démocratie chrétienne. Principes romains, expériences françaises*. Paris, 1986.

Mayeur, J.M. et al., eds. *Histoire du christianisme*. Vol. XI: *Libéralisme, industrialisation, expansion européenne (1830-1914)*. Vol. XII: *Guerres mondiales et totalitarismes (1914-1958)*. Paris, 1990 and 1995.

McLeod, H. *Religion and the People of Western Europe, 1789-1990*. Oxford, 1997[2].

McMillan, J.F. 'Remaking Catholic Europe: Louis Veuillot and the Ultramontane Project'. *Kirchliche Zeitgeschichte, 14 (2001)*, 112-122.

Menozzi, D. 'Regalità sociale di Cristo e secolarizzazione. Alle origini della "Quas Primas"'. *Cristianesimo nella storia*, 16 (1995), 79-123.

Menozzi, D. *Sacro Cuore: un culto tra devozione interiore e restaurazione cristiana della società*. Rome, 2001.

Metternich, Klemenz von. *Mémoires du Prince de Metternich*. Paris, 1959.

Migliorini, L.M. *Metternich. L'artefice dell'Europa nata dal Congresso di Vienna*. Rome, 2014.

Miko, N. *Das Ende des Kirchenstaates*. 4 vols. Vienna-Munich, 1962-1970.

Millon, C. *René de la Tour et la philosophie sociale du catholicisme au 19e siècle, face au libéralisme et au socialisme*. Paris, 1973.

Millon-Delsol, C. *L'Etat subsidiaire. Ingérence et non-ingérence de l'Etat: le principe de subsidiarité aux fondements de l'histoire européenne*. Paris, 1992.

Millon-Delsol, C. *Le principe de subsidiarité*. Paris, 1993.

Milza, P. *Napoléon III*. Paris, 2004.

Misner, P. *Social Catholicism in Europe. From the Onset of Industrialization to the First World War*. New York, 1991.

Molette, C. *Albert de Mun (1872-1890). Exigence doctrinale et préoccupations sociales chez un laïc catholique*. Paris, 1970.

Montalembert, Charles de. *L'Eglise libre dans l'Etat libre*. Ed. Louis Le Guillou. Paris, 2006.

Montalembert, Charles de. *Journal intime inédit*. Vol. VII: *1859-1864*. Paris, 2008.

Montero, F. en Robles, C. 'Le mouvement catholique en Espagne dans les années 1870' in: E. Lamberts, ed. *The Black International*. Leuven, 2002, 427-446.

Morsey, R. 'Konrad Adenauer (1876-1967)' in: J. Aretz, ed. *Zeitgeschichte in Lebensbildern*. Vol. 2. Mainz, 1975, 186-201.

Morsey, R. *Franz Hitze (1851-1921). Sozialreformer und Sozialpolitiker des Zentrums*. Münster, 2001.

Moulinet, D. 'Le Comité de Genève et la mobilisation des catholiques en France' in: E. Lamberts, ed. *The Black International*. Leuven, 2002, 319-344.

Moulinet, D. *Laïcat catholique et société française. Les comités catholiques (1870-1905)*. Paris, 2008.

Multon H. 'Géographies et mémoires de la culture politique blanche dans la France du XIXe siècle' in: *El Carlismo en su tiempo: geografias della contrarrevolucion*. Pamplona, 2008, 129-144.

Multon, H. 'L'Opera dei congressi. Aux origines de la politisation des catholiques italiens (1874-1904)' in: C. Langlois and C. Sorel, *Le catholicisme en congrès (XIXe-XXe siècle)*. Lyon, 2009, 29-44.

Mun, Albert de. *Ma vocation sociale*. Paris, 1908.

Murat, A. *La Tour du Pin et son temps*. Versailles, 2008.

Newey, G. *Hobbes and Leviathan*. London, 2008.

Niel, A. *Die grossen k.u.k. Kürbaden und Gesundbrunnen*. Graz, 1984.

Nipperdey, T. *Deutsche Geschichte (1800-1866). Bürgerwelt und starker Staat*. Munich, 1998.

Nipperdey, T. *Deutsche Geschichte (1866-1918)*. Vol. I: *Arbeitswelt und Bürgergeist*; vol. II: *Machtstaat vor der Demokratie*. Munich, 1998.

Novotny, F. *Die Vorarbeiter der Enzyklika Rerum Novarum*. Vienna, 1954.

O'Connell, M.R. 'Ultramontanism and Dupanloup. The Compromise of 1865'. *Church History* (Chicago), 53 (1984), 200-217.

Opitz, E. *Schleswig-Holstein. Das Land und Seine Geschichte*. Hamburg, 1997.

Orfei, R. 'Notizie sul primo movimento cattolico. Il Consiglio di Permanenza italiano e il duca Salviati'. *Vita e Pensiero*, 44 (1961), 101-109.

Ouvrard, R. *Le Congrès de Vienne (1814-1815). Carnet mondain et éphémérides*. Paris, 2014.

Palmer, E.H. et al., eds., *The Holy Bible, New International Version: Containing the Old Testament and the New Testament*, Grand Rapids, MI, 2011.

Papenheim, M. 'Il pontificato di Pio IX e la mobilitazione dei cattolici in Europa'. *Rassegna storica del Risorgimento*, 88 (2001), 137-146.

Papenheim, M. '*Roma o morte*: culture wars in Italy' in: C. Clark and W. Kaiser, eds. *Culture Wars*. Cambridge, 2003, 202-226.

Parturier, M. *Morny et son temps*. Paris, 1969.

Pauley, B.F. *From Prejudice to Persecution. A History of Austrian Antisemitism*. Chapel Hill, 1992.

Peijnenburg, J.W.M. *Judocus Smits en zijn tijd*. Amsterdam, 1976.

Peijnenburg, J.W.M. *Johannes Zwijsen, bisschop, 1794-1877*. Tilburg, 1996.

Pesci, U. *I primi anni di Roma capitale*. Florence, 1907.

Petersen, K. '*Ich höre den Ruf nach Freiheit*'. *Wilhelm Emmanuel von Ketteler und die Freiheitsforderungen seiner Zeit*. Paderborn, 2005.

Pfeiffer, M. *Der Kulturkampf in Genf (1864-1873) mit besonder Berücksichtigung der Ausweisung von Bischof Mermillod*. Zurich, 1970.

Pflanze, O. *Bismarck and the Development of Germany*. 3 vols. Princeton, 19902.

Pflaum, R. *The Emperor's Talisman, the Life of the Duc de Morny*. New York, 1968.

Pfleger, P. *Gab es einen Kulturkampf in Österreich?* Munich, 1997.

Photiadès, C. 'Maria Kalergis-Moukhanow, née Nesselrode (1822-1874)'. *Revue de Paris*, 30 (1923) Oct., 627-658 and 877-907; Nov., 124-161 and 391-432.

Pierrard, P. *Louis Veuillot*. Paris, 1998.

Pinon, R. 'Henri Lorin, apôtre et théoricien du catholicisme social'. *La Chronique sociale*, April 1952, 187-197.

Plongeron, B., ed. *Histoire du christianisme*. Vol. X: *Les défis de la modernité (1750-1840)*. Paris, 1997, 301-478.

Pollard, J.F. *Money and the Rise of the Modern Papacy. Financing the Vatican (1850-1950)*. Cambridge, 2005.

Pollard, J.F. *Catholicism in Modern Italy. Religion, Society and Politics since 1861*. Oxford, 2008.

Ponlevoy, Armand de. *Vie du R.P. Xavier de Ravignan*. Paris, 1860.

Poulat, E. *Intégrisme et catholicisme intégral. Un réseau secret international antimoderniste: La Sapinière (1909-1921)*. Paris, 1969.

Poulat, E. *Catholicisme*, démocratie et socialisme. Le mouvement catholique et Mgr Benigni de la naissance du socialisme à la victoire du fascisme. Tournai, 1977.

Poulat, E. *Eglise contre Bourgeoisie. Introduction au devenir du catholicisme actuel*. Paris, 2006.

Preda, D. 'Dalla Communità Europea di Difesa alla Comunità Politica Europea: il ruolo di De Gasperi e Spinelli' in: *I movimenti per l'unità europea, 1945-1954*, Milan, 1992, 367-392.

Prévotat, J. *Les catholiques et l'Action française. Histoire d'une condamnation, 1899-1939*. Paris, 2001.

Prudhomme, C. 'Léon XIII et le nouvel ordre international à la fin du XIXe siècle' in: B. Plongeron, ed. *Catholiques entre monarchie et république. Mgr Freppel et son temps*. Paris, 1992, 203-216.

Prudhomme, C. 'Léon XIII et la curie romaine à l'époque de "Rerum Novarum" in:'*Rerum Novarum'. Ecriture, contenu et réception d'une encyclique*, Rome, 1997, 29-48.

Pulzer, P. *Die Entstehung des politischen Antisemitismus in Deutschland und Österreich, 1867-1914*. Gütersloh, 1966.

Radvany, E. *Metternich's Projects for Reform in Austria*. The Hague, 1971.

Raggi, P. *La nona crociata. I volontari di Pio IX in difesa di Roma (1860-1870)*. Ravenna, 1991.

Rak, C. *Krieg, Nation und Konfession. Die Erfahrung des deutsch-französischen Krieges von 1870/71*. Paderborn, 2004.

Rambeau, M.P. *Chopin. L'enchanteur autoritaire*, Paris, 2005,

Rawls, J. *Political Liberalism*. New York, 2005.

Rémond, R. *Les droites en France*. Paris, 1982⁴.

Rémond, R. and Poulat, E., eds. *Cent ans d'histoire de 'La Croix', 1883-1983*. Paris, 1988.

Reytier, M.E. 'Karl Heinrich zu Löwenstein (1834-1921): un prince ultramontain au service de l'Eglise'. *Chrétiens et sociétés, XVI-XXe siècles*, 11 (2004), 48-60.

Rezsohazy, R. *Origines et formation du catholicisme social en Belgique (1842-1909)*. Leuven, 1958.

Riall, L. *The Italian Risorgimento. State, Society and National Unification*. London, 1994.

Rill, R. and Zellenberg, U., eds. *Konservatismus in Österreich*. Graz, 1999.

Rivain, J. *La Tour du Pin précurseur. Un programme de restauration sociale*. Paris, 1926.

Rivière, E. *Réimpressions des thèses de l'Union de Fribourg, 1883-1893*. Tours en Blois, 1903.

Rogier, L.J. *Katholieke herleving. Geschiedenis van katholiek Nederland sinds 1853*. The Hague, 1956.

Rohrer, M. *Kurorte als Treffpunkt politischer Prominenz*. Graz, 1990.

Röhrig, F. 'Die katholische Kirche: vom Josephinismus zum Politischen Katholizismus' in: R. Lill and U. Zellenberg, eds. *Konservatismus in Österreich*. Graz, 1999.

Rollet, H. *Action sociale des catholiques en France (1871-1901)*. 2 vols. Paris, 1947-1958.

Roman, E. *Austria-Hungary and the Successor States*. London, 2004.

Ross, R.J. 'Enforcing the Kulturkampf'. *Journal of Modern History*, 56 (1984), 456-482.

Ross, R.J. 'The 'Kulturkampf' and the limitations of power in Bismarck's Germany'. *Journal of Ecclesiastical History*, 46 (1995), 669-688.

Ross, R.J. *The Failure of Bismarck's Kulturkampf. Catholicism and State Power in Imperial Germany, 1871-1887*. Washington DC, 1998.

Rumpler, H. *Eine Chance für Mitteleuropa. Bürgerliche Emanzipation und Staatsverfall in der Habsburgermonarchie (1804-1914)*. Vienna, 1997.

Sandoni, L. *Il Sillabo di Pio IX*. Bologna, 2012.

Savoye, A. and Cardoni, F., eds. *Fréderic Le Play: parcours, audience, héritage*. Paris, 2007.

Sawallich, A. *Die Geschichte der päpstlichen Armee unter dem Pontifikat Pius IX (1849-1870)*. Vienna, 1970.

Schatz, K. *Vaticanum I, 1869-1870*. 3 vols. Paderborn, 1992-1994.

Schmidt, M. and Schwaiger, G., eds. *Kirchen und Liberalismus im 19. Jht*. Göttingen, 1976.

Schmidt-Volkmar, E. *Der Kulturkampf in Deutschland (1871-1890)*. Göttingen-Berlin, 1962.

Schöpfer, G. *Klar und Fest. Geschichte des Hauses Liechtenstein*. Riegersburg, 1996.

Schroeder, P. *The Transformation of European Politics, 1763-1848*. Oxford, 1996.

Schroeder, P.W. 'Die Habsburger Monarchie und das europäische System in 19. Jahrhundert' in: A.M. Birke and G. Heydemann, eds. *Die Herausforderung des europäischen Staatensystems. Nationale Ideologie und staatliches Interesse zwischen Restauration und Imperialismus.* Göttingen-Zürich, 1989.

Schwaiger, G. *Papsttum und Päpste im XX. Jht. Von Leo XIII zu Johannes Paul II.* Munich, 1999.

Schwarz, H.P. *Konrad Adenauer. A German Politician and Statesman in a Period of War, Revolution and Reconstruction.* 2 vols. New York - Oxford, 1996.

Scott, H.M. *The Birth of the Great Power System, 1740-1815.* London, 2005².

Senestrey, Ignatius von. *Wie es zur Definition der päpstlichen Unfehlbarkeit kam. Tagebuch vom Ersten Vatikanischen Konzil. Ed. K. Schatz. Frankfurt, 1977.*

Serman, W. *La Commune de Paris (1871).* Paris, 1986.

Seward, D. *Metternich, der erste Europäer.* Zürich, 1993.

Siebertz, P. *Karl Fürst zu Löwenstein. Ein bild seines Lebens und Wirkens, nach Briefen, Akten und Dokumenten.* Kempten, 1924.

Siemann, W. *Metternich. Staatsman zwischen Restauration und Moderne.* Munich, 2010.

Silberbauer, G. *Österreichs Katholiken und die Arbeiterfrage.* Graz-Vienna, 1966.

Simon, A. *Catholicisme et politique. Documents inédits.* Wetteren, 1955.

Simon, A. *L'Hypothèse libérale. Documents inédits (1839-1907).* Wetteren, 1956.

Simon, A. *Rencontres mennaisiennes en Belgique.* Brussels, 1963.

Sked, A. *Metternich and Austria. An Evaluation.* London, 2007.

Slapnicka, H. 'Friedrich Graf Revertera-Salandra (1827-1904). Botschafter auf wichtigen Posten, Diplomat in schwieriger Zeit' in: A. Sauner and H. Slapnicka, eds. *Oberösterreicher, Lebensbilder zur Geschichte Oberösterreichs.* Vol. 3. Linz, 1984, 83-96.

Soderini, E. 'Le cardinal Wladimir Czacki'. *Le Correspondant*, 151 (1888), 237-259.

Soderini, E. *Il Pontificato di Leone XIII.* 3 vols. Milan, 1932.

Sofka, J.R. 'Metternich's Theory of European Order: A Plan for Perpetual Peace'. *Review of Politics*, 60 (1998), 115-150.

Sommerville, J. *Thomas Hobbes. Political Ideas in Historical Context.* London, 1992.

Sorgenfrei, H. *Die geistesgeschichtlichen Hintergründe der Sozial-enzyklika 'Rerum Novarum'.* Heidelberg, 1970.

Sorrell, T. *Cambridge Companion to Thomas Hobbes.* Cambridge, 1996.

Srbik, H. *Quellen zur deutschen Politik Österreichs, 1859-1866.* Vols. I-II. Berlin, 1934-1935.

Srbik, H. *Metternich, der Staatsmann und der Mensch.* 3 vols. Munich, 1979-1984.

Stadelmann, R. *Das Jahr 1865 und das Problem von Bismarck's deutscher Politik.* Munich, 1933.

Stadler, P. *Der Kulturkampf in der Schweiz. Eidgenossenschaft und Katholische Kirche im europäischen Umkreis,1848-1888.* Stuttgart, 1996².

Steinberg, J. *Bismarck: a Life.* Oxford, 2011.

Sydow, B. *Correspondance de Frédéric Chopin.* Vol. III. Paris, 1960.

Szenic, S. *Maria Kalergi.* Warsaw, 1963.

Talmy, R. *Aux sources du catholicisme social. L'École de La Tour du Pin.* Paris, 1963.

Talmy, R. *René de la Tour du Pin.* Paris, 1964.

Thibault, P. *Savoir et pouvoir. Philosophie thomiste et politique cléricale au XIXe siècle.* Quebec, 1972.

Ticchi, J.M. 'Ubi Roma, ibi Papa. Les projets de fuite du pape hors de Rome sous Léon XIII (1878-1895)'. *Rassegna storica del Risorgimento*, 88 (2001), 355-400.

Trincia, L. *Il nucleo tedesco. Vaticano e Triplice Alleanza nei dispacci del nunzio a Vienna Luigi Galimberti, 1887-1892.* Brescia, 2001.

t'Serclaes, Ch. de. *Le Pape Léon XIII.* 3 vols. Bruges, 1894-1906.

Vailhé, S. *Vie du P. Emmanuel d'Alzon.* 2 vols. Paris, 1934.

Valente, M. 'Pio IX, il Sacro Collegio e il Corpo diplomatico di fronte alla questione della partenza da Roma dopo la caduta del potere temporale'. *Il Diritto ecclesiastico*, 110 (1999), 784-833.

Van Isacker, K. *Werkelijk en wettelijk land. De katholieke opinie tegenover de rechterzijde (1863-1884).* Antwerp, 1955.

Van Isacker, K. *Averechtse democratie. De gilden en de christen-democratie in België (1875-1914).* Antwerp, 1959.

van Kersbergen, K. *Social capitalism. A Study of Christian Democracy and the Welfare State.* London-New York, 1995.

Van Megen, B. *The Concept of Perfect Society from Pius IX to the Second Vatican Council.* Rome, 1996.

Van Molle, L. 'Croissance économique et éthique catholique: les points de vue de l'Union de Malines dans les années vingt' in: E. Aerts et al., eds. *Studia historica oeconomica. Liber amicorum Herman Van der Wee*. Leuven, 1993, 317-336.

van Schewick, B. *Die katholische Kirche und die Entstehung der Verfassungen in Westdeutschland, 1945-1950*. Mainz, 1980.

Vasili, P. [Juliette Adam]. *La société de Vienne*. Paris, 1885.

Vasili, P. [Juliette Adam]. *Roma Umbertina (La société de Rome)*. Milan, 1887.

Vermaut, C. *Het Katholiek Comité van Genève (1870-1876)*. Unpublished master's dissertation. Leuven, 1978.

Viaene, V. *Belgium and the Holy See from Gregory XVI to Pius IX (1831-1859). Catholic Revival, Society and Politics in 19th-Century Europe*. Leuven, 2001.

Viaene, V. '"A Brilliant Failure". Wladimir Czacki, the Legacy of the Geneva Committee and the Origins of Vatican Press Policy from Pius IX to Leo XIII' in: E. Lamberts, ed. *The Black International*. Leuven, 2002, 231-256.

Viaene, V. 'The Roman Question. Catholic Mobilisation and Papal Diplomacy during the Pontificate of Pius IX' in: E. Lamberts, ed. *The Black International*. Leuven, 2002, 135-143.

Viaene, V., ed. *The Papacy and the New World Order. Vatican Diplomacy, Catholic Opinion and international Politics at the Time of Leo XIII, 1878-1903*. Leuven, 2005.

Viaene, V. 'Wagging the Dog: an Introduction to Vatican Press Policy in an Age of Democracy and Imperialism' in: V. Viaene, ed. *The Papacy and the New World Order*, Leuven, 2005, 326-331.

Viaene, V. 'Question d'Orient et Question d'Occident de Pie IX à Léon XIII (1877-1878)' in: P. Levillain and J.M. Ticchi, eds. *Le Pontificat de Léon XIII: renaissances du Saint-Siège?* Rome, 2006, 399-420.

Vidotto, V. *Roma Contemporanea*. Rome, 2006.

Vitzthum, K.F. von. *London, Gastein und Sadowa, 1864-1866. Denkwürdigkeiten*. Stuttgart, 1889.

Vocelka, K. *Verfassung oder Konkordat? Der publizistische und politische Kampf der österreichischen Liberalen um die Religionsgesetze des Jahres 1868*. Vienna, 1978.

Vocelka, K. 'Die Gegenkräfte des Liberalismus in der Donaumonarchie' in: L. Kammerhofer, ed. *Studien zum Deutschliberalismus in Cisleithanien, 1873-1879*. Vienna, 1992, 122-142.

Voisine, N. and Hamelin, J., eds. *Les ultramontains canadiens-français. Etudes d'histoire religieuse*. Montreal, 1985.

Volker, U. *Die nervöse Grossmacht, 1871-1918. Aufstieg und Untergang des deutschen Kaiserreichs*. Frankfurt-am-Main, 1999.

Wandruszka, A. 'Österreichs politische Struktur. Die Entwicklung der Parteien und politische Bewegungen' in: H. Benedikt, ed. *Geschichte der Republik Österreichs*. Vienna, 1954, 301-310.

Wandruszka, A. 'Il cattolicesimo politico e sociale nell' Austria-Ungheria degli anni 1870-1914' in: E. Passerin d'Entrèves and K. Repgen, eds. *Il cattolicesimo politico e sociale in Italia e Germania dal 1870 al 1914*. Bologna, 1977, 151-178.

Waschkuhn, A. *Was ist Subsidiarität? Ein sozialphilosophisches Ordnungsprinzip: von Thomas von Aquin bis zur Civil Society*. Opladen, 1995.

Weber, C. *Quellen und Studien zur Kurie und zur Vatikanischen Politik unter Leo XIII. Mit Berücksichtigung der Beziehungen des Hl. Stuhles zu den Dreibundmachten*. Tübingen, 1973.

Weber, C. *Kardinäle und Prälaten in den letzten Jahrzehnten des Kirchenstaates. Elite-Rekrutierung, Karrieremuster und soziale Zusammensetzung der kurialen Führungsschicht zur Zeit Pius IX (1846-1878)*. Stuttgart, 1978.

Weber, C. 'Dans les couloirs du Vatican. Der Kampf der Kardinäle Czacki und Galimberti um die politische Richtung im Vatikan 1879-1896 im Spiegel der Literatur, Presse und Diplomatie'. *Historisches Jahrbuch*, 101 (1981), 38-129.

Weinzierl-Fischer, E. 'Aus den Anfängen der christlichsozialen Bewegung in Österreich. Nach der Korrespondenz des Grafen Anton Pergen'. *Mitteilungen des Oesterreichischen Staatsarchiv*, 14 (1961), 468-486.

Weiss, A.M. *Lebensweg und Lebenswerk*. Freiburg im Breisgau, 1925.

Weiss, J. *Conservatism in Europe (1770-1945)*. New York, 1977.

Weiss, O. 'Der Ultramontanismus. Grundlagen, Vorgeschichte, Struktur'. *Zeitschrift für bayerische Landesgeschichte*, 41 (1978), 821-877.

Weissensteiner, F. *Liebe in fremden Betten*. Munich, 2002.

Wetzel, D. *A Duel of Giants. Bismarck, Napoleon III and the Origins of the Franco-Prussian War*. Madison, 2003.

Williams, C. *Adenauer, the Father of the New Germany*. New York, 2001.

Wilson, P.H., ed. *1848. The Year of Revolutions*. Ashgate, 2006.

Winkler, H.A. *Der lange Weg nach Westen. Deutsche Geschichte vom Ende des Alten Reiches bis zum Untergang der Weimarer Republik.* Munich, 2001.

Wolny, J. *Fünfzig Jahre für Kirche und Papst. Chronik der Erzbruderschaft vom heiligen Erzengel Michael in Wien (1860-1910).* Vienna, 1911.

Wulf, P. 'Vormundschaftliche Rechnungsablage. Die Verwendung der Mündelgelder des Grafen Gustav Blome auf Salzau'. *Rundbrief der Arbeitskreises für Wirtschafts- und Sozialgeschichte Schleswig-Holsteins*, Dec. 2006, 26-29.

Wulf, P. 'Salzau-Paris-Salzau. Die Hochzeit des Grafen Otto Blome mit der Prinzessin Clementine Bagration'. *Jahrbuch für Regionalgeschichte* (Leipzig), 25 (2007), 71-85.

Yon, J.C. *Le Second Empire.* Paris, 2004.

Zaal, W. *De vuist van de paus. De Nederlandse zouaven en het einde van de Kerkelijke Staat, 1860-1870.* Amsterdam, 1996.

Zagar, J. 'Aquinas and the Social Teaching of the Church'. *The Thomist*, 38 (1974), 826-855.

Zamoyski, A. *Rites of Peace. The Fall of Napoleon and the Congress of Vienna.* London, 2008.

Zöllner, E. *Geschichte Österreichs.* Vienna, 1990.

Zweybruck, F., ed. *Bismarck und Österreich.* Leipzig, 1915.

ACKNOWLEDGEMENTS

This study is based on a wide-ranging search of sources and literature, which required a helping hand from a great many archivists and librarians. In particular, I would like to thank the following for their cooperation: Heinrich von Hoyningen-Huene (Landesarchiv Schleswig-Holstein), Leopold Kammerhofen (Haus-Hof und Staatsarchiv Wenen), Otto Chmelik (Staatsarchiv Litomerice-Decin), Jan Kahuda (Nationalarchiv Praag), Joseph Leisibach (Bibliothèque cantonale Fribourg) and Joachim Salzgeber O.S.B. (Stiftsarchiv Einsiedeln). Special thanks are due to Count Romedeo von Thun-Hohenstein, who provided me with all the facilities for consulting the surviving personal documents of Gustav von Blome at Gut Salzau, to Prof. dr. Moritz Czàky, who gave me access to the papers of Anton Pergen, and to Count Dominik Revertera who put the extensive Herrschaftsarchiv van Helfenberg at my disposal.

At a preparatory stage, this study received an important impetus from my former student Claudia Vermaut. Magda Pluymers put me on the trail of some interesting archives and so also contributed to the book's development. Carine Dujardin and Luk Schokkaert were my IT consultants and have enabled me master the extensive documentation. Guido Goerlitz and Eric Wychlacz helped me to transcribe hundreds of Gothic German letters. Bart Preneel and his assistant Christophe de Cannière succeeded in deciphering the letters written in code.

The scholarly insights developed in this book have been enhanced by the research of my former doctoral students, Jan De Maeyer, Annelien de Dijn and

Peter Van Kemseke. Most of all, Vincent Viaene's in-depth research was foundational for the work. For the broader scientific framework of this study, I owe many thanks to the Documentation and Research Centre for Religion, Culture and Society (KADOC) of KU Leuven.

The Academia Belgica in Rome repeatedly served as a base for research in Italian archives and libraries. The FWO-Flanders supported my work with a research and travel grant. A research stay at the Netherlands Institute for Advanced Study in the Humanities and Social Sciences (NIAS) in Wassenaar, as a guest of rector Wim Blockmans, was particularly stimulating and inspiring.

The original Dutch edition of this book was published by Prometheus / Bert Bakker Publishing Co. in Amsterdam. The English translation is the work of Maria Kelly, who devoted much dedication and expertise to the task. For this edition I am also deeply indebted to KADOC, especially to Luc Vints and his team, and to Marike Schipper, Director of Leuven University Press.

INDEX

COLOPHON

FINAL EDITING
Luc Vints

COPY EDITING
Joke Depuydt

TRANSLATION
Maria Kelly

LAY-OUT
Alexis Vermeylen

LAY-OUT COVER
Johan Van Looveren

COVER ILLUSTRATION
Caricature in *Kladderadatsch*,1875. Berlin, Bildarchiv Preussischer Kulturbesitz (see p. 231).

KADOC
Documentation and Research Centre for Religion, Culture and Society
Vlamingenstraat 39
B - 3000 Leuven
www.kadoc.kuleuven.be

Leuven University Press
Minderbroedersstraat 4
B - 3000 Leuven
www.lup.be